John Hervey Bristol, Sir Thomas Hervey

**Letter-Books**

Letters During Courtship and Poems During Widowhood, 1651 to 1750

John Hervey Bristol, Sir Thomas Hervey

**Letter-Books**
*Letters During Courtship and Poems During Widowhood, 1651 to 1750*

ISBN/EAN: 9783337005665

Printed in Europe, USA, Canada, Australia, Japan

Cover: Foto ©ninafisch / pixelio.de

More available books at **www.hansebooks.com**

# LETTER-BOOKS

OF

# JOHN HERVEY,

FIRST EARL OF BRISTOL.

*WITH SIR THOMAS HERVEY'S LETTERS DURING COURT-
SHIP & POEMS DURING WIDOWHOOD,*

1651 TO 1750.

IN THREE VOLUMES.

Vol. II.—1715 TO 1725.

*WITH THREE PORTRAITS.*

Wells:

ERNEST JACKSON, 5, HIGH STREET.

1894.

# CONTENTS OF VOL. II.

————:o:————

## ALPHABETICAL LIST OF THOSE TO WHOM LORD BRISTOL'S LETTERS ARE WRITTEN.

## ILLUSTRATIONS VOL. II.

*ERRATUM.*  On the above illustration of Elizabeth, Lady Bristol, for Æt. 61 read Æt. 64.

# LETTER-BOOKS OF JOHN HERVEY,

## FIRST EARL OF BRISTOL.

**453.**  Lady Bristol to Lord Bristol.*        London April 28, 1715.

I never thought I coud have been guilty of a deceit to my dear dear angel, which I now find I have, when I told you so long and so often that it was impossible to love you better than I did at that time; but I find by this short (though tedious) absence how much less able I am than ever to live without you, (thou joy of my life,) therefore I beg, if you love me, (which were a sin to doubt,) that if you think either business or pleasure will keep you beyond next week, that you woud send the coach for me ; I hope in a few days I might be able to take a journey, though the illness you left me with has been so violent that I am very weak and faint ; I believe every thing concurring with your absence to teaze me is the cause of it.   Yesterday morning I thought it impossible but that my Lord H: must meet with Mon: B:, he having appointed him to come in the morning, and he being (as you know) up and dressd so early ; however he loitered here till near 3 before he went out, so missd of him ; the same thing has happend to day, though I told him I woud deferr my writing till he coud tell me something ; tis now eight a clock, and he has just sent me word he cant meet with him ; things so managd can never come to any thing ; therefore pray write your letter as soon as you can, for there is nothing else to be depended upon.—I find tis yet uncertain who will be P—se; I venturd out this morning to the Countess of Buquenboy, who

---

*He had been created Earl of Bristol in October, 1714. Lord H. in this letter is Carr Hervey.—S.H.A.H.

Vol. II.    A

desird me to make her compliments to you; she said I was so much in the spleen I shoud stay with her, which I did till six a clock. The king dines to day with Lord Halifax at Hampton Court; Lady Doch: has miscarryd; the Dutchess of Marlborough has been very ill, as I have been, and so has abundance more. Pray God keep you and the dear children well is the constant prayers of, my dearest treasure, your faithtul E. Bristol.

P.S.  I hope Jack is with you, and that you find him well.  I must again beg you, my dear, if you stay to send for me, for I am not able to bear it, but dont let that hasten you to Town, because I think the country good for your health; I had rather come to you.

454.    My ever-new Delight            Ickworth, April 29, 1715.

As I know the news of my safe arrival here with my cargoe of children will be the welcomest news to you, I shall begin with telling you we passd our journey (God be thankd) without any ill accident; ney, which is yet more wonderful, not one of my company was guilty of the least fault; even Lady Louisa behavd herself so well as not to cry (but whimperd only when she wanted the bubby) between London and this place, and passd her night so well at Newport as never to awake once till they took her up in the morning. Felly has had many kisses on his own account, but more on his Mamas, whose image and superscription he wears to that degree of prettyness that he scarce injures (which seems incredible) the original. My mental counterpart, Lady Ann, is now setting by me, reading of Cowley whilst I write to you; she begs your blessing, and that I woud recommend her to your favour by telling you how much she loves Papa; I cant forbear doing her the justice to tell you she behaved herself with as exemplary prudence and fitness on all occasions as if she had been Gouvernante to the rest. I cannot for my dear mother's sake close this paragraph (tho long) without putting in a good word for Lady Bab, who, like her resemblance too, the more one knows of her, the better by much one likes her. Ickworth has every thing that's sweet or charming except thy self; but what is or can anything be to me where thou art not but emptiness and disappointment? The place seems stript by thy absence of its chief necessary ornament to make the others tasted. The many new beauties my imagination promisd me the pleasure of beholding here seem all to vanish like visions, and I know will nor can never appear but with you; therefore as I hope you love us both a little, and find how essential your presence is to the happyness of the one and the advantage of the other, I hope all other places put together will for the future never be blessd with half the time you'll pass at this for the satisfaction of us both; since unless you are pleasd & easy too in every circumstance of life, twill be impossible for him to feel either, who is with the utmost passion of affection your constant lover, Bristol.

455. Lady Bristol to Lord Bristol. London, April 30, 1715.

Even now that I am conversing with you, thou darling of my heart, cannot raise my spirits to day; for every thing I meet, with conspires to vex me. In the first place I have sent 3 times to day to enquire if the coach was come back that carried the children, in hopes of a letter, but can hear nothing of it; in the next your son is just come to tell me he cant meet with Mon: B: neither this morning nor afternoon, so that he is now (by my advice) writing a note to leave at his house to desire an appointment with him, but he is of opinion that nothing but your writing will signify any thing; I believe and hope that might do good, for things are quite unsettled till it is resolvd who shall go to Ireland; for Lord Sun: is going in a few days to the Bath; he is in Town, but sees no body, he is so extream ill, and vomits every thing he takes. The Princess has been extreamly ill with a fever; she was light-headed all night on Thursday, but was so well this morning that she saw the ladys, and has invited several to come and play with her in her dressing-room ; I am going there now. I dined with Lady Ann Hervey, but hear no news but what the prints will tell you, only every body is in great joy to see Nicolini again, except your poor disconsolate E. Bristol.

Eight a clock and no coach come back; I expect yours here to morrow to fetch me to my dear dear angel, till when I shall have no rest.

**456.    My ever-new Delight**          Ickworth, May 2, 1715.

The kind deceit you acknowledg your self guilty of towards me is of so singular a nature that it ought to be valued for its being a rarity onl,y had it no other quality to recommend it ; but tis full of so many other welcome considerations to my mind that it needs no other thought to make me throughly happy; may I hope that unless I had made you a little so, your heart woud never have ledd you from time to time into such pleasing errors ? I am afraid Carr perceives in those persons you make him apply to in my favour that the King has already done enough in his to hope he might have been troubled no more in mine ; and if that be the case, then writing will availe no more than speaking, and I should be extreamly sorry, after having never offerd or card to serve any Prince but the present one to have any, overtures of that kind rejected ; it woud be very long (if ever) before I coud recover inclination or assurance enough to make a second tender of my service should it once be refusd, and there-fore I woud not willingly expose my self to a denial in form which my writing must occasion ; therefore weigh this method well before tis pursued, and if at last you woud have such a desperate measure taken, I will prepare as proper a draught in my mind for the occasion as I am able, (altho' there is no subject so nice and delicate to speak or write of as one's self ;) but I am at present so full of business that I have time to think of nothing but that and thee. The chaize is gone to fetch Jack, altho' I know not how farr his journey hither may interfere with his intended publick exercises. I should be much concernd to find I gratifyed my own desires so much at his expence as to be the occasion of his losing any time from his studies, knowing by fatal experience that if this critical season of his life for learning be once slipt, years instead of days must be employd to retrieve it; and as he is the first fruit of our love, I have a more than ordinary passion to see him perfectly accomplishd, and thereby first among mankind too. The children are all as well as you can wish them; Lady Louisa goes constantly abroad every day with the rest in the coach, and seems to like it very well. As to my own health, it wants nothing but to be with you; when that can be is not yet to be known by your impatient friend and constant lover, Bristol.

**457.** Lady Bristol to Lord Bristol. London, May 3, 1715.

My first moment of ease is dedicated to my dear angel, though even now I am so very unfitt to write that I desird my Lord Hervey to tell all the business, that I might have nothing to do but to tell you (if possible) how much and dearly I love you, which sure must be extream, since the pain of your absence has been greater then what I felt last night and to day, which has outdone every bodyly pain except labour; Sunday night I began to be ill with mighty sickness in my stomach and pain in my back and side, as you have seen me lately; I was pretty well in the morning, and went to dinner to my Lady Dalkeith's, but was taken there again so very ill with the same complaint and the cholick with it, that I was forced to come home without eating a bit; but meeting with your dear letter revivd me so that I got well enough to venture to the Princess in the evening, but in the night my pain returnd more violent again than ever, that I was forcd to send for Sir David; I have taken Daffy's elixir and waters to day, and am to take a quieting draught at night to ease my pain and prevent the return of my vomiting, which has been off all this afternoon, though I am still sick and loath every thing ; to morrow I am to take the waters again, and Sir David flatters me that I may be well enough after to dine with the Dutchess of Grafton & Sir Thomas Hanmer who have invited me, so that, I hope, will make you easy concerning me ; but that you may be more so, you may depend that if my fit returns (which God forbid), you shall have a messenger on purpose; and now I have taken care to make you easy, pray make me so by sending the coach for me, for I believe you will have no business here this fortnight, and I am sure you'll have more pleasure where you are ; if you love me, my dear, let us meet, for in sickness or health I am not able to live without you, less, much less than ever. My blessing to the dear children ; tell Felle the Princess askd how her little favourite did. Good my dear, send for me.

**458.**    My ever-new Delight            Ickworth, May 5, 1715.
                  I am very sure no pain you felt could be worse than that the reading of your letter put me into, till I came to that part of it where you spoke of dineing with the Dutchess of Grafton, and in the other where you suppose your self well enough to think of coming hither, and that you faithfully promise, shoud your complaint (at all) return, you woud send a messenger express to fetch me to you ; these circumstances put together were but just sufficient to stop my journey till another post, which if it shoud not bring me intire satisfaction as to my dearest's health and ease, (neither whereof shall I feel in the interim,) will be undertaken the next moment. Every symptom of this last indisposition of yours shews it to proceed from gravel, and I perceive Sir David has applyd to it as such. That medicine which gave me present ease in the same case this time two years was diacodium and syrrop of marsh-mallows, of each an

equal quantity; and as an additional cordial know your son Jack is now sitting by me very much grown, and never lookd so healthfully in his life, till I told him by my eyes in reading the first part of your letter that you had not been so, which made him change countenance also, till I reassurd him by saying you had been very ill, but was something better again, a representation may make him easy I hope, but nothing can make me so till I hear again from you, my whole happyness being bound up in thy welfare, even to that degree as to render every other thing incapable of pleasing me, ney, or so much as keeping me tolerably easy where that is in any suspence; for since this allarm arrivd, my children, (which are without comparison the very finest in the world, thanks to God and their dear Mama,) have not been able to entertain me or furnish me with a more cheerful thought than how lost and forlorn a creature shoud I be, (altho' at present surrounded with blessings on all sides,) shoud it ever please that gracious God to deprive me of that one thing, which alone gives a relish to the rest of his favours; the continuance whereof is humbly hopd and prayd for with some sort of confidence from a consciousness of its having been receivd with gratitude, and enjoyd with the utmost chastity, by thy constant lover, Bristol.

**459.** Lady Bristol to Lord Bristol. London, May 5, 1715.

My head and heart are full of a thousand things I have to tell my dear dear angel, that I shoud not know where to begin, but that I judg by the tenderness I feel and have always found from you that you woud in the first place have an account of my health, which is I thank God much better this afternoon then I have been these four days, though both this night and the night before I have had some return of my pain (but not vomiting) notwithstanding my sleeping draught, but the waters I hope have got the better of it, but I am extreamly faint & vapourd, which you woud not wonder at if you knew how many, very many things I have to vex me, besides what I suffer by your absence, which I desire and beg upon many accounts you woud shorten as much as is possible to be done with convenience, so that I give over the thoughts of seeing you at Ickworth, finding your presence here so necessary; this change happens from my having dind yesterday with Sir Thomas Hanmer and the Dutchess of Grafton, (where I venturd to go, it being very warm in that part of the day,) he was more open than ever I knew him, and we have projected several things upon what he told me too long and hazardous to be venturd in a letter, but every thing lies still till you come, which is no advantage in any cause, as I find by the affair you left in my hands; I wonder a less penetration than yours coud not find by my letters, as well as what you have formerly seen, where the fault lay, and that you had no reason to be discouragd from writing by what has happend; therfore I desire you would think of it as soon as you can, for I can give you more reasons for it then ever when we meet; one is that you may do me some kindness in it, since I am like to meet with a second disappointment in my own affair, and that very soon, if your presence and assistance dont prevent it. I have had so many proofs of your tender love, that I cannot doubt of your taking the first minute for your coming to ease the impatience of a longing faithful heart, that loves and doats of you to madness. My head is so giddy I can say no more, but my blessing to all ye dear children, and something particular to Jack. Poor Betty has had a sad fit of the cholick. I am still so very sore that I am not able to put on a pair of bodys, but hope to do it to morrow, that I may see the Princess, who has still a very bad cough. If I am well enough, I go to the Opera a Saturday with Madam Shulenberg & her niece. Nicolina sings, but what is that to me.

**460.** Lady Bristol to Lord Bristol. London, May 7, 1715.

I hope the many pressing instances besides (I hope I may say both) our longing desires to meet will make this letter useless, and that it may meet you on the road; however, I write for fear I may not be so happy, and the missing a letter might give my dear dear angel as much uneasyness as I sufferd by the want of one by the stage-coach, that went with you to Ickworth. I am in some hopes that my affairs woud not be quite desperate if you were here; in the mean time I have done what I coud by Mon : Ber:, who is extreamly kind and civil to us both, and the Duke of Ar : the same, who I have spoke to also, but by the advice of my friends I have not yet spoke myself to the principle person till these have made my way and I have your assistance; there is too many and hazardous things to say in a letter upon this occasion in particular, and many more that I long to ease my heart of in my tender partner's bosom; I have this comfort, if my own affair miscarrys, that will and must promote yours, both from what I have said, and what I heard by Mon : B—. I write in such a hurry that I am afraid there is more nonsense than ordinary; you will not wonder at it when I tell you the Dutchess of Grafton and Sir Thomas Hanmer were with me all the morning till I went to Court, where I was receivd more graciously than ordinary, and stayd till 3 a clock, and am to be at half an hour after four with Madam Shulenberg to drink coffee before we go together to the Opera, and to morrow night I supp at Madam Kilmansack's; you will find by this diary I leave no stone unturnd. After this account I think I need not say any-thing of my health, but indeed tis far from being well, had not this unforeseen alarm rousd me up. The Princess askd me last night when you came, and told me she had heard of my vapours, and how many tears I had shed, notwithstanding all the Countess of Buquen : had done to divert

me.  I told her that was no new thing in your absence, but that I hopd for
my cure in a few days.  My hour is so farr past that I may justly repeat
those verses—

With thee conversing I forget all time,

and, my dear dearest life, I hope tis but a short Adieu.  Betty is pretty
well again.  God bless those with you ; I rather hope you have left them ;
if not, I beg you woud set out a Monday.—Tis now ten a clock, which
makes me fear my dearest life does not count the minutes as I do, at least
not find them so tedious as your absence makes them to me; if you did, you
woud not be long from your ever faithful loving E.B.

I have only time to tell you the Prince expects to supp here, but has
desird he might have but little company and but little meat; pray, if you
love me, come home ; but if it is not convenient to you, you need not come
till ten, but put me at ease by saying you wont fail then.

**461.**    To Mr. Geffes.              London, May 13, 1715.

Having been called up to Town much sooner then
I allowd for when I went into the country, & my nephew being returnd
hither also, impatient to know whether you think him & his estate worthy
of your daughter, with £10,000 for her portion, who I must do the justice to
tell you likes her well enough in all other respects to take with a much less
fortune, would the present circumstances admitt of it, but as that sum is
absolutely necessary to discharge the incumberances left upon his estate
by his grandfather, as the inclosd will throughly satisfy you, which I
herewith send you, nott only to confirm that fatal truth, but also that God
has blessd him with as good an understanding as was alwaies warrented
to you by your friend to serve you.

I desire my service to ye young lady.

**462.** To my son Carr.                                    Sept. 17, 1715.

Your coming into the world this day 24 years, was so sensible a pleasure to me that I then vowed never to forgett God's goodness in sending me and my family a son & heir; that you might live to prove both a blessing & ornament nott only to us but your country (too barren in present patriots) was alwaies the predominant wish of my heart; but believe me, ye modern scheme of augmenting standing armies and revenues can never produce that security to liberty in the conclusion, which I am sure you have (even now) as much att heart as your most affectionate father.

**463.** To Sir Thomas Hanmer.                             Sept. 21, 1715.

For a man of fivety to plead pleasure-partys with fine ladies could thus long keep him from the conversation of one he has a friendship for passing the love of women, would seem as inconsistent an excuse for my staying so long in Town as they generally make use of for themselves. However, as that happend to be the true reason why I could no sooner be in the way of injoying ye favour you promisd us, I hope no more time will be lost in granting than you (now) find there is in claiming it by your most affectionate kinsman & obedient servant.

My thanks for your kindness to Tom must be adjournd to our meeting.

**464.** To Sir R. Cockes.                     Ickworth, Sept. 27, 1715.

I was nott unmindfull of your brother's affair before I left London, but I found the frank declarations I had made according to the double duty of an old Whigg and of every free born Englishman against the increase of standing armies & revenues were so very improper introductions to ye success of any suite which was to pass through my hands, that ye only compensation I can make him is to give you fair warning nott to depend (at least for the present) on any great assistance from him, who, if ever his sincerity suffers him to get any credit, will with all readyness shew you how very much he is your most faithfull servant.

**465.** To Sir Richard Cocks.     Ickworth, Oct. 22, 1715.

    I was so unfortunate in timing the last officious proposal I made concerning your brother, (tho' that was throughly well meand,) that I know not how to venture a second; otherwise I shoud be glad if you coud conveniently put off your intended journey to London till I might meet you there; which I can do in a month or 5 weeks hence, when I woud give you every convinceing proof of my wanting neither strength of inclination or endeavour to make any naile drive in favour of ye worthy doctor which you shall bid me strike. I am very much' obligd to you for communicating to me your excellent discourse you entertaind your countrymen with at the Quarter Sessions. I think ye rest of ye kingdom might be no less edifyed by the publication ot that than ye whole may be by your printing the History of Henry ye 3d of France, a second perusal whereof after your emendations will yield a fresh pleasure to, Sir, yours etc.

**466.** To the Right Honble the Lord Hervey.     Dec. 16, 1715.
Dear Son

    Next to ye good news that the rebells strength shortens daily, I was glad to hear that the time of my enjoying the peace and pleasure of this place was lengthend to the 10th of ye next month. We country politicians concluded indeed matters could not be prepard for ye P. to proceed upon against ye 14th instant, seeing ye chief lord of ye articles was persuing much smaller quarry in Norfolk till Munday last. If ye

Whigs in, as well as out of, Parliament are at last grown jealous, I woud fain know under what denomination to rank those M——rs who have made the one as well as the other so; for to give the former thier due, they shewd themselves such willing titts to tugg through any tolerable drudgery in ye last session that measures must be very monstruous to make them restive in ye next, altho' I perceive Mr. Soll—r has provd so par avance, which I woud know the particular reason of. If ye present dispute be only which shall be ye sacrifice or the scape goate between Lord Oxford & Lord Lansdown, that's a point will never break squares in ye conclusion ; wherefore something more material must fall out before the publick affairs are placed in such hands as will with more disinterestedness transact them than any sett of men yet seen these 30 years by your etc.

**467.**    To ye Honble Thomas Newport Esq.

I perceive my butler has treated you with quite as little ingenuity as he did me on ye present occasion; for had he lett you know that instead of acquainting me (as he ought to have done) with your having written to or promoted him, he framd a formal story of his father's lying at ye point of death, in whose hands he pretended he had effects of value, & he begd leave only to go see him, promising to return in 5 or 6 days etc., I'm confident you woud not have made it a question whether he had done any thing wrong or not in offering to quit my service in so abrupt & so unfair a manner, which he had never come into but for ye character you gave of him to, Sir, yours.        P.S. He has no discharge for ye Plate.

**468.**    To Lady Bristol.        Hockeril, April 3, 1716.

It is impossible for me to omitt any occasion wherein I do but think you will be one way (tho' never so little) better pleasd than another ; and therefore notwithstanding Mr. Maynard promisd me to let you know we were all got well hither, yet I coud not go to rest till I had told you so my self, and that I find my self more uneasy than ever to be without you, even to that degree (tho' with your children) that tis not (I feel already) long to be born with by your faithful lover, Bristol.

**469.**    Lady Bristol to Lord Bristol.    London, April 5, 1716.
                                                    Poor twins birth-day.

         It was a very welcome and agreeable surprize when the porter gave me a letter from my dear dear angel yesterday just as I was setting down to dinner, which gave me a much better stomach than otherwise I shoud have had ; for I must confess (tho' perhaps you will think me a little illnaturd for it) I cant be sorry for the uneasyness you express by our absence, since I hope you will never let it be so again, and will the sooner ease the torment I feel from it now ; but I am afraid what I am going to tell you, joynd with the charms of Ickworth, wont answer my wishes, since I am told from very good hands that it is at last resolvd that the great affair shall certainly begin in the House of Commons, and that it is at present thought that Wednesday will be the day ; it is so farr believd that I know some members that have wrote to all their friends not to fail to be here on Tuesday night, for tis thought the struggle will be so hard that they will be glad to take any advantage ; the lord that I told you I woud depend upon for intelligence every post day has sent me word this morning that he beleivd no member will be absent on Wednesday; from what has past between us before, I took that to be a hint that you shoud give the earliest notice you can in your neighbourhood, which I hope you will, for I hear by all hands that day is fixed ; my doctor was here just now, and told me the same. The Town has disposd of Mr. W——'s place (who continues very ill) to Mr. Met—e. I wish I coud tell you a story between a great Duke and his brother, for I am sure it woud divert you, but tis impossible to make you understand it well without naming names. You know how unfitt I am to write after dinner, so I am doing it now, but if I hear any thing more you shall have it in a postcript after the Play, where I am going with Lady Pembroke ; till then or Saturday, my dear dear angel, Farewel.

I hope the children got well to Ickworth last night, though I was in great pain that you got no farther than Hockeril a Tuesday. I hope you will find the wine safe at Ickworth that I sent a Wednesday, the best I coud gett.

**470.**    My ever-new Delight            Newmarket, April 5, 1716.

I woud not begin my letter till the messenger I expected from Ickworth had enabled me to tell you the children got all very well thither, as your son Jack and we did hither. I must do my representative, dear Nann, the justice to relate a passage between us, as we were walking up a hill together on this side Newport. Said I, Child, do you ever think of any body when you are absent from them ? Yes sure, said she. Have you ever thought of dear Mama, said I, since we left her crying in bed ? Yes indeed I did, said she, last night, and could not help crying too. Why did you cry when you thought of her ? said I. Because, said she, I am sure she must have had at least as much a mind to come with you as I had ; and beside, as she was not well enough to come with us, I am sure too you will soon go back again, and I shant see you at Ickworth may be at all. Tnese being her very words and sentiments, and the child of such a mother, judg if it be great weakness to be as fond of her as you, and God alone (whom I ought to bless, praise and adore, day and night, for all his mercies and benefits towards so unworthy an object of them,) know I am.

Felly was kissd and caressd at every stop and stage as your representative, and as such shall expect great gratitude and kindness, notwithstanding Jack's judgment of his nature and disposition, which will only serve to enhance the value of those returns he makes me, by shewing himself more particular in my regard and letting me engross his whole affections, which was the monopoly I ever aimd at from the mother, and whereby alone his poor father could have been made so very happy as he is in beleiving he so entirely possesses so valuable a treasure as your heart, the chiefest comfort to his own, who is with all possible, ney, incredible returns of tenderness and passion your most constant faithful lover, Bristol.

**471.**    Lady Bristol to Lord Bristol.        London, April 7, 1716.

I wish what I am going to tell my dear dear angel may be as great a pleasure to you as it is to me, that this is the last letter I shall have occasion to write, for it is absolutely necessary that you shoud be here on Wednesday, time enough to be in the House; you may depend upon my intelligence, though I dont care to name names, but I believe you will know when I tell you that it is the son of that lord that sent for you some time since to speak with you from the Play; the Duke of Kingston and several lords more are to be in Town on Monday; it is the great affair that makes all this bustle, which is at last fixd to begin in the House of Lords, and certainly next week, but the day is not known yet, but my intelligence hopes to be able to let me know this evening or to morrow, that if it shoud be sooner than what I have told you, I may send a messenger on purpose, but I believe it will not, because the Dutchess of Rutland (who was here last night) told me she expected her lord then; but so much I value your pleasure and the good you may get by this fine weather in the country above my own satisfaction in your company, that if I learn from any good hands that the day is deferrd, you shall not fail of a reprieve by the Stage-coach on Monday; what makes them so very irresolute is the uncertainty of Mr. W— fate; his bloody flux is something abated, but they are forcd to lay on two fresh blisters again this morning.—Lady Sunderland is very ill at the Gravel pits; she was taken yesterday with a violent vomiting, has had a very ill night, and continues very ill.—The King and all the world is to be at the Play to night for Mrs. Santlow's benefit; I am to be at the Countess of Buquen :, where I think it is not likely I shoud hear any news, but if I do you shall hear of me again.—This minute a message is come to me from another of my intelligence, Lord P—, that the business is certainly in your House first, and that Wednesday is thought to be the day; I shall be uneasy till I know whether this letter comes safe to you; therefore pray make Jack (with my thanks for his last) write me word by the coach a Tuesday how and what you do. Kiss the dear children for me, and Nann in particular, though I grudg it, for I am really jealous of the least love taken from your constant and faithful E. Bristol.

**472.** My ever-new Delight      Newmarket, April 7, 1716.
       The reason of my making no mention of the pewits eggs in my letter was because there was none to be had in all this town when Fountain's letter came to Webster, and I was fearful to remind you of them till I was sure of satisfying your longing; in order wherunto I dispatchd several messengers, who brought me in 4 dozen of them time enough to send by the children's coach, which I hope you receivd as soon as it arrivd, according to the strict command I laid on the coachman. Mr. Shepherd being here I have had an account from him of ye state of your uncle's condition, which is certainly much worse than ever; he hath been bed-rid for above eight weeks, hath taken very little sustenance, and his continuance hath been reckond a kind of miracle. May God-Almighty's

Vol. II.    c

accustomd goodness to me but preserve my heiress in perfect health and happyness, and let the inheritance be as long in falling as pleases his Providence, the possession whereof cannot add one mite to my affection, which is already too great to admitt increase from any accident of that kind, or diminution from any other but death ; ney, twill be proof beyond the power even of that too, if any sense survives of what past here below with the better part of (my present angel) him, who hopes to know and love thee evermore in Heaven.  Bristol.

**473.**    Lady Bristol to Lord Bristol.        London, April 8, 1716.

I am afraid when my dear dear angel receives this, you will hope it brings a reprieve for Nann and Ickworth ; but farr from it, tis to confirm my last night's letter by the post, which was of too much consequence not to be afraid it might miscarry, which all your friends here are in great pain about, and woud have had me sent a servant for fear ; Wednesday seems fixd to be the day.  Lord Burlington desires me to tell you that if the Duke of Somerset is still at Newmarket, that he begs you woud see him as you come by, and let him know Lord Carlton (with whom he has left his proxy) will not be in Town till the week after this, so that if he does not come himself it is a vote lost, which is of great consequence.  Lord Carlton has left his proxy with Lord Burlington ; Mr. W— they think will recover ; but there is great doubt of Lady Sunderland, who is worse to day then ever, and in great extremity of pain from an artery being cut with letting blood, which has occasiond this violent fever.  Your friends expect you with great impatience, but not with that longing desire as your faithful E. Bristol.

I was mightily disappointed to day in not having heard from Mo: Trevey, who promisd to bring me a letter from you ; but pray dont let me be so by the coach a Tuesday, to let me know if you've receivd this and last night's letter safe. I hope to hear something of you by Sir T. Hanmer to morrow.

**474.** My ever-new Delight          Newmarket, April 9, 1716.
The only match of this meeting being to be run this afternoon, I shall not get to Ickworth till this night; and as I cannot possibly beleive that a Bill which so nearly concerns the priviledges of all the people shoud be first meddled with by the Peers, I shall not leave Ickworth till I hear tis actually begun there; whereof you may give me notice by express in case so extraordinary an accident shoud fall out, which can never be believd (no more than the thing itself) till seen by your most faithful friend and constant lover, Bristol.
Woud you have any more pewitts eggs?

**475.** My ever-new Delight          Ickworth, April 9, 1716.
Altho' it is not above six hours since I wrote to you from Newmarket, yet I cannot help thinking (from my own experience) you woud be disappointed should the post bring you no letter; and therefore I send this to let you know I shall be extreamly so, if I receive none from you on Wednesday after you have heard (by that Mr. Nurse brought you) my opinion of the very great improbability, not to say impossibility, of the monster's first appearance in our House; for shoud that happen, a day must be appointed to consider of it, and all lords summond by circular letters to attend, and then it will be time enough for me to leave this place, which I've been long enough here already to find wants my presence more than you can imagine, there being little or nothing done since I left it, beside the necessity of Jacks and my taking a little more of this sweet air to repair our healths, which without exaggeration has in five days made little Louisa's face almost as broad again as I parted with it, and Robbon

Wildman very near as fatt as Mary Claxton ; but as he does not want the company and conversation of his wife quite so much as I do of mine, I fear its good effects will not appear so soon as Louisa's, nor so much as Wildman's, in me. I hope Mr. Negus will have done what I desird of him before this arrives, which was to pay you the 100 guineas I sold Lady-thigh to him for, not knowing but you might have more occasion for it there than I here ; for your purse has procurd me good luck enough to bear my charges in the maine, altho' my boys and my expences there amounted to four pounds a day, an allowance I shoud contentedly increase to live with thee, but a most insupportable rate for time spent without thee, and will accordingly be shortend by all the means & methods in the power of your longing lover, Bristol.

Many thanks for the wine.


**476.**    Lady Bristol to Lord Bristol.        London, April 10, 1716.

I have been in such a frett ever since I receivd my dear dear angels letter by Mr. Nurse this morning, finding I was like to be disappointed of seeing you to morrow morning ; and being assurd last night at Court that the Bill woud certainly be brought in to day has made me very uneasy as well as all the rest of your friends, though I cant say mine was quite upon the same account. The particulars of what has past you have from a better hand, and one that was present, though they woud not set their name ; I suppose you are acquainted with the hand. I believe the length of time given to the second reading is not out of favour to the absent lords, but that the Duke of M— and Earl of S— is not fitt to attend by the great danger his lady is in ; she is worse then ever, and they are afraid her arm is gangerd. The King askd me last night if you were come, and when you woud be here ; I told him I expected you to morrow.

Pray Gcd bless you and send you a good journey, and bring you safe to the longing arms of your impatient E. Bristol.

Thank you for the eggs, though they were not for me but the Dutchess of Grafton; however, the letter mistook the person.

**477.    To Sir Thomas Hanmer.          London, Sept. 1, 1716.**
The kind enquiry you make after my wife's health deserves the earlyest acknowledgment and information; and therefore you see I loose no time in sending both.    Every symptome attending her condition is as promising as my heart can wish....I am in the next place to thank you for the trouble you gave your self in the conveyance of Mrs. Manleys letter to me, which is full of the sense she has of your great goodness to her and her family, more especially in giving up her husband's bond, the circumstances of whose estate are so commiserable by the long continuance of land-taxes as turns your generosity in to a most well-placed charity, for which she has conjurd me in most pressing terms to joyn with her in owning thier obligations to you.    Since you have given me this opportunity of writing to you, I cant conclude without condoling the publick loss, as well as my own, in missing your speech among those deliverd at ye fatal funeral of the Triennial Bill; whereupon I'm almost tempted to say, as Mr. L'Abbée de St. Real did of Atticus's modesty having been the cause that his letters were not published att ye time Cicero's & others were, Quand on luy en attribueroit quelque mauvaise le prejudice qu'il nous a porté par sa reserve meriteroit bien cette punition. Lastly, in answer to my share in ye wellcome compliment you've made us on our absence from Ickworth, lett me end with Cicero's words : nimis abes diu, præsertim cum sis in propinquis locis; neque nos te fruimur, et (may I be vain enough to hope & add) tu nobis cares.    I am with the utmost esteem your most faithtul humble servant.

**478.**   Dear Jack                                    Sept. 13, 1716.

Knowing how equally you admire ye Archbishop of Cambray's booke, both for ye nobleness of its design and ye beautyfullness of its execution, makes me conclude you must approve Mentor's rules of conduct for Telemachus's travels as very proper for your own.   Qui n'arrestoit ce jeune Prince en chaque lieu qu' autant qu' il le falloit pour excreer sa vertu et pour luy faire acquerir de l'experience.   And as I depend on your prudence & principles for making every occurrence in all places subservient to the former purpose, so I doubt not but your industrious curiosity has by this time left few things at Paris worth notice to escape your observation towards attaining the latter;  wherefore I would have you be sure to leave that place as soon as ye month you mention in your lodgings is determind, & to that end have herewith sent you such directions for creditt as is necessary for ye route you intend to take thro' Austrian Flanders & Holland in your way to Hannover, where I would not have you faile to arrive some time before his Majesty speaks of leaving it, which will be the very beginning of November att ye latest, & therfore you must not propose to stay long at any place in your passage thither, where I would have you take up your winter quarters.   You could not have sent me a much more agreeable piece of news than that Mr. L'Abbee Terrasson is about publishing any new worke, ney, tho' Operas be ye subject of it, for Midas-like every thing must become gold that he thinks fitt to handle. Could Madam Dacier have imagind that her praise of Mr. Des Cartes would have provd so just a prophecy of his dissertation on ye Iliade, she would have suppressd it: viz., on auroit dit qu'un Dieu etoit venu de brouiller ce cahos, dissiper les tenebres, et creer la lumiere.   I never looked over that matchless criticism but I pronounce, (tho' not apt to be dogmatical in any opinion about other matters,)

Cedite, Romani scriptores, cedite, Graii.
I read him over with a lover's eye ;
He has no faults, or I no faults can spy,
He is all beauty, or all blindness I.

I know but one body in this world, and another in ye next, who can find any thing amiss in him, which are Madam Dacier & poor Homer, for having so closely copyed Galatons picture of that poet a vomitting, & placing her in the servile scituation of his blind admirers, licking up all without distinction that falls from him. I am glad to hear of his intended voyage hither, & am yet better pleasd to find a man of his exquisite taste should value your conversation enough to make him deferr his journey till your return, a compliment you may be justly proud of, & one I could feel a thrô satisfaction in, were it not attended with ye allay of keeping him longer from us. Mrs. Oldfield has made your Mama a visitt, & was wellcome to us both, because she brought me a letter from you, which entertaind us better than she with all her witt & ridicule on France could do; your simile of the Invalides was worth her whole conversation. The justice you do that country in owning how much greater encouragements are given there to ye industrious in all arts & sciences than here, may be a just commendation of ye Prince; but then at ye same time it reflects on ye scarcity of its genii, since thier performances in painting, sculpture, musick & architecture have been very indefferent, wherin—Mediocritas esse non licet—I have heard it said ; but since they have been so particularly kind and courteous to you, I can find partiality enough to think allmost as advantagiously of them as they do of themselves, a weakness you are so utter a stranger to (notwithstanding you possess as many tempting endowments to betray you into that vice as most young men) that it makes none of the smallest beauties about you, whenever a general survey is taken of you by ye pleasd imagination of your most affectionate father.

**479.**   To Sir Thomas Hanmer.                    Sept. 25, 1716.

Dear Cousin

If you had not been so kind as to give me the authority of your own desire to trouble you again on this occasion, I should nevertheless have sent this to lett you know my wife was safely brought to bed between 4 & 5 this morning of a girl, & tho' the largest of all the twenty children God has blessd me with, yet He was pleasd so wonderfully to answer the fervent, reitterated prayers we put up to ye throne of Grace for her speedy & favourable delivery, that she never had a more remarkable good one in all respects, nor better after it; a blessing so signal that joyning your thanks with ours to ye mercifull author of it is ye due request of your most affectionate kinsman & faithfull servant, Bristol.

**480.**   Lady Bristol to Lord Bristol,      London, Oct. 18, 1716.

The dismal night that I have past is not to be expressd, nor woud I if I coud, since I am sure by the experience I have had of your tenderness it woud grieve you too much; therfore no more of that subject. I wish I had any other to entertain you with, but I heard not a word of news yesterday, nor I dont expect to hear any to day, for I believe I shall not see a mortal, for even Lady Charlott is engagd. The Duke of Grafton is gone to day, but her Grace has put off her journey for a few days longer. Sir John and Lady Betty Germain came last night. The pleasure I had in receiving a letter from Jack was a good deal allayd by the difficultys he met with in his journey, and the not having it to his own mind, which is always so reasonable that it is pity when it is not gratifyd; but I foresaw his nicety woud not let him do anything without particular order. I just now receivd my mantua and petticoat by Lady Warwick, who came last night, and that letter for Betty, I beg her pardon for opening of it, but

she must expect it when I saw dear Jacks hand, for that is a pleasure I cannot deny my self, especially at a time when so few can be tasted by, my dear dear angel, yours most entirely.

Harriott is very well, as I hope you found the rest: God bless you all, and send me soon with you. Bid Betty write soon to Jack, for I can send it safe. Nine a clock and not a word of news. I have grieved all day at the bad weather; I dont know if you had the same accident with you; a little before four a clock it grew by degrees darker and darker, just like the eclipse and very near as dark for two or three minutes, and then in the same manner lighter again; I have heard no remarks upon it yet but by my Lady Suffolk, who said her parrot went to sleep at that time, which he never does but in the night.

**481.**   My ever-new Delight          Ickworth, Oct. 19, 1716.

Why woud you let me leave you, when twas so entirely in your power to have prevented it ? Could you judg so ill as to believe I could be well without you ? So farr from it that even this place, with the finest day I ever saw to enjoy it in, seemd to have lost all its charms for me by thy absence ; even Felle's flights of wit and humour (which much surpass all I ever saw or heard of his age) appeard not near so entertaining as when you were by ; ney, though my next friend, Nann, receivd me with all the modest transport a heart desirous to be particularly distinguishd by her could desire, yet there still wanted my one thing necessary to taste the rest, which till I am repossessd of neither Betty can be beautiful, Bab quick, nor Louisa lively, so forlorn am I. I have lookd into both the places you directed, where I found six tea canisters in all, only two whereof were full, the other four having little or nothing in them. I have also enquird after your side-saddle, as you desird ; the house-keeper tells me she has the velvet cover in her keeping, and Emmet has the saddle and the rest of its furniture

Vol. II.   D

in his.  I took the first and readyest opportunity of conveying Jack's letter
to you, as soon as I had given it a hasty reading.  I hope the very ill entertainment he met with in  the village he was forcd  to take his lodging at
near  Brussels will  teach him providence enough for  the future to arrive at
all fortified places before their gates are shutt, and also to relish those good
beds and bitts you will provide for him at his return with a better gusto than
formerly.  That this and every other occurrence of  his life may turn to his
benefit and your satisfaction  shall be  part of  the prayer of  your  constant
friend & lover, Bristol.

**482.**    Lady Bristol to Lord Bristol.      London, Oct. 20, 1716.

          I suffer the last impatience till Monday's post to
hear how my dear dear angel past his  journey this miserable  weather, and
if you have not got cold ;  I repent I did not bid Baldwin write by the stage-
coach a Friday ;  I had  the  pleasure of hearing yesterday you  got well to
Hockeril, but was mightily  mortifyd when I opend Will Clevers letter to
hear how  unlucky  you had  been with your trees, but  I  believe my two
drunken sotts at  their first setting out helpd it forwards.  I have seen the
Dutchess of Grafton since I  wrote last, and  find her  journey was put off
by Sir Thomas's advice, he not  knowing but he shoud come to Town if the
news was true of the Parliament  meeting so soon ;  whether he had his intelligence from  her Grace or any better  hand I  dont know, but by what I
hear there is nothing more uncertain or unlikely ;  but tis  possible we may
both ground  our opinion according to  our wishes, I having as  much desire
to go to Ickworth as she has to stay here ;  that I  may be able to gratify my
inclinations the first minute I can, pray let the horses be here next Saturday.
Though I  believe you may  know more  certainly by the Duke of Grafton
or Sir T. Hanmer any thing relating to the Parliament, yet I will endeavour
to get  the best intelligence I can  by Tuesdays post, for I design to go out

that day if this very bad weather does not continue; to day I know nothing, nor dont expect to hear any thing, for every body is gone to Hampton Court, being the Crownation day; if any of them shoud come here afterwards with any news, you shall have a postscript. My aunt Felton was here yesterday; she said my aunt Effingham is much as she was. Mrs. Meggot's breast is broke, and she is easier since; mine is much as it was when you left me; I have some pain in it by fits, but I believe the weather is the occasion of it. They have made such a noise this morning at my Lord Radnor's that it kept me awake, and has given me the head-ach intolerably, so that I am sure, if you were here, you woud say, Pray, my dear, have done writing; and whatever I think you woud have done if you were present, shall be punctually observd in your absence by, my dear dearest life, your ever faithful E. Bristol.

If you love me, take care you dont get cold in the park; Lady Harriott is very well; nurse says she turnd & listend to the great guns, but I dont believe it.

**483.** My ever-new Delight        Ickworth, Oct. 22, 1716.

The knowing you have passd any dismal nights since I left you will make me spend every day with much anxiety till we meet again; ney, even then I shant be perfectly easy, for fear your kind impatience to make me throughly so shoud put you upon undertaking a journey before you can perform it with safety; and shoud any ill consequence attend your future state of health from stirring sooner or farther than you ought, I coud never forgive my self the putting of it into your powers to be here before the time you at first proposd; which since you desire it, (and I so secretly wishd you might do so,) the coach shall be at London on Saturday next; but when it is there, I conjure you not to venture one day sooner than Sir David will ensure it shall not nor cannot hurt you; for I am not so selfishly abandond to my own pleasures as to have them gratifyd at so dear a rate as the breach of your constitution, and the pains and perils incident thereto. The feast of the full moon is celebrated this night at Bury, whereto I have been invited, not only by a message from my cousin Hanmer this morning, but also by a visitt from Mr. Duncomb, who told me the company woud be very much disappointed by my absence; but I told him I was engagd to a lady who woud not be there, and as she has engrossd my heart to such a degree as to make pleasures (coud I feel any) punishments where she cant partake, so I was resolvd to spend this evening in an entertainment wholly dedicated to her, which was to tell thee, if I can, how much I love thee, and how much I long to see thee again, being much more than ever yours for ever, Bristol.

Our sweet children, God be praisd, are all wonderfully well, & in order to keep them so were all about the park to day, as your son Felle said, like themselves in the coach and six, except sister Betty, who accompanyed me on horse-back, and is full as careful in every thing that concerns me as your heart can wish, and altogether as commendable in her whole conduct as mine can possibly desire.

**484.**    Lady Bristol to Lord Bristol.    London, Oct. 23, 1716.

How coud you, my dear dear angel, be so cruel to me as to reproach me for letting you go. Is not what I suffer by your absence punishment enough, without making me a cause of any to you for whose sake alone I did it, the thought of which has been the only thing that has supported me since, and indeed I dare not tell you how much I have wanted comfort, since I am afraid it has been to such a degree that it has put back what I wish most, which is my journey, for I am not well enough to venture out to day as I did design, the weather being very bad, so have been churchd at home; but I hope to go to morrow to take leave of the Dutchess of Grafton, who sets out on Thursday for Suffolk : (O how I envy her.) Pray, my dear, let the coach and horses be here a Saturday, though if there is any inconvenience in it, I'm afraid Tuesday will be time enough ; but I shall be glad to have it in my power to come the first minute I am able. I hope you have receivd the book and Jacks letter by Mrs. Fisher ; my Lady Portland sent me word he intended to set out for Hanover the Thursday after she came away, which was the 18th. I wrote to him last Friday, and got Lady Sharlot to inclose it to Madam Kilmansack, who will keep it for him, if he is not there ; if you or Betty write, I can send it the same way. I hope he will not find the same reception there he did with some in Holland, for which I hate them heartily. Here is not a word of news, but that the Pretender is dead, or at least given over. The Princess comes to Town a Saturday. The Dutchess of Roxbourough says she is not enough recoverd to go to the Birth-day ; but Lady Gar: Stanhope says she does not see but that she is as well as ever she was in her life, and her complexion so fine that she believes she will be a new toast, which will supply the loss of poor Lady Lichfield, who has got the small pox, but is like to do well ; her lord wont leave her, though he has never had it. All the ladies that were here a Sunday sent for Harriott to see her, they had heard so much of her, and she behavd herself as if she designd to increase their admiration by turning and looking upon every body. The Dutchess of Devonshire told me the greatest news she heard was what her lord had told her, that you had passd through Newmarket without calling upon any of them to enquire what was doing. Lord Hervey is come to day, but I have not seen him. My eyes are so weak I dare not read over this long letter, so you must pass by all the faults in it, as you have done many others of hers, who has no merit to pretend to but being so entirely & unalterably yours.—It is a strange request for one who longs so much to see you ; but

I beg you woud not think of coming as you once spoke of, for I had so much rather come to you as is not to be imagined.

**485.**    Lady Bristol to Lord Bristol.          London, Oct. 24, 1716.
          This letter came from Jack to day by the Dowager Lady Portland.  I have sent you the book the Duke of Buck : commended so much, hoping it may divert you.  I know not a word of news since last night's post that I wrote to you.  Mrs. Ramsey and Mrs. Eatton dine with me, and send their compliments and miss you very much, but that is nothing to what she feels hourly that dies every minute for want of you, as does your most faithful and tenderly affectionate E. Bristol.
    This box is for Nurse Tuer's breast.

**486.**    My ever-new Delight          Ickworth, Oct. 24, 1716.
          I resolvd not to put you in mind of your breast, hoping you would be troubled with no farther remembrances from it ;  but since you have felt any returns, (which I devoutly deprecated,) tis some ease to me that they seem so slight....I just now receivd Jack's letter and the book you sent to divert me, but nothing can please without you ; could anything have done so in your absence, it must have been the stranger in the enclosd lyste to be raffled for by the ladies, who it seems was known by no body at first, but made so good use of his time as left none to seek what sort of man he must be before the ball began ; for my Lady Gage descending from her seate to salute my Lady Bacon at her entry, the gentleman finding good places already grown scarce ascends into Lady Gage's, without offering to make any room for either of the ladies, who both stood near him in the area destitute of any.  See, what a sacrifice I made to your wish I woud not be there.  O, what an irretrievable loss to miss of so much beauty, witt, and gallantry ! beside the vast improvement I might

have made in good manners from the polite behaviour of that bell' ignoto. You can do no less in return than let me see you without faile on Tuesday next at Newmarket, which I long more to do, much more, than ever I did in all my life; for tho' that is drawing towards its evening, yet my love and friendship for thee are fixd in a meridian can never know declension, being fed by the fuel of such charms as (like the elementary fire) must be everlasting, because pure. The last word putts me in mind of my cousin Hanmer, (whose meritt has the least alloy of most mens,) to tell you he was so kind to come and dine with me yesterday, for whom your daughter deputy (like her principal) musterd up a very good entertainment on as short notice. I shall send you half a doe by your own coach on Friday, hopeing that will be sufficient for your own use till you gett hither, where after all I have said, and more that I must suffer in your absence, I had rather not see you this month than have your future health impaird to the shortening that life one moment, which is become so necessary not only to the happyness but the being of, my dearest life, your most faithful friend and constant lover, Bristol.

If the fruit trees are not come from France, lett the porter enquire for and take care to send them at the Dover carryers at the King's Head in Southwark.

487.　My ever-new Delight　　　　　　Ickworth, Oct. 25, 1716.

The long letter I wrote to you this morning by the post would have sufficed any heart less inexhaustible than my own; but as there is no end of your kindness, so my love has no bound, and makes me ever uneasy but when I am imparting its sentiments to the worthy object of it, and consequently cannot let slip any opportunity of conversing with thee this way till I am made happy by doing so in an other more agreeable to us both; in order wherunto I herewith send you the coach, but on the express and solemn condition that you do not venture out of London (keep it there or me here ne'er so long without you) till I can be sure of seeing you with the satisfaction of knowing you did not run the least hazard for my sake. Upon reading that part of your last letter where you complain of wanting spirits to such a degree as to disable you from going even out of doors, and that it might retard what you most wishd, I took a thorough resolution of coming in it my self, till I came to your postscript, which seemd to carry so sincere and hearty a prohibition in it to the contrary that I at last chose to gratify your desire rather than my own; and in return only beg you would not come to me one moment sooner than with the utmost safety to your self, since on this occasion poor Lady D'Ewes's reading woud be rightest of Ziphares's admonition, viz., Remember, O Semandra, my invaluable Semandra, that on thy conduct all his fortunes hang, who next to the infinite pleasure of living with thee would be glad to dye for thee, or suffer any other thing which coud shew thee the extream affection and matchless tenderness of your constant lover, Bristol.

If you find yourself not entirely well enough to begin your journey on Monday, let me know it by Saturday night's post, that I may not, as dear Felle says, meet with a baulk instead of my dearer bride on Tuesday at Newmarket. Even sister Betty allows Lord Hervey has servd us but a slippery sort of trick in getting back to London without baiting here by the way; however, give him my blessing and thanks for his letter, tho' there was no news in it, which I shall expect from him altogether whenever you leave London. The children are all well, and want nothing but dear Mama.

**488.**    Lady Bristol to Lord Bristol.        London, Oct. 25, 1716.
            I can now have the satisfaction of telling my dear dear angel that I have been abroad, which is one step to dear Ick-

worth. I was only at Prayers in the morning, and to take leave of the Dutchess of Grafton ; the afternoon was spent with my aunt Effingham; she is much better, and sends her ,compliments to you; she says she wants you mightily, which every body must do that has been blest with your dear company; I came home before seven, and thought I was much better ; but the first body that came to see me I found I coud not get up, nor make a courtesie without great difficulty for a great pain in one of my knees and hip ; but I took some Gascoins powder when I went to bed, and find my self much better to day ; however, I can bear that better than any of my other complaints, because it wont hinder my journey, which I am afraid they will till this day sennight, my first day fixd, but I am glad you are so kind to let me have it in my power to come sooner, which, if it is possible, you shall know by Saturday's post ; but I must assure you I have com- mitted no irregularity to keep me so weak and so much leaner then I believe you coud ever think to see me, but I believe the country air, joynd with the ease it will be to my mind, will sooner recover me then any thing I can do here. The only debauch I have made was with your son last night ; he sat with me in my chamber till the clock struck one. I have been all this morning employd in buying lace for him for the Birth-day; he woud have persuaded me (and so would my aunts) to have worn my fine cloaths Jack has sent me ; but I told them, if I were well enough for that, I could go to Hockeril, which woud be a much better entertainment to me then the Ball. Lord Hervey is gone to Hampton-Court; I will keep my letter open till he comes home in hopes of some news, though they make such a practice of opening letters that one dare not say any thing but what is in the prints. The Pretender, they say, is certainly in great danger, if he is not dead. The old Dutchess of Hamilton is dead. Mr. Gardener was with me yesterday ; I find by him that if he had not gone to see your trees that they woud have come all wrong ; I got him to write a note of what was to come, that you

Vol. II.    E

might be sure you had what he orderd ;  he says there is fewer filaroys then was first designd, because he has  sent 20  English bays  instead, he having had  great  experience how  well they thrive :  but not  better then (I  thank God) our  young plant Harriott does ;  she is coated to day, and is  as hand- som as an angel, and so like your dear self  that I kiss her to pieces.   I am sorry I cant tell you the same good news of the rest, but poor Harry is much out of order ;  I sent my  chair to  fetch him  home this morning ;  I hope it will  prove nothing but a  great cold, though he  has a pain in his side with it, but since  he has dind  he is  better, so I hope  it is chiefly wind ;  Mr. Graham  will give him  something to sweat, and I  hope to give you a better account of  him next  post.   The day is fine, so I will go out  to harden my self a little to the air.   I receivd a  100£  of  Mr. Wanley the  day after you went out of  Town ;   there was  remaining of  yours besides  230..16..6 ;   I suppose there may be more since ;  if you have any orders about that or any thing else, let me have it by the next post to, my dearest treasure, your most constant E. Bristol.

**489.**    My ever-new Delight              Ickworth, Oct. 26, 1716.
           I flatterd my self with the agreeable hope that the second letter I sent you by Adam would be the last I shoud have oc- casion to write during this absence at least, (trusting in God's goodness that very few, if any more, will ever happen again,) but by yours which I have just now receivd I despair of seeing you at Newmarket till next Friday ; and since your strength returns so slowly, and that your finery is come from France, you cannot with any good grace stay in Town and not appear on the Birth-night, which I desire you woud do, to shew them

> Our loyalty is still the same
> Whither it winns or loose the game ;
> True as the diall to the sun,
> Altho it be not shind upon.

You know I never desird any thing more than that they woud govern so wisely as to make themselves belovd as universally as they might have been and may still be, woud they choose such honest and honourable Councellors to be about them as have not only the inclination but the courage to tell them truths they have not yet had the advantage of hearing, and which they never can be truly popular till they encourage such advices as none but those of independant fortunes dare tell them. I have a double interest in the security and prosperity of the Royal family, both as a subject and an original stickler for settling the succession in their House, where I woud have it remain in full fame and true glory till time shall be no more.—Pray let your aunt know how glad I am to hear she is better, and that those who love to hear good things said on all occasions as well as I do must miss her good company much more than she can do mine.—I cant but suspect from Harry's constant good looks that his occasional fitts of sickness are only learning-qualms, that return on every knotty task that proves too difficult for the day ; and if he finds a sanctuary at home to excuse the performances his present station binds him to, he will in time fall from his Captain's post into the rear of all his company, which of all things in the world I woud have you be aware of indulging in him or any other of our cadettes.—By the complaint you make of the return of pains in your hipp and knee I conclude you gatt cold in going abroad the first time, which you may remember among other sound advices I chiefly cautiond you against ; but since they seem in the power of Gascoigns powder to allay, I hope they will not prove obstinate. As to your leaness, as long as I hear of no cough it does not at all alarm me, since I trust in God and Ickworth air to make and keep you in as embonpoint as shall be best for you or desird by your constant lover and faithfullest of friends, Bristol.

The babes are all well.

**490.**   Lady Bristol to Lord Bristol.      London, Oct. 27, 1716.

I please my self with the hopes that this will be the last letter I shall have occasion to write to my dear dear angel, except any unforeseen accident shoud prevent my setting out on Wednesday next, as I design, and hope to have that much longd for pleasure of seeing you on Thursday at Newmarket. I am sorry it cant be sooner, though I had settled every thing last night for Tuesday, but my rest was so broken with the pain of my hip & knee that I am fainter then ordinary to day, though I am still so weak that I cant be out above two or three hours at a time; I believe the impatience I have to be with the joy & pleasure of my life keeps me so back; my aunt Effingham is now of that opinion, though she was once much against my taking a journey, yet she bid me yesterday—for God's sake be gone, for it does you more hurt to sit fretting here then the journey can— she bid me be sure to tell you you had not a friend or relation in the world that lovd you comparable to her besides my self; her expressing so much kindness for you gives her a great deal of my company; I satt and read over your letters to her yesterday; she says she doubts you practice some- where else, or you coud not say such pretty things after 21 years. Mrs. Meggott is better, but her child is dead. The prince & princess are come to Town to day by water, that being thought the safest passage for her Royal Highness. The Town is grown very full, but as empty as ever of news : the most agreeable to me is just now happend, the Coach is come, and Adam's peeping in at the door has given me new spirits, which increasd so at the reading your dear dear kind letter that I sent for my chair-men to consult how farr they coud carry me off the stones, and upon the whole matter have resolvd to set out on Tuesday, and hope to meet you on Wednesday at Newmarket; let what will be the consequence, it will be more supportable then your absence, which can no longer be supported by, my everlasting happyness, your ever constant doting E. Bristol.

P.S. Harry, thank God, is almost quite well again. The inclosd letters came after Robbon had been at the carriers; my Lord Hervey and I have consulted about them; I have desird him to advise with Mr. Row about them, (he is one of the Custom-house officers,) which he will do on Monday, and expects your farther direction by Wednesday's post, in order, if possible, to get them sent by Thursday's waggon to Bury.

**491.**  To Lord Hervey.  Ickworth, Oct. 29, 1716.

Dear Son

My wife having given me hopes of seeing her at Newmarkett on Wednesday next, the trouble of getting my fruit-trees out of ye Custom-house will fall to your share, wherein I hope you will not meet with any difficulty that your friend Mr. Rowe may not easily remove; but in case you shoud want the assistance of a Commissioner, Mr. Thomas Walker will readily do any service in his power as soon as he is told who they belong to. I woud not have you move in this matter your self further than to employ Loyseul with your commands to ye two officers above namd, & whatever the charges amount to, do you give me credit for the discharge of them till I can know what they come to, & I will send you a note on Mr. Wanley for it by the first opportunity.—Now I am writing to you, I cant but take notice to you of a thing which concerns your interest at Bury, where there are two troops of dragoons come to quarter, a sort of guests ye town has never been acquainted with since King James's time, and they will think it very hard that at ye same time they send a Collonell to Parliament, they shoud not be exempted from troops, especially conscious as they are of being not only barely loyal, but ye most zealous Hanoverian Whig-Ministrymen in all Brittain. How your friend Mr. Pultney coud appoint them these quarters without your privity, or how you coud consent to it if he did, I & they must wait the eclaraisment of. As I had ye happyness to make them

the soundest subjects the King has, & ye most heartily affected to his succession and family, I hope no just occasion will be given them to abate of
their wonted goodwill to the present establishment.   I cant conclude without
letting you know how great a disappointment it was to me to miss of ye visit
you made me hope for in your return from Aswarby to London; and as the
pleasure I take in seeing & hearing you are both very great, so your
voluntarily depriving me of either is one of ye few things I coud with
reluctancy forgive.   You have but one way to make amends, and that is
when you are almost weary of those repeated rounds of entertainments this
dead season of the year yet affords at London, you woud come & stay twice
as long as you promisd at a place & with a person to whom its increasing
beauties become so many additional satisfactions, as often as he reflects
they may possibly yeild you as much pleasure as they have afforded to your
most affectionate father.

    **492.**   To Lord Hervey.        Ickworth, Nov. 10, 1716.
          Dear Son

                At the same time I am to thank you for the care
you have taken of the fruit-trees, which are got safe to this place, I must
trouble you again in behalf of Captain Gage, whose case I have inclosd sent
you; & desire you'd press Lord Townsend either to restore his comission,
or give a good reason why it hath been so long detaind to ye starving of
him & his family; if he hath been guilty of any fault which will justify
such usage of him, I shoud be glad to know it, that I might withdraw that
favour I have shewn him purely on the account of his father's forsaking
him, & all his other friends abandoning him ever since he forsook ye errors
& corruptions of ye Church of Rome; but if none such are to be assignd, I
hope power & prejudice are not yet arrivd at that formidable height as to
take away both a man's bread & reputation without deigning to give a

reason why he is so treated. Mr. Frezier gives no better a relation of the Inquisition establishd in Peru. On ne donne aucune connoisance aux accuser de ceux qui les accusent; il n'y a point de confrontation de temoins; ainsi tous le jours on arrete des innocens dont tout le crime consiste á avoir des gens interresser a leur perte. But as such proceedings are justly abhord by all honest men even in slavish & Popish countrys, I trust in God they shall never gain footing here; and as he is my relation, (tho' that may prove the poor man's greatest fault,) & that I obtaind his first commission for him, I shall positively insist on a reason at least why he is not restord at ye repeated instances of your etc.

**493.** To Mr. Walter Ray, Alderman of Bury.

Mr. Alderman                 Ickworth, Nov. 16, 1716.

           Having receivd a letter by last night's post from my son, wherein he tells me that he had no sooner obtaind an effectual order from Mr. Pulteney for removing the dragoons from Bury but he had the concern & surprise of seeing a letter writt to him by one of ye officers there, who gives him an account of ye greatest part of ye Corporacion shewing themselves much displeasd at hearing such a thing was stirring in ye Warr-office, and informs him that there has been a hall held at Bury on that subject, & that ye majority of ye Body have declared their desire to have the troops continued there; I think it behoves your selves, as well as me, to undeceive Mr. Pulteney in this matter as soon as ever you can by a letter from your self to my son by this very days post, which I hope you will not fail to do, & send me a coppy of what you write to him, that I may second it accordingly by another from my self. Whenever there can be a majority found in Bury of so senseless & slavish sentiments as to counter-petition for ye continuance of dragoons amongst them, even when they are not necessary, & can find friends to rid them of 'em, I shall think

it high time to beg I may be excused from interposing any farther in its
affairs; but as my native love to ye place has made its welfare & prosperity
necessary to my own, I hope that fatal day will never be beheld by ye eyes
of their most faithfull friend & your servant.

**494.**   Dear Tom                                    Ickworth, Dec. 3, 1716.
                            The just concern you shew for being suspected
only of a fault, and the satisfactory apology you have made to ye supposed
charge, has luckily servd to verify Pliny's observation in you: nulli
patientius reprehendunter quam qui maxime laudari merentur.   And
therefore I take ye first opportunity of releiving your mind by sending you
this acquittal in form from your share in the indictment, altho' I must still
so farr justify ye accusation as to say, since frater est fere alter, twas not
to be imagind you was ignorant of what was befallen Harry; his part was
neither right towards his parents nor your self, which I hope he is so
throughly sensible of as never to be guilty of the same omission.   Pray
give my humble service to Dr. Friend, & let him know his kindnesses to
you & your brother shall no more be lost on me than I hope they will prove
ill bestowd on you; as I remember you told me he lovd venison, I shall
therefore send him half a ha ..., ye first fatt one can be met with by your etc.
Your mama loves you, & wishes to see you a great & good man.

**495.**   To Mr. John Ward at ye Inner Temple.
                                            Ickworth, Dec. 14, 1716.
                            Mr. Thornton having some time since told Mr.
Milles that unless I woud throw ye advowson of ye Vicaridge of Digby into
his purchase he woud not proceed any further in it, I sent him word by ye
very next post I shoud never do it; so that if he does not think fitt to leave
that out, or pay the accustomed rate for it, & lett me have his answer quickly,

I shall look on my self at liberty to treat with those who will without any chicane not only allow the utmost value for the perpetual right of presentation, but pay for every stick of wood on the premisses, & be very glad to deal with me for Dunsby & Branswell estates also, and take it as a favour from your humble servant, Bristol.

**496.** To Mr. John Hervey. Ickworth, Dec. 14, 1716.

Dear Jack

The agreeable letters your fruitfull brain has furnishd your Mama and me with must make us regrett the miscarriages of any of them with as much greif as is naturally paid by parents to abortions of ye most hopefull progeny ; & such I cant but conclude is due (and felt accordingly) to the loss of that large bratt you mention in yours of ye 10th instant, which never reachd your father's sight ; and since their passage by ye ordinary posts is so precarious, I hope you will omitt no opportunity of writing to us by every courier which ye multiplicity of business on ye tapis will weekly require. As to your farther travells, I find your Mama's tears & fears are both so very predominant whenever Italy is but mentiond, that rather than put my self into ye uneasy scituation of standing answerable for all accidents that may happen in such an expedition, I am forcd not only to sacrifice my own judgment but your improvement to her foolish fondness ; and therefore when you see and are sure ye foundation in Prince Frederick's favour (the blooming beauties of whose person & character I wish my country & family as true joy of as so great a blessing in prospect deserves,) is laid as indelibly deep as you know I woud have it, and I know you are capable of contriveing, you may think of returning homewards ; but whether it will be convenient for you to come back at ye same time with ye King is a question you shoud consider well of, since those who have travelld with a Court & were not officers in it have

often wanted necessary accomodations; & shoud those who attend his
Majesty there take no more care of providing for ye son than others whom
he has thought to intrust here ever did for ye father,

> Then those who have their interests trulyest servd
> May thank their own estates they are not starvd.

However, be to them (I conjure you) like your constant father,

> True as ye dial to ye sun,
> Altho' you are not shind upon.

Methinks some of the smaller rays might fall on you, whatever reason has
intercepted them from me; & therefore since your return is determind, &
that idleness is rightly stiled ye Devill's shop, & your genius tending to
some military employ, your Mama woud be extreamly well pleasd if you
coud find any way to make his Majesty think you worthy the promise either
of ye first Guidons post or company in ye Guards that shall prove vacant.
She bids me tell you the lady who promisd to spend the first moment she
coud call her own in Mama's service cannot possibly employ it half so
much to her satisfaction as in assisting you to get something that may be
honourable for & so agreeable to you; put her but in mind of your bleeding
heart, & it must soften her own into a complyance with so just a request.
Make Mama's & my compliments to her & every other body on your side
the water, as you see proper; & believe it none from me when I tell you
how very much you are valued and beloved by your most affectionate
father.

**497.**   To Mr. Jouneau.                Ickworth, Dec. 14, 1716.

I am very much concernd to hear my son could
be capable of making so false a step towards you & me as well as him selfe
as to be presented to the King without you; were his travells to be of much

longer continuance, I should take effectual care to prevent a second error of that kind; but as his mother is not to be persuaded to lett him go into Italy, & that there is very little, if anything, worth seeing on this side the Alpes, I have by this post left him a latitude of returning home as soon as he finds he has securd ye prime point which carryed him where he is, viz., the favour & good opinion of Prince Frederick, near whose person I should be very glad to place you in the post you desire were it in my power; but as I have neither courted creditt, nor would be supposed to have any, till councils more agreeable to my judgment come to be given and taken, I can only at present recommend your pretensions to all the assistance my son can give them, which has been done accordingly by your friend to serve you.

I have received your accompaniments.

**498.** To Mrs. Burslem. Ickworth, Jan. 7, 1716.

Madam

Tis pity a pen that can so well please other people & might entertain your self so much should never stirr but when acts of charity or beneficence are its motives. I am very ready to second (& shoud rejoyce to succeed) your kind endeavours for Mr. Ellis; but being still here I cant assist him so effectually as I coud & woud have done had I been at London. However, I have written to severall of ye Mercer's Company not only for their own votes but all the interest they can make in favour of him, depending on your sincerity for ye truth of that character you give him, as I did for Thickbrooms. I most heartily congratulate ye happy return of those welcome hopes which will support you thro' all difficultys or discontents. May they all prove true prophets in every pleasing prospect, and all your doubts and fears as false impostors. God's power & goodness are both so infinite as to have retrievd even worthless

sinfull me out of a state of wretchedness & misery to a condition of ye most
perfect humane happyness, who knows how to make him no better returns
for his innumerable blessings than the sacrifice of praise & thanksgiving
which are daily, I may say hourly, offerd up for their continuance by etc.
My wife is very truly your friend & well wisher.

**499.** To Mr. Robert Reynolds. Jan. 18, 1716/17, just 37 years
Dear Cousin from ye death of my dear uncle John Hervey.
I have alwaies preservd so just an esteem for
those very valuable qualities you are owner of, that I have ever wishd you
had seen enough of them in me to have afforded me as much of your conversation as my relation alone lays claim to, had not a true affection desird
it also. Lett not then an immoderate humility so injurious to us both any
longer deprive me of a pleasure I may challenge sometimes as my due; nor
lett thinking over ye past suffice ; but sett your self to enjoy those future
happy daies you may yet make your own. Had God Allmighty's wisdom
thought me worthy of being intrusted with any talents, I should have
thought them better employd & improvd in my country's service than putt
to any other humane use; & next to that in doing good to my friends or
family; wherein as you stand doubly related to me, so not only you but
your son* (whose modest meritt I should be glad to have as much power as
will to gett advanced) may depend on ye readyest inclination to serve
either on all occasions from your etc.

**500.** To Lady M—n, who supposd she had engagd me to goe to ye
masquerade with her. March 4, 1716/17.
The plain sincere part I have chosen to act in life
has satisfyed my soul too well to think of wearing a disguise at last. Could

---

*Lord Bristol's marginal note says, Now Lord Chief Justice in Ireland.—S.H.A.H.

any consideration tempt me to assume one, twould be the mighty bribe of being some hours with the agreeable gipsy.  Plain-Dealer.

The pleasure of being rememberd by so very fine a young lady\* at my time of day has made me seem young again ;  may the cause & its effects continue ever.

**501.**  To Mrs. Burslem.                London, April 11, 1717.

Knowing  how  much  more  concern  you  must naturally have for Lady Fox's health than mine, I would not give you the trouble of setting you right as to my own till I could at the same time assure you her Ladyship is well also.  I have brought my soul to such a pitch of resignation that I can subscribe to that character of a true Christian :

He dares not wish nor his own fate propound ;
But if God sends, reads love in every wound ;
And would not loose for all ye joys of sence
The glorious pleasures of obedience.
His better part alone he fears to loose,
And all God's will can bear, can do, ney choose.

I can give you also ye satisfaction of knowing your daughter came off with great applause ;  the whole was so well performed that itts thought ye Princess will desire to see it acted once againe upon ye advantagious report made to her of it by ye Countess of Picbourg.—Branswell & Dunsby will both be sould, but not till I come into Lincolnshire, which will be about ye middle of July, when I hope to see you at Aswarby, and by word of mouth to assure you with how great truth I am your frind & well wisher.  My wife is very much yours.

---

\* Lord Bristol's marginal note says, Mrs. Balladine.—S.H.A.H.

**502.**   To Mr. Foulkes when dear Tom went to Oxford.

Sir                                                                              April 22, 1717.

The Bishop of Bristol having been so very kind as to take ye trouble on himself of directing every thing necessary for my son's reception in Colledg, there remains nothing for me but to recommend him to your best care & instruction. I flatter my self you will find such natural & acquird foundations laid in him as will encourage your industry to form as virtuous and as substantial a man out of both as is not only wishd but (I must add) expected by his affectionate father & your servant.

**503.**   To Mrs. Eliz: Manley (in Wales).           July 28, 1717.

You will find how powerfull an advocate you make use of toward me when ever you employ ye name of my kind and good uncle Hervey, since it has prevaild with me to send my picture with the tea you desird, a request I have denyd all that ever askd it except my two wifes, to whom I never refusd any thing. I hope Sir Thomas Hanmer will send you his also ; if he shoud want to be reminded of it, I am now got to my center of rest, sweet Ickworth, where I shall have frequent opportunities of solliciting that favour for you ; but I know his good nature is such, that ye very first minute I can convince him how great a pleasure twill give you to comply with your desire, a second petition will prove unnecessary from etc.

**504.**   To Sir William Ellys (then at Bath).

Aswarby, Aug. 28, 1717.

Your kind remembrance of me at so great a distance was too sensible an obligation not to draw upon you the trouble of my thanks for the present you ordered me from Nocton, which tho' the best of its kind, yet coming from a place which usd to afford me a much more valuable pleasure in your conversation till ye Bath began to rob me of it, I can never forgive the injury that place has annually done me, till I am assurd its waters have done your health as much good as has been constantly wishd you by your etc.

**505.** To Sir Samuel Garth, after his visitt to me at Bury.

Bury, Oct. 1, 1717.

Your readyness to oblige & your success in pleasing all you converse with makes every civillity you meet with so much your due by anticipation, that coud I have shown you many more than I had time or opportunity to perform, they woud not have deservd ye least of those acknowledgments you sent me. The fair which we found so full of wit & gallantry whilst you was here, has wore as different a face since you, the soul of both, withdrew, as when you saw the whole turnd into a masquerade. The loss of your company has made many proselytes here to her Grace of Grafton's opinion, that tis better never to know the taste of right champaigne, if tis not always in our power to drink it, since it destroys the rellish of our pallates for all other wines; but notwithstanding I am one of the greatest sufferers by the sad experience of this last truth, yet I cant conclude without giving you ten thousand thanks for that great favour to which we owe ye refining all our tastes, & in particular that of your etc.

**506.** To Sir William Ellys. London, Dec. 5, 1717.

Concluding the letter I wrote to you some time since miscarryd, I give you this trouble of a second to lett you know again that your goodness to Mr. Hervey when alive, and your charity to his children now dead, added to that constant kindness & civility I have ever experienced from you since my marrying into your neighbourhood, has made me think you have the best right to nominate any person you care most to oblige to ye Vicarage of Metheringham, whose choice shall be most readily approvd & confirmd by, Sir, your most faithful humble servant.

**507.**    To Mrs. De la Riviere Manley, (near Oxford).   Dec. 11, 1717.
            Had your nine neighbouring sisters clubbd thier joynt assistance, they could not have producd a piece so finishd in its kind as this unequal one comes to thank you for; Oxford being reinforced with the inspiration of such a tenth Muse may now surpass her learned corrivals in all polite performances throughout the world, since sure that praise was first pronounced in prophecy of you;

> Minerve pour l'instruire eut si peu de reserve,
> Qu'elle juge de tout comme feroit Minerve.

And as a demonstration of my sincerity in that belief, I beg you would without delay send me the essay you mention, knowing nothing falls from your pen but what is excellent.

> From what I've seen what is to come I've guesst,
> And most impatient grow to know the rest.

The complaint you make of a barren education only serves to sett the force & fruitfulness of your natural genius in ye strongest light, which as I had the pleasure & advantage of being early acquainted with, so I've from thence justly dated all those helpes, which have since taught me to distinguish true from false meritt either in persons, words or workes. In a mind not naturally ungratetul, conscious of such endearing benefits, you may easily imagine many more pleasing remembrances have passd than yours could possibly experience, since the share your superior talents furnishd to those entertaining ideas must ever farr, very farr, exceed the vainest valuations of your etc.

**508.** To ye Rev. Mr. Thomas Foulkes. March 18, 1717.

This comes to thank you for your last letter, which has sett my heart at ease for my son, whom of all the twenty children God has blessd me with I ever expected the nearest pattern of possible perfection from bearing throughout a most surprising resemblance to his good grandfather Hervey, whose piety, chastity, charity, truth and justice, mixd with wonderful witt and innocent mirth, made that comprehensive character entirely his own:—ita in singulis virtutibus eminebat quasi cœteras non haberet :—who, pray tell Tom, never playd at any game but whist, and at that only in Christmas-time for six pence a corner; wherefore I depend on his following such parts of that shineing example at least as are wholly in his power to practise. Play is become so epidemical a vice that few people of fashion can plead not guilty. I wish—video meliora proboque, deteriora sequor—were not my own case ; but as experience hath acquainted me with its numberless ills and inconveniencies, and that you have been so faithfull as to lett me know tis his predominant passion, I intend to write him a long letter on that subject, when he has entitled himself to such a marke of my favour by renewing his correspondence with me, which whether thro' shame or laziness he has much too long already discontinued, especially if he believes himself of consequence enough by his silence and our ignorance of his condition to have given his mother some pain, and more uneasyness yet to your assured friend.

**509.** Lady Bristol to Lord Bristol. Richmond, May 1718.

I have but a moments time to tell you I shall not have the pleasure of seeing you at Kensington to day ; we have lost the hopes of a young prince, but that you must not take notice of for the world, neither here nor elsewhere ; thank God the princess is better, but has been very ill. Adieu, my dear dear ; I have a hundred pretty things to say to

Vol. II. G

you from her Royal Highness if I had time; you must get all the news you
can for her; Richmond is a pretty airing after this rain, and woud do you
good.

510.    My ever-new Delight            London, May 14, 1718.
                    Courts may perhaps deceive the time, especially
where the most agreeable princess in the world makes every moment
entertaining to those who have the happiness to be near her; but mine I'm
sure passes tediously without you.

> Nor sleep, nor ease, thy absent lover find ;
> Sleep flyes my eyes, as quiet flyes my mind.

I ever foresaw your waiting weeks woud prove so many years, unless the
priviledg of being with you in them was permitted me, it being certain that
when one has lovd any thing without division or remission half so long as
I have you for its own sake, time and use grafts our only pleasures so
essentially upon that sole stock that our happiness can receive nourishment
from no other root.   I hope you have been so just as to let Lord Grantham
know by some remote occasional hint that I deservd a sack-possett, though
I had none; and that as short absences are sufficient to constitutions of my
constant, loving family to make new bride-grooms of, I hope he'll order one
against the next visit, which I intend to make you on Sunday, (as the
Dutchess of Grafton says she'l do too,) though having thee again nothing
else can then be wanting to your most affectionate Bristol.

P.S.  Make prince & princess sensible how well I love them & theirs.
The black was the prettyest, genteelest horse I ever bred.

511.    Lady Bristol to Lord Bristol.    Richmond, May 15, 1718.
                    I am so uneasy at being absent from you that I
cannot find words to express it my self, but have given orders to a little

Secretary* of mine to assure you in my name of the grateful sense I have of all those happy years I have enjoyd with you, and how I owe it all to your indulgent fondness of me, and that real protection I have found in having given my self into the arms of a man of your merrit. If I coud chide you for any part of behaviour to me, it shoud be for that unkind surmise that Courts have charms to engage me when you are not there ; how little can I deserve all you have done to make me the happyest of my sex if all my thoughts of pleasure did not centre in spending my days with you ; this absence, however esteemd short by those who do not love like me, the pain it gives me instructs me that I have never known till now how dear you are to me. I have read what my secretary has writ, but I find it impossible to answer your letter with the tenderness it deserves and I feel for you ; so that I order her to conclude after she tells you from her self she has the merrit of having curd me of a fitt of the cholick, and she resents that so well a bred man as you are woud not remember her in a postscript.—My secretary's penetration has found out so much of my own thoughts, that there woud be little left for me to say if I had time ; but there being a great deal of company here, which is very scarce, I can only tell you that the Prince is so fond of his new horse he carries every body to see him ; but I dare not press the other upon him, because they say he has been more gracious to me than ever he was to any body in his life in accepting this ; his Royal Highness has done me the honour to make me a visitt in my chamber, which has put my old friend in a fresh ferment of envy with me, and I am afraid will give him a fitt of rheumatism. Duke & Dutchess of Argyle dind with me yesterday. Pray, my dear, come early of Sunday, because I am to go to London soon in the afternoon to stand godmother for the Princess to Mon : Shutes child ; and if you coud imagine how much I

* Lord Bristol writes in the margin, Lady Suffolk.

long to see you, you woud meet me at the young Princesses lodging at Kensington to morrow between seven & eight a clock; I will take care you shall be let in, and will leave one of the Princesses footmen to shew you the way to your constant mourning turtle, E. Bristol.

P.S.  The Speaker tells me to day that Lady Dorset will be in Town on Saturday night; therfore I desire you woud send my service to her, and that I hope she will be here a Sunday at dinner or early in the afternoon, because I am to obey the Princesses commands at London. They make such a noise about me I don't know what I do.

**512.**    My ever-new Delight            London, May 17, 1718.

Though I was an utter stranger to your little secretary's hand, yet I soon discoverd by the beauty of the sense and sentiments Mrs. Howard only must have been your amanuensis; who I concluded had understood finesses so well as to have chosen rather than condemnd (had she card one farthing for the husband) being omitted in a postscript to a wife's letter. I know she has a magazine of wit sufficient to cure any maladies of the mind, but were your vapours occasiond by my absence, (which by a fellow-feeling, exclusive of the vanity natural to our sex, I can easily imagine,) I woud not methinks have had them quite allayd till Sunday, when I hope our meeting will reciprocally banish all uneasynesses between you & your most affectionate Bristol.

I will take care of your message to Lady Dorset.

**513.**    To Mrs. Bradshaw.            May 16, 1718.

I shall be so throughly pleasd to see my house at Bury made again the temple of vertue by two such worthy successors to my chaste and constant parents as Sir John & Lady Rebecca Holland, that you may lett them know they shall have it for thier own time & on thier own terms. If I have had the good fortune to prevent the least ill one from attending you, the greatest share of satisfaction resulting thence will be more sensibly felt by, Madam, your most humble servant, Bristol.

**514.** To my niece Meggott on ye death of her very good husband.

Dear Niece                                                            June 4, 1718.

Had I heard any certain account of ye great loss it has pleasd God to send you before your brother told me of it yesterday, you would sooner have receivd my wife's & my condoleance upon it. I have trodd ye same thorny path before you, & can assure you there is no relief or remedy in your case but by a through resignation to ye will of infinite wisdom & mercy, which, if you can obtain grace enough to acquiesce in, both can and will (tho' not, it may be, now conceivable by you) recompense every dutiful submission to it. That you may in his due time putt off nature just enough to reape the benefitt of such a necessary piece of true Christianity, shall be ye prayer of your most affectionate uncle.

If I can be of any service to you, lett me know wherin.

**515.**    Lady Bristol to Lord Bristol.        London, July 20, 1718.

If I shoud tell you I am well come to this place, I shoud forfeit a truth that has ever been kept sacred since the first moment I knew you ; for indeed, my dear dear angel, I never had so dismal a journey in my life, notwithstanding Jack did all he coud to divert me; at my getting into the Coach at Born-bridg I burst out into a flood of tears to find I was going still farther off the centre of all my happiness, and indeed a greater than ever fell to any mortal's share ; but if I were to say all my heart is full of upon that subject, I shoud have as little sleep to night as I had last night, which coud not be calld resting, for indeed I never was farther from it in my life, which made me the sooner here to day. I was at home between one & two a clock, where I found Lord Hervey, who told me he had wrote to you last night all the news there was; he goes with me to morrow to Richmond. I dind to day with Mrs. Dunch according to my appointment, but coud learn nothing, though Mr. Secretary Craggs was of the party and the Duke of Grafton, who sets out on Tuesday for Euston with the two Dutchesses. The Dutchess of Shrewsbury has been dying, but is better; the Princess came to see her a Friday. Sir John Jermain and Lady Betty are come to town again, he being much worse, and is to have a consultation of physicians to morrow to determine whether he goes to France or Bath; but notwithstanding this I had two messages and Lady Betty to call me to go to the Spanish ambassadors, the most dismal place I ever saw, and the Knight to every bodys thinking just expiring at the table, while the lady had a swarm of lovers upon the near approach of being a rich widow. In the mean time I satt gasping with impatience to tell my dear dear life (if it were possible) how much and dearly I love him and long to see him, which I depend upon for the Bath, else I am sure I cannot have the good I find by this journey I have so much need of, as well as what is Sir David's opinion, who has been here to night.

**516.**    Lady Bristol to Lord Bristol.    Richmond, July 21, 1718.
            I find that time (that they say is a cure for all things) does but add to my uneasyness; for though I have been receivd here with all the kindness imaginable by my Master & Mistress & indeed the whole family, yet I fear I cannot dissemble enough to receive it with the pleasure I ought. I have inclosd Mrs. Howard's letter to you, which I found at London; I hope you will bring her a horse your self, for it is upon that hope alone I can subsist, for I really am not well neither in body nor mind, and to help both I am to wait upon the Prince & Princess at five a clock to Epsom-Wells, with three coach-fulls incognito, to all the diversions there,

and to supp after it. Lady Burlington & Lady Pembroke dind with me, and they stay for me, therfore I can stay no more, for I expect to be calld every minute. Though this is but a few hours before the post goes out, if any thing happens before, you shall hear from me again, though Jack said he woud write. Lord Hervey did not come with me, nor I have not seen him to day.—The painters are intolerable, if you dont write a word or two to quicken them, for I coud not see any of 'em, and every room is in a litter and nothing done, they are so idle.

**517.** My ever-new Delight        Ickworth, July 21, 1718.

I hope this will find thee well arrivd at Richmond, and that you found the Prince and Princess so too, to whom I trust you will always take care to make my duty acceptable. I already find how precarious the pleasures of this place are without you, and how beholden Ickworth was to your presence for all its charms, since your absence has robbd it of every one I used to see in it; the park and gardens (though both the creatures of my contrivance more for your entertainment than my own) are now unable to afford me the least satisfaction, unless in the sweet remembrance of those blessd hours I have spent in them with you, which yields at best but a pleasing sort of melancholly to a mind inured like mine to constant better cheer. How I am like to bear the long remainder of that tedious time I am to pass here by my self is a secret I must keep from you, because I know twould grieve much more than please you ; were it not for the children who frequently feed my famishd eyes with pretty copies of their amiable original, I shoud have no comfort left to subsist on ; but they seeing how much I want to be diverted, by turns endeavour (tho' in vain) to supply your room. Felle, as the surest means to please, undertook to represent your self in settling oeconomicks with your housekeeper, wherin he shewd not only a marvellous memory, but as close a resemblance in speech & action as the good God of nature has bountifully bestowd on him in beautiful features. May he grant him half the grace his Mama is mistress of, and his wife will be almost as happy as you have made your most affectionate husband, Bristol.

**518.**    Lady Bristol to Lord Bristol.    Richmond, July 22, 1718.
Miserable as I am in body and mind, to whom shoud I complain but to the dear kind partner of all my happiness and distress, which indeed at this time is very great, for I am hardly able to stand or go, for we did not come home from Epsom till six a clock this morning, but I must say, to make amends for the fatigue, I never saw people in so good humour as the Prince & Princess, and consequently all the rest of the company; but I am so much out of order that my company that dind with me to day have made me lie down till this minute that I gott up to make my complaint where I know I shall be pittyd ; and now I think I am easier, but that will not be lasting, for the coaches are come to go to Kensington, so that I must bid my dear dear life, Adieu. The Prince is charmd with his horse; I hope he will like the fawns as well, and be as much pleasd as I shall be to see any thing out of Ickworth-park, but a letter more especially, which is what I long for. I am calld, and can no more. Adieu.

**519.**    My ever-new Delight        Ickworth, July 23, 1718.
Truth is so invaluable a jewel that I woud not have you sully the luster yours has ever shind with, even to prevent the pain I must feel whenever I know you are not so well as I alwaies wish you ; were I so strictly sincere as I shoud be towards you in all things, I coud not send you a much better account of my self; but reciprocal complaints will be farr from mending either of our conditions, though I dare

answer we woud not have each other less sensible than we are of our present separation, whatever other uneasynesses indolence might free us from. Pray tell your secretary, if ever my heart proves capable of falshood, she best knows who must be chargeable with the crime of making me like any woman at all beside your self; and least that new-born inclination shoud grow stronger, I am religiously resolvd to mortify rather than indulge my self the dangerous pleasure of her bewitching correspondence. As to a padd, you know I have none but that I bought for you, which neither proves good or handsome enough for her; but I will lend her Union, if she pleases, till Prince Frederick comes, (for whom, being like himself a nonpareil of his kind, I ever designd him,) whose size will suite her symmetry better than my letters woud her witt and vivacity. I hope the fawns are gott safe to you; if they are not, tis not for want of all the care & caution that coud be thought on to have them so, but from the nicety of their nature when taken too late from the does. I have this night sent a buck to go by Bury-coach, with a letter directing Robin our porter to send a messenger with half of it to Mrs. Nevills, and to go on with the other half to Richmond for your self. These are things you may excuse a sharer in, since you so entirely engross the heart & soul (unless you'll admit your little secretary to a small dividend) of your constant friend and lover, Bristol.

**520.    Lady Bristol to Lord Bristol.    Richmond, July 24, 1718.**

O my dear dear, imagine (if you can) how much I suffer when I date a letter to you the 24th July without the least hopes of seeing you to morrow to celebrate that blessed day, blessed indeed to me, and therefore so much greater is the pain of absence, which I hope you'll relieve on Sunday the third of August, else (though rackd as I am with my rheumatism ever since I came hither) I am determind not to go to the Bath;

Vol. II.    H

I woud not give my dear life the pain of knowing what I endure but upon
this occasion, but my leg is so swelld that I am hardly able to stand while
the Princess is dressing ; I walkd last night (with my stick) to the farther
end of the terrass, but there the Princess had the goodness to force me to
stay till she walkd to Que-Green, a mile & half farther, to Ma : Buquen: ;
as I was satt upon the bench, the messenger came by with your dear letter,
and gave it me over the wall, which I read over so often that I was overtaken
with darkness, and all alone by myself coud hardly find my way through
the wood, but by good luck I rememberd a cut that led into the great walk,
where I mett the Prince, who laughd ready to kill himself to see the fright
I was in ; I made your compliments which they return with thanks ; I told
the Princess how you were charmd with that evening's conversation ; she
bid me tell you she will not believe you are sincere without you come again ;
I am afraid you will think this is a speech of my own making, but upon my
word it is not, though it is the only artifice I woud be guilty of to you. The
Prince and Princess (thank God) are both very well, and in such good
humour that they inspire every body else with mirth but such a forlorn
creature as I.   My brethren, the lords and grooms of the bedchamber,
entertain me to morrow at the tent to keep my wedding-day, where the Duke
and Dutchess of Argile & Lady Delorain are to meet me at dinner, and Mrs.
Howard & the Maids are of the party ; they have offerd me a ball, but I am
to go to Kensington with my mistress.   Lord Hervey came here yesterday ;
I conclude he is well, but I have not seen him, though as he came into the
house I invited him to dinner & supper with Lord Delorain (who is in
waiting) and does both with me every day, I believe out of discretion, for
fear of drinking, after his fall from his horse, which he has been very ill
with, the horse having kickd him on the breast.   The Dutchess of Kingston
has miscarryd and goes to the Bath, and her lord with her ; you see what

is still uppermost in the mind and heart of your ever faithful mourning turtle, E.B.

P.S. I hear nothing of the fawns ; pray kiss mine for me, and Felle in particular for entertaining you so well.—Just as I finishd my letter the fawns are come, six of them safe and well, the other dead ; the Prince is extremely pleasd with them, and came in from shooting on purpose to take care of them; he fed them with his own hands, and has walkd me about all this morning to see his birds and other creatures; and as soon as the Princess was dressd, the Prince took her and all the court (men & woemen) to see the fawns again, so that I am quite tired. Lady Suffolke & Lady Burlington (who dind with me) present their services to you. Lord Hervey told me he woud write, so I have nothing to say from him. Once more, my dear, Adieu.

**521.**   My ever-new Delight                    Ickworth, July 25, 1718.

Our wedding day.

As when the bird of wonder dies, the matchless phœnix, (says Shakespear somewhere) her ashes new create an heir as great in admiration as her self ; so upon this blessd day kind Heaven largely recompencd ye loss I bore with such submissive resignation by giving into my arms the worthyest woman of this or any other age ; beauty, good sense, truth & honour, in strict perfection ; yet even all these rare and valuable qualities coud never have made me the happy man I am without that humble heart you have shown in being not only contented but throughly pleasd these three and twenty years with those poor objects niggard Nature had unequally bestowd on me toward attaching and engrossing so much superior meritt as dwells in thee.

O ! were woemen all like thee, men woud adore them,
And all the business of their lives (like mine) be loving ;
The nuptial bed shoud be the pledge of peace,
And all domestick cares & quarrels cease ;
The world shoud learn to live by virtuous rules,
And marriage be no more the test of fools.

With what transports of pleasing passion have I daily gazd & thought on those winning charms, which have all along so powerfully preservd a Joseph-like virtue in a soul naturally prone to amourous sensualities ; your kindness clippd the wings of a most high-flying fancy, & sweetly confind a wandering heart at home by the laws ot its own contentment ; so that

There's now no room for change, nor need there be,
Where one contains such vaste variety.

To this auspicious day, beside the treasure of your love and the preservation of my virtue, I owe the additional blessings of so many beauteous babes as now surround me ; coud any thing content me but their all-sufficient mother, they might ; but alass ! that's impossible ; without her there's neither peace nor pleasure for their forlorn father.  The morning of this day I spent in fervent prayers that the future scene of our love & lives may prove as prosperous as the past.

Hear me, bounteous Heaven !
Pour down your blessings on her beauteous head,
Where everlasting sweets are always springing,
With a continual giving hand ; lett peace,
Honour & safety always hover round her ;
Feed her with plenty ; lett her eyes ne'er see
A sight of sorrow, nor her heart know mourning ;
Crown all her daies with joys, her nights with rest,
Harmless as her own thoughts, all lasting as her virtue.

This oraison thus ended, the next petition I put up was to this effect ;

> Gránt me but life, good Heaven, but length of daies,
> To pay some part, some little of that debt,
> That countless summe of tenderness and love,
> For which I stand engagd to this All-excellence ;
> I shall have livd beyond all æras then
> Of most desird time, when once I've made
> This exquisite, this most amazing goodness
> Some recompence of love & matchless truth.

The conclusion of my hymn, sacred to this dear day, ended in a gratefull chorus, wherein I hope you have been made so happy by it as cordially to joyn with me.

> Thro' each revolving year may this day be
> Distinguishd in the rounds of all eternity ;
> And lett's to Heaven our annual tribute pay
> For the great blessings of this happy day :

I chiefly, who enjoy so farr the happier lot, possessing thee preeminent by so much odds. To God's infinite goodness, for this in particular and all other his blessings and benefits vouchsafd me, be all praise & thanksgiving for ever paid by thy most happy husband, faithful friend & constant lover, Bristol.

Thy dear kind letter is just come in, for which I'll thank thee more at large by next post.

**522.** Lady Bristol to Lord Bristol. Richmond, July 25, 1718.

I believe I shall take up all the time you shoud do your business in with reading my letters, for this is the fourth I have wrote this week, for every moment I have to my self is this way employd, as you will know when I tell you, my dearest life, I am now at Kensington waiting upon the Princess, and with great impatience expecting your letter, which I have sent for from London. I have been most magnificently entertaind to day at the tent, where your health was drank. The Prince & Princess did me the honour to compliment me upon this happy day, as did all the Court; but I am too sincere for one of that society, for I coud not dissemble enough not to let them see I wanted a large addition to my entertainment, for which they plainly saw I had been crying. But I will indulge this subject no longer, and tell you the news here. The King had an express to day at twelve a clock, which brings word that the peace is signd between the Emperor and the Turks for 24 years instead of 12 (which was the first agreement), and the Venetians included in the same agreement.

**523.**    Lady Bristol to Lord Bristol.    Richmond, July 26, 1718.

Saturday morning in my bed, to rest my poor legs, which are very bad; Jack is sitting by me at breakfast; he lay last night at Lord Hervey's lodgings; they both of them dind & supd with me yesterday; the rest of the company I told you in my last. I did not receive your letter till I came home last night; I think since my secretary had so large a share in it, you might have sweetend it with telling me I shoud see you to morrow sennight; for though I think myself sure of it (after all I have told you), yet it woud have pleasd me better to have had it from under your own hand. I hear nothing yet of the venison, so that if it comes at all, it must be in all the heat, which is extreme to day. I am so generous a rival that I have promisd to leave her room for a postscript, therfore must bid my dear dear angel adieu. Kiss the dear children for me.—I am orderd to send the inclosd without reading; you may guess if I obey; I find she woud be very glad of a scrub horse.

**524.** My ever-new Delight                    Ickworth, July 28, 1718.

Could you imagine into what strange perplexities
of mind your pressing my journey so to the Bath has thrown me, you woud
either never have done it, or will yet let me know that you will try to
undertake it without me. There is so long a roll of reasons against my
thinking of it, that to enter into the detaille of them woud take up more
time than I am master of, it being now late, Sir John Holland having dind
and stayd here till it was near night, after which I walkd with Betty to
take her leave of Mrs. Duncombe, and am but just gott home by moonlight to tell you, that if you cant resolve to go with young Jack and leave
the old one at home, but that he must exchange the health, the good hours,
the quiet, the innocence, the frugality (which considering the condition of
my finances is to be thought on) of this place for the noise and nauseous
company, intolerable heats both in and out of doors I ever mett with at
Bath, I say think throughly of it; and if the last result be (which I shall
expect by Friday's post) that you will not if I dont go too, rather than your
life shoud want the prolongation of an hour in my power, (though I woud
almost as soon make Orpheus's tour to redeem his lovd Euridyce,) I will with
pleasure resolve to sett out when you desire. Judg first how weighty &
powerful those considerations must be that can come in any competition
with the necessary pleasures I ever feel in being with thee, and then
determine as you think fitt of him, who devotes all his daies to come as
well as past to make you easy & happy. Good night, my angel : yours for
ever, Bristol.

**525.** Lady Bristol to Lord Bristol.    Richmond, July 29, 1718.

O my dear dear life, how can I ever return thy
wonderous tenderness and love : the entire possession of my poor unworthy

heart can never half repay the rich treasure of yours, who was surely born
for my eternal delight and comfort in all my distresses; for I receivd your
dear letter last night at a time when nothing else coud have revivd me
almost from the dead; if I have strength enough, I will tell you all. On
Sunday night I waited on the Princess to Kensington, and then to London;
I came home very much fatigued, eat only an egg, and went to bed; in the
morning I was calld up in a great hurry to go to the Princess at the summer
house, so that I woud not stay to eat my breakfast, and put my self in a
great heat to make hast; we went immediately to Kensington to see the
Princess Amelia, who was not well; by that time I fell into a violent fitt
of the cholick, and thought I shoud have died in the coach coming home;
I went immediately to bed, and some time after I fell into a violent vomiting.—My lady is so very faint that she is able to write no more. Mr.
Graham has been up with her all night; she took a quieting draught that
gave her five or six hours rest towards morning; and is so much better to
day that she hopes your Lordship will have no uneasyness on this account.
My mother charges me not to ommit telling your Lordship how most
particularly kind the Prince & Princess with their whole family have been
to her during her illness. Mrs. Howard's good nature carryd her so farr as
to offer her service to sitt up all night, but that being refusd she insisted on
being calld in case of a relapse. My Lady hopes by to morrow's post to
hear that this is the last letter it will be necessary to write before she has
the happiness of seeing your Lordship, without which she despairs of a
perfect cure. I am, my Lord, your lordship's most dutyfull son & humble
servant, John Hervey.

   I must once more take my pen to tell my dear I am much better since I
gott up; the Prince has just sent to know how I do, and Mr. Hill has been
so kind to come to see me, and offer me to be at his house while I am ill,

but I hope to morrow to be well enough to wait again. Sir David (who is now here) has given me leave to go down to see the Princess. Pray, my dear, dont be uneasy, for if I am worse I will certainly send a messenger to you, my only cure.

526. Lady Bristol to Lord Bristol. Richmond, July 31, 1718.

How, my dear, coud you be so cruel as to keep me so long in suspence of a pleasure you never designd me; it had been much kinder if in your first letter, instead of telling me how hard it was to live without me, you had set forth (as you have done in this) how agreeably you pass your time with polite Sir John all day and mad Sophy at night; good God, that I should live to the day that a visitt to that romantick fool shoud be thought reason enough (to one that loves like me) to shorten the pleasure you know I always take in your letters; at least you shoud have allowd a little more time to sweeten the bitter draught you have given me in this, in which you might have spard half the ingredients to a soul so tender as mine, and yet it woud have been sufficiently strong enough for me to have desird you not to come; not that Jack (dear as he is) is any equivalent to his much dearer father, to whose ease and quiet I ought (as well by duty as inclination) to sacrifice my own ; and sure there never coud be a greater tryal of such a resignation than now, and what I have sufferd this night to bring it about I dare not tell you ; but sure the tempest in my soul was greater than that in the air, and had more showers] to allay it, and with as little success, for every body says there never was such a night of thunder & lightning known in England, nor so hot a day as this after it, which increases my faintness very much, though, thank God, my fever is quite gone, and the little pain & sickness that I have now & then I believe only proceeds from weakness and soreness in my stomach. I began yesterday to wait again, but the Princess is so good she woud neither let me stand or walk; nothing but this last shock of illness shoud constrain me to this hated journey to the Bath; not but that I hate Ickworth as bad, since you can be pleasd there without me, and I believe that hatred will be increasd if people that live within two miles can come and spend whole days; I am curious to know how he coud entertain you, (for I know he must talk,) whether with an old story of his grandfathers, a pun of his fathers, or some scraps of the sublime parts of his she-friend, Peggy. I suppose Betty has been so taken up with that correspondence had made her not do me the honour to write. I had hopes of your being in town on Saturday to fetch me home on Sunday, for I find it absolutely necessary to be one day in Town before I go to the Bath. The painters have left the house in such disorder there's never a room to be in; they have not been there since I came. I am afraid to begin another sheet of paper for fear of contradicting what I wrote in the last, to tell you not to come. O my dear, both hand & heart trembles at those words; I am upon the rack for fear of saying too little or too much; I hope—I dare not say what, will be in Town on Sunday, for I begin to pay for my lodgings at the Bath Wednesday the sixth of August. It is impossible to be without the cook, which I think I forgot to speak of. Mrs. Howard waited with great impatience the opening of your letter, to see if there was any thing to her; when I told her there was not she said, Is that possible? Has the varlett said nothing to me? O monster of ingratitude. She begd mightily to see the letter, but she soon read it in my eyes, and indeed my pride woud not give me leave to shew it, for fear it shoud confirm all their opinions, that the rest (I have braggd so much of) were but flattery. God forbid, for there needs but that to compleat the misery of E. Bristol.

I think I am like Lady M. Wortley, who has wrote me four sheets of paper from Constantinople; I wish I coud send it.

**527.** To Mrs. Howard. (Now Lady Suffolk.) 1718.

The bel esprit your billet so abounds with
throughly shows the man had some sense, who, conscious of ye vast
inferiority of his own to yours, woud prudently have waved a correspondence must necessarily expose his insufficiency to maintain an equal
one with her, whose stile

> Like a delicious streem it ever ran,
> As smooth as woman, yet as strong as man.

However, since the price we pay for pleasures shoud be proportiond to ye
satisfaction they afford us, I am now content rather than have it discon-
tinud even to suffer the mortifications I shall frequently feel in being so far
surpassd in ye beauties of diction as well as sentiment by that very woman
you most unjustly abuse with ye epithet of simple. You might easily
account for Lady Bristol's crossness to you if you'd please to reflect a little;
in short she finds she caught a Tartar in recomending that simple person
you wott of to my friendship, whose meritt begins to usurp a much larger
share in it than she can possibly with ease allow to any. Things are
grown already to that taunting, testy pass as in her last letter to tell me,
" since my secretary had so long & so particular a paragraph in my letter,
you might have sweetend it with telling me etc." And indeed I must
needs say one ought to be endowd with a double portion of patience (which
she was never blessd with) to bear such trying accidents with courtesy.
You advise me as a friend to appear at Richmond to plead off some high
crimes imputed to me there; but if, instead of acquitting my self from
those, I shoud chance to incur the guilt of any misdemeanours too, what
woud become of so incorrigible an offender.

**528.**   To ye Worshipful Mr. Cary, Alderman of Bury St. Edmunds.

Sir                                                    Dec. 2, 1718.

You being chief magistrate of a town I have ever felt a most innate affection for, makes me address my self to you as the properest person to contrive ye best disposal of a small Charity I intend towards the relief of those poor families who are afflicted with ye small pox. My steward Oliver has direction from me by the same hand which conveys this to you to pay one hundred pounds to such person or persons as you & your brethren of ye Corporation (to every member whereof I desire you would make my service always acceptable) shall think fitt to appoint ; and when yee are mett to deliberate on ye most impartial method of distribution, which I'm sure by these means will be observd, I hope you will do me the favour to make them accept of six dozen bottles of wine, which will be likewise orderd for such meeting (whenever you'l appoint it) by, Sir, your etc.

**529.**   To Mrs. M. on ye verses* she made of dear wife & our family.

Madam

Your poem is so perfect that I would as soon attempt mending ye Magnificat as making any alterations in it. I woud have waited on you to tell you so my self, but am obligd to pay my court in Leicester Fields, where I've not been since I saw you. Ye first hour of leisure I have shall be employd to bring you ye joynt thanks of the whole House of Hervey, and particularly those of, Madam, yours etc.

---

* These verses by Mrs. Manley are copied into the 2nd of the two quarto volumes containing the correspondence between Lord and Lady Bristol. I have printed them after the letters. From an entry in Lord Bristol's expenses it would appear that Mrs. Manley received 20 guineas for writing the verses.— S.H.A.H.

**530.**    To ye Reverend Mr. Butts.                    Dec. 26, 1718.

The plentiful fortune God's good providence has graciously allotted me would have provd but half a blessing, had he not also vouchsafed me a heart farr from being insensible of my neighbour's poverty. I had not only ye advantage of having some humanity conveyd to me from both my dear parents natures, but also ye benefit of their bright examples in all acts of charity : sequiturque patrem non passibus æquis. However, as I ascribe most of my prosperity to God's blessing on their unfeigned virtue and piety, & as twas rightly said of Lord Chief Baron Manwood's being so charitable, that he and ye poor had but one revenue, that he therby made ye very best settlement ever lawyer drew of a lasting estate to have and to hold to him and his heirs for ever, so by ye grace of God my children & posterity shall never want ye efficacy of ye best entaile my circumstances will admitt of in ye same kind ; & since ye bowels of ye poor are so rich a soile as to bring forth an hundred fold, sure no money can be put out to near so good an intrest on any other fond by your assured friend.

**531.**    To ye Dutchess of Marlborough.                    Jan. 18, 1718/19.

When I first proposd that ye trustees (if ye mortgage mentiond any) should give thier receipt for ye interest-mony, (they in that case being as I conceivd ye only persons who could legally discharge it,) then your Grace was of opinion ye Duke of Marlborough's acquittance might be sufficient; to which having signifyed my consent, you now seem to dislike my acceptance of that expedient, because exclusive of ye trustees; so that I being wholly at a loss how to please, must waite your Grace's fixd resolution, both as to ye form of ye receipt & ye time to which your Grace would have ye interest paid, even to ye very day tis due, if you so

please. The last part of your Grace's letter was, I must confess, so incredibly surprising to me that I cannot but hope you must have mistaken
your information, or I ye reading of it. You are pleasd to say, "You think
"it one instance of thier (ye trustees) being careful & just men, since they
"would not advise ye Duke of Marlborough to change a real security for
"one that is already ingagd by ye settlement on your first marriage etc:"
which plainly intimates that I had offerd lands in lieu of ye present
security, which were pre-ingaged ; a charge, if true, would make me ye
worst of men, except ye person who could tell your Grace so foule a falshood; for such I will undertake to prove it, whenever your Grace will give
me ye opportunity (a piece of justice I expect & insist on) by letting me
know who could be capable of endeavouring so basely to traduce an integrity,
for ye preservation wherof all other interests in life have been all along
sacrificed by, Madam, etc.

532.   To ye Dutchess of Marlborough.      Jan. 20, 1718/19.
        If, when for form sake I was advisd to take ye
trustees receipt, your Grace seemd dissatisfyed that ye Duke of Marlborough's
was not as well proposd, & that after I had expressd all readyness to accept
of his your Grace then wrote me word you could not think I was less safe in
taking a receipt from ye trustees or any of them, since they were men of
honour & substance etc., what could I conclude from this but that neither
were agreeable in thier turns as soon as they became my choice? However,
it being now near a week to ye time ye interest will be due, Mr. Guidott
may draw such an acquittance as will discharge me when tis paid, he only
knowing what will be effectual, having all ye deeds in his own hands. And
now, Madam, as an honest reputation is of farr greater value than ye
interest or principal of any mony can amount to, so I must again take leave
to renew my request that you would not treate mine in so very slight a

manner as to tell me tis a subject of no use, after having given it one of ye deepest wounds it can possibly receive; but to do me justice in letting me know from whom I receivd it, that, if found to have been deservedly given, it may bleed on to shame and reproach; but if unjustly, that those who would murder in ye darke may be exposd to infamy, and all due reparation made to, Madam, your most injurd servant.

**533.**    To ye Dutchess of Marlborough.    Jan. 23, 1718/19.

I am satisfyed with ye draught of ye receipt, & will send your Grace a bill for ye interest mony on ye day it will be due; but for ye very same reason your Grace now says ye discharge can be given by no body but ye Duke of Marlborough (ye mortgage being in him), so surely had it been vested in trustees & no trust declard, none but they could have given a legal acquittance for it. However, as I declared my self safe in the Duke of Marlborough's hands in all events, methinks that ought to have been so farr from furnishing any just grounds of resentment, that where there had not been the keenest appetite for exception prepard against me by repeated ill offices done me with your Grace, it would rather have been well receivd than laid hold of as a fitt opportunity to retaliate a supposed & (at last) imaginary fault with an imputation of the most flagitious nature; I take the liberty to call it supposd, because there is not one single word I am very sure in any of my letters, that can bear ye least shadow of a distrustfull or disrespectfull construction towards ye trustees, had there been any; & as there are none, it proves imaginary too. As to ye other more heinous crime so unjustly suggested to my dishonour, your Grace owning your mistake and desiring no more mention may be made of it, ye only amends I shall expect for the wrong you have done me is that for ye future your Grace woud not lightly believe any thing to ye prejudice of one, who has been with a most peculiar faithfullness your Grace's etc.

**534.**   To Doctor Clopton.                Ickworth, May 13, 1719.

I am obligd to you for ye favour of looking over Dr. Mead's prescription for my daughter, & am much more easy than I should otherwise have been to know there is nothing in it but what is proper.  She gains ground daily, & as long as she does so, I cannot think of altering ye course she is in, nor of putting her into other hands during her present distemper; but as to ye rest of my family, whenever it shall please God to make your assistance necessary, I shall alwaies think them safe in your skill & care, & hope no prejudice can or will happen to you from his being otherwise ingagd on this occasion, who on all others will gladly shew how much he is your friend etc.

**535.**   Lady Bristol to Lord Bristol.        London, July 5, 1719.

Weary and tird to death with the most tedious journey that ever poor mortal endurd, I am come home from visiting Lady Suffolk and Aunt Effingham to take a little refreshment this way, being the only cordial can give me any comfort this fortnight; indeed, my dear, I dare not tell you what I feel, for I know your kind tender nature so well that it woud make you too great a sufferer with me; but why do I enter upon a subject that woud more than fill this paper (large as it is). O my dear dear, my poor heart is ready to burst, and I am afraid I shall have as little relief from my pillow to night as I had last night, for every new place where I have been happy gives me fresh trouble; I have not slept since three a clock this morning, when I was wakd with a violent tempest, which lasted till five; then I sett out, but did not get hither till past two, the horses were so fatigued with the heat.  As soon as I got my dust off I went to dinner to the Dutchess of Graftons, where Mrs. Ramsey was as full of spirits as ever I saw her; we all drank your health; Mrs. Ramsey is so impatient to be in the country, she says she will come with me if the

Dutchess of Grafton wont bring her sooner ; she recommends a sermon of Dr. Hairs to you to read, which I have sent for to the booksellers with what other pamphlets he thinks you will care for. This is the best I can do for you, for the Town is so dull and empty there is not a word of news ; all I coud pick up is these verses. If I can meet with any thing at Richmond before Tom Harvey goes, you shall have it, for though there are but few hours difference between his going and the posts, I chuse him, because they say they open all the letters ; and sure every thing relating to our loves shoud be made as secure as our hearts are to one another, which till death you will find unalterable in your E. Bristol.

**536.** Lady Bristol to Lord Bristol.     Monday morning 8 a clock.

Just rose from my mournful bed with very little refreshment but this minute conversing with you, and praying to God to bless you till our happy meeting again. O my dear dear, how much and tenderly I love you is not to be expressd. God bless the babes.

**537.** My ever-new Delight     Ickworth, July 6, 1719.

I trust in our good God that this will find thee well arrivd at Richmond, notwithstanding the excessive heat of your first days journey, which your usual happy stars nor my prayers coud not prevent. I hope you found the effect of both in the sweet shower that fell the morning after, without being awakd and terrifyd by the thunder which attended it, and that you found the dust laid and the sun coverd with clouds (as it has been here) all this morning to make the end of your journey at least as easy to you as I wishd the whole woud prove. Nothing can make them so to me, since they occasion your absence, which even your very fine and entertaining children poorly compensate. Jack seeing me very low in spirits has tried to raise them (tho' in vain) with a ludicrous composition

Vol. II.     K

of his own, supposd to be an amourous epistle from Clack to Squire on their separation ; which though excellent in its kind I shall not send you, unless you'll tell me mirth is scarce at Court, and promise never to let Squire know a tittle of it ; for it woud break her pious heart to hear but such a character in jest, although her gallant Roger Clack-stone has much the worst share in it. . . . . If you hope to find me as you left me, you must shorten my pennance, which I cant but tell you is born with inconceivable uneasiness by your constant friend and lover, Bristol.

Present my duty and hearty services to your good & gracious Master & Mistress.

**538.**    Lady Bristol to Lord Bristol.    Richmond, July 7, 1719.

I know I shoud be glad to hear every hour in the day from my dear dear angel, so judging by my self I sett pen to paper again, (for as the Dutchess of Grafton usd to say, I know I am welcome,) though I believe this and that I wrote by the coachman will arrive together; but I must vent some of my complaints to you, for indeed they are great both in body and mind, though I had a very kind reception from both my Master & Mistress, and what made it the more agreeable to me was the many kind enquirys after you, and why you woud not come with me ; these obligations give me the more uneasiness, because I am in so ill a condition to perform my duty ; for my rheumatism is so violent both in my knee and ancle as to have swelld them both extremely, especially the latter, that I am hardly able to bear a shoe ; I was forcd to call Cathraine this morning at seven a clock to rub it before I coud gett any sleep, though I did not go to bed till two a clock, for I had a great deal of company at supper, and sitt an hour with Lady Pembroke in her chamber after, hearing a description of Mr. Addison's death, who provd himself a second Cato ; the particulars are too moving for me to write at this time, but I had no patience to see his play burlesqued as it was last night for the entertainment of their Royal Highnesses; I need not give you any other description of it than telling you who acted; Cato by Dicky Norris, Juba by Penktheman, Marcia by young Wilkes, Lucia by Shepherd, Porcius by Fieldhouse, and the rest sutable; their audience was much too good for them, for there was a great many people of quality. Now, my dear, I must trouble you with the directions of what I sent by the coachman; there is half a yard of lute string for Nann; two yards of damask for my saddle; if there wants more, pray let me know that I may bring it; there is also 21 yards of silver binding; what he does not use must be returnd when the horses come for me; O when will that happy day come, that I may again & again repeat how much & dearly you are belovd by your faithful E.B.

Thank God I am a little better since I gott up, but there is so little walking that I hope I shall have but little difficulty. Some venison will do well when the weather will bear it, which I have said is now impossible.

539.  My ever-new Delight  Ickworth, July 8, 1719.

You may see, though my subject naturally led me into it, that I waved the description of my own uneasy condition, because I knew it woud augment your own ; but you have inlargd so much upon that topick in the letter Tom Harvey just now gave me, that shoud I suppress the whole set of sentiments I ever feel when from you, my tenderness towards your heart might justly draw a suspicion on my own ; and therfore I must e'en plainly discover the truth of it for my own quiet, whatever effect it may have on yours. Know then that since we parted, all sorts of satisfaction have taken their leave of me too, and so farr seem they from returning but with thee, that every day gives strength to my disrelish of every pleasure your presence alone was the sauce to; even Ickworth's boasted beauties are all turnd nullities, meer Chimeras, that seem never to

have had  any existence  in nature but  what thy  powerful  charms created;
tis to you alone I find they've been beholden for all their pleasing sen-
sations on my soul;  even my bed affords no rest, nor my meat nourishment,
without my dearest partner in all.  See what an inexhaustible spring your
own  complaints have opend;  mine  coud run  on  incessantly till we meet
again, but that I will  not ease my self at  your expence, altho' you are (I
fear) every way the innocent occasion of them.  I thank  God all our sweet
children are wondrous well;  Betty owns now she finds  herself so, and
Jack's  eye  is  almost  as  well  as t'other;  I  have  taken  more  than  one
opportunity to let fall such  strong hints in relation to what you desird that
his future fears will keep him, I hope, from ever offending in the least tittle,
where  he now  knows each  peccadillio will  prove  irremissible by  your
affectionate lover, Bristol.

  P.S.  How coud you sett  up till two in the morning after  my injunctions
to the contrary, and not expect something worse than a swelld knee or ancle
by  way of  just punishment ?  Pray  be kinder.  If Lord Godolphin  be the
man I have alwaies taken him for, he will  thank us heartily for putting it
into his power to do so much good as his nature will prompt him to of course
on this occasion.

  **540.**    Lady Bristol to Lord Bristol.      Richmond, July 9, 1719.
              Five tedious days are past, and  not one word of
comfort from  my  dear dear  angel to  bless  my  longing eyes ;  by  what
unhappy accident your dear letter (for I know there must be one) is not yet
come I am  still  to  learn, for  I thought  I had  taken all the care that was
possible to have it last night, and a bottle of Epsom  waters which I have
great need of, not  being  able  yet to put on a shoe ;  but I hope I shall not
have occasion to use it much, for they say the Princess has not given any
of her ladys the trouble of walking farther than the terrass, where we were

last night with a very great Court to hear the fine musick the Prince has taken for the summer; last night we had the addition of Mrs. Robinson's singing; but I woud willingly have exchangd it all to have heard you pipeing in the summer house; but wishes are vain, else I shoud not be writing here, notwithstanding all the honours that are done me, for the Prince came up to my room yesterday and stayd above an hour. They just bring me word to be ready by ten a clock to go with the Prince & Princess to Kensington. Just as I was going down stairs, I receivd your dear letter, but have not time to give you all the thanks it deserves, for the Princesses footman stays to carry my letter to Town. I suppose the news tells you of the Spaniards having beaten the German troops, and of the Duke of Sholenberg's death. That which we heard of Tom Killigrew was false, but he is still very ill. Peg dind with me, and desires her compliments to the family. I desire Jack's verses the more, because they were wrote to divert you, though that, nor nothing else, can have any effect till we meet upon your faithful, ever constant E. Bristol.

The whole family is broke in upon me according to custom. Mrs. Howard says she woud have said a thousand pretty things to you, but they that have nothing to say to her, she has nothing to say to them. Pray send me word the day of Ipswich assembly in August, for I have a particular reason. They plague me to death, and I cant read what I have wrote, they snatch my letter away every minute.

541. My ever-new Delight                Ickworth, July 10, 1719.

The Spaniards having beaten the Germans is nothing near so strange as a piece of news I have to tell you in return for it from this place, which is that there has happend a time wherin I have thankd God you was not with me; for the night before last, after I had recommended thee and thy sweet children to the divine protection, (which

I never omitt,) I heard a fluttering noise move swiftly round our room,
wherat I rose up and opend the curtains, but coud see nothing on neither
side of the bed, so composd my self to sleep again; but I had not been
long laid before the same noise began again, and immediately a huge batt
flew in at the beds-feet, which had it not been one of your antipathys I
coud have sufferd rather than have rose to kill it, which at last I coud not
compass, so was forced to open the windows, and let it escape that way
rather than make any farther acquaintance with your lodging.... Your kind
disinterested wish to exchange the pompous elegant pleasures of a Court
for the humble pastime of my pipe and cottage was truly welcome to your
faithful shepherd, though it has made him more uneasily impatient, if
possible, to see and hear and talk with his Amarillis. I herewith send you
Jack's composition, which I told you was an epistle and in prose, but
nevertheless entertaining for that, knowing the parties concernd so well as
you do. Your epitome, Felle, burning with emulation to do something
that might divert my melancholly in Mama's absence as well as brother
Jack, broachd a new representation upon us, which surprisd the rest of the
family as well as my self, being all equally strangers to it; who after
dinner made himself a most ingenuously contrivd pulpitt by the conjunction of four chairs, and having a cushion placd before him gave out his
text (after a short prayer first ended), repeating a second time with a louder,
more distinct voice, looking round his congregation, and then proceeded to
his preachment, which he deliverd in pronunciation, gesture and tone of
voice so surprisingly like Dr. Clarke, even to the pulling forward his wigg,
& uncovering his book at pauses to look over his notes, then throwing his
handkerchief over them again etc, that Jack ownd himself but a bungler
to him in mimichry; and yet you know he is farr from being an ill one,
though not quite so good a son of late to thee as I must have him, if he

cares at all to have me so kind a father as I woud be. Mrs. Howard's meritt has alwaies had all the secrett worship of my soul, which was consistent with that paramount adoration I have and ever must pay to thy superior attributes of kindness, constancy and truth, you being my Goddess, she my saint only, will hardly be satisfyd with this distinction (and more cannot be allowd) by your idolizer, Bristol.

**542.** Lady Bristol to Lord Bristol.　　Richmond, July 11, 1719.

I believe there never was such a letter as what I wrote to my dearest life last post, but you coud easily see the occasion of it; but they found I grew so peevish with them that they all run out of the room at once, saying, Let us be gone, or she will never let us come again. But in that minute his Royal Highness came up to see how I woud pass the evening; (for the Princess having a great many letters to write dismissd me for the afternoon ;) I being a cripple it was determind for the Water, where there was a great deal of mirth for those that were in humour to tast it ; (which God knows I was not ;) at our landing between nine & ten, coming down the great walk, we saw an extraordinary sight in the air, like fire, which lasted about a quarter of an hour ; but the description is too much for my pen, therfore must let it alone till we meet. O when will that longd for day arrive, for though ages are past yet there are ten thousand more to come in that number of days, which to shorten as much as may be, I hope you will order the horses to be early in Town a Sunday morning, because I may want them in the evening to carry me to London. Last night the Princess suppd at Lady Padgets, which though an ugly place and ill kept had been a bitter night of walking for poor me, if Lady Grantham had not been there to assist me. Lady Padgett was in great pain that I did not eat ; upon which the Princess told her, Madam, though you dont know the reason, I do, for it is her being so farr from her lord,

and she does not know now that she is with us, for I am forcd to wake her
sometimes out of a dream when she is at omber.  We came home by water
this morning at two a clock, yet I am forcd to take the waters, this being
the only day I have a chance to be regular, being to go to Kensington, and
then I am commonly dismissd at eleven a clock without walking.  I am so
faint & giddy with my physick that I am sure you woud take the pen out
of my hand, if you were here, but I am afraid to trust to an afternoon again,
therfore I woud have begun yesterday, but that Lady Suffolk was here by
eleven a clock, and stayd till I went out ; but here comes a cordial, if I
was quite fainted ; your letter is just arrivd, which though it brings me such
welcome news has some allay in it, by your thinking I coud disobey any of
your commands if I coud have helpd it ; for that late night I did not leave
the Princess till twelve, and had a dozen people to supp with me after.  O
my dear, coud I as easily relieve my heart as conscience towards you, I
shoud not suffer what I do now ; but though you say I have enlargd upon
that subject, assure your self I have not, nor never can tell you half the
love & tenderness my soul feels for the adorable charmer of it ; but since I
dare not trust my self upon that subject, I must bid you adieu.—I said
nothing to you of Mr. Wanley, because he said he woud write you word
that he knew nothing about your tickets ; if I am to do any thing more
with him, pray order him to come to me a Sunday night about ten a clock,
for I shall go before they are stirring a Monday morning.  I suppose all
the news there is is in Peg's letter.  General Davenport and Sir Ja : Ashley
are dead.

**543.**   My ever-new Delight              Ickworth, July 13, 1719.
              Tho' your letters give me the only pleasure I am
capable of tasting in your absence, yet I had much rather refuse my self
that sole satisfaction which is left me till thy much longd for return, than

have it indulgd at so high a price as putting you to any pain ; therefore even for my sake, as well as your own, never write a word after finding your spirrits faint or your head giddy. Why would you extend your last letter to such a length, after sitting up till two a clock again and drinking waters ? And why would you lett the unwellcome news of your being a cripple have any place in it ? You can make but one complaint that creates not much more pain in me than any you can feel ; which is how much you want me ; that is, I must confess, a sort of uneasiness I would not have you quite insensible to, tho' God of his goodness grant the occasions of it may be few and short. Could you tell (which is the only secret I have kept from you) how frequent and how long, very long, even the shortest of them have seemd to me, you would never suffer any consideration but of the utmost necessity to cut off one moment of that remnant I ought to be so justly covetous of ; the past has taught me how chearily I should husband every future minute of my time, since all have been worse than barely lost that were not spent in thy belovd society. The Princess, remembring her own condition when his R.H. came hither before her, judgd your case by her own, and I hope not wide of the mark, however short my merit must be reckond of his ; since your gratefull humble heart has supplyd every defect, and heightend every appearance of desert, with all the industrious kindness that could not only have been desird but wanted by, my dearest life, your most obligd lover and faithfull friend, Bristol.

The children are all well, as also Jack's eye ; he wears no more his silk over it. Mr. Wanley will leave the ticketts with Robin the porter to give you for me. Fear not but the horses shall be with you before the time you can use them.

**544.**   Lady Bristol to Lord Bristol.   Richmond, July 14, 1719.
            Tis well I have the refreshment of thinking it is not now quite a week to the happy minute of my seeing my dear dear angel

Vol. II.   L

again, for I have had none from my pillow, having been unable to sleep
four hours to night,....ney, were my mind enough at ease, your old enemys
the knatts would not let me sleep, for they have bit my left arm that it is
swelld almost as bigg as two; I hope you have not found (my mortall foe)
the batt half so troublesome....Therefore I will drink your dear health in my
chocolate, and tell you the occurrences of this place. Yesterday there was
an horse-race for a saddle etc. the Prince gave; twas run under the terrass
wall for their Royall Highnesses to see it; their was an infinite number of
people to see them all along the banks, and the river full of boats with
people of fashion that doe not come to Court; among whom was the
Dutchess of Grafton, with Mr. and Mrs. Berringer. They all stayd till it
was late upon the water to hear the Prince's musick, which sounded much
sweeter for the share every one took in the Princes and Princesses pleasure
in having this place securd to them when they almost despaird of it, and,
tho in such a trifle, no small pains taken to disappoint them. That party
has made a ballad in answer to the B kings, much beyond what could be
expected from them; if I can gett a copy of it before I must seal this letter,
you shall have one for I am sure there are some things in it will make you
laugh, and more to please Jack, who I must love in spite of my resolutions
to the contrary. The Princesses letter from Madam last night brought the
news of the Dutchess of Berry's being at the point of death, but mighty
resignd, (tho' but 23 years old;) she says she thanks God she has nothing
to trouble her conscience, but goes out of the world with as much innocence
as she came into it. Now if that religion has such an healing quality, sure
this age will produce them a world of death-bed converts; however, the
Countess of Buquenbourgh thinks herself very happy to have savd her sons
from 'em. They are now with her; the eldest is a very pretty gentleman;
he dines and supps with me almost every day; the youngest is not bigger
than Charles, but very well bred; but now I am talking of breeding I must

tell you the compliment the Princess made Betty; she said she should think her self very happy to have her daughters as rightly behavd. I hope this news will perfect her cure, as well as make her endeavour to deserve it. God Almighty bless them all, and send their dearer father long life and health to have the comfort of them with his faithfull tender partner, E.B.

P.S. I am invited to dinner at the Tent, but shall not be very good company, for since I begun to write a knatt has bitt my eye-lid, so that I can hardly see, and gives me great pain; tho' every body is bit, no one is such a martyr as my self. I cant gett the ballad; Pegg got it away last night, and carryd it home; I hope she will send it,

545.    My ever-new Delight            Ickworth, July 15, 1719.

Were not this to be ye last letter before I am restord to my usial happiness in thee, I am confident I could not find strength or spiritts enough to write many more. Betty has done her best endeavours to keep up both by getting me all the good things Syer's industry or housewifry can help us to, but all attempts are vain of that & every other kind tò supply your absence. Judg how near tis being compensated to me, since I'm reduced to seek for ease & pastime out of Ickworth Park-pale, being this moment come from Haustead, where I carryed my flute & fiddle to compare notes with honest innocent Sir Dudly Cullum, (whom most will envy in the next world, tho' not many will do it in this since his choice of my god-daughter;) but tho' musick is physick to other distempers, I find it nourishment to mine, & therfore made haste home to meet thy kind letter, which is but just now come. I'm more pleasd with the news it brings of your Master's being quieted in the possession of what he likes so well than in any other has happend since I saw you; may thier malicious souls who would have disappointed him therin (& yet you know I'm farr from being ill-naturd in the main) be transmigrated into your antipathy a batt, or my aversion (much improvd by hurting you) a knatt. I have perfected your daughter's cure by telling her ye Princesses compliment ; ye applause of so nice & through a judg in all ye graces & decencies of conduct and breeding is much more worth than the plaudite of ye fullest amphitheater. I cant help telling you Felle is become my shadow, as he is so very pretty a part of thy (otherwaies) inimitable substance. He has been with me at Saxham, Horringer & Haustead ; & like his sweet original the more I have of his engaging company the more I covett of it; there never was his fellow. Tho' tis late I cant conclude till I have thankd you for all your letters & your news, ye only comfort or cordiale I have tasted since I saw you. I know you will not lett me want them till I shall stand in need of nothing by having thier dear author here. Your horses will be at London Saturday at night ; therfore lett Tuesday evening be ye latest, if thou ever lovedst me. I have taken care your saddle shall be finishd this week, & tho' I have used all the dilligence possible to know when Ipswich Assemblee is to be in August, no body could yet inform me. Keep but you your time, & all things beside will be indifferent to your longing lover, Bristol.

    **546.**   Lady Bristol to Lord Bristol.    Richmond, July 16, 1719.

        Something extrodnary has happend to hinder me of the only pleasure I can tast, which is writing to my dear, dear angell as I woud do, the perteculers of which you shall know by ye next post; & in the mean time I must comfort my self with my happynes on Tuesday, which is longd for with ye utmost impattience by, my dearest treasure, your faithfull E.B.

    I beg a letter by Tom Hervey to live upon on Monday.

    **547.**   My ever-new Delight    Ickworth, July 16, 1719.

        Remembering how glad I was to see a letter from thee by Tom Harvey, altho' I had just receivd one by ye post, makes me hope there may be no love lost between us, & that you'l be as pleasd to see a second of ye same day, having sent one already this morning to Bury to lett you know I am so lost, so lifeless, so wretched a creature without thee, that I am sure you will not keep me one moment in pain after your waiting is over, nor renew it again for all ye salaries of ye whole Civel lyste, if you could but tell what perpetual uneasynesses this fortnight has occasiond to your insatiable lover & faithfulest of frinds, Bristol.

**548.** Lady Bristol to Lord Bristol. Richmond, July 18, 1719.

Forgive, my dear dearest life, the only fraud I ever was guilty of towards you, since it was to save you the pain of knowing what I then labourd under; endeed a more sever fitt of ilness I never had in my life; it began Wensday morning with a voielent fitt of ye cholick, but purging with it, I was in hopes it woud have gon off; instead of that at night it increasd so much that with the flux & vometting I kept nothing I took, which flung me into a feaver, that held me above 20 hours, & was but just then off when I writ you those few deceetful lines, saying I had busness, & God knows what I said, for I hardly knew or was able to hold my pen; in a little time after my feaver & all my other complaints returnd again about the same hour it had done the night before; twas then, my dear dear angell, I dispaird ever to see you more; I cant give you a juster image of what I sufferd than by telling you 2 batts came to my bed-side one after another without moveing me any more than if they had been butterflys; but God Almighty's infinett goodness be praisd, the bolluses Sir David Hambleton gave me (every 6 hours) suceeded so well that with that & a quietting draught Mr. Grimes (who satt up with me) found necessary to give me, I had a very good night, and misd my feaver, so that I seem to day in Paradice, & hope to be in my earthly heaven a Tuesday, tho' they tell me I am much too weak to compase my jurney in two days, but I shall

certainly sett out on Monday morning ; however, for your ease be assurd
I will not go farther than my strength will bear. I am now going to pay
my duty & thanks to their Royal Highnesses for the kind and oblidging
honers they have done me, for both Prince & Princes came into my room
as soon as I got up, & kept their (little) court their tell diner ; this was
Thursday, when I was not able to be out of my bed but very few hours,
consequently very unfitt for such honers ; endeed the kindnes I have
receivd from all the famely, both men & women, (nay, even from strangers,)
upon this occasion, will, I am sure, when you come to know it, give you a
better oppinion of the world than the generalty of it deserves. My hand
trembles so, I fear you wont be able to read this ; I am really amasd when
I see the lenth of it ; but what will not love like mine cary one threw to the
dear object belovd, dear dear, far dearer than can be expressd by your E.B.

I dind below, & (thank God) am well to a meracle, so well that I think
of going with the Princes to Kinsington ; theirfore pray, my dear, be easy
till the happy muinett of our meeting ; how much that is longd for, no toung
can expres or heart conceive.

**549.    To my son Tom at Oxford.**          July 23, 1719.

Tom

Could I make you sensible of but half the pain &
uneasyness your late surprising misbehaviour has given me, I'm confident
you would never have venturd to occasion it for ten times the pleasure you
might have vainly proposed to your self by it. It seems after previous
admonitions (which I was kept a stranger to, but hope to be so no more) &
solemn promises passd thereon that you would never again neglect your
studies, the first honourable step you made in performance thereof was to
absent your self from Colledge without the leave or knowledg either of the
Bishop of Bristol or your tutor, a fact incredible had not the information

come from so very authentick an hand as his Lordships. You cant be
ignorant of the great affection I have alwaies borne you, & as a genuine
effect thereof how much my heart is set on making you an accomplishd
gentleman in your generation ; neither can you have forgott how often I
have told you that tho' Providence has placed two before you in the succession to your good grandfather's estate, yet I have ever pleased myself with
the prospect of your inheriting as large a portion of his virtues & learning
as you do of his likeness ; and then you'd make your self heir to the most
valuable part of all his riches ; but as neither virtue nor learning is to be
found in idle company at Astropwells, if you will not henceforth resolve to
seek for both in the place I have appointed you with that regularity and
application his Lordship thinks fitt to injoyne, & shall hereafter approve,
I am determind immediatly to remove you where you will find it necessary
to take much more pains & to undergo many more hardships than you need
to do where you are ; a change I hope your future conduct will wisely prevent, it being contrary to the natural disposition of yours etc.

**550.**    To my son Henry at Oxford.              Oct. 12, 1719.

Tho' all ye prints & common report make mention
of the Bishop of Bristol's death, yet I cannot believe it true, because neither
you nor your brother Tom have writ me word of it.  Should it prove so, I
am confident tis without precedent that ever any man should have two sons
under the same roof where such an accident happend, & not one of them (at
. least) to have had either duty or diligence enow to acquaint their father
with it, especially in such a case where ye loss would be common to us all,
but more particularly your own, he having been so truly your friend & well
wisher as to give himself (to my knowledg) more trouble and thought in
consulting ye best means of reclaiming you from idleness & ignorance than
you (I begin now almost desperatly to fear) will ever live to deserve by

growing the better for it. You cannot but be conscious of having given me more anxiety & disquiet than all my other children putt together; & one might reasonably have hoped from any generous temper that as much has been forgiven you, so of course you would have loved much; but alass! I've found no such worthy fruits from my indulgence or your gratitude; for did you bear but an ordinary affection towards me, it would naturally shew itself by your doing & becoming what you know I injoyne & approve; but so directly contrary has your past conduct been to both, that I am not able without tears (which you, not I, should shed,) to read over the following passage concerning you in his Lordship's last letter, viz :—"But the younger "is very idle, & is not by any thing which either his tutor or I can say to "him to be prevaild with to apply himself to his studies, so that there is no "prospect of his improving that very small stock of learning which he "brought from school; when I talk with him, he seems to be convincd of "his error, & very readily promises to do better; but those promises are "soon forgott, & wee find no effect of them.  He has very good natural "parts, but no inclination at all to cultivate them by study."—And can you survey so worthless a character without conceiving ye utmost indignation at your slothful self for it, & solemnly resolving to read your eyes out rather than be any longer known by it.

> Unhappy he who does this work adjourn,
> And till to morrow would his search delay ;
> His lazy morrow would be like to day ;
> But is one day of rest too much to borrow ?
> Yes tis ; our yesterday is gone, & nothing gaind,
> And all thy fruitless daies will thus be draind ;
> For thou hast more to morrows yet to ask,
> And wilt be ever to begin thy task ;
> Thou'lt like ye hindmost charriot wheels be curst,
> Still to be near, but never reach ye first.

I would fain have seen you foremost among ye most learned of your contemporaries, & deeply versd in ye invaluable laws & customs of your country, whereby you might have made your self every way as considerable, ney more so, supposing them to be less knowing in that useful science, than your elder brothers ; but if you can be so farr infatuated as to throw away all those advantages you may make your self master of (for you have yet one to morrow left to acquire them in, but no more,) in exchange for ignorance, contempt & poverty, you must after so fatal, so foolish a choice, expect no farther countenance or support from me than what is barely necessary to maintain an ideot, from one whom you may otherwaies still preserve for your most affectionate father.

**551.**   Lady Bristol to Lord Bristol.       London, Oct. 11, 1719.
From my bed, Sunday night, 10 a clock·

Tho' weary to death, I cant go to rest till I have told my dearest life I have obeyd his commands to Lady B. Germain ; after that I went to Aunt Effingham, who has been il some time, but is extreemly full of her acknowledgments for all the trouble you have given your self in her affairs.   I found ye Bishop of Norwhich with her, who ses ye king will certainly be hear the 10th of Nov.; from thence I went to my grandmother Suffolke's, who not being well was gon to bed ; after that to Pegg, but so dead I was not able to speak, as you will easyly beleive when I tell you that before these visetts, as soon as we got to London, Jack & my self tooke the first Hackney coach we mett & went in search of Betty's new doctor, such was my impatience to sett her mind at eas, (finding by sad experience at this time what it is to be otherways); after all our pains he was unluckly out of Town ; but Mr. Grimes will write you word what he ses, as soon as he can speak with him.   I was forcd to send my excuse to Lord and Lady Essex, who weir so kind to invite me both to diner & super; and now I have finishd my days jurnale I will conclud; for the whole night woud not suffice to tell you the passionet love and tendernes my constant faithfull heart feels towards its most dear valueable & worthy object.

Monday morning but 7 a clock, yet no rest for me, or more papar to vent my greifs; theirfore must bid my dearest life Adue for this time.

**552.**    My ever-new Delight          Ickworth, Oct. 12, 1719.

The poor mare you sent back with her shoulder out of its place could not feel half ye pain I did in parting with thee; which was not a little aggravated by the inconveniences I was afraid you might meet with in being so long retarded by that unlucky accident; but I trust in God (to whom I never made more fervent prayers for his powerfull protection in thy preservation] that was ye only one attended you in all your journey, & that this will find you well settled in your waiting, which I know will pass with much more ease and pleasure to you ye better you found your Master & Mistress in body and mind ; if any thing could make my time wear away with either till I am restord to thy sweet society, it would be in ye company of those pretty pieces of thy dearer self you left behind; the perpetual assiduities of Nann to entertain or assist me in thy absence are particularly endearing, notwithstanding Herrietts endeavours to divert my melancholly have much surpassd ye usual abilities of her age; Betty's cough decreases again daily, & as that gradually abates, her strength & appetite will consequently return.   Lord Hervey came back to us this day, & brought Mr. Blomberg to diner, who going away late this evening will make this letter something shorter than it would have been, since ye sole satisfaction now left me is to be telling thee (tho' very imperfectly) how much I miss thee, how much I love thee, how much I already long for thee again; wherfore pity thy most disconsolate frind and lover, Bristol.

553. Lady Bristol to Lord Bristol. Richmond, Oct. 13, 1719.

Sure every thing that is agreable is denyd to me in this journey, for this whole morning I had (with pleasure) dedicated to the charmer of my heart, to vent some part of its tendernes towards you ; but I am orderd to be ready by ten a clock to go with ye Prince and Princes to Kingsinton; so that thees few moments must be borowd from sleep, to which I am a great debter since I saw you, & indeed dispair of any rest. To my great mortefication I proposd yesterday to Lord Grantam for my lady & I to change weeks, but he told me twas imposable, so that it will be a whole month before I can be releasd ; for you may remember, (my dearest,) I told you that when I had paid the 2 weeks I owed, Lady Grantam was to wate one, and I to come after in my own turn. I am in ye last distress by this disappointment ; for Lady Dorsett is in such deep mourning she cant appear at ye birth-day, so that I have no resource but your comeing to my releife, which I am sure you woud do, if you coud guess but half what I suffer. Therefore for God's sake, my dear, releive me by next post, els I am afraid (if you dont give me hopes of seeing you soon) I shall break threw all decorems to come to you, which woud be very indecent after ye kind reception I have mett with both from my Master & Mistress; a great adission to it was their oblidging inquirey after you ; the Princes (who remembers every thing) said she was in hopes the Term & your law sute woud have brought you with me, but if that dus not she saw the Parliament must soon, for by her letters yesterday from Hanover ye King setts out the second of November (our stile) certainly. The Prince tells me their is now a vacancy at Alborough by ye death of Sir Ha: Johnson, & askd me if you & Sir Thomas Hanmer woud not try for Jack to gitt in there ; ye most zealous of our Court woud have had me send you an express on purpos, for they say General Harvey is gon down with one Plumer of Hertfordshire to set up their ; so that I hope you will loose no time in seeing Sir Thomas,

& that you will say as much as you pleas from me to him, how much my heart is sett upon bringing Jack into ye House of Commons; ye coming of the high Suffolk gentelmen to Bury happens very lucky upon this occassion, and tis ye only one that coud make me wish you to be at the Assembly.—As often as you see my pen has been changd, so many different places I have writ in; part was at Kingsinton, from whence I am just now come, & Mr. Douglas is waiting for my letter to cary to London; thees frequent interuptions I hope will excues the blunders of my pen, as love must those of my head, which is too full of that passion for sence or reason to be found in your faithfull E. B.

**554.**    My ever-new Delight

From forsaken Ickworth,
Oct. 14, 1719.

You will see by ye letter I wrote by Tuesdays post ye part I took in ye accident of ye mare after all ye precautions I had taken to prevent any of that kind. Emmitt & his three pages stand stiffly in ye assertion of her perfect soundness when she went out; and if not, why did not Lawrence acquaint you with ye contrary when Jack perceivd her otherwise; ye rider may better feel a lameness than an other see it; but we have not ye good luck to have many servants in all ye number we keep to do either well. Tho' I am put at some ease by ye kind letter which Tom Harvey brought me this night, that this negligence of ye grooms was attended with no worse consequence than your being an hour in ye moonlight, yet I cannot forgive ye lazy carelessness of those who exposd you to ye least fears or inconveniences; may all adverse accidents that are to attend you come off as well. Mr. Graham has punctually performd what you made me expect from him concerning Betty, having sent me Ferns conditions & an account of his method & medicines, which are exactly ye same as Dr. Pake told us in the Norfolke ladys case, as you will find by the counterpart sent you by Mr. Graham; there seems to be but one difficulty, which I fear may have arisen from Ferns and Grahams misunderstanding each other; which is that Fern will undertake no person till he first sees the patient & views ye sores; now you know there are none in our case; therfore I have written by this nights post to Mr. Graham to explain that point particularly to Fern, and to know of Fern whether, as their are no sores nor ever were on this present patient, he will not send her his flasks of water & other ingredients for ye infusion into ye country, for her going to London & returning immediatly (which it seems Fern says will be necessary for any patient, & to stay at least two months in ye country after it,) will make more eclatt by farr with me than if she had gone when you went on account of her foot. Lord Hervey came from Newmarket as I told you on Monday, and could not spare me more of his company than till next day at dinner; after which, as I was oblidgd to meet Sir W. Gage at Westley to terminate all differences between our tenants there, (wherin I have made many more concessions than I should have mett with had he been in my place,) he went for Bury, where he lay at my house, & rode post for London this morning. His absence & Jacks resolution of seeing this place or me any more this year would sett much more easy on my mind were not you from me too ; but I must confess, as things have happend, I feel my self more unable than ever to bear that circumstance in conjunction with other disquiets & disappointments. I used to find that alone in my best days of prosperity more than a match for all ye philosophy I could muster up : what then tis now become in company of several other trying incidents shall never be describd for your sake by still your constant lover without division or remission, Bristol.

555. Lady Bristol to Lord Bristol. Richmond, Oct. 14, 1719.

This is the third letter I have begun but hope shall not end before I have receivd one from my dear, dearest life : the

pleasure I have with ye thoughts of that keeps up my poor drouping spiretts
for this day, for allase

> How slowly time when cloggd with greif dus move,
> But O how swift when born upon ye wings of love;
> Hardly three days they tell me yett is past;
> Yett tis an age since I beheld you last.

And almost an eternety (to an impatient love like mine) is yett to come,
if my kind and tender dear dus not releive me, which, to confess ye truth,
past experience of your goodnes to me has made me so much depend upon
that ye disapointment woud prove ye greater if any thing shoud happen to
hinder you. I hope in God by this time your health is so well establish'd
that that will be no obstecale in ye way; for if you think you shall have the
least prejudice by the jurney, I am sure I had rather suffer much more (if
that weir posable to be bourn and live) then that should happen, or as a
lesser uneasynes condesend to ask Lady Grantam (once more) to change
weeks with me, if I can find a time that her lord is out of his vapours, for I
beleive their lys the only diffeculty, for tis a week every body that weir
not in my circomstances woud wish to avoid, the removeal of ye Court and
the Birth day both happening in it, though ye Prince said last night he
thought he could hardly hold out to stay tell ye 27th, the wether being so
very bad, & that is a reason why ye Princes goes now always in a morning
to Kingsinton, which is every post day, so that I am forcd to write the day
before, as you see by ye date. General Harvey dind hear to day, & gave
him self the air of haveing sent one down (meaning Mr. Plumer) to be chose
at Alborough. I thought it not worth while to speak to him about it; when
he declard himself elswhere, he said Lord Strafford had sent to make interest
for some body els, but that he made very light off, which is more then I can
do of my misfortune not to have receivd your dear letter to night as I
expected. I am afraid being at Court may make you expect some news,

but the place is as dull as my self, who am remarkably enough so for a proverb. Pegg promist to send Betty all she coud pick up at London; what she writt us word of this place is very true in every perteculer, which dus not add to ye sweetnes of their tempers who are consernd in it, but makes them fitter company for your forlorne E. B.

**556.** Lady Bristol to Lord Bristol.   Oct. 15. Jack's birthday.

I am just this muinett come from Kingsinton, and did not receive your dear letter tell I was just going their. I had hopes of meeting with some news, but found nothing talkd of but lottry ticketts; ye £20000 is drawn to day; Lord Tenham has £10000, Mr. Gibson £5000; the best prize I coud gitt woud be to have my dear angell with me again. The Arch Bishop was last night with ye Princes, & ses they have had no news yett from ye fleet, but the King is expected by ye 8th or 9th of next month. Lord Hervey & Jack are both hear, & I am calld to diner, so must bid my dearest Adue.

I am so hurryd I fear this is wors nonsense then ordinary. The whole famely dine with me, & Jack is seasd upon to ly hear to night.

**557.** My ever-new Delight         Ickworth, Oct. 16, 1719.

Did you know how very earnest an invitation I receiv'd from Mildenhall by Welch Tom to make one at this nights Assembly, you woud think my absence some sort of reprisal for ye many plotted contrivances to disappoint Lady Bristols favours to Mr. Wood. O! but tell him I expect & insist upon meeting him there, & will never forgive him if he failes us. Mr. Bowes was also planted to sollicitt my daughters & my presence there by a messenger last night, which he dispatchd from Horringer hither to disire we would take his house in the way to Eastlands, to rest our selves there & drink tea first etc. Sir John Vanbrugh too, who is with his lady at Bury, sent me a message to excuse his not coming to Ickworth to day, but hoped he should see me at night etc.  I am sorry I can add no more weight to ye sacrifice I find so great a pleasure in making to your disires, unless it be in ye care I took (which I never did before) to prevent both Mrs. Battelys & her sister Sideys appearance, which I effected ; but I beseech you to engage me in no more of these factious requitals, for my mind wont be quite easy till I have given Eastlands wife & children ye last five shillings I hinderd them of.—Yesterday 23 years was productive of too much pleasure to us both ever to be forgotten by me, & would have been rememberd with much more warmth of affection had not his late mis-behaviour to you as well as my self bred a coldness, which so old a stomach as mine must be a long time in recovering; his being a part of you must prove ye sole restorative at last to the heart of your disconsolate lover, Bristol.

Tis now beyond my usuale hour of going to bed (near midnight), & ye messenger not returnd with ye dear letter which I impatiently expect from thee, so must wish thee a good night....Can you gett no good naturd wife to wait for you after your fortnight's out ?  This first week has seemd an age ; ye next will pass yet more heavily ; how then can a third be born ?

**558.**    Lady Bristol to Lord Bristol.    Richmond, Oct. 16, 1719.

The want of time on post days setts me a scribling every muinett.  Kattern, give me pen & ink, is ye first thing as soon as I wake in ye morning, which is so early as to make her pevish ; for I have never slept after 7 but twise since I saw you ; that happynes would soon be restored to me if my wishes weir as effectuale in that as they have been for ill wether hear, for it has raind every day sence I came, so that I have had no walking ; endeed I dont know how I shoud have born it if I had, for tho' my sholder is better yett my hipp & knees are very lame ; and now

I am makeing my own complaints (my dear), I must ask you why you did not add to all ye kind expressions in your letter that of letting me know how you do; endeed, my dear, if you knew how esenceial it weir to my repose I am sure you woud not have omitted it, for it gives me a thousand imagenations that I hope there is no foundation for but in my silly nodle ; however, that among many other nameles thoughts of tendernes (for that the discours turnd upon) made me burst out a crying at supper, which put me sadly out of countenance, being before Lord Pagett, who is yett but a stranger in ye famely, els he woud not have been surprisd at me. Jack is just come to breakfast with me; he lay last night in Mr. Selwin's room, & I beleive will do so as long as he is in waiting; his wife being hear one room serves them; Lord Lumley has alsoe been so kind as to let him have one of ye Prince's coaches when he pleases, so that he is much at his eas.

**559.** Lady Bristol to Lord Bristol. Kingsinton, Oct. 17.

12 a clock.

I had so much company yesterday at diner that I had not a moments time all day to write more ; among ye men that dind with me was the Speaker and Mr. Hill, who inquird very kindly after you ; he promist to write to Sir Thomas Hanmer to day to lett him know how agreable it woud be to our Court to gitt Jack chose at Alborough ; I long to hear if there be any hopes, your letter last night makeing no mention of it ; I conclude you had not receivd mine by Tuesdays post ; yours came to me just as I was satt down to play, so that I had ye penance of sitting three hours with it in my pockett unoppend ; upon which Lord Grantam told the Princes she might win what money she pleasd of me while that letter was kept seald up ; I told him he was much mistaken, for ye pleasure I had in prospect from it raisd my spiretts to that degree that it was imposable I coud loose ; but I was soon dashd at ye reading of it from ye sympathy I

Vol. II. N

felt in your complaints, & finding no releif for my own either by your giveing me hopes of seeing you in Town, or puting me in a way to gitt to you ; for I have tryd Lady Grantam again, but cant gitt my week changd, so that I live upon ye rack tell I have some prospect of our meeting soon. There is not a word of news but a flying report that the fleet is at Vigoe, but this wants conformation.  My letter is staid, for I have time to say no more, but pitty and love me, my dear dear Angell.

If there is a nessesity of Bettys coming (which I cant think), you need have no uneasynes about it, for I have taken care of that.

    **560.**    My ever-new Delight           Ickworth, Oct. 17, 1719.

                  Tho' I sent one letter by Tom this morning to ye post, yet remembering it does not go away this return till towards evening, I could not omitt thanking you for your two kind letters which I receivd together this morning (ye best breakfast I have had since I saw you) by as many ; but I must tell you tis as impossible for me to live at London & preserve that little stock of health I have but lately recoverd, as it would have been for me to execute your other desires of not going to ye Assembly, and yet making use of that opportunity of ye high Suffolke gentlemens being there to promote your sons pretensions at Aldborough, had I receivd ye intimation time enough.  Jack & you may see what ye professions of this world's frindships ought to pass for by the part Lord — has acted on this occasion, after having been so lately sollicitted by you to bespeak his assistance on any future emergency ; since your heart is so sett upon it, I will try what Sir Thomas Hanmer can do for him, tho', unless he can resolve to take more proper pains for himself, not only to make interest to gett into Parliament but to make a more significant figure when he is in it than ye perpetual pursuit of poetry will enable him to do, I think twill be but loss of time & expence to attempt any thing of this kind.—As my whole life has been but a due sacrifice to your satisfaction ever since God Allmighty's goodness was pleasd to bless me with ye possession of so rare a jewel as your gratefull heart, so my death shall readily be made one too, by my leaving this place immediatly, if you'l tell me there is no other way to be made easy by your most passionate lover, Bristol.

**561.**    Lady Bristol to Lord Bristol.    Richmond, Oct. 19, 1719.

Il news always comes time enough, and I was unwilling to add to ye uneasiness (you have given me the torment to know) you feel, els I beleive I should have oppend my letter on Satterday to tell you I had the misfortune to have a sad fall just as I was going to diner; you know the stones there are very sharp, so that twas a great mercy I was not wors hurt; one of my hands is brusd, & my ancle & knee, but I made shift to put on a shoe yesterday to go to Church with ye Prince & Princes, & after that to take ye air; I am afraid you will think this wholey owing to my awkard walking, but endeed it was not, for their had been a great storm of hail & rain, that had made it as slipery as glass. Ye Speaker & Mr. Hill was so obliding to come to inquire how I did. I should have conceald this from you, if I had not been afraid he might have mentiond it in his letter to Sir Thomas Hanmer, & by that you immagen it wors than it realy is, for I have no skin broke, so that I hope the present pain is all I shall suffer from it, for I have not been wanting in any waiting, which is much easyer now then in ye sumer, for the Princes has company but 3 times a week, the other days I have ye honour to be of the Prince's partys; he did me ye favour last night to come up to my room to invite me to play in his appartment; there he told me he was afraid they shoud make me grow lean, for the Princes intended to go again this morning to King-sinton, (where I now am,) which has oblidgd me to be up & dresd thees three mornings by ten a clock, but the Princes has been so good to lessen (at least I could not feel it so much) ye fattegue by saying so many kind & oblidging things to me all the way in ye coach as none but your dear self can have partiality enough for me to beleive.  Jack is so admird hear that they wont let him go to London till we all go ;  he is now at ye Count La : lips lodging, Mr. Selwin being gon ;  Mr. Hill was so kind to invite him to diner yesterday with ye Speaker &  a great deal of company, but he was ingaged to Mrs. Howard.  I am afraid I have never said any thing of ye other poor babs, I am always (both head & heart) so full of there dear original that I can think of nothing els, & they'r too happy in being with you to want any thing ;  I am sure I shoud not.  My next greatest pleasure is to hear from you, which I hope to do by & by, for the Maids are gon to London, & have promist me to stay till ye post comes in for my letters.  The Prince asks me every day if I have had any answeir about ye election ;  tho' I shoud be glad to hear of that, yet I have much greater pleasurs in view when I see your dear hand, for then I am sure of fresh assurances of your love & tendernes for one that has no other merett but the most faithfull & sincer passion that ever dwelt in a hueman brest for the worthyest of objects ;  but then wheres ye merett.—       ·

Oct. 20.  Ten a clock, & no letter come yett :  ye post was not come in when ye maids left London last night, but our buttler promist I should have them this morning by 8 a clock; a true Court promis ; but I dont wonder at all my disapointments, when my good genious is so farr from me, & (to my great mortefication) like to continue so, for I cant prevail with Lady Grantam to change, and it would be unreasonable to send to Lady Dorsett to come to town on purpos ; besides that I believe she coud not, if I did, Lady Betty Germain being with her; Lady Pembrook dus not come this 3 weeks, & you know ye other 2 ladys are not to be depended upon for waiting.—But hear is come a cordial, 2 letters at once ; O happyness ; my other breakfast must be laid aside for that more nourishing one.  I find I have prophetically answeird ye most matterial part in either of them by the account of my waiting, which is a consequence of our meeting. O my dear, how could you be so cruell to name death as an attendant on ye greatest happynes in life, our being together, without which I am sure there can be none for poor me, but rather then purchase it at a much less prise then any you name, I woud bear this rack three weeks longer, for tis just that time from this day before I can gitt to Ickworth if no happy expediant is found, which at present I cant forsee; after what you have said I dare not name ye only one, nay, (what I thought I coud never have brought out) shoud dread it; yett among all thees greivances I must own my self so true a woman to have a little pleasure in ye disapointment you gave to the Assembly, & ye more becaus there was so much pains taken about it; but I cant conceive how my letter by Tuesdays post came to reach you no sooner, for Mr. Douglas told me sence he deliverd it that night.—I conclude Betty is pritty well, becaus you dont mention her, & Jack told me he had a letter from her which was very gay; to make her more so pray tell her the Princes wishes her maids would take example by her, & that she has a great mind to make her mother of them when she comes to Town. That coming to Town runs strangly in my head; and not to say more of it there is no other way but to say no more at all, but that I am, my dear dearest life, for ever & ever yours, E. B.

Lord Hervey is very well, & was hear yesterday at ye musick. I have pritty well recoverd my fall.

562. Lady Bristol to Lord Bristol. Thursday night, 10 a clock.

Since I sent my letters to ye post, I am come to see Lady Essex, & hear the news of ye takeing of Vigo; ye parteculers are in the inclosd papar. I sent to Mr. Burgett to inquire after Will; he sends me word that he is well, & ye fleet coming home. Lord Essex talks all this while, & will lett me say no more, els I coud go on for ever as if I had not sent you four sides of papar an hour agoe.  Once more a good night to my dearest.

**563.**   My ever-new Delight                    Ickworth, Oct. 20, 1719.

My amanuensis has orderd my epistle to & from Sir Thomas Hanmer in so aukard a manner that I must intercept between both ye one & ye other.* I send them to you, that seeing how matters stand you may send me your & your sons ultimate resolution upon them ; but in order to your forming them right he ought to know that could I find out such a person to send of this errant as Sir Thomas describes, (which is no easy matter to meet with,) yet unless he finds himself well enough & willing enough to leave London & make his appearance at ye place to second such overtures as shall be made in his favour by his frinds, the very attempt can turn to no better accompt than exposing him to a rejection, which I would carefully avoid ; he must be told there are but two waies of succeeding in making an interest, the one by down right bribery, (which I hope no child of mine will ever practise,) the other by his infusing into ye electors an oppinion of his ability and integrity.  This can never be attain but by a personale acquaintance, & unless he can resolve to use such condescensions as are necessary to ingratiate himself with them, he had much better determin to lay aside all thoughts of getting into Parliament till he can push his pretensions in ye upper house.  However, if you two shall think otherwaies, & will appoint me my part in it, I shall for your sake act it in ye most effectual manner.  I cannot yet learn wether Mr. Holt has no views on that burrough, (he having been lately on that side of ye country ;)

* The following note (in, I think, Lord Bristol's writing,) at the end of this letter, in the first of the two quarto letter-books, will explain this passage :—*The two letters mentiond in this, which weir too & from Sir Thomas Hanmer, were both coppyd in ye same sheet of papar of this.*—The letter to Sir Thomas Hanmer is in the folio letter-book.  I have printed it a little out of its place, so as not to come in the middle of this batch of letters between Lord & Lady Bristol.  *See* No. 577.—S.II.A.II.

if he should, ours ought not to clash with his interest. You may remember I once for all told you (& with which you then seemd sattisfyed) that whenever I made no mention of ye children's or my own health for want of time or room in my letters, you might conclude of course we were all well; but indeed had I not supposd it so understood between us, I should seldom think mine of consequence enough to write of; but as your kind concern has now made it so, I must tell you it is in as good a state as a mind ill at ease will suffer it to be; I cannot so farr prevaricate with you as to say I sleep so serenely as I used to do, but that I impute to the universal cause of all my other disquiets, your absence, which being farr from being shortend, as I once hopd you could contrive it, makes me much more impatient to bear what remains, even to that paradoxical degree as to feel my self much more unable to live long without you now than in my younger daies; therfore as you' give creditt to this truth, you'l shorten my future pains & uneasynesses by never letting me loose one day of your dear company, which is now become as necessary as nourishment to ye life of your disconsolate lover, Bristol.

Betty rides abroad every day, but does not find so good looks nor appetite from it as formerly; she now complains of a pain in her ankle; the surgeon has advisd her to foment it, which she will do to morrow; we both wonder at not hearing from Fern by Grimes the last post. Pray never write longer nor oftener than tis easy for you; more can never truly please me.

**564.** My ever-new Delight                    Ickworth, Oct. 21, 1719.

If these two last charming daies have not made your Master repent of his resolution to remove, this I hope will find you well at ease in our own house at London: tis some satisfaction (tho' not near enough to make me half so easy as I know you alwaies wish me,) to my impatient soul to know ye distance of space as well as time is shortend;

Sunday come sevenight is I hope ye longest term my tedious expectation has to suffer in, tho' all good nature should be fled to heaven with justice, & since you could not meet with charity enough to take this next week's waiting off your hands, yet I hope you will contrive your next turn so as not to be obligd to go again before ye Parliament meets, which I have heard one of my best birds sing will not sitt till after Christmass. Poor Betty acquainted me this day with a new complaint from a swelling in her knee on ye same legg her ankle has given her so much pain in, which is not that she has been lame of by the leeches, but without having any communication with that ankle; she has found uneasyness in her knee at times in bending it for above a week, but never visibly swelld till this morning; tis not at all discolourd, & about ye breadth of a crown-piece, & ye pain in her ankle so farr from being abated that last night she was forced to foment it; her cough is rather better, never troubling her but upon motion after sitting long still. Mr. Graham has at last answerd my letter, & says Mr. Fern will by no means consent to send his medicines unless he first sees the patient, which he will come hither to do if I chuse to have it so ; wherupon I put it to her choice either to go with her or to send for him, & she has by this nights post wrote to Mr. Graham to send him hither, not finding her self strong enough to think of undertaking two such journeys at this season of ye year as to & from London, for Fern says she must be in ye country at least two months during the course of his physick. There is nothing I would not do, even to hazard my life, to save hers ; & therfore I offerd her ye alternative, which I would not have done but upon one more occasion I can think of. She is capable of making a much finer woman than any of her contemporaries, being blessd with a strength of understanding that will enable her to subdue all ye follies & foibles of her sex ; she wrote a letter to Mrs. Murray full of finer thoughts & more masculinely expressd than to be found in Balzac or Voiture. I know her surpassd by none but the mother who bore her, where ye preferrence in that and all other virtues that adorn our species are justly given by your constant admirer, Bristol.

**565.  Lady Bristol to Lord Bristol.  Richmond, Oct. 21, 1719.**

The great hurry I shall be in to morow all day makes me begin to write now, for we are to go early to London, becaus the Prince & Princes intends to call at Kingsinton in there way, (it being Princes Ann's birth-day,) & ye evening is to be spent in ye citty. However, I shall have a good deal of time now, haveing been waked ever sence 6 a clock with removing of goods, & I shall make use of it to settle the cheif bisness of my life, (our being together); in order to it I have wrote to Mr. Mills to know if he has any call for you to Town & when ; & I have wrote alsoe to Mr. Graham to know what is determind (by Fern) about Betty ; & expect both answeirs (and I hope your dear letter with them) to night ; for if neither of thees things bring you to Town, I cant think of your taking a jurney purposly for me, especialy after what you have said may be the consequence of it; for that would give me (if possible) more uneassines then I already suffer ; so to prevent it I have resolvd to send an express to Lady Dorsett to morow morning time enough to have her answeir before I send my letters to the post. Mrs. Howard seeing my distress (which is but too visable for a Court, my eyes being sweld almost out of my head,) has promist to write in my behalf, which I am sure will succeed if tis posable. And now ye great affair is put in a way of being settled, I wish I had any news to entertain you ; but Mr. Hill, who was with me an hour yesterday morning, said there was not a word ; he & ye Speaker dine with me to day ; the last of thees has given me so much of his company that the Princes tooke nottis of it, & told me, though she dispaird of makeing you uneasy about me, she woud try what she could do with Sir Thomas Hanmer, if he woud not be jealous. The Prince too dus me ye honour to

come every day to my room when I have no strangers. But what is all
this to Maximus & me; torn from his lovd breast, like gatherd flowers I
dye.

**566.**    Lady Bristol to Lord Bristol.        London, Oct. 22, 1719.

We are safely arived at this place with vast
demonstrations of joy by all people, ringing of bells etc. I pertake a little
with them, tho' I cant tell why, unless it be in ye hopes of a new place
giveing me eass, that change of air may be as good for ye diseases of ye
mind as it is for the body; or may be tis ye being ten mile nearer ye center
of all my wishes; but I rather think it is ye hopes I have of seeing you
soon ; nay, I depend so much upon it that I have not sent to Lady Dorsett,
for sure you will think it absolutely nessesary for Betty (as well as me) when
you receive Mr. Graham's letter ; for fear that should miscary, I have sent
that he wrote to me ; I have sent Mr. Mills's alsoe to give a lift, tho' I believe
by your account of Betty you cant but think ye sooner she is put into other
hands ye better, & as I have orderd the matter, her coming will not be
wonderd at, since tis for some body els to see her foot, & if ye town dus not
agree with her, she may go back with us after my waiting is over. Jacks
eyes are il again this 2 daies ; we both agree to give you no farther trouble
about Alborough, for niether his purs nor (I hope) his principles will agree
with it. You bid me never write oftener nor longer then is easy to me, &
God knows I never am easy but when I do, as you may well see by what I
do write that it must be purely for writing sake, for I realy beleive in ye
way I have done it at Richmond I have often repeated the same thing over
& over, for I have seldome had time to read any letter I have sent. I
dind at Leister house, & have not seen a mortale sence, so that I can tell
you nothing that I hope will ever be news to you, which is, dear dearest
life, I love you with all my soul & heart. Adue.

**567.** My ever-new Delight                    Ickworth, Oct. 23, 1719.

How could you be so careless of my quiet as well as of your self to gett an other fall after all ye precautions I have given you to prevent them. You used to lay those accidents upon your being with child, saying you never stumbled but in that condition, ruminating alwaies upon ye time of your travel; but now tis plain that was not ye cause; wherfore pray take better heed, or I must introduce ye mode again of a gentleman usher to conduct you. I hope my fears over-allow for its consequences, (which I know your tenderness for me will make less then they are,) & that therfore my pain is greater than your own; ye most comfortable circumstance I can pick out of your description is that you neither faild in your waiting on her or his Royal Highness in such good as well as great company. Tis doubly kind in you to think of absent frinds with such reciprocal wishes & impatience of returning to them again; but that disird period was, it seems, as remote when you wrote last as I flatterd my self the whole absence was to be (viz-3 weeks) when you first went from hence. Were not your Mistress as gracious to you as you tell me she is, I should grudg every moment of that time she robbs me of, but as I know she both values & possesses virtue in ye highest degree, so she must have a true tast of your merett, & as her discernment is more penetrating than any womans I ever observd, so as she will love you better ye longer she knows you, that thought alone calms my mind into a tolerable submission to Sunday (still) come fortnight, in which time I hope her Royal Highness will make you so perfect a good housewife as that you'l be dressd every day hear before ten, & then we shall not stay at dinner for you after two. If example would teach ye maids what she would have them learn, her own would preach more to them in a day than poor Bettys could in an eternity; however, she is very proud of her place; I am now with her, & have askd her what account I am to give you of her; she says she cant say she is better, tho' Mr. Holt & Balladin have been with her all this evening, as all your 3 cousin Howards were last night, who staid till midnight ; as long as they talkd of & commended you, they entertaind me as well as your daughter did them with a very good supper; they leave this country on Tuesday come sevenight.  I have written a very long letter & in ye strongest terms to our son Harry about his learning, which he is so almost incorrigibly tardy in, that if you have ever a spare moment, I desire you would employ it in seconding my admonitions, which unless they take place now at this critical season of his life, we must expect instead of an eminent useful person to see him an ignorant,· empty, contemptible one, which God of his goodness avert.  Ye word incorrigible putts me in mind of a person & piece of news I know will surprise you ; tis that Tom Harris & I are for ever parted ; he gott drunk (as is said at Saxham) with brandy, which made him much more mad than any body in Bedlam ; in short his behaviour was so incredibly monstrous & extravagant that had he been shott, as they do mad doggs, no body ought to have been questiond, at least not punishd for it; he has writt me ye most penitential epistle was ever pennd, & so orewhelmd with confusion that I am afraid he should offer some violence to himself; but what coud he expect should better befall him after having offended you ?  It alwaies proves ominous to ye loss of my favour when ever they have ye greater misfortune of falling into your displeasure. Judg now of my forlorn scituation, left alone to Adam & bereft of my better Eve, without whom this parke is farr from being ye usual Paradice to your now solitary hermite, Bristol.

**568.**    Lady Bristol to Lord Bristol.    London, Oct. 24, 1719.

O my dear dear life, what did I not suffer yester-day at ye reading your letter ; ye pain it gave me even surpasd ye pleasure

I alwaies feel at ye sight of one from you ; to find my self so disapointed in the hopes I had of seeing you hear, with that aggravating circomstance that you must be as much so, if you expected me to leave this place before Monday come fortnight, that was a grievance ·lay much at my heart from ye first day I gott to Richmond, (for then Lord Grantam refusd me changing ye next week with my Lady,) as I believe I have more then once told you, & how the case stood, but I find (by your dear letter) not plain enough, so that you must bear with a repetition of it. This fortnight is what I owed for Lady Dorsett & my self last turn, when I was sick; Monday next is Lady Grantam's right to come inn for her self; & as mine in cours alwaies follows hers, I concluded ye change would have been no difficulty for one week. This is what I believe has made you mistake ye whole affair, & reckon BUT 3 weeks when it was a month ; BUT did I say ? O, tis an age in love like mine; theirfore to have shortend it, all ye favour I askd was to wait next week instead of that following, so to have paid my dutty to the Prince ot his birth-day & my waiting all under one, & by that a week saved ; for I reckon all time lost that is absent from ye treasure of my heart; but this very smale request has been twise refusd me ; so that (my dear) you will easely beleive I did not nead ye addission of hearing poor Betty was wors to all thees troubles, which have quite overwhelmd me, & sett me into such a passion of crying as made me in a sad condition to attend ye Princes to Lord Essex's christening; so that I was oblidgd to say it was my daughter's being worse and not able to come to town that had given me so much consern ; but I went, before the time I was orderd to attend, to the resource of all my (Court) greivances, my dear mistress, in ye condision I have mentiond to vent my troubles ; I found her to my wish alone with as much tender compassion to my distress as coud be expected ; for she told me I should go away to day rather then she would see me suffer so much, being truly sinceable what it was to be from a sick child, without its being a Lady Betty. I told her how much I thought my self obligd for this great goodness, but that it would add to my uneasynes to go before the Prince's birth-day at a time when so few of ye ladys weir in town ; all that I wishd was to have my waiting & that over together, that I might stay the longer in ye country ; she said that was so smale a thing, & so very reasonable, that I nead only to speak to Lady Grantam to change ; I told her Royal Highness I thought it so, or I had not askd it at first, but that I had been twise refusd ; upon which she bid me take no farther care about it, but be assurd it shoud be as I desird ; and accordingly I found it, for even before our going to ye christening ye very same lord & lady that had twise refusd me came to ye room where I was sitting with a great many complements to offer ye change I disird, nay, to give me 2 days, that I might sett out ye sooner ; theirfore, my dear, I beg you would lett ye horses be hear, so that I may leave this place early enough on Sunday to gitt to Newport that night ; I shoud have been glad it might have been on Satterday ; but I am afraid after 3 weeks waiting, & ye fatigue of ye birth-day on Fryday, I should never be able to rise time enough ye next morning to gitt to ye Inn before tis dark. I am so very lame now that I have not slept 4 hours to night with pain ; but I am sure what ever I suffer next week will seem light, becaus tis to shorten our absence. I beleive the reason of your not hearing sooner from Mr. Graham was his being out of town, which he is at present ; so that if I had not sent for his son this morning, & made him open Squirs's letter, you would have been again disapointed of an answeir, which I have taken ye best care I could to prevent by desiring him to go early to Fern & hasten his jurney (as much as possible) to Ickworth ; but I have not yett had his answeir, tho' I have sent 3 times for it ; but he promist me to write you every perteculer by ye post, wether his father came to town or not. Pray let me know if I shall bring any Renish wine, & how much, or any other commands that you have,

which are always obeyd with pleasure by, my dear dearest life, yours &
only yours whilst I have life.

Mr. Graham is just come to tell me Fern will sett out Thursday next by
Bury coach.—Sure I nead say no more about ye horses coming; for positively if you dont see me Monday ye 2d of Nov. in a coach, I shall come
to you in a herss.

**569.** My ever-new Delight          Ickworth, Oct. 26, 1719.

I can safely swear I have not passd one un-
desturbd night since I saw you till ye last, which your kind letter procurd
me by letting me know I should be made happy again a week sooner than
I expected. Your true affection in contriving, & your Mistresses most
gracious goodness in effecting it, are of a sort of benefetts never to be forgotten as long as ye memory of any thing remains in us. Ye gratefull
sence of your inviolable truth & tenderness towards me will be ye very last
thing that will live in me; for that thought administers ye highest cordial
to my heart in all its conflicts; when that failes its pulse may beat no
longer, but still I hope ye pleasure of remembering thee may survive even
in ye land where all other things may more easily be forgotten. These are
ye constant sentiments which continually sitt uppermost on my soul when
ever you are from me; but as I find they soften me too much, I've paryd
them with all ye strength & skill I'm master of till you are with me again;
when of course they & all other malancholly ones soon vanish. Most
prophets are pleasd when their predictions are punctually verifyd; but I
cant help feeling ye reverse as to Jacks eyes, notwithstanding his running
counter to sense & common experience, as well as to my dissuasions, in
removing out of this into London air, in exchanging ye wholsome diet &
good hours of this place for ye irregular way of life in all kinds where he
is, not to mention the expence too, when he had all things gratis, which
will be worth thinking of if he intends ever to be in Parliament, for tis

never to be obtaind without some extraordinary charge at best. I have
this day written a second letter to Sir Thomas Hanmer to thank him for
ye readyness he shewd to serve him.  As I was telling Betty (who I cant
say is much better, or hopes to be so till ye Doctor comes,) that you had
been so good to desire I would send you some commands before you left
London, & asking her if she had any thing, ye whole nursery (who are, God
be praisd, all well,) threw in thier several requests ; but I shall trouble you
with those only of absolute necessity ; as a pair of shooes for Herriett (who
is without exception ye finest child in ye world) of ye fifth size ; a quantity
of limons ; four pair of knitt thred stockings for my lordship ; more chocolate, there being but three pounds left; as for Rhinish, I think you nead
remove none, but I must desire you to send for Soleirol, & to tell him you
have orders to pay him for ye ten dozen of wine he has sent down at thirty
six shillings ye dozen, tho' ye first two dozen that came was so foul & very
bad that no body could drink it, & is most of it still in ye house; neither
would I give him so many pence a dozen for any more of it ; but if he has
any better than he has yett sent me, I will give him ye same rate for ten
dozen more, which he may send in two hampers.  The butler says that all
the sack is out ; so that if Soleirol has any that is pure & excellant, or
knowes who has any such, at or under eight shillings a gallon, I would have
nine gallons sent in pint bottles.  If all or any of these commissions should
be at all inconvenient to you, being in waiting and before a birth-day, I beg
you woud give your self & me ye ease of knowing when we meet they were
laid aside ; for I had rather want every thing but your self than have it on
the hard terms of troubling you for it ;  your eass & happiness being the
cheif aim in this life of your most faithfull friend & constant lover, Bristol.

570.    Lady Bristol to Lord Bristol.       London, Oct. 26, 1719.
                    I find nothing that is ye least agreable to me
can happen without an alay ; for when I had pleasd my self with ye hopes

of seeing you on Sunday or Monday at farthest, tho' that is an age to
impatience like mine, yett being so much sooner then expected made it a
great pleasure to me ; but I was not long to injoy even that, for good Lady
Grantam told me that since I changd ye week I must go threw with it, for
she could wait no part of it, and that she had more than once repented
haveing changd, since she understood my daughter was not so il but that I
might have staid. I dont much wonder at her, poor soul ; it may be she
has no notion of anybodys having any thing better than a Lord Grantam
to go to, & then endeed it weir no great matter how long one was absent ;
but I did not nead so shocking a thing to be said to me to aggravate ye
disapointment of staying hear till Monday, which her crosnes makes
unavoidable ; theirfor disire you would not lett ye horses be hear till
Sunday, for it can only put me to an unnessesary expence, besides fretting
that I cant make use of them ; their nead come but two sadle horses, without you woud have me bring you another footman ; I cant wonder at your
parting with this ; but how you coud bear with him so long would seem
strang to any but me, that have experiencd such a nature in you that no
creature was ever blessd with, or that ever blessd so many, or extended it
self so farr ; what then must be the share of a wife and children in so
uneversale a goodness ; which makes my pain ye greater when I know of
any that dont diserve it, (at least as farr as they are able ;) but be asured
(my dear angell) nothing that I can say to Harry upon this occassion shall
be wanting, & Jack has promist ye same on his part, for I think nothing
shoud be left untryd, though I much fear if he hears not my prophett,
neither will he be perswaided though one rose from the dead.—The yachts
that went for ye King are driven back to Margrett by ye contrary winds,
which is ye only thing can keep him, for he was to leave Hanover as yesterday. You and Sir Thomas Hanmer are desird (I nead not say by who)
not to give any creditt to those that tell you the Parliament dus not sitt at

ye time fixt, if ye King can gitt over, or ye first day after his arivall, & not
only for you to depend upon this your selves, but to undeceive all your
frinds that may be misled into a contrary oppinion.  I shall tell you nothing
of ye secrett expedision, for tis made such a jest of hear that I never can
distinguish when they are in ernest about it.  All that was talkd of last
night was that Lord Bristol's goldsmith had one of ye 10000 pound lotts,
& a cooke maid had ye other.  The lights in ye sky appeard last night &
three nights together in a more extrodnary maner than ever.  You will be
surprisd when I tell you Mr. Balladins Phis was the brightest constellation
that has appeard to me a great while.  O what a joy it was to see him enter
ye box at ye play, that I might ask him a thousand questions, & all of you,
tho' I was glad to hear a little of poor Betty by ye by, & with a great deal
of pleasure that her cough was better.  I am writing at Leister house to
loose no time before ye drawing-room, & have made Howard write to you
that I might be quiett; but now her own letter is done she has no more
pattience with me, & ses she will blott it if I say a word more ; but in
spight of her I will again repeat, dear dearest, how much I love & value
you is never to be expresd.

> **571.**     My ever-new Delight                    Ickworth, Oct. 28, 1719.

Having computed that ye horses will be in
London some hours before ye post, I chose this conveyance by my
Governour in hopes to make him once welcome to you ; you know tis a
point I have long labourd without much effect, but that's a history methinks you should be almost as much ashamd of as he or I ; pray lett me
at last be ye happy instrument of a peace between you, as he vainly
imagines he was one in our blessed union.  The plan of ye articles which I
have drawn are short & pithy; tis only that you would suffer your name to
be used to Mrs. Jones, that if she will take one of his daughters to keep,

you will make his son your page. Your saying you should have been glad to have gott away on Saturday has made me send ye horses a day sooner, only to putt it in your power to do just as you like best; but I beseech you, dont think of me in the determination farther than is intirely consistent with your ease & safety; after having been fatigued with 3 weeks waiting & setting up to celebrate your Master's birth-day, (may they prove as many & as prosperous as his own wishes & our happiness in him can dictate,) I would not for ye world (that is for ye best thing in it, your all-satisfying society,) have you think of breaking your rest or heating your blood by beginning a journey before you have sufficiently recruited your spiritts, & enabled your self to bear it without any complaint; for should I hear any on this occasion, it would almost cancel ye comfort I propose to my self in seeing you again ye 2d of November, which I can with strict truth affirm is more impatiently longd for than ye 25th July, 1695, could possibly have been by your faithfull Bristol.

Sent by Welch Tom, directed, To the worthyest woman in ye world, I nead not say the Countess of Bristol.

**572.** My ever-new Delight                    Thursday morning.

Tis now past midnight, & your letter but just come, which, as it hinders me a day at least from ye sight of you, will I am afraid prevent my sleeping so well to night as I have done ever since I receivd ye welcome news of your being to be hear on ye 2d of November at farthest; but now I see it will be ye 3d first. I had formd a project in hopes to have seen you here on Sunday, Tom Harvey having receivd his last orders to go away to morrow morning 2 hours before day with ye horses, & Welch Tom with him, who has a letter of mine for you in his pocket. Tis well I sett up till this time, (which is more than I have done since I saw you,) or ye horses would have been with you two days before you want them; however, I cant help sending them away on Fryday, that they may rest on ye Sabbath, in case you cant come away sooner than Monday; but even then I can never consent to have you attended by two horsemen only, & therfore must still retain that part of my plan, because your safety is consernd in it, which is to send Mr. Morris up with them, (who has a mind to see his sons,) & he has promist to return again with you; 3 horsmen will deterr any band of highway men from attempting you, wheras having but two may invite one. Pitty my disapointment, & believe me more than ever your most faithfull lover, Bristol.

**573.**    Lady Bristol to Lord Bristol.

Oct. 28, 1719, between 9 & 10 at night.

I am sure you will say, this is an early hour indeed, I wish she has always done so; and realy I have as believing it your desire, (which is ever sacred to me,) for I have never faild to come home when I was dismisd from my Mistress, except one night that I supt with Mrs. Howard, & then I was so stueped that I might very well have been spaird; for Jeny Smith (who was their) said, Prithy, Howard, lett us wake ye Countess, for I beleive she has slept near a month, & I think it down right an affront to us all; so they will think it alsoe to night at Mrs. Southwells, (where ye whole town is to be,) that I have chosen rather to come home than to share in there entertainments. Alase, they little think I am injoying much greater by my self in reading over & over your dear kind letter; I wish I could answeir it; but words are as much too poor for that as they are to express what my heart feels for thee, thou dearest treasure of it; so I must return to my old cours again, that is telling you how missarable I spend my tedious hours in your absence. To day Jack & I was very kindly entertaind at diner with Lady Griz: Baily; she, Mrs. Murry, Mrs. Lapell & I went to ye play together afterwards; but in my whole life I never was so tird or felt such impatience to come home to write, knowing how scars time will be with me to morow, for I have not yett tryd my birth day cloths, & am to go at 12 a clock to Kingsinton with ye Prince & Princes; but what ever is left undone, nothing of your commands shall be neclected as farr as lys in my power; yett you will think me very much at leasure when I tell you I have satt with my aunts two hours at a time, & have been thrise with them sence I came to town; it sutes my humour now as well as any thing els; they are both much out of order; Lady Suffolke has gott ye gout; every body has some distemper or other; mine (according to Dr. Gibens rule of seizing ye weakest part) took me with such a giddiness in my head last night at ye drawing-room that ye playing was forcd to be stopt tell I was better; they woud have comforted me by saying twas a genarale complaint; but that did not lessen mine. Thank God, I am much better to day, but for fear of a return I will conclude this like a sermon by leaving the rest to another oppertunetty.

574.    Lady Bristol to Lord Bristol.

Oct. 29.    Leister House.    8 a clock.

Weary & faint as I am, I cant go to diner till my letter is ready for the post, & I have given you an account of this days expedision. As soon as we came from Kingsinton this morning, the Prince & Princes went to Lord Mayor's Show, where we have been ever since, excepting the two hours we have been coming from Cheapside heither; their Royal Highnesses intended to be incogneto, so would not go in there own coaches; but they weir soon discoverd, and such demonstrations of joy was expresd by all sorts of people as I believe ye like was never seen upon any occassion; the mob accompanyd us home; many perteculer things happend not proper for a letter, if I had time; but as soon as I have eat a bitt, I must go home to try my cloths, that pece of work being still to do;

theirfore you will eassily beleive after that I shall be, glad of what rest my bed will afford. I have sent you the inclosd verses, said to be made by Tickell (& much commended) in contradiction to ye old proverb, and to show he can make a silk purs of a sow's ear. Diner stays for me, but I cant conclude till I have begd you woud not forgitt me by Tom Harvey with a line of comfort to live upon tell Tuesday noon; I should be glad then to meet you at diner at Newmarkett with Lady Thomond, if she is their, (& it is not inconvenient to you); els I shall go without stoping with all the hast & impatience an affection like mine can cary me to ye dearest of all creatures. Good night.

**575.**    My ever-new Delight          •          Ickworth, Oct. 29, 1719.

You will see by ye letter which my governour was gon to bed with in his pocket last night, (& which he will not part with, becaus he is sure I cant mend what was said in his favour by an other,) how great a disappointment yours brought me afterwards. I wish you dont find Lady Grantam's repentance founded in a mistake, when you see poor Betty; for I am farr from thinking her in so good a way as she seems to soppose; her swelld ankle has given her so much uneasyness that she has not been on hors-back till to-day since Saturday; & if she be onĉe more disabled from useing that sovereign restorative, her sole ressource must be in Fern's specifick; I hope he will not fail us to morrow, for our faith is great, especially since we have nothing wants to be made whole, which it seems he all along supposes to be ye case, otherwaies I cant but think he would have venturd his medicines without viewing the patient, unless a greater reward be his greatest view.—If Lord Hervey would write to Harry & tell him even without a good stock of learning he shall never be able to recommend him to any thing in a Court above a gentleman usher's place, beside that it will be a perpetual uneasyness to have an ignorant insignificant so nearly related to him continually in his sight, it would do more good than any thing I could say to cure him of all his vain expectations from that hand without some sound foundation for his brother to work upon.—I shall not trouble you to bring me a footman, having still too much of Adam; woud I coud live without any servants, ye bane of quiet. Pray do me justice to Mrs. Howard, especially since she says both my sons have faild to do so, by letting her know neither of them have true understanding enough to tast her meritt half so much as I have ever done ; that tho' my letter staid above 3 months for an answer, & it may be then thought a great condescension from a courtier to a plain countryman, yet hers shall be sooner acknowledgd ; but as for fine & pretty things, (you may e'en tell her ye truth) that as many of either sort as I am capable of affording are wholly & solely reservd for your sweet self by your 'faithful constant lover, Bristol.               Ye inclosd are Felle's native thoughts, touchd with a small file by Nan, his amanuensis.

576.    Lady Bristol to Lord Bristol.       London, Oct. 31, 1719.

This has been such a week that nead not have been grudgd one, for I am realy quite dead with thees last two days· Thursday I gave you an account of, & yesterday was as bad ; for what did it signefy to me to have the prittest cloths their, when all I woud wish to please was absent. My Master & Mistress admird me so much that they showd me about for a sight ; but those honours did not hinder me from being extreemly il all night; it was near two before I gott to bed with all ye hast I coud make, & nothing but a bitt of bread & a glass of wine for my supper ; about five I waked extreemly sick & voielent pain in my back, with all ye symptoms of gravell ; I was forcd to send for Mr. Graham, & tryd to gitt ye Dutchess of Shrewsbury to wait for me this morning ; but she being gon out of town, & no other lady hear but one I did not care to be oblidged to, I was forcd to gitt up & go with the Princes to Kingsinton. I am extremly faint for want of rest, but much freer from pain since dinner, where I was accompanyd by Welch Tom. Who coud have thought he shoud revive me? but ye precious tokens he brought of your dear love must always have that effect; but the monster kept me an hour after he came to town in ye last impattience for your dear letter ; yett notwithstanding that prejudice to him, I have granted his request, as it was your disire ; all ye rest of your commands are alsoe obeyd, tho' one is not exactly as you orderd ;  but as I did it for ye best, I hope you will think it so.  Hear is great talke of an invassion by ye Duke of Ormond with 2000 men on ye West, & arms for 10000 more ; after this I nead not tell you the Parliament is near meeting ;  ye King is to sett out this day, & is expected ye latter end of next week hear.  And now I am at ye end of my news, I must be so of my letter ; for my poor head is so giddy I cant see what I have writt ; but I dont expect to be better till I am lodgd in those dear arms again, which (with God's permission) shall be on Tuesday ; I am very sure no earthly power shall prevent me ; till that long time farwell, my dear dear.

I beleive I might have been releasd to morow, but that tis ye first Sunday in ye month, & courtiers care only to pay their devotions to an earthly Prince.

**577.**    To Sir Thomas Hanmer at Mildenhall.        Oct. 19, 1719.

There being a vacancy at Aldburrough by ye death of Sir Henry Johnson, & my wife having (as you may remember on a former occasion) nothing nearer her heart than to see her son Jack in Parliament, has written to me on purpose to desire I would (with her most humble service) give you this trouble, & in both our names beg ye favour, not only of your recommendation to ye town & to all the gentlemen who live near and have any interest in it, but also to advise him & us what other proper measures must be taken in order to gett him elected there. Your friendship & assistance on this weighty occasion, I must needs tell you, will be a work of pure generosity & supererogation, since it can only heap obligations on those who cannot possibly esteem & love you better than they do already. Had not I been long acquainted with your beneficent, disinterested nature, this should have been kept a secret; but to such a mind as you are master of, twill double every endeavour in ye service of such friends as sett so just a value on you, among whom do me alwaies ye right to allow ye very first place to, Sir, your most affectionate kinsman.

**578.** To Mrs. Howard.     Ickworth Park. Nov. 10, 1719.
    (now Lady Suffolk.)
    Madam
        I took you to be one of those rare woemen who possessd perfection to such a degree as renderd you (of course) indifferent to praise, & therefore never thought of commending you with any other view than to show my own discernment; but since you voluntarily confess your weak side lyes most exposd that way, it woud be impolite in me not to ply it accordingly. However, as this letter of mine comes only to thank you for one of yours, which are always fine beyond flattery, I cant on this occasion begin to sooth your general vanity on that head, & shoud all your other good qualities appear the same when examind in their turn, as I am too apt to think they will, what a bankrupt in panegyrick must such superiour meritt reduce your humble servant to?

**579.** To Lord Hervey. (Carr.)     Feb. 1, 1719/20.
    Dear Son
        Altho' ye answer you thought fitt to give me when I last spoke to you of marrying might have made any parent less zealously concernd than my self for the prosperity of our family resolve

Vol. II.   Q

never to renew ye mention of it any more, yet since you once told me, if I could find out such a party as would both build Ickworth & recruit again those necessary diminutions of my estate which suitable provisions for eleven younger children must occasion, that you would readily receive any such proposal, it has at last pleasd Providence to afford us such an opportunity, there being a gentleman* of £7000 per annum, who having an only daughter whom he would gladly dispose of into so honest a family & to a man of your meritt & reputation, who offers me almost charte-blanche as to what part of it we would ask at present, & will settle ye whole to descend at his death. This seeming to be ye crisis of our familys fate, that God of his undeservd goodness to me would inspire you with such right resolutions as may determine you to true happiness, & that to a perpetual plenteous independancy, shall be ye fervent prayer of your most affectionate father.

**580.**    My dear daughter†                         May 20, 1720.

I take ye first opportunity (with safety to ye secret) to lett you know how throughly pleasd I am (even amidst no small uneasynesses for another) that I can call you by that indearing name. My son has shewn ye nicest skill in choosing you, since in you alone he could securely promise himself not only every quality essential to his own happiness, but has also made a wise provision to intaile good sense & virtue (its constant concomitant) on our (now) flourishing family. My wishes for your mutual welfare were too warm to suffer him to leave me without offering all ye good advice I thought necessary to it ; but (to do him right) I find he wants none in any thing where you are at all concernd ; since then yee

---

* Lord Bristol's marginal note says, Mr. Tilney.—S.H.A.H.

† Lord Bristol, who has himself copied both this letter and the preceding one into the folio letter-book, has added "now Lady Hervey." The marriage of John Hervey and Mary Lepell was not publickly announced till five months after this. Mr. Croker suggests a possible reason for the secrecy of it in his preface to Lord Hervey's Memoirs p. xxiv.—S.H.A.H.

have made your selves so compleatly happy in each other, I hope and earnestly desire that yee would think of making my wife & me so too by living with us, where ye daily satisfaction of being witnesses to your bliss will prolong ye declining daies of your most affectionate friend & faithful servant, Bristol.

**581.** To Lord Hervey. (Carr.)        Ickworth, June 25, 1720.

Dear Son

After having rejected so advantagious an opportunity as Providence had thrown into your power of making me, your self & our family, not only easy, but great and independent for many generations, notwithstanding ye great number of children that must be provided for out of my estate, I cannot think ye matter you desire my advice in can prove of much signification to either ; yet since you have thought fit to ask it, I will give you my best thoughts upon it. In ye first place, ye value of mony is so sinking & consequently that of land so rising, that ye most foresighted men in these matters cannot at present guess where ye proportion between one & t'other is likely to fix ; & untill that be known you must deal at random. But, besides, what could you do with money now, when nobody knows how to employ any but by investing of it into Stocks, which are all near trebled above their orriginal intrinsick values, & South Sea even farr exceeds those. Then if any thing that is right can possibly proceed from ye latter, it must be by occasioning ye reduction of ye national interest to £3 per cent, (after ye annuities are bought in,) that British merchants may trade on a level with ye Dutch & others at forreign marketts ; so that ye rents of land will in that case almost doubly answer ye produce of money ; all which considerd, (& that you seem indifferent,) I think your best way will be to keep as you are at least for the present.—I am very glad I can now assure you that Betty is so visibly mended, that we may all promise our selves the pleasure of her continuing long among us, whose value is likely to prove inestimable.—I hope Mr. Mills made you understand that ye security you enterd into upon my account was only that I shoud not run away, in case no error shoud be found in the judgment Mr. Minshull obtaind in our £500 wager.—I have been so farr from being able to pick out any true joy to congratulate upon, that ye more I see, hear or think of it, the less reason appears to approve or excuse ye conduct or council of those who concluded it, unless it be those parts of ye Treaty only which relate to ye managers personal interests, whose honours or profitt no wise or honest man will envy. I cannot conclude without letting you know your Bury friends are very inquisitive when they may expect to see you, & that all advantages have been endeavourd to be taken both of your long absence from them & their service, but without much effect, I hope, by ye care of your affectionate father, Bristol.

P.S. I know nothing of Mrs. Scott's demand, neither when, where or for what ye money was advanced. I can only tell that Will has been allowd all, nay, more than I can well spare him, & that whoever will give him or any other of my children creditt without my privity, shall do it at their peril.

**582.**    To Sir William Barker.    Ickworth, July 12, 1720.

I did not receive the favour of yours of the 5th instant till this day at noon, which brought me the very first notice I ever had that any Court was to be held at Trimly since the death of Sir Compton Felton; other waies I should have sent one sooner to let you know that I have lately found in a letter from Sir C. Felton to me in ye year 1710 that there was a fine of fourty seven shillings only paid by Sir Henry Felton in the year 1658 for his son Thomas's admission to the Marsh in question, and he inferrd from thence (ye quantity it contains being about 24 acres) that ye fine was certain at 2 shillings per acre. Now being altogether a stranger to what agreement you & he afterwards came to for his own admission, I must beg your patience and information from ye Court books in that point; because as I hope you would not insist on more from me, so the same terms would be readily complyd with by, Sir, etc.

**583.**   To Mrs. Manley.              Ickworth, July 12, 1720.

Madam

Your "lovely Bristol" and "bright Eliza"* having both been dangerously ill at the same time you were so, it seems kind Providence (with all the faults & follies I stand punishable for) thought it not fitt entirely to break the bruised reed, & so conceald your sickness from me till they were better & you well enough recoverd to tell me so your self. May the country air convey as long and large a share of health & happiness to you as your Muse has of praise & reputation to every branch of the Hervey family; and may that part of it which you have thought worthy of interesting your self so zealously for, (& who for that reason I shall take more particularly into my protection,) live to deserve but half the trouble you have given your self for him, & then I shall think all the cares of his education throughly repaid to, Madam, your etc.

**584.**   To Sir Henry Bunbury.         Ickworth, July 18, 1720.

I shall always think my self extreamly obligd to you for the kind trouble you have given your self in acquainting me with what must ever nearly concern me, the good or ill state of Sir Thomas Hanmer's health; as also for the just opinion you express of my sentiments for him; which put me into more pain than can be imagind by any one that knows his value less than I do till releivd by your second letter, on the welcome news whereof I most heartily congratulate her Grace of Grafton,

---

* See Mrs. Manley's poem at the end of these letters. —S.H.A.H.

Lady Bunbury, your self, my self and country, who are all so deeply interested in his preservation. When'ere such souls as his are called to Heaven, (from whence orriginally they spring,) twill be the worst of omens for those who stay behind, since nought but evill can be to come; but as he is now likely to be lent much longer to the world, we may hope for halcyon days, if either his advice or example be at all followd, both which shall be the imitation as they have been the admiration of his and your most faithfull, much obliged servant, Bristol.

My wife joins in all services to Lady Bunbury, ye young ladies & Sir Thomas Hanmer.

**585.** To Mr. William Astell. Aug. 4, 1720.

Altho' in ye course of our treaty you demurrd for some time upon several articles, which would have given most men but such as you & all ye world shall ever find me many allowable opportunities to have declard it void, as land has almost doubly increasd in value since ye time I first fixd for your final answer, & more especially too after the intervention of a proposal, which, had I kept my self master of those estates you are purchasing of, would have enabled me to make a most advantagious match for one of my many children, yet rather than suffer my self to do any thing that might but seem to deviate in ye least punctillio from ye strictest rules of just & honourable dealing, I have sacrificed all family & other interests to secure & preserve ye more valuable character & conscience of a thorough honest man ; & have therefore sent you ye articles (executed in form) by this bearer, my son, (Tom,) who as he is ye very person that will be ye chief present sufferer by his father's nice principles, so I cannot but lay hold on this occasion most earnestly to recommend him to your friendly advice & assistance in improving that small fortune I am able to give him in some other way than by this wife, whose friends insisting peremptorily on a settlement in land it will not now be in my power to comply with, & therfore I hope & trust God's good providence will provide some other way for his happiness, which is ye firm belief & dependance of your etc. Bristol.

**586.** Lady Bristol to Lord Bristol. Hockerell, Aug. 5, 1720.

I wish I coud tell my dear angell I were well gott to this place, but that woud be an untruth, which is what I never was guilty of in thought too thee, thou never failing spring of that & love; yett thus much I can say, that I am better then I expected after so dismale a setting out. O my dear, what did I not suffer; what addisional pain to our parting was it to see such a storm of rain, & not be sure you weir not in it, & I the unhappy cause by bringing you so farr from home; but I think I shall never be able to forgive old Frampton if he did not keep you by force till ye afternoon, which was very fine, & then I hope ye jurney coud not hurt you; however, I cant be easy till I hear of you, & how you do after it, which I hope I shall not fail of by to morow's post, no more than you shall from your faithfull E. Bristol.

Jack is just arrivd, so every body hear is happy but poor me; I know ye time when I shoud have been so to at ye sight of him;

Butt now nor that nor nothing els can please;
Those were injoyments for a mind at ease.

**587.** My ever-new Delight Ickworth, Aug. 6, 1720.

If ye pious prayers of a repenting reprobate can in aught avail thee, this will find my faithfull fair one safe & at ease from all kind of pains at Richmond, except some small uneasyness for being from me, which is ye only one I can never wish you without, it being a debt I have run you into so great an arrear of that you must loose one of your best qualities, that of being nicely just, not to be perpetually paying me some share of it whenever we are absent, especially since I solemly assure thee that I have in these last four & twenty hours since I parted from thee been giving thee more creditt of that kind than ever I could before, because I have now known & possessd thee above that number of years.... Since I am never able to give you a better account of my self when thus left by my self, I will endeavour to give you ye best I can of our daughter Betty; her appetite seemd to day as good as you saw it at Sir Dudly Cullums, & is like to continue so by continuing ye use of ye Pyrmont watters, which agree wonderfully well with her. Dr. Pake was here this morning in so great a shower of rain & so dreepd with it, that he was forced to call for a dram to repell ye dangerous humidities that might penetrate through three setts of Bavarias & Brandenburghs. The rest of our sweet children are all well, & very good except Felly, who was grown so very naught, even by ye report and allowance of his partial frind Betty, that I was obliged to whip him before I had been one hour in ye house; but I doubt he found it in so superficial a manner that he'l be little ye better for it; his eyes are so like yours that wheneer they weep or whatever is then askd, must of course be complyd with by your faithful friend & constant lover, Bristol.

Pray make my honest duty & sincere services acceptable where you are.

**588.**    Lady Bristol to Lord Bristol.          London, Aug. 6, 1720.

I am afraid, my dearest life, you should be under any uneasiness for want of your coach, which woud be doubled upon me as being ye occassion of it; but I am sure, if you had seen ye difficultys we must have undergon by making use of the Prince's coach, you woud have been sooner determined then I was to take my own on, for you will find by the inclosd letter that was not intended when I went to bed, though I dont send it to sattisfy you in that point, but in a much more matterial one, which is to show you how you posses all my thoughts as well as heart; for that little dab of papar was the first thing I satt down too in ye inn, & the conclussion ye last thing when I went to bed, as I beleive this will be to night, for ye first bell is gon for letters. I have not ben out of the house since I came to town, nor indeed am fitt for any thing but my bed, as Sir D. Hambleton (who has been hear) disird me; but I believe he has added more to my uneassiness by saying how absolutely nessesary tis for me to go to ye Bath to prevent il consequences that may attend my complaints; this, he said, he woud give you an account of more pertecullerly; therfore I will dwell no longer upon this dissagreable subject, but enter upon a more pleasing one, which is to tell you that Lord Hervey has been to see me, & looks very well, & grown very rich (as he tells me), tho South Sea is extreemly fallen; he has securd 6000 & odd hundred pounds by selling only part out, beside a very good stock in; I find him mightyly bent upon selling Aswarby at 40 years purchase, which, as he makes out to me, must turn to very good account, but he will tell you more at large then I am able to do at this time, being extremely sick, (as I was at Newmarkett, but I hope it will go off as well after I have slept,) els I think I could give you many good reasons why the complying with him in this will answeir every purpose you have so long labourd to obtain, besides that he reckons when all is together to be in possession of £4000 a year without your assistance. Tom has ben hear, & I think looks very thin; he will be with you on Wensday in our coach; I thought that woud be his best conveyance, beside that I beleive Lord Hervey will go with him, if he can leave his affairs hear for a few days, which I hope will settle every thing to your liking, with ye addissional pleasure of my having some hand in it. O may I ever be an instrement of happyness to you & yours, thou eternal source of all happyness to your faithfull E.B.

Vol. II.    R

**589.**   My ever-new Delight          Ickworth, Aug. 8, 1720.

If my (or rather your own) coach proved of ye
least use towards your greater ease in your journey by going on to London,
an apology woud have been much more necessary for your leaving than
taking it ; for how can any thing be right or wrong to me but as it is better
or worse for you ; tis by that standard only ye value of all things rise or
fall in my esteem, & for that very reason found my self better pleasd even
in those storms you mention, because suffering for both our satisfactions-
sake, (tho but for a few hours,) than if I could (without that circumstance)
have fared never so deliciously elswhere ; I tast too much delight in being
with you to feel most inconveniences it can be purchasd with, and as a
pregnant proof of this profession I will without hesitation resolve to go to
Bath with you, if Sir David Hamilton (to whom my servis) will seriously
assure me tis necessary for ye prolongation of your precious life, tho' but
for one moment,—I am glad to hear for our son's as well as my second she-
frinds sake  that Jack mett you at Hockeril, becaus I plainly perceivd she
expected him, & disappointments would come too soon to such hearts as
hers even if deferrd to ye winter, as tis ye spring of her life & love.  Should
my other son's calculations prove true as to ye patrimonial part of his
concerns, (wherin I doubt he reckons without his host,) yet I am at a loss
to find out how my complying with what he is about would answer every
purpose I have been so long labouring to attain by all just & honest means
for ye independant establishment of my family ; I make no question but he
has drawn a very plausible scheme of ye whole in his own imagination, &
could accordingly sett it well off to you, but I much fear twill never bear so
strict a scrutiny as I ought to make into it before I can consent to it; his
dear mother's meritts are so daily refreshd in my memory by what your
goodness incessantly pays me that I could yett be as well pleasd to see him
throughly happy as if he had never disobligd me in so sensible a matter &

manner as you your self was a witness of, especially since you have interposed your good offices, which shall ever meet with the most sacred regard from your most faithful lover, Bristol.

Betty has complaind these two days of a little soreness in her throat, but not to any such degree as to cause much abatement in her appetite or good looks. Ye rest, God be for ever thankd & praisd for it, are all (even Charles & Bab) very well.

**590.** Lady Bristol to Lord Bristol. Richmond, Aug. 9, 1720.

I did not nead so vast addission to all my pains of body & mind (as I now labour under) to be dissapointed of a letter from you last night, which I sent to London for, but how was I struck to ye heart when Jack came & told me their was only one from Betty to him, & that mentiond not any thing of you, which they all agreed might sattisfy a reasonable body that you were well; but who is reassonable in love, & such a passion as mine for you was never felt from one mortale to another. O my dear, tis impossable to discribe, & by that I find how impossible it will be for me to think of the Bath without you, though I find by such sad experience (sence I left you) how much nead I have of it, besides ye frightfull apprehensions I live under till I can be freed from this complaint. Thank God, I was not near so bad yesterday as I was on Sunday, which I wonder at, hear being a great Court in ye morning as well as at ye drawing-room at night, where ye Princes stood a great while (before she satt down to play) to hear ye musick, which is extreemly fine. Both their Royal Highnesses inquird very kindly after you....Lord Cooper dind with me, and seemd very well entertaind with a whole sett of ladys that talkd of nothing but stocks; the Dutchess of Grafton was one, & has gott something; Lady Pembrook is a considerable gainer, & now his Lordship is convinced ye stock is worth above 98, & is come in to it himself as deep as

any body; two of his daughters has alsoe increasd their portions; in short
every body but you & 1 grow rich; Mrs. Howard has got £20000, & How
£10000; ye cheif of ye famely has gott vastly; tis endless to tell of all ye
wealth; but I dont know a mortale that has not gott somthing, which has
drawn me into £500; theirfore I disire you to know of Betty (by ye next
post) wether she will go share with me & how much; it shall be just what
she declares to you; but this has nothing to do with our present stock; I
go this with Mr. Poltney & Mr. Berenger; but that she may not be
deceived, pray tell her we may loose ye whole or double it very soon; Jack
woud have had me declared her inn, being ingagd with 2 such lucky
people; I wish he were so himself, for he told me yesterday that he should
be forced to give 10 per cent for five or six thousand pound against ye
oppening of ye books to save himself from being a looser by this last fall of
ye stocks; so that if you shoud agree with Mr. Astell before that time, I
beleive you might contrive to lett him have his mony, & save him from
this extorsion.  Thees great gains has made such deep play that 2 or
3000 £ at a sitting is nothing.  Mrs. Poultney invited me to diner last
Sunday, and both were extreemly kind & civell to me; they come no more
to our Court; but that's a history to long for my time or papar; but being
nothing relating to politticks, tis not material.  I was to see poor Aunt
Felton, a most dismale sight; half of her is quite dead to every thing but
pain, yett her spiretts are good, tho' her spech is alterd.  Lady Suffolke
is gon to Kingsinton for ye air, so I calld of her in my way hether; she is
in great danger.  Lady Mary Benett is mared without her father's consent
to a gentleman of £1500 a year besides mony; Lord Tankervill is blamd
for haveing several good offers for her & not excepting any but one she had
an aversion for; one cant wonder at children's disobedience where they
have such parrants; but when tis to such a father as you, what punishment
ought they not to suffer, tho' ye bare reflection of so much ingrattetude to a

sinceable soul is enough in it self without any other consequences ; this I take to be ye unhappy case of poor Tom, who's ruien is inevettable if your kind care & wisdom dont prevent it now he is with you ; for upon inquirey (as you orderd me) I found he has very often satt up whole nights with Lord Hervey, & he has brought him to be bed hear, or els carred him to ye Banjoe after ; he has alsoe been twise with him at Richmond & lain their ; he is endeed very kind to him, but tis a fatal kindness, I am sure tis so to ye quiett of, my dear dear life, your ever faithfull E. Bristol.

You may be better informd by Tom's own man, who I am told is so faithfull to be much consernd for him. I have not time to read what I have writt, so you must take it as it is.

**591.** My ever-new Delight        Ickworth, Aug. 10, 1720.

I have not slept soundly one minute, nor shall do so, unless this night's post brings me ye agreeable news of your having awaked at London on Sunday morning (as you did at Newmarket on Fryday) freed from all ye pain & sickness you complaind of before you went to bed ; tis uneasyness enough to a heart like mine to suffer a seperation only from ye cheif, ney, almost sole object of its happiness, without ye insupportable anxiety of living in ye least doubt whether you are well or not. I hope my sins will not require so severe a chastisement as to be left in such a miserable state much longer. The coach is just now returnd, & twice welcome Tom has brought me ye sattisfaction I most impatiently expected of hearing you were better on Sunday than you gave me an account of ye night before, for which God's goodness be blessd & praisd by me & mine. Had Lord Hervey come with him, (as you said he intended,) we might then have considerd & agreed what terms would be reasonable for him to insist on for parting with his interest in ye £34..18 J (?) and I am with other farms selling to Mr. Astell, which now I must desire by you

he would attend Mr. Ward for (who is Mr. A's council) at his chambers in
ye Inner Temple; for till that be settled to his satisfaction, it will not be
adviseable for me to proceed any farther; as I am to be in town ye latter
end of next week, he may stay till then before he goes to him. Altho' tis
now very late, your dear letter is but this moment arrivd; & because I conclude you would not have me make it later by entering into an answer of
the particulars it contains by this ordinary, yett I cant rest till I have
assurd you of my being wholly blameless in ye disappointment your letter
begins with as to having missd one from me. I have beat up ye stable
quarters upon it (late as it is), & find upon ye strictest inquiry that it was
certainly given into Jore's ye postmaster's hand by Jack Offord on
Saturday before six in ye evening, which is near six hours sooner than ye
post ever setts out on that day, so that ye fault must lye at ye London
offices. All your arguments relating to my going with you to ye Bath, you
will find seasonably anticipated by ye second letter (unless by my run of il
luck that has miscarryed too) from your irreproachable lover, Bristol.

**592.**    Lady Bristol to Lord Bristol.
                                    Richmond, Aug. 11, 1720.
        I have been unluckely hinderd all this day from
ye only pleasure I can tast, & tis now five a clock, so that I have only time
to tell you that I was yesterday agreably surprisd with both your dear
letters together; where ye falt lay I know not that I had not the first
sooner. I hope next post to be able to thank you for them more parte-
culerly; till then, my dear dear angell, Adue.

**593.**    My ever-new Delight        Ickworth, Aug. 13, 1720.
        I am in ye first place to lett you know Betty has
declard to me that she will go a tenth part with you in ye £500 you are
concernd with Mr. Pultney & Mr. Beranger, for she says if ye whole should
be lost, as you say tis possible it may so happen, that she can spare; but

is not willing (how promising soever ye project or prospect may seem) to wade out of her depth. In ye next, as to what you mention concerning ye speedy paying of Jack's mony, you know how my treaty stands with Mr. A :, which one would not precipitate for many weighty reasons ; but since your son has involvd himself afresh in South-sea difficulties, (as I always apprehended would be his case,) I woud willingly be bound with him for ye sum he now wants rather than expose him to ye extortion he speaks of at ye opening of ye books, which I would know the precise time of, that, if possible, I may gett it elswhere.—The dismal accounts you give me of your grandmother Suffolke & Aunt Felton should serve to assist all those repeated admonitions I have so often made in vain to you for ye preservation of your own health ; tis evident that a London life will destroy ye best of constitutions & ye most regular regimen from ye instance of ye former. Having written to your son by this post, I must desire you to tell Lord Hervey that I do not understand his scheme throughly enough to send him any opinion or advice upon it, but hope when I come to town (if I must do so) the latter end of ye next week that he will then be able to make me master of ye whole, so as to give him both. What you write of Tom came very unseasonably, for it has broke ye bruised reed in such a manner & to such a degree of desperation of ever seeing any of my children come to good, if he who has his pious grandfather's seal so strongly impressd upon him can fall to evill, that no medicine but thy presence can in any measure heal ye multiplyd disquiets of a mind, which in all its extremity of distress & disappointment can still with pleasure reflect on its being so wholly & only thine, Bristol.

**594.** Lady Bristol to Lord Bristol. Richmond, Aug. 13, 1720.

It is a great addission to my present uneassiness for fear my unaptnes to dissemble shoud make you suspect any part of my

sufferings when I writt last (tho' with great diffeculty) that bitt of a letter;
endeed it was farr beyond what I ever felt in my life; that extreem sickness & trembleing that I have of late been so much troubled with increasd
to that degree on Wensday night that it threw me into a voielant vometting
& purging all that night & the greatest part of ye next day, so that I kept
nothing I took, either of medcin or any other kind, which gave me a
severe fitt of ye cholick & such voielent histericks that I fainted away
several times. It is impossible to express the kindness of ye whole famely
to me upon this occassion; the Princes was so good as to come up ye
muinett she was out of her bed, & satt by me a great while; I have ben
told since that she expressd a great deal of fear & consern for me; however,
by the help of Sir David & very good nursing I made shift to wait, & hope
to continue out my time, tho' I am very faint & sick by fitts; every thing
goes against me; I dont think I have eat an ounce of meat since Wensday
at dinner; ye cheif thing I live upon is toast & clarett, which was ye first
thing staid with me on Thursday. I dont know if it will be any more sattisfaction to you then tis to me, that this great disorder has proceeded from
no ireguellaretty of any kind either from eating or drinking, & cold is
impossible, for I have not been out of doors since I came, & keep as good
hours (almost) as if I were at Ickworth; for ye Princes is still much out of
order; but if I have any skill, it may turn to good account; she bids me
tell you it will be a great deal of pleasure to her to see you hear; but now
(strange request) I must beg you, if you love me, as I am very sure you do,
dont think of coming one day the sooner for this; for if you leave any of
your bisness undone, it will make me very uneassy the whole time I am at
ye Bath, which it is now time to provide for, theirfor I must putt you in
mind of bringing a dussen knives, forks & spoons with you, & if Betty
Morris has not thought of my trunk, pray lett it come by Mondays waggen.
I hope you bring ye old coach, for the other will be quite spoyld. I wish

I had any news after this maloncholy history, but I have none but what I fear will be as little pleasing to you ; Mrs. Tinley's marrage with Lord Craven is all concluded ; this brings Lord Hervey into my thoughts ; but I beleive it will not be nessesary to enter into perteculers about his affairs tell we meet, which I hope will be before you settle anything with him.   Lady Anabela Benett was following her sister's example, but Lord Tankervill overtooke her, so what will become of her I know not ; for they say he threatend to kill poor Lady Mary if she did not marry the man he had a mind to, tho' he was her averssion, which was ye cause of her runing away.   Thees balletts must supply the want of better entertainment ; if they dont devert you they will Betty.   Lord Townsend inquird much after you ; Mr. Craggs alsoe made me a visett yesterday.   I hope this long letter will convince you how much better I am, & that nothing can ever be wanting to prove how much & dearly I love you, & am to all eternetty unalterably yours for ever & ever whilest E. B.

I hope ye dear childeren are well, becaus you say nothing of them. Depend upon it, if I am wors, you shall have another letter before ye post goes out, so for my sake pray be easy ; this is from my bed.   Pray lett Nan's stays come with you, and full directions to fitt another pair by.

595.    Lady Bristol to Lord Bristol.

Richmond, Aug. 13, 7 a clock.

Since my last letter went I have eat some diner, and find my self so much better after it that I coud not help giving you ye pleasure to know it, tho' I have time for nothing more.   I hope you will bring Betty Morris to town with you ; I cant tell wether I mentiond it in my last or not, but if I did you must excuse me, for my poor brain is farr from being settled yett.   We have had a vast Court to day ; Lord Sunderland & Lord Stairs tooke leave being going to Hanover; ye former of thees was graciously pleasd to own me for an old acquantance. I am just calld for, & can say no more to my dear dear etternale pleasure of my life.

**596.**    My ever-new Delight                Ickworth, Aug. 15, 1720.

I find my fears too truely fore-boded what I was to expect after your very short letter of ye 11th instant, neither subscribd nor addressd by your own hand; there is not a circumstance in all ye maloncholly history of your sufferings but my busy fancy had already anticipated. Oh! what an insupportable load of torment & perplexity has this present pious fraud of yours prevented in my soul: but then think how impossible it will be hereafter to make me one moment tolerably easy, whenever I am to be so wretched again as to live but one day without you; sure this thought should make us both so mutually tender of each others quiet (loving intently as we I hope shall ever do) as to resolve & contrive to cut off all future occasions that may possibly produce ye shortest absence; for tis a state my heart was never framed to bear but with uncommon misery ; & am therfore now determind to shunn it till death shall make one unavoidable. Your second letter of ye 13th has afforded me just releif enough as to your self to be able to comply with ye most sacred injunction (if I love you) in your first ; for being in ye very middle of my Steward's accounts, which are of two years' standing, & because I would leave no other part of my affairs unsettled behind me that may break ye peace of your mind when at Bath, I shall stay hear to finish all till Saturday, and hope to meet my mistress on Sunday night at London, unless any worse news comes by Wednesdays post, which God of his great goodness & mercy avert. The kind & gracious condescensions which your Royal mistress has shewn to her sick servant shall be rememberd & acknowledgd upon all occasions, & in every action of my life towards her & hers ; God's protection & such a nurse will I trust make you as well even as you can be & are wishd by your etc, Bristol.

If you would have me bring your strong box with me, you must say so by Thursday's post, for I am alwaies so grievd at parting from you that I never know what is said to me then but what relates more immediately to our loves. The children are all well.

**597.** Lady Bristol to Lord Bristol.  Richmond, Aug. 16, 1720.

I should have infinett pleasure in thinking this letter might be ye last I nead write before I see the delight of my eyes & charmer of my heart, if I had not found by reading yours last night (for what can scape a lovers eye,) how uneasy you weir in your mind, & much I fear this journey is a great part of your trouble, of which I am the fattel tho' innoscent caus ; how great a weight this must be upon my poor spiretts (already quite sunk) I'le leave you to judg, & how little I am able to bear this addission you may guess, when I tell you I have as much reason to be dissattisfyd with my children hear as you have to be with sum of those with you ; however, I shoud have ben glad to have easd them of any trouble ; but I am afraid ye kind assistance you offer will now be too late, for ye South-sea books oppen next Monday, which I fear will bring both your sons into great diffecultys, for their bargains is not so good as ours, (tho' upon ye same foot ;) Betty shall be sure of ye share she dessirs ; ye stocks fell yesterday, which posted Lord Hervey & Jack to town after they had supt with me & a great deal of other company ; I conclude you will find them their at your arivall, but if they keep you a moment longer then is neadfull for your rest, twill break my heart.—Oh ! tis in vain to struggle with desires strong as my love to thee; for every moment I'm from thy sight ye heart withen my bosom moans like a tender infant in its cradle whose nurse had left it ; come & with the songs of gentle love perswade it to its peace.

Fly swift, ye minutes, & contract the space
Of time that holds me from his dear embrace ;
When I am there, I'll bid you kindly stay,
I'll bid you rest, & never glide away.

I could not help breaking out into this extacy, it suted me so well ; you are too well read for me to nead to quote my auther, though I wonder I had any but my own heart, which is fuller of passion & tenderness than can be expressd to its dear object by his ever faithfull wife, E.B.

I hope you receivd both my letters by Satterdays post, becaus ye last woud sattisfy you that I am better. Pray, my dear, dont forgitt my box.

**598.**    My ever-new Delight            Ickworth, Aug. 17, 1720.

I have condemnd my self oftner for not going to you in ye place of my last letter than there has passd seconds since I wrote it, even tho' I had over & above all those reasons I therin gave you many more to determine me to live uneasily ever since (& must do so now till Sunday) rather than make you do so at Bath, whence no benefitt can be expected without ye concurrence of a quiett, tranquile mind ; how great a stranger mine has been to that blessed state since it was bereft of thy belovd society you shall never know, unless never parting more were to be ye price of so dreadful a discovery. Mrs. Duncombe has been here all this evening, who continues very kind to Betty & every other branch of our family, as you shall know more at large when we meet, (which as I told you in my last will I hope be on Sunday evening in St. James's Square, or I shall be most heavily disappointed,) & what has made me love her much better than ever I did was her shewing so much real concern for ye valuable stem of it, (I nead not name Her,) as not to go away till ye letters came in, which tho' very late, yet, considering ye welcome news they brought of your continuing well after so severe a shock, was well worth a weeks watching for me to have known, since I could not sleep one wink till assurd of it. That you may rest in full peace that the Bath journey has no share in any of the uneasynesses I have lately felt, know that since Sir David only thinks tis necessary to restore your health, (whatever the consequence may prove) the very bare hope of lengthening your precious life a day will infinitely over pay every inconvenience that may or can be felt in it by thy devoted faithful friend & lover, Bristol.

Did not Lady Cowper send you the key by me on Sunday night from ye Dutchess of Shrewsburys? Why then need you stay longer at Richmond, unless you have a mind to make me very ill company to both my sons, shoud I find them there.

**599.** Lady Bristol to Lord Bristol. Richmond, Aug. 18, 1720.

If I had suspected my injunctions would have kept you to such a lenth of time, I am afraid (nessesary as it is) I shoud never have been able to perswaid my self to make them, for (oh! my dear,) tis impossible to express the great disapointment your letter gave me in saying you would not be hear till Sunday, & expected to meet me at London. Sure, my dear, you forgitt I am pawnd hear till ye coach comes to fetch me; besides that you are expected hear by both Prince & Princes to come for me your self; happy was it for me that the rest of your dear letter was full of so many kind & tender expressions, & the dearest of all that we shoud meet to part no more; oh happy sound to a soul & body oppressed with all sorts of uneasinesses to such a degree that even near as the time draws to an end, I am yett afraid to sink under them before tis expird. After I had wrott to you last post, (which was ye easyest hour I have had a great while,) I was taken again in ye evening with ye same disorder of sickness & vometing that I had before, but the fitts not so voielant as ye former, but yett enough to make me chuse to leave my bed &

sitt up In a great chare tell day light; you may immagin what I suffer in the days after such nights; however, I waited yesterday and have never missd but that once I told you of; the Princes has never been out since I came, & is oblidgd to keep still, which sutes my present condission, els it would have been impossible for me to have staid hear so long. I had a new medcin from Sir David last night, which gave me some rest, & I hope will make me pass this day better than ye former, which you shall know ye latest muinett I can keep my letter; but now I am sure if you weir hear & saw me, you woud take the pen out of my hand, & not suffer me to tell you (if words coud express it) how truely and dearly you are lovd by E. B.

Tis now 6 a clock, & I have been eassier all day then usual, which is some releif to my body, tho' very little to my mind, for I have such suden changes that I never know when or how long I shall be well. Sure, my dear, if you ly at Hockerell, it woud be as easy to you & your horses to come over London Bridg & bait hear & carry me home in ye evening; you see by this schem how I grudg every muinett that will keep me from you. Adue, my dear, heaven's choicest blessings ever attend you. Their is dreadfull robing; for Gods sake dont resist.

**600.**     *Lady Bristol to Lord Bristol.
Richmond. Aug. 21. 1720, 8 at night.

I have just gott time to tell you that I must live upon ye rack till to morrow, for ye Princes is so very ill that it woud be monstrous in me to leave her, besides that she has orderd me to sitt by her bedside, where I have been for above two hours already, & dont find her ye

* This is the last letter in the first of the two quarto volumes which contain the correspondence only between Lord and Lady Bristol. The hand that has copied this letter into the volume, (which I think is Lord Bristol's own hand,) has added, Here end all the letters to Aug. 1721. Another hand, which I imagine to be that of George, 2nd Earl of Bristol, has added this couplet:
With such delight I read his letters ore,
His presance only ever gave me more.

least better, so that it would be after twelve before I coud leave this place, which I am sure you would not have me do with such disorders as I have every night upon me, & dont expect any rest till I am lodgd again in those dear arms, the center of all happiness for your E. B.

601.   My dear daughter*                    Bath, Oct. 2, 1720.
        If my letter to your husband had any thing more kind or tender in it than usual, he ought to ascribe all ye excess in either to your interests being so essentially blended with his own that they are now become more than doubly my wonted concern, since you have made his so entirely your own ; this is a sort of secrett I would never have trusted in your keeping, had I not known he loves you so much above himself that he will even value my affection ye more for its being so much better disposd of. You will doubtless wonder how any love or kindness once placed on him should ever be transferrd to an other ; but that is only for want of knowing your own superior meritt, which is ye sole piece of ignorance has been remarkd in you by your etc.

602.   To Mr. Thomas Folkes.          London, March 11, 1720/21.
        I am so unfeignedly fond of every opportunity to shew my sincere affection for ye town of Bury, that I must alwaies remember those with kindness who lay any occasion in my way that will serve to demonstrate the truth of my professions towards it ; & as I esteem ye friendly part you have taken in ye present transaction to be of that nature, I have accordingly signd ye letter as you desire to Mr. Serjeant Reynolds, & shall readily concurr in any other measures that will tend to attain ye end proposd by ye rest of ye Governours, being thier & your etc.

* Here Lord Bristol, who has himself copied this letter into the folio letter-book, has added, *now Lady Hervey.*—S.H.A.H.

**603.**  To ye Dutchess of Marleborough.          April 10, 1721.

Madam

I have carefully read over ye case your Grace was pleasd to send me, & according to ye best observations I am at present able to make upon it do find cause enough of complaint against ye decree appeald from, if it has nothing farther to warrant it than ye facts & proofs as stated in it; insomuch that tho' I was just about taking my leave of London from finding how very vain & insignificant my constant endeavours have hitherto provd in promoting any good or preventing any evill to the perishing publick, yet as long as I can but serve the sacred cause of private justice, & especially where ye Duke of Marleborough & your Grace is concernd, I shall think my self doubly bound either to stay or come back again on purpose in order to do right to those, who I on all occasions have acknowledgd (ever since the payment of them has been unhappily prevented) to have ye justest title to ye best services of, Madam, your etc.

**604.**  To ye Dutchess of Marleborough.          April 12, 1721.

My curiosity had already prevented ye care your Grace took yesterday to inform me of ye several proceedings in ye House of Commons relating to ye Duke of Marleboroughs great & seasonable services, whose just sense of them, in concurrence with ye Queens, seemd to me to leave little room for any doubt at whose expence ye building at Blenheim was to be ; so that ye pending point will solely turn upon ye proof of ye Duke of Marleboroughs privity or consent to ye warrant given by my Lord Godolphin to Sir John Vanbrugh, which for fear of ye fatal consequences that may happen to any other man in ye same scituation, I should think ought to be most plainly & fully made out before it should affect ye Duke of Marleborough's estate. This being a dictate & principle of natural justice, ye declaration only of what is so can (I hope) be deemd no transgression of the nicest rules of it in, Madam, your etc.

**605.**   To Sir William Barker.

Not having yet seen one skrip of evidence re-
lating to the Feltons estate, I thought it no unreasonable request to desire
you would respite the setting a fine on Falkenham Marsh, till I could inform
my self whether it held of your Mannor at 2 shillings per acre, (as Sir
Compton Felton once wrote me word he conceived it did,) or was at the will
of the lord ; if upon perusal of the writings, (which I intend to take into my
possession the latter end of ye next month,) it shall appear that the fine is
not certain but arbitrary, I will then readily comply with your demand of
twenty guineas rather than have any other dispute about it, lawsuites being
the aversion of your humble etc.

**606.**   To Mr. Alderman Turnor, Comptroller of ye ffree-school at
Bury St. Edmunds, April, 1721.

The season of ye year aproaching wherin most
buildings are generally begun, I suppose my brother Governours of ye free-
school would be glad to know what success my sollicitations have mett with
from ye persons mentiond in thier letter to me, that they may take thier
measures upon it accordingly ; & therfore I now send you the following
account, viz. the Duke of Grafton hath promisd to subscribe, but hath
not yet named ye sum ; Lord Cornwallis hath done ye same ; the Bishop of
Norwich hath actually subscribd ten guineas ; Sir Mathew Dudley five
guineas ; & Mr. Maynard five guineas ; Sir Marmaduke Wyvell told my
messenger he would come & see me, & would then subscribe, but I have not
yet received ye favour of a visitt from him ; Lord Guilford excusd himself
from ye hardness of ye times & ye scarcity of mony ; & I cannot hear of
any such person as Sir Ralph Carr in all this town. This being ye result of
my best endeavours to serve ye school & them, I shall depend on your good
offices to make them as acceptable to them as you can, knowing with how

Vol. II.   T

sincere an affection every thing that relates to ye interest or ornament of Bury has been & ever shall be most cordially espousd by thier & your most faithful friend & servant.

**607.**    To Sir Thomas Hanmer.                    May 6, 1721.

Dear Sir Thomas

I cannot any longer refuse my self ye satisfaction of enquiring after ye progress of your health, which I hope you find by this time so well establishd as may relieve your self & friends from all future fears of your relapsing into your late painful, dangerous distemper ; ye terrible description you once gave me of your exquisite sufferings under it has ever since given you a place in my best prayers & wishes, that you may never feel ye least return of it, which thro' God's blessing on your own wise & temperate treatment of a young & strong constitution, we may reasonably promise our selves for you ; should you tell me ye Bath hath contributed to so meritorious a worke, it would at once cancell all my former prejudices to it, & from being my aversion become a favorite ; such changes we know have happend, even in cases ye very reverse of this.—Monsieur Diharce telling me you referrd ye choice of his two sorts of Burgundy to my decision, I have pitchd upon ye vin de Beaune for you as ye best (I think) in all respects. You do your self some right in allowing me to have a through good taste, since there is no body breathing who rellishes all your good qualities with a more distinguishing palate than your etc.

**608.**    To Mr. Henry Barrell, Chapter-clerk to ye Church of Rochester.
                    July 11, 1721.

The whole estate I hold of ye Church of Rochester having been lett by lease for a long term of years to John Ellys (ye immediate predecessor of ye present tenant) for no more than £120 per

annum, & he having dyed considerably indebted to my father even at that
rent, ye Dean & Chapter A.D. 1684 thought then fitt to accept of £80 as a
fine from my said father when he renewd his lease, ye same being just one
whole years clear profitts of ye estate, deducting ye reservd rent of £36..8, &
ye £4 per annum payable for ye Vicar's pension : a rate that ye Bishops of
Norwich never aimd at exceeding in all my transactions with them upon ye
same occasions ; neither do I believe there is any instance where more has
ever been demanded, or at least complyd with, above that known rule of
income. If my present masters are resolvd to insist upon more than ever
was hitherto thought of being askd by any of thier predecessors, I am fully
& positively resolvd not to create a precedent so much to ye prejudice of my
successors & all who hold by ye same tenure. I hereby assure you & them
that ye utmost improvd value of this estate after all my expences in repairing etc is no more than £200 per annum, out of which must be deducted
ye said reservd rent & Vicar's pension, & if they are so much strangers to
my person or character as to doubt of ye truth of that assertion, any one
shall see ye lease between me & my tenant that they shall appoint, to shew
them that nothing but what is fair & equall is meant, & ye same is expected
from them by yours etc. Bristol.

**609.    Lady Bristol to Lord Bristol.**

7 a clock Tuesday.   Aug. 8, 1721.

I am just arived at Reading, & (judging by my
self) conclude you will be glad to hear I am come safe thus farr, but till I
gott to Slough I sufferd a rack in my body as well as mind, for so voialent a
pain in my back I never felt ; thank God I am much easier this afternoon,
& hope to hear you are so when I gitt to Bath. I am forced to keep ye post
boy while I write ; the promis of 6 pence has prevaild till now that he is
calling to me under ye window to make hast ; so I can say no more, but

wish a good night to my dear Angell.  I am much better then I coud hope for after such a morning ;  I beleive tis oweing to this little conversation with the life of my life.

**610.**    My ever-new Delight

London, Tuesday 10 at night.  Aug. 8, 1721.

As you may be capable of some satisfaction, which God knows I have not been since you left me, I send this after you to lett you know I intend to pursue your advice, which has alwaies provd much more fortunate to me than my own, and have accordingly appointed a sett of Blunt's horses to take me out of this forlorn abode to morow at 5 in ye morning, finding it impossible for me with all the submission & resignation I am master of to endure it an other day without my dear companion, who alone can make all times & places agreeable to her (now) more wretched friend than shall or can be told (because your friend) by your dejected, almost despairing Bristol.

**611.**    Lady Bristol to Lord Bristol.        Bath, Aug. 11, 1721.

The coach & post setting out both of a day, I choues to write by ye former as the safest and quickest conveyance, for I beleive you will know by that one day sooner that we are safe arived at this place, I cant say well either in body or mind, for I have had the cholick all this morning ; tis impossible to guess at the caus, unless the watters may have stird ye unhappy humours that attend my poor carcase ; but I'm in hopes what they dont cary off to day, my ruebarb will to morow.  I wish to God I had as good hopes to  ease the distempers of my mind ; but there is but one cure for them ;  when that will be, God & you only know;  my poor heart must still be rackd with uncertainty ; I fancy if I knew ye end of my missery, I coud bear it better. Wont you then be so charettable to tell me when you think it may be; endeed it was some releif to me last night to find by your kind letter that you were by this time with the dear babes at Ickworth, just when I gott to this cursed place, cursed indeed when I reflect upon the cruell distance it has put us at; it makes my blood chill & my head turn round as if I weir upon a precipeice as often as I think of it. O my dear, for God sake ease me as soon as you can without inconvenience to your self or affairs; though I know (by all the tenderness I have been blessd with) this is a needless request, yett I cant help making it.— They just now bring me word ye posttillion horse is lame by being pinchd in his shouing at London; I am sure nothing could happen in the jurney, for we had always time before hand, for we weir never laiter (hardly so late) in our inn as when I writt to you from Reading, & always baited above two • hours. I passd ye last two days with much more ease to my body, though with greater pain to my mind the farther I went from the center of all my happyness. Pegg exerted her uttmost to devert me, but I am afraid I shall not be able to return it to her now she has so much nead of it, for she is taken very ill with ye cholick; I am much better this evening, & so is ye poor horse, and I hope will perform his jurney well as I have orderd the matter, which is to have the posttillion lead him upon his other horse, & the Coach to go with four; I hope you will think I have contrived admirably or els I shall be disapointed, for as great a disire as I have for ye Coach to be with you, I have, however, orderd Tom Harvey, that if he dus not find ye horse well to morow, to stay another day. I have been tormented this whole day with vissetts, tho' they say hear is less company then ever was known in ye town. Betty Southell is just arived from Marlborough, & woud fain tempt me out, but I have neither curiosity nor spiretts enough for the expedition, but am returnd to this more agreable entertainment, where I woud tell you (if it weir possible) how much & dearly I love you, my dear dearest life, but as no toung can express it, no pen can write what is in the heart of your faithfull E.B.

I hope you found all ye children well ; I long to hear their senttements about their new nephew.  If Betty finds her old complaints enough removd to think of this place, I must know it soon ; for at present there is not a room unlett in this house.  Poor Pegg is forcd to ly above stairs ; she saith I shall not seal my letter till I pay her respects to you & Madam Betty.

**612.**    My ever-new Delight              Ickworth, Aug. 11, 1721.

Knowing it will give you some satisfaction to see me date my letter from this place, I have transposd its usual scituation for your first view.  Our children, I thank God, are all well, even Betty much better than I expected, notwithstanding I found her very much allarmd by what Mr. Graham suggested about her late complaints,....If you expect as good an accompt of thier poor, disconsolate papa, I can not be hypocrite enough to deceive you ; ye pain I felt at parting with you was so much more sensible than ever I experiencd before, that I was just upon ye point of sending for you back again, had I not been restraind from it by reflecting that as your health was in ballance with my ease, (wheron all my future peace & pleasure depends,) I ought to suffer any thing rather than retard ye success of that; how dear that determination has cost me since, you shall (can) never know, in spight of all ye faith & resignation I could muster up, assisted too by a providential help I chanced to find in a book I took down for my journey, where I dippd into the following passage ; tis ye 10th command of the shepherd sent to St. Hermas :—*Putt all sadness farr from thee, for sadness is ye sister of doubting ; tis the most mischievous of all spiritts, and ye worst to ye servants of God ; it destroys ye spiritts of all men, & torments the holy Spiritt ; wherfore cloathe thy self with chearfulness, which has alwaies favour with the Lord, & thou shalt rejoyce in it.*—This accident, & ye apposite advice it containd to

cure my malancholly, was too singular not to be imparted to ye dear &
valuable cause of it, with ye assurance that when I have heard (which I
wait for with ye utmost impatience) ye only news can please me, that thou
art gott safe and well to Bath, I will endeavour as farr as possible to
compose my mind into such a frame as may be more suitable to ye principles I profess of an entire submission towards God in ye first place, & of
that thorough regard I pay to every thing wherin your desires, much more
your quiet, is concernd, as well as that of your at present forlorn friend,
Bristol.———My servis to Mrs. Bradshaw.

**613.** Aug. 12.
Your letter from Reading I have just now receivd,
as I hope you have mine of ye 8th from London. Could you think ye pain
in your back would mend that of my heart ; however, that it may not be
increasd by doubts, lett me know ye truth by every post. Felly came to
see me yesterday, who having gott a little cold, & ye evening being rainy,
I as readily as he laid hold on ye first excuse to keep him with me till
Sunday, tho' Mr. Butts told me this was to have been his repetition-day,
he being so agreeable and entertaining that were he not your very image
in beauty, his witt would charm my soul into some remission of grief for ye
otherwise irrepairable loss of his much more inchanting originall.—Thanks
for ye postscript that your back was better.

**614.** Lady Bristol to Lord Bristol. Bath, Aug. 12, 1721.
Though I sent you 4 sides of papar but a few
hours sence, I cant lett a post go away without somthing, for fear you
shoud be as much disapointed as I was this morning ; for though I knew
twas impossible to have a letter from you, yett I hoped for the comfort of
hearing from Ickworth, which might have been if Squire had writt by
Tuesdays post, as she was ordered (by a letter from Cornforth this day

sevenight), I then coud not have faild of it to day. I hope I shall not be as much out in my calculation on Monday, for I reckon if you thought of writing by ye coach that caryd you to Ickworth, they woud be back time enough for the post this night at London, els it will be an age before I can hear from you. Betty Southel & her brother came back to us last night & staid supper; they went home this morning to his house; what woud one not give for her spiretts, for in the little time she was from hence she contrived to be at every place in ye whole town, and came back from Lindseys loaded with silver and a bitt or two of gold she had nickd Syms out off at hasard; he is by what I hear the cheif beau upon the place; but sure so many fine ladys will not be long destitute; hear are the Dutches's of Kingston & Warton & Mrs. Cook; Lady Harrald & her sister came last night; poor Pegg is very ill again to day, which is a great addission to all my other troubles, tho I thank God I am better my self, only the watters are much in my head, which must shorten this epissel. I beleive you will think there neads no excuse for that after what I have already sent you by the coach; but I cant depend upon your having this or what I writt upon ye road, for ye mail has been robd this week, & all ye letters thrown in a ditch; they say ye reason was a fair at Bristol, where they hoped to find returns; the same thing may happen now with us, hear being a fair at Lansdown.—The sun begins to appear, & we have a fine evening; may it prove a good omen to me, for we have had nothing but rain ever sence I came to this place, after a terable dusty jurney, which woud have vext me if their weir room for such triffels in a heart so over loaded already as is your poor forlorn E. B.

To morow fortnight is ye 27th of August,* a most blessed day to me; oh may I never know a disapointment on it; I dare say no more; pray bless all ye children for me, & chide Squire.

---

* Marginal note says, Lord B's birth day.—S.H.A.H.

**615.** My ever-new Delight                    Ickworth, Aug. 14, 1721.

Sir John Holland, Sir William Gage, Mr. Sergeant Reynolds & other company, having just now left me, were presently succeeded by Mr. Milles, who lyes hear to night, & as he is to go away again to morrow I could not decently leave him till tis now too late for one who is trying to retrieve an almost ruind constitution by ye late hours we kept at London (to) say any more to you by this post, (having sent you a very long one by ye last,) than that my eyes are famishd since they beheld you to behold at least a letter from you, they having livd upon that you wrote from Reading & your picture these six live long daies, & must starve on till Wednesday, if then they can have ye satisfaction of seeing you gott safe & well to Bath, a piece of news they still languish after with such restless impatience that I neither eat nor sleep so well as I hope I should do, were those good tideings once arrivd.—I have written to Lady Felton to lett her know I intend (God willing) to be at Ipswich on Monday the 21st instant, in order to ridd her of ye trouble of our goods, since she seems so impatient to have them taken away, as by a renewd request she has made me for that purpose, a copy wherof you shall have by the next post. Your son Jack has written to me to lett me know he has been told that since the King & Princess are ye other gossips, it will be expected I should not stand by proxy; but my last journey hither does really & truly stick too much in my old bones to think of a new one in haste, & must therfore return answer that I beg to be excusd, & cannot see why a representative of my own rank (of which he has his choice in London) may not be as acceptable as my self to ye Lord & Lady of the Bedchamber in waiting.— Tis now later by two hours than I have made my going to bed since I came, (which is at ten,) and therfore, as I am sure you would have made me, I will wish thee a good night & all other kinds of good, as being necessary to the well-being of your lover, Bristol.

Vol. II.     v

Betty is ridd of all her fears, looks, eats & sleeps well, even 12 hours together; ye rest of our children (God be praisd) are all very well.

**616.**   Lady Bristol to Lord Bristol.       Bath, Aug. 14, 1721.

I will not tell you my dear angel how much I am disapointed in ye hopes I had of receiving a letter from you this morning, becaus I know it woud greive your tender nature; but sure the not hearing from Squire yett is such a pece of neglegence as never was known ; but tis as if every thing in this fateal journey conspird to torment me, & poor Pegge's illness is no smale addission to ye rest ; for she is so much worse that I thought yesterday she would have dyed ; she has Docter Beaston (by Sir John Shadwell's recommendation), and Mr. Skrine is her apothecary ; they think her somthing better to day, but she is so very weak that they orderd she should be kept very quiett, and desire I woud not be with her, for fear it should tempt her to talk ; so that I think I shall go out this evening for ye third time since I come to this place; endeed I beleive if I dont, I shall be laid up my self; for every thing together has vapourd me, so I am hardly able to bear it. I had my histerick disorder very bad on Satterday after I had writt to you; but to day I begun to drink the watters at the pump, and find they agree much better with me there then at home, & so I shall continue that way.—I had a letter from Jack this morning, in which he tells me he has wrott to you that it will be expected you should stand your self at his Christening, and hopes I wont wish him hangd, because it will be but a days journey out of your way heither. Thats true ; but is not a day, nay an hour, an age in love ; I am sure it is to impattience like mine ; however, I coud the easyer bear it if twer nessesary, which I am sure tis not, without ye King or Princes stood themselves ; you may remember it was determind so when I was Godmother to ye Duke of St.

Albains's son with Prince George; besides I dont see how tis possible if Betty comes with you; for it would be unreasonable to bring her so much out of the way; but I hope you remember what Dr. Friend said, that if she felt any heat or any thing upon her lungs, she must not think of it.—I am afraid you will say I have transgresd your orders in ye lenth of this; but you will think the punishment greater then ye crime deserves if I tell you it effects my head; for I am so very wretched that even ye venting my troubles is an addission to them. Adue, my dear dearest life.—Since I wrott this I have been to see the Dutches of Kingston & Mrs. Cook, & they both confirm what I have told you conserning ye proxy, and wonder any body could think of your taking a journey on purpose, as a thing never done; this I have wrott Jack word.—Poor Pegg is better, but so very weak you cant hear her speak without laying your head close to ye pillow; she is, however, out of pain.

Ickworth, Wednesday, Aug. 16, 1721,

**617.** My ever-new Delight past nine at night.

Was it not enough for my poor soul to bear the pain & punishment of your absence at so great a distance, but that I must also endure ye additional affliction of living so many daies as I have done under the cruel and tedious uncertainty of your having gott safe and well to Bath ; which at this hour I am still ignorant of, after having expected that releif all yesterday & thinking my self sure of it to night; but tis now dark, & no news yet that ye coach is arrivd, which I am so inquisitive after and so disturbd at ye answers they bring me that I can hardly write a line without interruption; neither could I find resolution enough to proceed were not my ressource in ye infinite goodness of God, who never failes to order all things for the best where such virtue as thine & so firm faith and resignation as mine is concernd; what merciful purposes his immense wisdom has to bring about by laying me under such a series of mortifying tryals as I have experiencd withen these few years, his omniscience only knows; this I can only tell, that no messages of his salutary correction ever mett with, or ever shall, a froward or repining reception from me; but such a submission as is due to the bountiful author of so many blessings as he's vouchsafd to me his unworthy creature.—See how they are rewarded who not only preach but practice my infallible principles; for ye coach is at last returnd with thy dear letter, which has sett my heart at ease as to thy being safe at thy journeys end; for which, on reading it, I devoutly thankd our common protector; could I give yours the same as to the time of our meeting again, this should convey it to you; but as it is yett impossible to make any near calculation of it, I not having yet had leisure to enter upon any business, visitts and writing having engrossd this first week, (Sir Thomas Hanmer & his two nieces having dined here yesterday,) and I being to dine with ye Corporation to morow, & they being to elect their preacher the next day, I shall not be able to settle to Will Oliver's accompts till I have dispatchd all my affairs at Ipswich with your Aunt Felton & ye tenants, which I forsee will require a longer stay than I ever allowd for, part of Playford House being blown down, & 12 workmen putt into it by Lady Felton to repair it; beside my dispute with Sir John Barker concerning ye copyhold Marsh at Falkenham etc. But why nead I enter upon so ungratefull a detaile to us both, since you do me the justice to conclude I can never live one moment longer without thee than absolute necessity imposes on me. May you do my heart as much right in all other points that relate to you, & then you would find it worthy of the utmost affection & tenderness you can pay it, which I acknowledg is more than most others can possibly deserve, may I not say none but that of your matchless, faithful Bristol.

**618.** Lady Bristol to Lord Bristol. Bath, Aug. 16, 1721.

When I reflect tis but 8 daies since we parted, I look back with wonder; for to me it seems as many years; this is ye fifth time I have (in part) recounted my greifs to you; all I cannot, for as is said in the Orphan,

No toung my pleasure or my pain can tell;
Tis heaven with you, and without you hell.

But I should not indulge my self in these flights tell I coud know an end of my missery; may be to morrows post may bring it me; oh how I long for it; endeed I am very wretched, for besides my own uneasiness I live in a continual terour for fear poor Bradshaw should dye; for sure never creature sufferd so much in stomach & bowells as she has done; yesterday morning she was so easy that I breakfasted by her bedside, & ye Dr gave her leave to rise; but she had not been up an hour when all her complaints returnd again;....and such a hickup that we thought she would have fallen into convulsions; they weir forcd to give her somthing to quiett her, but in ye night she brought it up again as she dus every thing els; this morning she has taken another, & is quiett ever sence; if she relapses again, it will go hard with her, & I believe not very well with me, for I was so vapourd last night with seeing her & ye closnes of ye room together, I coud hardly bear it, having had a voielant head ach all day, I beleive occassiond by drinking ye watters at home; it raind so hard that I coud not think of stiring, but I am resolved no wether shall keep me in again, I find so vast a difference at ye pump. I have been but three times at Lindseys since I came, & once at Harissons to see a medly ye Duke of Warton bespoke; he would fain have had me sett play a going there, (for he has had none yett,) but I told him I never did that in your absence that I would not do in your presence, for you had determind neither of us should play their; he seemd to be

mightyly surprisd & consernd thåt you should be angry with him, for he
said if you had any farther trouble about ye bill, it was without his knowledg or consent; so that it seems to ly at Nashes door, who is not yett
arrived, but is to come to day, as dus several others.  The Dutchis of
Queensborough's journey is put off, Lord Rochester being very ill; pray
God keep you well & send us a happy meeting, is ye constant daily prayers
of, my dear dearest life, your ever faithfull & truely affectionet wife, E. B.

I have been abroad, & hear tis Lord Essex, & not Lord Rochester, that
is so ill; he vomets blood, & is thought in great danger.  Poor Pegg has
been pritty well since 6 a clock, and if she continues so all night I hope
she will do well.

**619.**    My ever-new Delight                Ickworth, Aug. 18, 1721.
That you may know ye naked truth of every
thing wherin you are concernd or I for you, I have sent you copies of both
my Lady Felton's letters ; I hope ye contents of them will not give you
much disturbance, since she must make good all dammages during her
enjoyment of Playford, which I already beleive she is weary of.  On
Monday I begin my journey thither, but what to do with the goods without
my meet help God knows, I am sure I do not, unless I can persuade her to
lett them remain there untill you can go & give better order about them ;
ye very taking them down & ye carriage in removing will eat up a good
part of their value, beside that they cannot be disposd of in any place that
I can think of, where, without more care than any servants now take, moths
& mouldiness will not near consume ye rest ; but, however, as they are my
dear heiresses, she may depend on my very best contrivances to serve her.
—Yesterday I dined with ye Corporation, who receivd me with more
universal kindness & respect (if possible) than ever, except ye two Hovells,
whose measures were so unexpectedly disconcerted by the choice of my

very true & zealous freind, Mr. Alderman Wright, for their new elect instead of a creature of thier own, that I beleive this, together with an other step I've taken since I came, which was to persuade Mr. Butts to declare he declind standing candidate for ye lecturership, (seeing two relations of Mr. Macro's & Mr. Hovell's were his concurrents in it,) has so dashd Collonel Norton's pretensions, that I cannot think he will make love much longer to a mistress where he is like to find so cold encouragement; were not my son the most negligent Buzlum that ever courted so likeable a lady, your cousin would never have attempted to rivall him; I have been ye more particular in this narrative, becaus I am sure twill please you to know that any plott is disappointed which was laid to give me more uneasyness then in your absence I could well bear.—Instead of chideing poor Squire as you desire, I must make her apology, for twas not her fault you did not receive ye letter you orderd her (by Cornfourth) to write; which she for the sake of expedition sending by ye flying-coach, I mett it on ye road, & containing nothing but an account of Betty's biles, & having no convenience to seal it up again I kept it, & sent you ye contents of it by the very next post.—I intended to have begun this letter where my last ended, which was to tell you your epistles have been so farr from wanting an excuse from the short-ness or frequency of them, that if they stand in nead of any, tis for trans-gressing that self-denying injunction I laid on you at parting, not to sacrifice your health & ease to my satisfaction by writing too often or too long letters, since it takes away all my pleasure when I find they are not to be had without giving you pain. I depended much on Mrs. Bradshaw to be your secretary for imparting all common occurrences ; as for those which are mutually particular between us, I am glad to hear you find them as undescribable as my self by any language but ye private dictates of my heart, which towards you yet speaks more tender passionate things than are expressible by ye tongue or pen of your faithfull lover, Bristol.

Tis now near midnight that your letter by ye post is brought me, which I shall answer & thank you for by ye next. I cant seal this till I have begd you not to writ such long letters, so much more I value your health & ease above my own pleasure, I may say at present my only one.

**620.**    Lady Bristol to Lord Bristol.        Bath, Aug. 19, 1721.

As I was revived by your dear kind letter of Thursday last, so was I as much cast down by this I received to day; to hear you sufferd so much in your last journey as to make you say so cruell a thing as that you could not think of another in hast, and in words so very strong as makes me not dare to press it; yett sure there is a vast differance in a spring coach & a hack; and ye going to or from ye person one loves is quite another thing; tis so much so to me that I think I could either ride or walk (the two conveyances I hate most) to Ickworth; some comfort, however, I find in this greivance, that it must certainly have made you lay aside the thoughts of going into Lincolnshire, as well as that unnessesary journey to London; that's so much time gaind; for I flatter my self still that after all I have said every post of my wretched & forlorn esstait, you will take some pitty of me, & not lett me remain so much longer. Poor Bradshaw is out of danger, & satt up yesterday, & begun to jokes again, but is still very weak; I cant bragg much of my own health, tho' I think I am rather better then when I came, if this daies disapointment dont sett me back again, for my companions tell me they never saw such a change in any body as my self between last night & to day, from ye vexation of not knowing when I shall be happy again. I must do them ye justice to say they take as much pains as lys in their power to make me forgitt my sorrows; but alass, tis all in vain;....my heart is ready to break, & all my griefs flow out afresh....; but I am runing on (as sure I could for ever) without telling you who thees companions are I have mentiond; the

Dutchess of Warton & her sister Mrs. Moor, (who is the late Bishop of Elly's son's wife,) with Mrs. Andrews (Generall Whitemans daughter,) all live in a house together, & as they are in eternal good humour & spiretts themselves, they woud indeavour to make me the same, & have never sufferd me to eat a meal alone since Pegg has been sick. Yesterday I began to bathe, but was very much vapourd with it ; but being better in ye evening I went to ye first ball has been this season, though they say hear is more company than ever was so early in the year. The plays begin to night, & I sopose all deversions will go forward now Governor Nash is arrived. Poor Gaye is exceeding maloncholy for the death of his frind, Lord Warwick, who dyd (as they say) without a will ; so all goes to Lady Betty, his aunt, who marred a country attorney, & poor Rich, of our famelly, is an earl without a groat. They talk mightyly to day that the plague is at a place over against Weymouth ; pray God preserve us all from that misfortune, and all other addissional ones to those already felt & hardly to be bourn by, my dear dearest life, your faithfull E. B.

I have been sitting with Pegg for the first time she has been able to bear a long vissett ; she presents her servis to you, & bids me tell you she shall not recover tell you come. Pray press Jack to remove his famely to Ickworth, for the town they say is very sickly. I am glad to hear such good news of poor Betty. God bless them all.

Ipswich, Aug. 21, 1721.

**621.** My ever-new Delight      From ye White-horse Inn.

          I am come very weary to this place, having seen your estate at Sproughton by ye way ; to morrow I am to go to Playford, where Colonell Norton & Captain Russell (who have been both with me) tell me I am to expect to see more ruin than could be imagind after all your father laid out there ; they also tell me Lady Felton hath been ill ever since

Vol. II.     w

she wrote to me to come hither, which I wish I had known sooner, that it might have prevented my taking a very maloncholly and I believe a fruitless journey too, seeing no possibility of settling ye goods in any tolerable posture without my heiress.   I have already so farr felt their pulse about them as to find my Lady Felton (in case I am driven to that necessity) will not refuse me ye use of ye great parlour to putt them all into under ye care of ye gardiner or his wife, untill we can tell where better to dispose of them; or if Lady Felton should lett ye house, (which Collonel Norton told me she could have done more than once to some ladies had it not been for our goods,) I cannot see why it would not be best to lett the goods with ye house, since no body sure would choose to bring furniture to so precarious a place as that must be by reason of Lady Felton's very ill state of health. How very unfitt I am at present to undertake ye management of this or any other business, you shall not know, & more especially since I receivd yours of ye 16th last night before I left Ickworth, wherin you tell me of nothing but vapours & headaches you are not able to bear, besides poor Pegg's desperate condition, which I know must have occasiond a good deal of your own disorders ; what effect ye ruminating on your & my own circumstances must at this time have upon a mind susceptible of ye deepest impressions from such a length of distance, absence & uncertainty of meeting so soon again as I know we both wish with equal impatience, is a discription I will spare you, knowing what it costs me whenever I hear you complain, which, however, I would not for all the world be ignorant of from your fearing to tell me the truth, since my doubts would give me perpetual torment.   I have written till tis so late, I am sure you would have me go to bed ; yet rest I cannot till I have desird you (since you say you find so sensible a difference) never to faile of drinking ye watters at ye pump, ye entire establishment of your health being ye only comfortable cordial my heart can taste, as ye want of it would overwhelm me more than ever with terrours not to be expressd, since I never so throughly felt as at this very moment how very wretched, how inconsolably miserable, how irretrievably unhappy, even to the wishing my self out of being, should you ever cease to be or not be easy and happy ; to make you both has been & ever shall be ye cheif business of his life who cares to live no longer than he can some way or other administer to your happiness, being solely & only yours, Bristol.

Since I finishd ye inclosed last night, I receivd yours of ye 14th this morning ; but instead of a feast to my breakfast, (which from former experience I reasonably promist my self,) it provd a fast ; the account you give of your hysterick disorder and Mrs. Bradshaw's ilness to heighten it spoiling my stomach to my chocolate, as will your vapours & affections of the head consequent on your writing much my appetite to your long letters, which tho' ye only comfort I at this distance can enjoy, yet I hope I have said enough on that head to convince you how much I preferr your ease to ye sattisfaction of my own desires, and therfore would never see a line beyond your strength or convenience to your faithful Bristol.

Our children, I thank God, are all well. I have not yet forgiven Harry ye anxiety he kept me in by delaying ye arrival of your letter a whole day, during my uncertainty how you had passd your journey.

622.    Lady Bristol to Lord Bristol.        Bath, Aug. 21, 1721.

Tis very hard that every (ney, the only) pleasure I can tast, which is your dear letters, shoud be allayd with so much sorrow as I felt this morning at the reading that dated the 16th. Judge, my dearest life, what a heart overchargd before (when I thought my happiness much nearer) must feel from such a disappointment, to have it lengthend to so long a time as not to have the end of my misery guessd at. O, I coud rave & curse all the unhappy causes that keeps us asunder, did I not fear some of them might reach where I hope all blessing will ever attend, whatever becomes of me; and as if I needed any additional weight, Jack sends me word by your letter to him you speak as if you coud not come at all; but if I coud suspect such a thing were possible, I woud hire a sett of horses & leave this cursed place, let the consequence of my health be what it will, though I really think it woud mend if my mind were enough at ease to let it, for I was better to day after bathing than I was last time, if I had not cryd so as to give me a fitt of trembling till after I had eat my dinner, which the Dutchess of Wharton came herself & fetchd me to, but I was so overwhelmd that I burst forth in the middle of it; she is a good deal in the spleen too, having expected her lord every day, & now hears he is gone for Ireland.—You dont tell me the reason why you had not the coach on Tuesday, or whether Harry went in it; I hope no accident happend either to him or the lame horse, which, thank God, was the only one we had in our journey; but if I had sett out of Monday as I designd, I shoud not have escapd so well, for I shoud certainly have been robd, not having so much courage as my Lady Stamford, who was sett upon in Marlborough Forrest the day before I gott there by five highwaymen well armd; she had but four horsemen, and two behind; however, was resolvd not to be robd, and before they gott up to the coach she gott out of it, and bid her servants guard that and not mind her, so that when they came to the coach and found they were to be resisted with guns & pistols, they rode off, and she heard no more of them.—I conclude the dear babes are well, because you say nothing of them; but I have dreamt of nothing else all night but them and their much dearer original; pray God bless you all till our happy meeting; till that long time farewell to my dear dear angel.—I think I have found out that it wont be disagreeable to Tom to let him know Mrs. Andrews enquires much after him, and sends her compliments; Pegg does the same to you and the rest at Ickworth; she is to come down stairs to morrow.

**623.** My ever-new Delight    Ickworth, Aug. 23, 1721.

The melancholly scene I saw yesterday at Playford made me not able to proceed on my journey to Shotley as I intended. I have taken the best care I possibly coud contrive of your goods, having taken them all into my own custody, and given Lady Felton a receipt for them at the bottom of both the inventories, excepting some things that were missing and broken, none of much value unless a bed & some of the linnen, on condition they may remain in the house as they are, the keys wherof I have given to one Simson, a neighbouring Quaker, who is one of our tenants for Shotley estate, and his wife, a very titey woman, who will see they shall take no more harm than they have already done by the roof of the house being open in four places, in the repairing wherof I found the workmen were prepard to persuade me to consent that instead of the brick lucums which are fallen, and others taken down that woud have done so too, they might have putt wooden ones in their places, saying the old walls woud not bear long the weight of new brick ones; but as I knew the cheapness of wood ones was their chief reason in favour of their lady, so I told them I woud agree to nothing on the part of mine till I had stated the matter of fact to her, and receivd her desires concerning it; in the mean time, I told them, every one knew that the house must be kept up & continued in the condition they found it, fair usage excepted; but that is so farr from having been its case that I never saw any place half so much impaird in double the time they have had it. For beside the four breaches in the roof of the old part of the house, the very new piazza built in the front of it by your dear father lett in wett so fast upon us (the morning proving rainy) that we coud not stand shelterd in any one part of it; the roof of that was laid so flatt, that tho' tis leaded it does as I have told you. Then the new pallizade, which was sett up too by him, is fallen down the length of a whole raile together, & there they lye rotting against the ground.

The bridge over the moate, that was made very tite & strong by him, is now in so crazy a condition that it is not very safe to pass upon it. The woods are rather more mallihackd and ruind than the Mansion-house, even to the impossibility of furnishing a load of timber to repair only a tenant's barn, the very venerable old trees that stood on the side-hill in the park being all croppd also, now wearing nothing but short bobbs instead of their venerable long perruques left on them by your ancestors. But why do I give you the trouble of knowing all this? woud any one say that knows not me; but I must answer, tis because my universal fidelity towards you in all things, even to the nicest scrupulosity in the minutest matters, will not sufferr me to conceal any thing but my former follies from you, wherin you have no interest, & especially since I can at the same time assure you that shoud your inheritance by any other accidents dwindle to nothing, yet as long as I possess that invaluable treasure of your faithful heart, my love & friendship can never feel the least diminution or decay; so much otherwise, that you were never thought of with so much true passion as at this moment by your at present unhappy friend, Bristol.

**624.**     Lady Bristol to Lord Bristol.          Bath, Aug. 23, 1721.

If life can subsist without sleep, I may hope to see my dear dear angel once again; for I am sure, if I were to put all my broken slumbers together, I have not rested five hours this night. O my dear, when shall my wearied soul have rest? for I expect none till I am lodgd upon that faithfull breast that has so often been my pillow. To any that does not love like me, (as sure none ever did,) this might seem strange, when all this little world strives who shall oblige me most; for besides my constant friends I have been invited to two entertainments at my Lady Lueys (Sir Berkeleys lady); she is a very agreable, good sort of woman, and one I am sure you will like. To morrow I expect Mrs. Meggett here, for Jack writ to me to take her lodgings for the middle of the week.—I receivd your kind message by Dards last night to take care of my self; I wish I coud be sure you did as much, for I am the pattern of regularity here, and I have made my companions conform to my hours, which is to dine at two, sup at nine, and rise at eight; the last they are not yet come to. I use all the exercise the weather will give me leave, for I never go in a chair but when it rains; but indeed that is allmost constant; I wish it does not hinder the pleasure at Ickworth, tho' I think I coud be jealous even of that, if I thought you had too much, or in any thing else in which I did not bear a part; but some joy I can give you that I have a. share in, which is I think I am better this afternoon than I have been since I came to Bath. I dont know if the hopes of to morrows post bringing me some better news than the former has done may not go a great way in what I feel, for tis observd here that I am allways sweeter temperd the night before the post comes in—but I am running on, and forgett your commands to the contrary, so hard it is to beleive any thing one likes can hurt one; therefore if I do transgress a little, sure I may be pardond, since all my fault is love, and that so tender a passion as never was felt in any heart but your faithfull E. Bristol.

Pegg sends her compliments (and I my blessing) to Ickworth; this is the first day of her going out. This copy of verses I found in a news paper; the name at the bottom struck me so, I coud not help copying of them to send you.

625.   My ever-new Delight            Ickworth, Aug. 25, 1721.

The fullness of my last letter and the fatigue of my Ipswich journey made me omitt acquainting you with two material circumstances in it. The one was that Mr. Frohock, Lady Felton's lawyer, made me unexpected overtures towards her Ladyships letting us have

Playford House in present upon terms, offering himself to be a mediator in the case; but I receivd them with the coldness they now deserve, seeing £500 will not putt it into the condition they found it at your dear father's death, and such she is obligd to leave it at her own; besides, I old him Sir C. Felton had so intangled it by his lease of it to Legatt with the Parke and other lands, that I questiond whether she coud during her life make us a title, were we agreed upon the terms, and they never so easy. The other is that I did not receive one penny of your tenants, they all too justly pleading the want of mony from the cheapness of corn and the deadness of all trade, especially that for their fatt cattle, which sell for very little more than they buy them in at lean. But the worst of my journey is still behind, for poor Will Oliver fell ill at Ipswich, which proves (as Mr. Ray calls it) one of those bilious feavers which are grown rife in this country, (for both your dairy-maids are fallen ill of it too,) so that I cannot proceed upon his accounts now I am returnd, till he getts well again. My Lincolnshire journey, tho' the most important and necessary of all others, (except that to the Bath,) must in this unlucky scituation of my affairs be postponed to another year, for tis impossible to leave this family and all my business within and without in such confusion, and no body to take care of any thing.

Aug. 26. I had written the other two sides yesterday before I went to the Assembly, where nothing less than a particular message from Sir. T. Hanmer the night before, hoping I woud meet him there, added to Lady Betty's betraying a more than usual inclination that I woud do so, coud possibly have prevaild with me to appear, knowing how unfitt I am in your absence to entertain or be entertaind, unless it was by your kind yet cruel letter, which I seperated from all the company to read over again and again, where I mett with so many welcome (tho' cruciating) sister-sentiments with my own upon the painfull uncertainties of our meeting, mixd with so many native strokes of true passion exactly tallying with my own sufferings, which by a most allowable hypocricy I have hitherto out of due tenderness to you most carefully dissembled, that I am determind to throw off all disguises and confess my own condition, which has been more unsupportably wretched and forlorn since I saw you than ever, even to that degree of disquiet as hardly to possess my soul in that decent patience I profess to God's good will, of which may no tryal or temptation ever gett the better, and that the present one may not do so, I will give yours and my own heart the releif of making you the mistress of appointing the day by which you woud have me at Bath, where had not many prudential reasons by your own consent prevaild I had been long ago, altho' I must have gone on foot, and every toe as full of anguish as that last year of the goute, there being no pain of body comparable to that my soul has lately felt in losing so much time from thy sweet fellowship at such a season of my life as ought to make me covetous in managing every moment of its short remainder in thy blessed society, a satisfaction too sweet not to have all other meaner considerations sacrificed to it by your ever faithfull friend and constant lover, Bristol.

Conclude our children are well, whenever I have not room to mention them. Harry came by our coach, and kept it a day longer on the way than it needed have been; but as I knew it woud be disagreeable news to you, as it had disapointed and displeasd me, I woud have conceald it from you. I am glad to hear Mrs. Bradshaw is so well again without me, for I much doubt my being able to make any body so but your dear self.

**626.** Lady Bristol to Lord Bristol. Bath, Aug. 26, 1721.

The eve to my great festival. O happy day that gave you birth, to make me the most blessd of women ; may your years be multiplyd to my fond wishes, and never know an hour of sorrow after this

Vol. II. x

cruel absence, cruel indeed to me, for three weeks is almost gone, and no
day set to releive my poor drooping spirits, which are lower now than
ordinary, occasiond (as I beleive) by some cold, for I have coughd all night,
and such an oppression and heat upon my chest that is very painfull to me.
Some people tell me the waters will some times have that effect; I sent for
Mr. Skreen this morning, and he says I must by no means drink the waters
or bath while tis upon me; he proposd asses milk, which you know I cant
take, & bleeding, which I am unwilling to do without an absolute necessity,
because I was so lately; so that tis concluded to take a quieting draught
with oyl of sweet almonds; I hope by this to compass one night's sleep,
which yet I have never had; I woud not enlarge so upon this ungrateful
subject, if it were not your positive commands, and that I hope no ill consequence will attend it, since he gives me leave to go abroad, (nay, desires
I woud,) the weather being changd, and my spirits so low, so that Madam
Bradshaw and I dine with the Dutchess of Wharton; they all dine with me
to morrow to celebrate your birthday, and the whole fraternity is to be set
forth as fine as the sun, and several in new cloaths, both men and women,
as the greatest compliment they can make me.   Lady Lucy and Colonel
Cotton (her nephew, who keeps house with her,) has invited me and the rest
of our company to finish the day with a supper and musick; tis impossible
to imagine how kind and civil this sett of people (which I have named to
you before) are to my forlorn estate.   I hope the telling you what I have in
view will make you easy under my present indisposition, which I hope will
not last long enough to break much of the course of my waters, which I
have great faith in to restore (at least) part of my health again.   Grant me,
kind Heaven, but length of days to pay in part (the whole I never can) this
wonderous truth and tenderness, yet be assurd, as far as the most gratefull
heart is capable of, the mighty debt shall be dischargd by your faithfull,
constant wife, E. Bristol.

I say nothing in answer to either of your letters about Playford, because you will be come away before you can receive it. I am sorry any thing relating to me shoud give you so much trouble. I thought my dear angel woud be glad to hear something of me as late as I coud, therefore I have staid as late as the post will give me leave to tell you I am better than I have been all day. Pegg and I am going to supper tete a tete, and then to bed; so good night to my dearest life.—Half an hour past nine.

627. My ever-new Delight                    Ickworth, Aug. 28, 1721.

My last letter will sufficiently show you how little able a heart which feels what mine does for you was to resist those pathetick questions you putt to me, desiring to know some sett time when our meeting might be guessd at; since you will there find I have made you absolute mistress under God's permissive providence of it; notwithstanding I coud add a thousand reasons to those I have already laid before you why I ought not to leave (even for your sake) this family without any head to it, either within doors or without, Will Oliver being still very ill, and not one article of two years accompts at this minute lookd into, and shoud he dye, as he thinks he shall, I shoud never be able to gett much out of his widows hands, whatever may happen to be chargeable in his, unless I am ready upon the place to receive it; besides, what will your son and daughter Hervey with their child do here till we gett to them again. Then as Tom and Harry call for their dozen glasses of wine each daily (which I desire you will take no notice of) in my presence, what do you think will be done in my absence. They are both young men of hopeful parts, (Tom especially, who has the solid as well as the brillant qualitys of the diamond,) and it woud be great pity to see them drownd in drink (like you know who) for want of giving a timely check to such fatal inclinations before they become habitual and so incurable. I have taken all the opportunities in my way of inveighing against the vice of drunkeness as the most pernicious of all others in its universal ill consequences upon soul, body, estate, reputation and under-standing, and I am not without hope that they both see and dread the deformity of it elswhere. These, together with the state you know my finances are in, will I fear prove too hard a taske for you to give tolerable solutions to (which I must expect) when you fix the time of my coming; and therefore (so strong is my desire of being with you once more) I will not enumerate several other objections that occur, least I shoud make you discreet enough to give way to so many prudential reasons as might present themselves, and so disappoint my expectation in conjureing me for the good of the whole to continue where I am, which I can faithfully assure you is so alterd a place in my eyes and sentiments by your absence that I daily wonder what is become of that pleasure I used to find in it. So farr is it from being a rivall to provoke your jealousy by giving me too much satis-faction without you, that your quarrel to it now ought to be from its inability to divert that spleen which preys upon my vitalls, and will do so till I am restord to thy much wanted belovd presence. Many thanks to thee, my dearest, and millions more to Gods goodness, for your most welcome news of being better by your own confession; tis a strong proof of recovery when the patient both feels and tells it too; O may it still proceed till such fast foundations are laid for a future stock of health as may enable you without pain or weakness to see your grandson blessd with as fair, as chaste, as affectionate a wife as your self, and his daughter married to as tender, as faithfull a fond fool as my self.—On Thursday next I am to treate the Corporation at the Angel in Bury; they have given the Hovells a fresh mortification, by choosing a kinsman of Mr. Macro's for their Preacher in exclusion of their nephew Symonds; this, they say, they may take for offering to sett up an interest in opposition to Lord Bristol's.—Bury Musick has been here all day, and the fagg-end of the family are now danceing, tho' tis near midnight. Good days and nights ever attend thee, is the constant prayer of thy faithfull Bristol.

**628.**  Lady Bristol to Lord Bristol. Bath, Aug. 28, 1721.

I had great hopes to days post woud have told me I need write no more; but after so many troubles as you have had of all kinds I dare not add to them (as I am sure I shoud) by telling you how great the disapointment is to me. I will only say the expectation was so pleasing as to wake me this morning by six a clock, and gave me such spirits last night that I have not been so merry since I came to this hatefull place; but I believe the honours done to your birth-day contributed a good deal towards it. I told you in my last how the day was laid out, which was performd in every particular; for tho' I staid at home all day to nurse my cold, yet I wrapt my self up to go to supper, which was impossible to avoid after the complements they had made me; your health was added to every other that was drank, besides a bumper in particular to your self. My Lady Lucy was so obliging (tho' she is in very deep mourning) to leave off her black gloves and putt on a new white manteau a purpose for the day. Pegg desires (with her compliments) you may know she putt on a new suit, and was very bright upon the occasion; and to crown the feast to my dear dear angel, I must tell you I hope I am quite recoverd of my late indisposition, att least so much so as to begin the waters and bathing again to day, and find my self pretty well after it, tho' it was twelve a' clock when I went to bed, and I told you the hour of waking.—Mrs. Meggett came to this place a Saturday, as did many others, and last night a great number; if the increase of our company produces any thing new, you shall have it at night.—I have been at the sweet recreation of visits where I can pick up nothing to entertain you. Mrs. Hamden and Mrs. Ellis are here, but not Sir William. Mr. Hutcheson and Mr. Broderick enquire every post when I expect you; I answer, I wish I coud tell you. When, my dear, will that long lookd for time arrive; tis ages since I saw you last, and so will the time seem that is to come to the impatience felt by your faithfull E. Bristol.

**629.**    My ever-new Delight                    Ickworth, Aug. 30, 1721.

What alternate hopes, doubts and fears have agitated my poor soul since I equally indulged my own uneasy heart as well as yours in making you mistress of my motions from this family, (knowing how many more reasons there are against than for leaving it in the condition it is,) you shall not now be troubled with any other description of than by the following distich:

> With much regrett I prudently persuade,
> And often wish my counsel disobeyd.

May God Almighty bless your determinations with his divine direction, and then they cannot faile in the event of proving best for us and ours.—I hear by my Governour, Welch Tom, who came hither yesterday, that my neice Meggott was to be with you as on Sunday last; if so, you will have a pair of very intelligent, entertaining companions between her and Mrs. Bradshaw constantly with you at home, beside the Duchess of Wharton, Lady Lucy, Mrs. Moor and many others, who you mention with such emphatick expressions of kindness and seem so well pleasd with, that I in my turn may much more justly be jealous of them than you have reason to be of Ickworth Parke, which being stript of its chief ornament by your absence from it,

> Soft scenes of solitude no longer please,
> Spleen enters there, and I'm my own disease:

which I find nothing can cure me of but being restord to the sovereign cordial of thy sweet society. I have just now receivd the next comfort to it, which is your kind letter of the 26th, wherin you allow more encomiums to the vigill than the festival deserves, unless it be in that part of its panegyrick where you stile your self the most blessd of women by my birthday ; were that so, I might modestly admitt I was born to one of the most eligible purposes in life, since I know no better end of being than to have the body of the world happy who best deserves to be so, not only from your own intrinsick worth, but as you have the additional meritt of having renderd me compleatly so too, which no woman I now know but your self coud have done. Tis late and I must conclude, tho' I coud run on infinitely.

> Farewell my soul's best object, pride of love ;
> All that obstructs our meeting Heaven remove ;
> May every joy love can or fortune give,
> For ever with my chaste Eliza live.—Bristol.

How coud you expose your self to getting cold after all the precautions I gave you against it, and your promises to observe them ? I heartily condole with you upon the death of Sir D. Hamilton ; but thanks be to God, all skill in womens waies are not departed with him ; besides I trust in his goodness that you may never have any future need of any.—On Saturday next I am engagd to dine with Sir Thomas Hanmer, and by Sunday's post, if I compute right, your decisive summons will come to your faithful friend and follower, Bristol.

**630.**   Lady Bristol to Lord Bristol.         Bath, Aug. 30, 1721.

This is a most uncomfortable post to an impatience like mine, to live two whole days and nights (and write twice) without being able to receive any releif to all my sorrows but what bare imagination furnishes; and that has been so kind to me to night in dreams as I realy thought you come; being willing to indulge so much pleasure I dosd on till I was calld to my wretched state again, and find it but a dream ; yet so farr it has workd upon my fancy that I have a glimering hope this (nay even the letter I writ a Monday) may not come to your hands before you sett out; let but to morrows letter tell me that, and my poor heart will have some ease; at present I have none, tho' company and diversions increase daily. I have playd four or five times at ombre, but now Mr. Herbert is gone to fetch his wife that entertainment is spoyld, and I have taken to hazard, which is very low, for most of the ladys play silver. Mr. Nash talks of several gamesters that are coming this week; fine ladys come in apace; the Duchess of Queensborough and Mrs. Berenger are expected to night, and Mrs. Poultney the latter end of the week; but if they dont bring some fine men after them, they will pass their time sadly, for here is such a scarcity in this place they are ready to be devourd. God send me my own; they shall willingly have my share of all the rest.—I wish I had any news to entertain you, but here is nothing worth repeating; two rediculous quarrells is now the entertainment of the place. Sir George Bing went from hence this morning; he was sent for by an express, some say to be made a lord, but Colonel Cotton told me twas to take care the ships performd their Quarentine, for they are now in great aprehensions of the plague, and they say there will be a proclamation out soon for the Parliament to meet to put a stop to the commerce with France; but all these affairs you are, I believe, better informd of than I can tell you, at least know better what to give credit to, for there is nothing to be depended upon in this place, unless it be the truth and sincerity of your faithfull mourning turtle, E. Bristol.

You will find this is not one of my spelling days.

**631.**    My ever-new Delight                Ickworth, Sept. 2, 1721.

    I hope the laudanum and oyl of sweet almonds releivd all your complaints as effectually as they did mine when I was so ill at this place. I was glad to know the result of the consultation upon

your case ended in a prescription that had succeeded so well with your
second self; sure where there is such a thorough sympathy of hearts, whatever medicine hitts one bloud must agree with t'other; so that I shall find
my self doubly disappointed if this nights letter does not bring me the good
news of your being perfectly well again, tho' the Bath Theater is but an ill
sort of a second to a physicians bill; and shoud you have increasd your
cough, or fixd that oppression you speak of upon your chest, (by getting
cold upon cold,) in celebrating my birth-day, so sad a consequence from so
kind a cause woud tempt me to wish I had never been born. May every
circumstance attending my life prove propitious to every accident of yours;
and if there be a day to come in mine which is to shorten or make yours
uneasy, may my death happen to be the vigill to it.—Yesterday I gave the
Corporation a dinner of twenty nine dishes (warm), at which there were
above fourty of our friends present, who all agreed there never was seen a
more noble entertainment at any time or place, and indeed I thought so
too; and such I beleive you will think it ought to have been, after I have
told you it cost above five and twenty pounds, besides my own beef and
mutton, veale and venison. Had it, or coud it have been better, they woud
have deservd it all, since they rememberd you with such particular respect
and esteem that I shall ever love them more for that than for all the trust
and confidence they have putt in me and my family, by sending them so
many years for their representatives to Parliament, especially Alderman
Chamberlain, who when I drank a health to all our wives, woud pledg only
to your own, saying that not only their but no other mens wives health was
worthy to be mingled with the virtuous, beautiful Countess of Bristol's.—I
have sett up in expectation of your letter beyond my ordinary hour, which
is now ten a clock, feeling I coud not sleep till I knew whether you were
better or worse for the 27th of August. Tis just now arrivd, and has sett
my heart at ease by telling me you are quite recoverd of your late indis-

position, and fallen to the waters and bathing again; for which mercy to
me and mine among many others, Gods goodness be for ever praisd. To
morrow I am to dine at Mildenhall with Sir Thomas Hanmer. I find by
Mrs. Bradshaws letter to Betty she is quite recoverd, and woud fain make
me sick with jealousy (mere spight), but pray tell her our hearts are (now)
both too sound to give or take that worse than pestilent infection. Yours,
Bristol.

**632.**    Lady Bristol to Lord Bristol.          Bath, Sept. 2, 1721.

The month 'is changd, and I remain the same
wretched thing I was; indeed, my dear dear angel, if the kind and tender
expressions in your letter had not in some degree aswagd the anguish of
my poor heart, I coud never have born it to find the day was yet to be namd
for your setting out, when I have expected every hour this week to have
you in my longing arms, where, if it is in my power, I will for ever keep
you, never to part no more. What consideration in life can be worth the
torment this has cost me; and as if this were not enough to bear, I at the
same time receive so very weighty an addition to my present sufferings as
the death of poor Sir David Hamilton; tis a cutting stroak to one in my
condition to loose the cheif (nay only) assistance I depended on to recover
my ill state of health; I dare not tell you all the aprehensions it has given
to my weak and depressd spirits; the surprise had such an effect upon me
yesterday that I was not able to stir out, neither was I fit to have been seen,
but I was obligd, having before ingagd company to dine with me. I had a
great assembly in the afternoon, notwithstanding the many diversions that
are stirring abroad; here was two commerce tables, (with nine or ten in a
sett,) & one ombre; for tho' there is great divisions in this little spot of
ground, I am so happy to have them all agree in being very obliging to
me; but between you and I, there is one of my new friends I am with-

drawing from as farr as good manners will give me leave; for she does not in the least answer the opinion I (at first) had of her, tho' she makes good the character I have heard since; I dont care to name names, but tis the lady I sent a message from to Tom; if you can sift any thing out of his closeness about her, I may be better informd; but why do I imploy you in such trifles, when I hope you wont lose a moment that is not of absolute necessity before you sett out. I own I grudg the assembly, especially since you say you coud not be entertaind there; yet how is that possible not to have some share in the pleasure one gives; and I will have the vanity to say that is only due where tis so truly tasted as by your faithfull love and constant admirer, E. Bristol.

**633.** Lady Bristol to Lord Bristol. Sept. 3, 1721.

I coud never have beleivd a letter from my dearest life woud have been an addition rather than a comfort to my present miserable circumstances, but such is my forlorn estate that by my greatest pleasure I receive my greatest pain; for sure no torment coud be added to my almost broken heart like all those reasons you give for deferring your journey; and as if those laid down were not enough, you say how many more you coud add, then leave it to me to determine your coming. O tis a cruelty beyond expression to putt such difficultys upon me; but I have said enough in all my letters to show which way my inclination tends; after that I must leave it to your better judgment; I dare not trust my own discretion, for who ever was discreet in love; yet some little hints I must venture at; first then the cruel distance between us makes it above a week before one can receive and answer a letter, so that by that time Will Olivers fate must be determind and that affair ended; then as to my sons, (who's conduct, if my full heart had room for more afflictions, woud be no small addition,) Harry I suppose you will leave at Oxford, and sure Tom may be trusted with the assistance of his sisters good advice for so little a time; as for Mr. and Mrs. Hervey, I beleive you need not give your self much trouble about them, for he sends me word she recovers her strength very slow, so that I beleive they will not think of a journey soon; however, I hope you will press them to send the child before the weather is to cold ; tis extreamly so here allready, therefore pray take care of your dear self in your journey, for I much flatter my self that you are near taking one, els I coud not subsist till that happy moment arrives to releive all the cares of your poor disconsolate E. Bristol.

The company I keep most, loves strong ale extreamly; therefore if you have very good for the credit of Ickworth, it woud be very acceptable if you coud bring a little hamper behind the coach.—Bradshaw sends her compliments ; she drones about in a pittious sort of condition.—Dont be in pain that I have writ to much, for the first letter, as you see by the date, was yesterday, when I did not drink the waters, for I have been forbid them again for two or three days ; to day I have begun again. Need I say any more about your coming; wont your own heart tell you what I woud have.

> **634.**    My ever-new Delight        Ickworth, Sept. 4, 1721.

As matters have happend here, I can hardly say I am sorry I had not an answer to my letter of license I sent you some time since to name the day when you woud have me sett out hence for the Bath, for I coud not have complyed with an immediate summons, being at present under the discipline of the goute in the very same part I had it before ; I felt several grumblings of it ever since Thursday, and woud not have venturd to Sir T. Hanmer's (as I did on Saturday) but that I had disappointed him once before ; I hope this fitt may yet prove favourable enough to permitt me to begin my journey as soon as my postillion and Tom my footman are recoverd, who are both ill of this new feaver, from which I am comforted with an assurance that my pain in my great toe will certainly exempt me; one other of the maids (the under one in the laundry) was taken ill of it lately, but I thank God all our children continue well. I have so much to think of and to take care in since Will Oliver's sickness, (who still keeps his bed, tho' out of all danger,) that unless I had been here I am sure the family woud have sufferd under such a state of anarchy as never was seen before. What then will it (likely) be when increasd by your son and daughter Hervey, our grandson and their servants, if left to themselves ; yet left they must and shall be as soon as my pain leaves me, (I wonder it shoud lett me forgett it long enough to omitt its name,) and that Will Oliver can furnish me with mony to bear my charges, which he this day sent me word he coud not do till he is well enough to receive my rents and give receipts. My pain (as before) seems less when I am on horseback than at any other time, so that I am all day long abroad.

> But like a ghost I glide thro' every grove,
> To visitt all our tresuries of love ;
> This shade th' account of thousand joys does hide ;
> As many more this murmuring rivers side,
> Where the dear grass as sacred does retain
> The print where thou and I so oft have lain ;
> Still those sweet times to my remembrance move,
> For oh ! how vaste a memory has love.

From this poetical quotation I woud have you inferr for your own ease that my bodily greif is not near so intense as the humours tis produced by generally gives. I wish I coud send you as good an account of my mental ; but as that proceeds from so heavy a cause as your absence, nothing can lighten or releive my poor heart ; no, not even your dear children, tho' they do many things to try to entertain me, but they find it all in vain. However, wretched as I am and feel I must ever be without you, yet I can find some respite from my melancholy thoughts whilst I reflect that your company and diversions increase daily, one part of the latter excepted, which is hazard, because I know it will ingage you long and daily in a hott room, which will frustrate all the good effects proposd from the waters, or at least make them require more time to do their work in, which I have alwaies livd in hopes might be shortend to six weeks, even by the advice of Dr. Freind, who did not think so many necessary in his own case, and I have alwaies had a presentiment in yours that a longer use than that of them might endanger laying a foundation of a dropsy in you, which woud at once irrecoverably drown me in such a deluge of misery and distraction as nothing but my own death coud releive me from, which in that case woud be courted as a favour from Heaven by your forlorn friend, Bristol.

**635.**    Lady Bristol to Lord Bristol.        Bath, Sept. 4, 1721.

I find my last was dated a day to forward. According to my usual custom (of post days) I have been awake ever since six a clock in expectation of your dear letter, which brought its bitter as well as sweets along with it, when I found there was no day namd for your coming, for I pleasd my self with the hopes after all I have said you woud not wait for my determination in that affair, which shoud you yet do must be the first moment that it were posible, and even that be thought as distant as dooms-day to an impatience like mine ; and see how unluckily the time must be lengthend, for your letter dated the twenty fifth of August gave me so pleasing (tho' difficult) a power I did not receive till Thursday morning, the only post in the week that one cant answer the letter the same day, for they go from hence a Wedensday nights, so that I receivd that of the twenty eighth of August (so full of difficultys) before I coud answer the other, by which you will see what a distracted condition you put me into, for fear I shoud say to little to express my love, or show to much how unreasonable that passion has made me; but when I reflect upon its dear and worthy object, I acquit my self of all its consequences and beg you again to come the first moment you can with ease to your self, which ought and ever shall be my cheif consideration in life. I have been to much affected with disappointments in this unlucky journey not to be very sensible of that you mett with last night in the kind expectation you say you had to receive my summons, which you see (by the account I have given you) was not put in my power till Saturday last, and then how unnecessary was it to tell my desires, if my pen has ever expressd but half the tenderness felt in the heart of your faithful E. Bristol.

Your saying nothing of Will Oliver makes me hope he is recoverd, and that great (and I think only) difficulty over that delays my happiness.— The inclosd is a song made upon Mrs. Howard, the Maid of Honour, at Tunbridg; if it does not divert you, it may Betty, who I conclude is well, because you say nothing of her; God bless her and the rest of ye dear babes. The company increases daily too much to give an account of in a letter.

**636.** Lady Bristol to Lord Bristol. Bath, Sept.— 1721.

I have great reason to hope this will not come to your hands, for if it does, I fear it will be an occasion of trouble to both of us, as I have great dependance upon your being sett out before this can reach you; if you are not, it must (since you have so strictly injoind it) bring you the unwelcome news of my being so very ill last night that I thought I shoud never see you more. O cruelty of thought; for God sake, my dear, prevent it the first moment you can; for there is no price I woud not have given for a sight of you in my hysterick disorder, which I think was as great as ever I felt it. I cant guess at any accident that brought it to such a heigth, unless it was over walking my self; I am sure you will wonder at that cause till I let you know I was yesterday with the Duchess of Wharton, Lady Cobham, and a great party to see Mr. Blathwates, and was so delighted with the gardens I coud hardly let the least part of them remain unseen, which you (that have been there) know was a great deal too much for me to undertake, especially since I am very farr from having recoverd the loss of Sir David, which I must own has sett me back in my health ; the sight of Dr. Cheyne this morning renewd my affliction, but he has given me something that has done me a vast deal of good, and I am to have a party at Ombre, so that before the post goes out I hope to give you a very good account of my self.—I am a good deal better, only dosd and heavy for want of sleep, but I hope a good nights rest will sett me as right again as I can be, till I am restord to my former happiness in your lovd presence, without which no joy, no peace of mind, can be found for your forlorn E.B.   —Wedensday night, nine a clock.—

**637.**   My ever-new Delight          Ickworth, Sept. 6, 1721.

Having nothing to entertain you with but the tedious relations of my goute and greifs, I am afraid of making you as weary of hearing them as I am of bearing them ; my pains are doubly irksome to me, as they for the present prevent the pleasure I had promisd my self of seeing you soon at Bath; and all the abatement I can feel proceeds from reflecting how very much this ungovernable family woud want me had I been in a condition to leave it at the time I intended; for as it is even the bread was left all night in the oven and utterly spoyld, and not so much as a toaste left for me to eat with my chocolate; then the very same night the hounds were lockd up in the kitchin, and broke thro' all the windows, which made such a noise as wakd and frighted Lady Betty so that she concluded thieves were breaking in, and sent Clack to beat up all the family to oppose them. Syer comes daily to me with complaints of the servants hideing more meat (showing me vaste quantities of her finding out) than woud suffice as many more as we now have, telling me she is quite weary of her life amongst them, especially since Will Oliver's sickness, for the four carters have learnd so well of the rest that they require more of all sorts than was ever allowd their predecessors, so that I have given them all warning at Michaelmass, and am resolvd to keep no more, but make my husbandmen do their work, which will be so much savd, beside the ease of having four less in family, which I woud gladly, if possible, retrench to near that number.—I am just now returnd from Barrowbridg, where I waited till twas almost night in expectation of my grandson, but the coachman losing his way (as your son Tom did when I came down) after he was out of Newmarket went in the Norwich road so farr that he never came near Barrow-bridg, (where a servant of mine had attended ever since noon to show them the best and nearest way hither,) but did however gett home above an hour before us, where they did not find one soul of all our numerous family who had either the presence of mind or manners to send a messenger to me to tell me they were safely arrivd, (which I was in great pain for,) so that I might have staid there still for them. The child, thank God, is very well, and so is his nurse. Mrs. Edwards came down with them, and returns to London by the same coach to morrow ; the parents come next week. I have sett up beyond my wonted hour to receive the pleasure of your letters of the second and third instant, which are but now near eleven at night arrivd ; my pains need no augmentation, especially at bed-time; but how much more uneasy am I made by seeing your ex-pectation frustrated as well as my own ? were not my toe still swelling and not near its heigth, (tho' red as scarlett,) and my servants sick, I woud venture being laid up at the Bath rather than be longer from you, which is the greatest expression I can make you. You rightly ask me what con-

Vol. II.    z

sideration in life can be worth the torment we mutually endure ? Why truly
none but your own life, which is become so essentially necessary to my
well-being that I shoud rather choose not to be at all than not to see you
enjoy your health and ease, the two only things coud posibly persuade me
to suffer what I have endurd since yesterday was a month with that submission and resignation that my piety professes, which great as it is, never
had much severer tryals than the present occasion has laid me under, being
more than ever yours, Bristol.

I will see you the first moment I am able.

**638.**    My ever-new Delight                Ickworth, Sept. 8, 1721.
                        I cannot help beginning this with a just reprehen-
sion for your condoleing the loss of Sir David Hamilton in the manner you
do, by saying his was the cheif, nay only assistance you depended on to
recover your ill state of health; since, blessed be God, you have still his
infinite goodness and power to protect you from all harms, if the ferventest
prayer of a sincere penitent can prevaile to preserve your life in health and
happiness, as the only comfort can render the remainder of my own tolerable ;
a truth He so well knows that unless my sins of youth were so numerous and
unpardonable as nothing less than the heavyest chastisement he has to
inflict can expiate, I have the humble confidence to hope his infinite mercy,
in which I thoroughly putt my trust, will prove the surest guard against
every evil your remotest fears can possibly suggest ; on Him therfore depend
as entirely as you know I do, and he will either so order events as that you
shall want no humane help, (which is best,) or send you at least as effectual
an adviser as the person he has thought fitt to deprive you of.   Were it not
for this and my other great principles of submission and resignation to the
wise appointments of his unerring providence, how do you imagine I coud
have borne your absence, my present pain, and the other disappointments

incident to my condition, with that due deference (I hope) I have shewn to whatever he pleases to ordain ? Oh! my dearest disciple, bring but your mind up to the same standard, and every accident shall fall out to your advantage.

> For they shall all their miseries transcend
> Who God adore, and on his will depend.

This was the maxim my dear father and mother constantly professd and practisd throughout their lives, and all things at last succeeded well with them accordingly.—Will Oliver's fate is, I hope, at last determind to a longer life, his feaver having left him now for several days without any symptoms of a return ; but he is yet much too weak to assist me in auditing his last years accompts, which are very long, and I coud wish were ballanced, because there is now another year at Michaelmass to be reckond for, and I dont find that either he or my tenants have near so much mony in their hands as I expected from the slender returns I have receivd from this Suffolke estate for a twelvmonth passd. How it will come out I cannot imagine ; since there has been so little mony laid out lately in lean stock to recruite what is sold or spent in the family, that had not I bought both sheep and bullocks my self within this week, there woud not have been enough for my own use (so farr from selling any), tho' the grass is grown up to the knees all over the Parke.—

Sept. 9. Having sent you word our grandson is here, you will expect an account of his health and behaviour; the latter is so froward whenever his mouth is not stoppd with the bubby, that I cannot think the child feels it self perfectly easy ; the nurse says he was not quite right in order before he left London, so that tis very well he is gott hither, tho' I am made more uneasy (which need not have been) by it, lest any accident shoud happen in its parents absence, who I wonder coud lett him come without them ; but I hear they intend to follow him sooner than I said in my last letter.—The best account I can give you of my self is to be gatherd from the beginning of this letter, and that, next to God, I love you farr above and beyond all other sublunary goods putt together, and hope this fitt will prove so favourable as to suffer me to be soon happy in thy much lovd and longd for company, out of which there is neither joy nor common comfort for yours ever, Bristol.

**639.**   Lady Bristol to Lord Bristol.          Bath, Sept. 9, 1721.

Tis with a most heavy heart I take my pen in hand again, but my joys of Thursday were too great to last; when there came a letter from Jack directed to you here, I opend it with an eager hast, and found my expectation answerd when I saw it was by your orders sent here, and I receivd another at the same time from Mrs. Hervey to wish me joy of your being arrived, a joy indeed too great for me to conceal, for Mr. Nash said my countenance informd them more of your being near at hand than all the bells coud do; to confess the truth I so much depended upon your being here that day that I staid at home till it was dark; when that disappointment was over I made another calculation, which was that you woud receive my letter a Wednesday (in answer to the kind power you gave me), and sett out a Thursday and be here to morrow; this I depended so much upon as to ingage the Dutchess of Wharton to carry me three or four mile upon the Downs to meet you; but alas all those pleasing prospects are vanishd, and even that I could not disguise, for I was asked at the pump what great misfortune had happend to me; sure some unlucky star reigns, or I have been too long happy, and not thankfull enough for it, else fortune woud not frown so long upon me; but I hope my evil genious will not prevail so long as to hinder your being sett out before this can reach you, for sure laying up ones foot in a coach must be easier than a horse for the gout, and the Bath waters are reckond a sovereign remedy taken in the beginning; I wish I coud say they provd so to me; but I am afraid you will be too sensible by my last letter (which I was hardly able to write) they have not yet had great effect upon me, tho I am a good deal better this afternoon; but tis impossible to be quite well without eating or sleeping, both which are grown strangers to me. I intend to write to Dr. Freind to night when I come from the Play, (where I am going with the Dutchess of Queensbourrough, Lady Draugheda bespeaks it;) but I dispair of any phycisian till I am blessd again with your much lovd presence, without which no joy nor comfort in life can be found for your poor E. Bristol.

Mrs. Meggott, I think, is in an ill state of health; she is very ill at this time. I hope dear little George is safe arrived; his father and mother are at Mr. Pultneys. Pegg is very busy answering a very diverting letter of Jacks to her, els I woud have got her to write Betty some Bath adventures, which are inumerable.

640. My ever-new Delight          Ickworth, Sept. 11, 1721.

The game of ombre never afforded you half the pleasure, ever since your acquaintance with it, as the name of it only gave me in your last letter; for had not the description you made me of your disorder concluded with that party you mentiond to play at ombre the same night, I must e'en have venturd to come in the place of this, (which I am sure you woud not have chosen, and therfore I determind accordingly,) tho' I am less fitt than ever to undertake such a journey, my gouty humour being not only in its former place, but also in the middle finger of my left hand, and in my neck and shoulders; these being the parts where I have felt pain before may be easily accounted for; but this fitt has attackd me in a new limb on the other side of my body, my right knee after sitting still to dine, supp or write being so weak and full of pain I cannot rise up from my chair without the assistance of my hands upon a table or my cane. This being the truth of my condition, I know you woud have been much more concernd to have been the occasion of my travelling in pain for so many days as it must have taken to gett to you, (for I coud have made but very short stages,) & after that, it may be, to have been laid up at Bath beyond your intended stay, or at best to have had such another expedition to gett home again in a fortnight, than you coud have been pleasd to see me on such terms and in such circumstances, whatever I might have been to see thy sweet eyes and be entertaind with thy kind conversation. If I have misjudgd this case, my tenderness towards you, not my self, led me into it.—How coud you, who are at Bath upon no other account but to lay in a lasting stock of health for my peace-sake as well as your own and your children's benefitt, think of exposing your self to such hazards of getting heats and colds only for a party of pleasure? Sure much greater than you coud possibly meet with in any such (I guess from my own experience) must fall very short of compensating for those mutual pains the consequences have cost us, the bare relation of them having exceeded those of my goute, which (to make you some return for your mentioning the ombre party you were ingagd to) seem to sitt on me in such a manner as I fancy one hours sight of and talk with thee woud charm them all into ease and health. However, to be sure of both those, I woud not have them purchasd by your leaving the waters a day sooner than they can have administerd all in their power to secure both those and every thing else that's good and safe for thy dear self. Our grandson is so wonderfully alterd for the better, both as to his looks and humour, since he came hither as is not to be imagind; it seems he was uneasy by being bound in his body, which was releivd by his taking oyl of sweet almonds and syrop of violetts, since which he has thriven prodigiously, and was in so good humour yesterday that he laughd near half an hour incessantly. Betty writes her self by this nights post to Mrs. Bradshaw, to whom I hope you never faile making my compliments, tho' I cant help saying I have never been able to love her half so well as I usd to do, since she, tho' but in jest, dard to prophane so sacred a thing as your conduct in your faithfull friends absence. Woud to God all my other pains and grievances were reducd to that one head, for then my heart woud be at rest, which for five weeks past it hath been an utter stranger to, and will be so till your next letter says you have had no return of your illness, and that I shall see you as soon as consistent with your cure. Adieu, yours, Bristol.

**641.    Lady Bristol to Lord Bristol.          Bath, Sept. 11, 1721.**

I never thought till now I shoud have cause to repent my sincerity, but indeed I do most heartily; for shoud the repeated instances of my impatience to see you bring you but one day sooner than will be easy under your present circumstances, or make you suffer a moments pain the more, good God, how coud I bear it! it woud be such an allay to that vaste happiness as my poor drooping spirits coud hardly bear; but I will not tell you in how bad a state they are; I rather wish I coud call back my two last letters again, for fear I have said or (by my writing) shewd too much, without I coud tell you I were mended, which I cant say, tho' I have not kept the house since Wedensday, for my doctor orders me to be abroad when I can crawl, and not to be alone a minute, which is an unnecessary prescription, for whenever I am missd this little city is in an uproar, so much am I in fashion; this is a great bait to the general vanity of our sex, and might prove so to me, were not my heart, soul and body immoveably fixd to one dear, dear object, without which no other joy or comfort is to be found for your poor disconsolate but ever faith-full E. Bristol.——I dont know if your commands woud prevail upon me to shorten my letter so much, if I had not lately found such ill effects from writing as to be expressly forbid either that or reading. Mrs. Meggott is better, and dines with me to day, which she does as often as I eat at home ; she and Pegg send their compliments to you. You say nothing of my grandson's beauty; sure he must be pretty.

**642.**    My ever-new Delight                    Ickworth, Sept. 13, 1721.
My inability to gett to you, joynd to the uncertainty I have livd under ever since Sunday night concerning your own well-being, (which I expect with the utmost impatience to be confirmd by this nights post,) have together putt my principles and patience to their last proof; but as I rightly conclude both coud never have happend at the same time unless designd as one of the severest tryals, so have I endeavourd, as farr as humane frailty is capable of, to deserve a favourable issue out of all my present anxieties by a becoming submission to the Divine will, which has thought fitt to order things thus, and to waite with an assured hope a good event out of all those evils which now seem to besett me. As to my own ailes, they depend in so great a measure upon hearing how you are, that till your letter comes I am not able to give you any just or good account of them ; my pains are doubtless greater during the suspension I am in with relation to your own ; were I sure you had felt no returns of those disorders your last complaind of, I coud bear mine with more philosophy ; but to live in doubt where one dotes so much as I do is almost as cruel a torment in my case and sence as poor Othello felt in another. To leave you in none about us here I can tell you the good news, God be thankd, that all our children have escapd this epidemick feaver, tho' my other footman is now taken ill with it, as well as Larner and his wife. Lady Cullum left my house ; I yesterday made a tender of it (by letter) to the Mildenal family, (not thinking to be at Bury Fair my self,) but twas refused with many thanks, they being ingagd elswhere.—Tis now later by an hour than I have yet sett up since

I had the happiness to be with you, and yet the messenger not returnd who went for the letters ; did not my pains and humours, which are flying about me and make me more than usually uneasy, admonish me to bed-ward, I woud yet stay up to expect them, knowing I cannot sleep for want of them.—

I was just going into my bed (past midnight) when your letter was brought me; I have putt on my stockings again to thank you for the welcome circumstance you have again acquainted me with of being well enough to go to a play, (for sure one cannot aile much and do that,) but on the other hand you must not wonder that the waters have wrought no thorough cure in all this time, since they have plays, Harrisons, Hazard, balls, and other country-partys and assemblies to struggle with, besides your other infirmities. You woud stand more corrected did you feel the pains of yours ever, Bristol.

Dear Nann desires (with her duty) to know if you will give leave to have her red and white tabby made up.

**643.** Lady Bristol to Lord Bristol. Bath, Sept 13, 1721.

Its better I shoud loose a letter than you be disappointed in the want of one, tho' I am fully perswaded you will have left Ickworth before this can reach you. Pray God send you a good journey, and that you may have no relapse by your venturing to soon; for if you shoud my poor unsettled brain woud be quite turnd ; tis almost so already by hearing such repetitions of troubles that you (my poor dear angel) have undergone of all kinds, as if such a cruel absence were not enough of it self ; I am sure I find it so, not that I have not my little greivances too, but they are all lost in that one great one. I am sorry to find Betty no better an assistant to you within doors, since you have so much upon your hands without by Will Oliver's illness ; but I hope by this time that is quite over, and your troubles lessend ; may they be so in every circumstance in life, and all your joys increase ; coud I but make them so, I were too happy ;

Vol. II. AA

yet I am sure I shall help towards it when I tell you I am something better, and that it is not any irregularity that has ever putt me out of order, for I am very strict both in diett and hours ; and for play there has not been temptation enough to make me transgress, tho' they are always so complaisant to play at Dames whenever I please, which has made it very bad for Harrison, for till last week (that I did not play much) he has had very little to do, tho' he has the Groom Porter and several of the deep gamesters arrived.  Banester I hear lost £300 t'other night at Pharon ; Mr. Nash is complaining according to custom ; a farther account of the Bath cannot entertain you, because most of the people are new to you, but some of them are very agreeable and what you will like, and the rest that are not so I have withdrawn from, that you may meet with nothing unpleasant when you arrive to your impatient faithfull wife.

I have sent you a ballad made by or for the Duke of Wharton at York. Bradshaw says she is much your servant, tho' almost dead with the headach.

**644.**      My ever-new Delight            Ickworth, Sept. 16, 1721.

It was so very late before your letter was brought to me on Wednesday night, that I had not half time or room enough in mine to expostulate with you on your going to Plays and Assemblies again, or setting at hazard in Harrisons stove, which I know from former woeful experience have constantly frustrated all or most of the good effects to be expected from a regular use of the Bath waters.  Did not I earnestly desire you woud not embark in any of them ?  Did not you kindly assure me you woud carefully avoid the former, and reason with me as if you coud not well enter into the latter when I was not there ?  Did not I solemnly conjure you to venture upon no one experiment which coud possibly retard or diminish the full efficacy of them ? knowing what I was still to suffer if your cure was but doubtfully delayd, and more inexpressibly wretched yet if finally disappointed. Coud I have given my self leave to tell you what bodily smart I have endurd in my foot, fingers, neck and knees, besides the keener anguish of my mind in their preventing the pleasure of my seeing you as I designd, you woud never have augmented both by letting me see my sufferings, great as they are and have been, may possibly end at last in having done no service to your health ; without the promising prospect of which most desirable blessing, God is my witness I woud not pass through the pains I have felt for six weeks of all sorts (but more especially those at and after our parting) for any other consideration in life. How then coud you find in your heart (mine woud never have done so) to run the least risque of meeting with any putt-backs in the progress of your medicines, since they must of course prolong the miseries I live under till your return ? Surely the virtues of that mineral are unavailable in your case, or your method of treating your self in the taking of them must be destructive of the benefit other people receive from them, since now by your own confession after so long a tryal you cannot say you are mended. O blasting news to all my hopes! O sad return for all my sorrows, which have already exceeded the price of most things but your recovery; and that not being yet begun, when are my troubles to have an end ? Must the grave alone releive me ? Gods will be done. Your last account of my neice Meggott was so melancholy a one, that I can find just spiritts enough to say I am glad for her poor childrens sake she is better, knowing by our own how much the temporary want only of a mother turns to their disadvantage. Little George is so well and thriven since he came, that that epithet will not long suite him ; as to his beauty, I have been so accustomd to contemplate the exact symetry of those features your miraculous mould has produced, that nothing now but an angel can surprise me enough to mention it particularly. His parents will be here on Wednesday; my coach is to meet them at Newport; they woud have been so mad and unadvisd as to come through in a day, if not prevented by the greater prudence of their parent, and your faithful disconsolate husband, Bristol.

**645.**    Lady Bristol to Lord Bristol.        Bath, Sept. 16, 1721.

O my dear, dear angel, what a cruel letter have you sent me; it has made me almost distracted; I dont know what to say or do ; to have all those pleasing hopes the last post brought me of seeing you soon, vanishd, and nothing but pain and misery in body and mind in its stead, tho' had your pain of the goute been a little more favourable and not prevented your journey, I cant but say I shoud have been glad of it, as I think it a means to keep you from all other distempers, and to preserve a life so essential to all the happiness of mine, nay, without which I can never know or tast any pleasure in life ; but alas, my distemper is of another kind, for the terrours of mind it gives me creates me many more, and gives me fresh occasion every day to regrett the loss of poor Sir David, for I have been wakd every morning for this fortnight past in great pain with my old complaint, except yesterday (that I took laudanum the night before) that I was so well that I begun to think I might receive the constant benefit I have always had from these waters ; but alas, it was but a lightening before death, for sure I am as near it to day as any thing can be that breaths and stalks about; and to expose my wretched state the more I did not receive your letter this morning till I was at the Pump, and then I misbehavd so that I was forced to gett Mrs. Cook to go into a corner with me behind the door, as if we had a secret, for my tears flowd so fast that I coud not (till I had vented a little) gett into my chair to come home, where I gave a loose to all my griefs, which are sure beyond compare, and have putt me into such a condition of mind that, as I am now, I can never hope for any good

from being here ; therfore beg you woud send the coach away as soon as
you receive this, if God Almighty is not mercifull enough to me to hear my
prayers and grant you ease and strength to perform a journey hither, which
I much wish, because every body that has skill in these waters say that
drinking them after a fitt will make the next more favourable, and very
likely secure you for the winter.  Pray God direct you to do the best for
your self, whatever becomes of your poor, disconsolate E. Bristol.

All dear Nanns requests are so reasonable that cant fail of being granted.
I wish it were as easy to do what Betty desires, but I much fear it will be
impossible, for Mary Bragg that makes the finest laces is just gone away.

**646.**    My ever-new Delight              Ickworth, Sept. 18, 1721.
                        It being to morrow six weeks since I had the
happiness of seeing you, and Dr. Pake telling me that the Bath waters
either do their work in that time or not at-all, (and you know Dr. Mead
allows him to be as good a judg as himself,) I think it high time for me to
undeceive you in the expectation of my coming to you, since I have been
all along wholly unable to take such a journey ; my living the last year
round in London has filled my bloud so full of peccant humours and
brought pains upon me in so many places, that I am very sure you woud
not have me think of travelling under the apprehension of increasing them,
and of being laid up all the winter at Bath, the place of all the world, you
know, I have ever felt an utter aversion for from my first acquaintance with
it ; so farr am I from being fitt for such a removal, that I have resolvd to
go into a course of taking the tincture of rheubarb as soon as my swellings
in my foot and finger, and the pain in my right knee, are abated ; you may
see by this submission of mine to any physick how much I stand corrected
by what I have lately felt, and how I dread any return.  Lett not any
thing I have said hasten yours one moment, if you think it will add one to

your life; mine is so essentially bound up with yours, that if I cannot live
I must dye with you; therfore for my preservation-sake take care of your
own.  If this severe seperation is not to be repaid me by the lengthening
of your daies, then have I passd many wakeful dismal nights in vain, for
even my dreams are disagreeable of late, (but yours it seems are otherwise,)
so very allarming and unwelcome that I am glad to find they are but dreams;
sure I was in one, if ever I let fall any expression that lookd as if Betty had
not done every thing on her part to take off all the trouble from me she was
able within doors; she is, I thank God, every thing I can wish her in the
fundemental principles of piety, strict honour and virtue ; and if she recovers perfect health,(which she is now more likely to do than ever I thought
almost possible but by omnipotence,) will certainly make the most valuable
woman by farr of all the rising generation.  May none but such proceed
from my loins, who will prove blessings (and not curses) in the families they
are destind for ; and shoud they not become so, how strangely must they
degenerate from the dear stock that bore them.  Thorns can never come
from such a rose-tree, nor thistles from the figg ; for this I have the authority
of divine writt, and the earnest of an almost divine creature.  Having made
all the search I coud before I left London after Mr. Bannister to pay him
fivety guineas I owe him, and written twice since to Mr. Skelton that he
woud send me word where he lodgd, that I might order my goldsmith to
attend him with it, but all without effect, I must desire you (hearing he is
at Bath) to write him a note for it upon my goldsmiths, Messrs Nicholls and
Fowler, who shall by this nights post receive direction from me to answer
it at sight.—The news of your being better has effectually made good what
you rightly judgd it woud bring to pass in me ; for it has both lessend my
troubles and increasd my joys ; God only knows, or shall know, besides my
self how seasonable any releif of that kind was to my mind, for love roves
restless in fond enquiries, suggesting ten thousand dangers, nor will beleive

its object ever safe or well enough.

The character of mine in this appears,
Quick to presage, and even in safety fears.

which I hope God will forgive, as a fault not ever to be overcome as it ought
by the enamourd heart of your Bristol.

**647.** Lady Bristol to Lord Bristol. Bath, Sept. 18, 1721.

Sure my last letter enough expressd my miserable
condition not to fail of haveing the coach sett out full or empty the first
minute you receivd it; in that hope alone I subsist, I cannot call it living,
for I can solemnly swear I have not known a moments ease since Saturday
morning that I receivd that cruel letter; this to day has made the full
measure run over; it has given occasion for a very just remark here of the
difference of wives; for as I walk about like a discontented shade for want
of my kind (and everlastingly pleasing) companion, so has another lady
expressd (if that were possible) as much sorrow for the arrival of her
husband last night.

So have I seen the lost clouds pour
Into the sea a fruitless show'r,
And the rude sailor curse that rain,
For which poor shepherds pray in vain.

These lines were never more applicable than now; see therfore how
partial is fate, to give the same thing to one as the greatest curse, and deny
it to another where it woud be esteemd the greatest blessing; in this
scituation of mind I beleive it will be needless to tell you my body is much
out of order too, because in my case one depends so much upon the other,
which made me always fear this unhappy journey (without my dear and

cheif comfort in life) coud never answer the expectations the doctors had of
it, and so it has provd, for I was extreamly bad this morning with my old
complaint, but being my bathing day I hàve been pretty easy ever since ;
and to make you so concerning any irregularity of mine, I must assure you
I am much the most regular of any body at the Bath ; as to hours, I always
sup at nine, whether at home or abroad, and to bed at eleven ; as to Harrisons, I am surprisd you name that, since you know by your own commands
(which are sacred to me) I never play there, nor have not been in his house
an hour at a time (even at balls or breakfasts) since I came; the company
is so complaisant to me that they play where I please, notwithstanding the
Groom-porter is at Harrisons ; but I seldom play at dice but in the
morning, and then the room is never hott ; and for plays, there is hardly
ever company enough to make it warm ; as for my country party, (which
was but once,) I took it by way of physick rather than pleasure. I think
now I have answerd all my accusations ; I wish you coud as well, or had
been half so discreet; then we had not been both so miserable at this
time ; for I cant but think this severe fitt is oweing to so much champaign
and Burgundy as you drank last winter ; but, however, by this time I hope
it may be over, that I may see you here, and not be under the necessity of
taking two journeys between this and the sixteenth of October, when I go
into waiting ; not but that I will certainly do it, if I can see you upon no
other terms ; for to be plain, I am not able to bear it any longer and keep
my sences ; tis the severest tryal I ever had in my life, or hope ever shall
again. O my dear, dear angel, woud I were inspird with some of your
wise precepts to enable me to bear the remainder of this cruel absence,
which tho' it may seem short to indifferent people, tis an age to love and
impatience like that which can only be felt by your ever faithful E. Bristol.

Tis impossible I can take a journey next week, which I never reflected on
till this minute, to add to my wretchedness.

**648.** My ever-new Delight                    Ickworth, Sept. 20, 1721.

Were not the world grown weary of wisdom, truth and all the lovely traine of virtues, I shoud be proudly pleasd to hear my friend was most in fashion ; but as vice and folly are much more the present mode than the contrary qualities which distinguish and adorn my chosen one, I think she rather prejudicd than praisd her self when she acknowledgd she was in vogue. I woud have all admire & revere those rare and valuable endowments you possess ; but alass ! they can be truly fond of nothing but what administers either to their sordid interest or sensual pleasures ; of which sort I am afraid you'l find your new acquaintance you desird me to pump Tom about, who, notwithstanding his natural dry reservedness, has said enough to make me aprehend there is neither safety nor creditt to be gaind by her company ; a little of your lover's cautious coldness in the choice of his associates you'l find hereafter to be of use to you in the adoption of your own ; but since your friendship has been contracted, you must contrive not to rend it asunder all at once abruptly, but let it gradually unripp, and in a manner unperceivable, lest the wounds of such a friend become after-wards more greivous than an enemy coud find creditt enough to fix upon you, shoud she feel her self neglected or suspected by you. Were you of my mind, you woud find so much pleasure in cherishing and frequenting your old tryd friends, you coud never care to seek out or admitt new ones.— Your son and his wife are both well arrivd here, which she woud never have been had not I prevented their coming thro' in a day, as their wise young heads had otherwise projected. They found their son so much thriven in the fortnight they had been from him that they scarce knew him, both for bulk and beauty. But this sweet air has wrought yet greater wonders on a poor footman they sent down with him, who was dying of an astma, yet this day at dinner told me he was already as well as ever he was in his life. I wish it were in my power to say the same of it in my own case ; but alass !

Vol. II.    BB

the seeds of those distempers which so long a lazy London life had sown in my bloud are lately risen up into too rank a cropp to be soon or easily subdued. I dont expect my pains shoud cease but with your absence; yet as your health depends upon the cure of mine, be sure you sacrifice not one day of your life towards it, even for the sake of your second self and sufferer, Bristol.

**649.**    Lady Bristol to Lord Bristol.        Bath, Sept. 20, 1721.

Notwithstanding all the regularity I boasted of, I can send you nothing but complaints; for I have been very bad again with my hysterick disorder after I writ my last letter, which I beleive you will not wonder at, when you see by it the distraction of mind I was then in, and am likely to continue so, if to morrows post does not bring me some comfort; pray God send it for both our sakes, that I may be easd in my mind, and you in your body, which sure if you are, you will not loose a moment to bless me with your dear and much longd for presence; so much longd for that sure I shall dye with joy once more to behold you. O what woud I not give this were the happy minute; for I do love you beyond expression farr more than ever (if that be possible); I was made sensible this morning in a dream what I might suffer by to morrows post; for I dreamd you were worse, and putt my self into such a passion of crying that I have not been able to recover it all the day, tho' I have had a good deal of company to dine with me, which I beleive you will think pretty necessary, (tho' 1 have a very bad cook,) when I tell you I have eat but one meal at home before this this week, so very charitable and kind to me are the most agreeable people in this place; and as the greatest compliment can be made to me, your health is constantly drank. I wish I coud tell you any news to entertain you, but really I cant, tho' the town is as full as possible, but such a mixture as was never got together at the building of Babel; yet one peice of news I must not forgett, which is that I threw fifteen mains yesterday morning, and I got but fivety pound by it; Mr. Nash said he had a great mind to write you word of it ; here is very deep play ; Mr. Stanup has improvd it since he came ; Nash lost fivety pound a Saturday at Harrisons, and as they say broke all the windows according to custom. There is several parties of ladys and gentlemen gone to Bristol to see a review, and General White- man is to give a ball there; I had the honour to be invited, but I neither likd my company, nor was fitt for such an expedition, if I had. To morrow I am to begin pumping by Doctor Freinds directions, which I shall follow in that particular, tho' not in his orders to continue in this cursed place longer than till I can gett a conveyance to carry me off, which I am sure you will not lett me be long without, if you feel half the torments I endure by my stay ; either come or send for me, for I am not able to bear it any longer ; I am wretched beyond expression, and shall not have an eye left in a little while to make my complaints to you ; I can bear no more ; adieu, my life.—My Lord Radner bids me tell you that these waters will certainly cure you, as he knows by experience; therfore hopes you will come for your own sake as well as mine, else I shall make them loose their creditt.

**650.**    My ever-new Delight                Ickworth, Sept. 23, 1721.

After having most devoutly beggd of Gods good- ness that he woud mercifully direct me to determine what woud prove best for both of us in the present exigence, I have resolvd at last (considering all things) to send the coach instead of venturing in it, as I more than once found my self strongly tempted to have done ; but reflecting how much more uneasyness than satisfaction you woud have found in my company, had the journey disorderd me so (as probably it must have done) that I coud not have gott home again before the winter, I thought it better to putt it alwaies in your power to come away whenever you found the waters had

done you their utmost service, (which I desire you woud take the best
advice upon,) for till we are assurd of that, I charge and conjure you, nay
require and insist upon it, as you tender my quiet, that you do not think of
leaving them, tho' God knows I long more to see you than the blind do for
sight, or the condemnd for a repreive ; yet shoud I ever be able to tax my
self hereafter with having purchasd my pleasure with your pain, it woud
make me miserable without redemption. O ! what exquisite torments woud
arise from the least suspicion only that I had any way been the fatal cause
of shortening thy daies for my sake ! The aprehension only of such a mis-
cheif, tho' never so remote, gives me present pains, even exceeding those of
my goute, tho' attacking me in many places at once ; therfore once more I
beseech you think not of coming till your health is wholly established.

651.    Lady Bristol to Lord Bristol.        Bath, Sept. 22, 1721.
        Was not the measure of my woes full enough
before but that you must give such addition ás to make them run over ? O
my unkind and cruel dear, (is it possible I shoud ever live to call you so,)
but even that I must bear as a weighty addition to all my other misfortunes;
how coud you break the bruised reed by laying all the blame of my ill
success in the waters to my conduct, which never kept so strictly to rules
in any journey I ever made to this place, nor never mett with so ill success ;
but that is so easy to account for, that even Mr. Skreen (with his little
acquaintance) coud tell me to day that except I coud be easier in my
mind, it was impossible I shoud receive any benefit from the waters,
therfore hopd I woud never come again without you ; see how soon I
am found out ; but my plain and honest heart is incapable of a disguise ;
woud you had a window to it, to see with what a tender passion you are
belovd ; sure none ever lovd like me, nor none ever had so worthy an
object.—I begun pumping yesterday (as I told you in my last), but I was
so ill with it, I was afraid I shoud have been quite laid up; for besides

giving me a fitt of the cholick, it set my blood and all my spirits into such a firment, that I thought it woud have putt me in a feaver, so that I must be forced to think no more of it, but continue lame rather than hazard my life, which is farr dearer to me since your kindness putts such a value upon it, and flatters the only pleasure I have in it, which is to make you happy; may that never have an end but in the grave; nay, after death (if possible) let our souls be united as our hearts are now.—

Sept. 23. Thus farr I writ yesterday, for fear bathing to day might putt it out of my power, but thank God it has not disorderd me in the least; I beleive it was your kind letter which I receivd in the Bath kept up my spirits, tho' it was a great allay to the pleasure to find by it I must not (nay coud not) hope to see you here; and a yet greater to hear how much pain and misery you have sufferd in body and mind; so much that I dare not give you the addition of a full description of mine; if I did, you woud find I was not in the least behind hand with you in my distresses either of body or mind; I hope you have not let me into yours without sending me a releif for both of us, I mean the coach, which I am afraid the going to meet Jack and his lady may have hindred for some days, till I shall not dare to venture without running the risk of being laid up upon the road. I wish it were here now; then I woud take the first minute to end all my sorrows in your lovd arms; till I can there is no rest, no peace of mind, for poor E.B.

I have obeyd your commands to Mr. Banester, and writ a note payable to him or his order, as he desird. Sure you wont be tempted to Bury-fair. Pray make my compliments and excuse to Mrs. Hervey that I dont write; indeed its impossible.

Bath, Sept. 25, 1721.

652.   Lady Bristol to Lord Bristol.      Dear Harriotts Birth-day.

May she live many, many happy years, and with mine all other blessings ever surround her; and as the cheif, may she have a husband as partially kind to her as her dear father is to me, and (if possible) be as doatingly fond as I am of him; then she will be as happy as I can wish her, or this world can make her. The day will have great honours done it, for Stanup gives a ball and a great entertainment, and desires Harriott may be told it is for her; it has been putt off for some days to perswade me to be Queen of it, which I woud by no means accept of, knowing with my general acquaintance, and so many relations here, I shoud disoblige more than I coud oblige, without making it a publick instead of a private ball; besides that, I never dance but in my own dominions; tho' if you were to see me here, you woud conclude this were so, I am so absolute a Princess.—Thus farr I writ before eight a clock that I begun my waters; for I was wakd with the bells (which are the plague of my life) between six and seven; it happend very unlucky to day, it has given me the head-ach prodigiously, for I took laudanum last night by way of prevention, for I venturd again to the Pump last night, but it was the dry Pump without bathing, which did not heat me in the least, nor give me the cholick, so that I intend to keep to that method as long as I am confind to this hated place, which I hope you will not let me be longer in then the coach must be coming after you receivd my letter for that purpose, which I reckond woud be with you last Wensday, and that I might have an answer to it this morning when it woud be here, which makes me surprisd you say nothing of it in your letter; and to make that and every other disappoint-ment feel greater, you dont (or I fear cant) tell me you are better; think, O think, my dear, what I suffer under these uneasy circumstances, and for God sake give me my release as soon as possible; I really think if I dont see the coach or hear tis coming by Thursdays post, I shall send for the next sett of able horses (with a good coachman) that is cried about the streets, such is the impatience of my aching heart to be with the only center of rest for E. Bristol.

I have sent to Mrs Howard to see if I can get a week changd to lengthen out my time at Ickworth.—This more than ordinary nonsense and ill spelling will I hope be taken for the laudanum that is still in my head.

**653.**    Lady Bristol to Lord Bristol.        Richmond, June 5, 1722.

The condition I saw you in at parting has left me upon the rack ever since, that I cant be satisfied with the common answer (I have every day) that you are very well, without having it under your own that you are so, or at least better; if any thing in my power can contribute to your ease, I shall think my self most happy (at present I am very much otherwise); in order to it I had a thought which I shoud think woud make the taking up money upon my estate very easy ; you know I have a power by the settlement to raise three thousand pounds, which I conclude may be done without the trustees with your consent and mine together, and your note to me for it will be all that I shall desire, or if it were never to be repaid; if it can make you easy under your present circumstances, I shall think it but a small return for all the happiness you have bestowed upon, my dear angel, your most faithful and affectionate wife, E. Bristol.

I hope my Lord Hervey has told you that Lord Cadogan said on Sunday at Court to me that he hopd Harry's business might be done in a fortnight or three weeks, which makes the more haste necessary in the other affair. My Lady Grantham will wait for me if I let her know the night before you woud have me come.

London, June 5, 1722.
**654.**        36 years since the death of my dear & excellent mother.

Having yet made no farther progress in the business which keeps me here than to know by trying others without success that I must at last putt my self into Gibson's hands, this comes te lett you know you need not think of troubling your self to come hither, nor of being obligd to Lady G. to wait for you, till you hear from me matters are much more ready for your execution. In the mean time lett me contentedly continue in that strict course of humiliation and mortification which Providence by such a series of degouts and disappointments seems to have ordaind for me towards this declension of my daies, to expiate for the sins and follies of my heedless youth; and if a submissive resignation to Gods wiser will can effect the errand they are sent upon, I shall bless the dispensation, however harsh to humane nature, which will at last enable me on any terms to enjoy his ravishing perfections thro' endless eternity, a state which tho' doubtless perfect in its self, yet till I can throw off this mortal coyle, can neer conceive how it can prove intirely so without you; therfore as the best thing can happen for us both, I intreat you to loose no opportunity of securing your title to it betimes, which was alwaies the friendlyest, and now the most passionate advice can come from your once most happy husband.

**655.** Lady Bristol to Lord Bristol. Richmond, June 7, 1722.

Your dear letters, that always used to releive my drooping spirits, found a far different effect from that yesterday. The melancholy stile you writ in, added to what I felt at parting with you in that condition, made the measure of my woes quite run over, which has sunk my spirits so to day that nothing but the seeing you can releive me, which I sent to desire yesterday by Mrs. Howard, (I coud not write, for she rose from table to go away ;) however, I hope this will come time enough to tell you I shall be at Kingsinton about seven a clock this evening, and if you will come to the gate and send for me out, I may have an hour or two to air with you in the coach while the Princess is there ; and to make me more welcome will bring Felly with me. I am sure the airing will do you so much good, that I will venture to say, if you dont come, it will be the last disappointment to your faithful E. Bristol.

I shall be at the young Princesses lodgings; if any thing hinders our going, you shall be sure to hear it.

**656.** London, June 7, 1722.

I had no sooner orderd my coach and horses to have mett you at Kinsington, (since you desird it so earnestly, tho' no proper rendezvous for me,) but I receivd a mortifying message by Lord Scarborough's servant that you coud not come. I have been of late so much accustomd to disappointments of all kinds, that I shall ere long find it one, I beleive, shoud any thing hereafter happen according to my wishes. One welcome experiment, however, has been repeated by this last, which is that tho' I have been weaning my self with the utmost industry from the world and most things in it, yet I cant but feel the sight of you and being in your society must and will be the cheif and last desire that is to live in the heart of your once most happy husband.

**657.** Lady Bristol to Lord Bristol. Richmond, June 8, 1722.

If you had felt half the disappointment I had in not seeing you yesterday, you woud have come to day and told me so your self rather then by a messenger ; it is much wonderd at here that you have been so long absent, (what then must I feel ;) business cant take up every day and hour, and I still hope your cheifest pleasure is here. The Princess came to my bed side this morning at a little after eight when I was fast a sleep ; she opend my curtains and endeavourd to make me beleive it was you. Recompence me for the disappointment, and let me see you to morrow if you can ; Sundays you know is a late day, because we go to Kinsengton

Vol. II.     cc

to Church, and Monday the Prince dines at the Camp.—I am calld to the Princess, and shant have another moment till the afternoon, so must bid my dear dear Adieu.

**658.**   Dear double heiress                    London, June 15, 1722.

Your requests to me at parting, (which as it always seems a sort of death to me I pay a most religious regard to,) being not only to take care but to send you an account of your late second providential windfall, this comes to lett you see I have used all diligence to satisfy your desires, and have in the first place carefully perused the pedigree of your family, and do find that your grandfather, James Earl of Suffolk, being the eldest son of Theophilus the common ancestor, Mrs. Giffords ancestor being one of the younger sons of the said Theophilus, as was also the present Earl of Berkshire's, Mr. Griffin & your self are undoubted heirs at law, not only to the estate Mrs. Gifford dyed possessd of amounting to near £900 per annum, but also to Mrs. Minshuls sisters joynture of above £600 per annum, (who is the widow of Henry, who was the elder brother of Robert Howard, grandfather to the late Mrs. Gifford,) when that falls. Mr. Webb of Grays Inn, being council both to Mrs. Giffords husband and your cousin Griffin, is very lucky, (as may all things else happen wherever you or yours are concernd,) for I gott him to write last night both to Mr. Griffin and Mr. Gifford ; to the former, desiring him to impower some person to concurr with me in speedy measures to make entries, that so, tho' Lord Berkshire may have gott possession, yet he may account for the mean profitts whenever evicted ; and to the latter, that he woud advise his late tenants not to attorn to Lord Berkshire or any other person, till we can satisfy them of our having the only good title to the lands in question, which in case there have been no mean entailes will not be hard to do. Mr. Webb tells me he knows of none, neither does he beleive there are any ; she was not above 18 years of age at her death, had been marryed but two years, and dyed of a consumption, having never had any children.  Shouldst thou thus miraculously (in a manner) succeed to this remote, collateral, unexpected estate, twould seem as if thy good grandfather, who lovd thee so affectionately, now knowing how ungratefully his widow had dealt by thee, has been applying to the Sovereign Disposer of all things to compensate what Lady Charlotte Montaigue has run away with of his from his deserving grand daughter and her numerous nursery by a most remarkable equivalent.  Be this as it will, I must say beforehand I cannot adore Gods goodness nor love you more than I did, and my strict fidelity towards you can claim no share in this good fortune, because that has been one of those virtues which has provd its own most abundant reward to your most happy husband, Bristol.

659.    Lady Bristol to Lord Bristol.*    Richmond, Friday morning.

The joy and satisfaction I had on Wensday in being with the center of all my happiness woud not be grudgd me by the worst enemy I had, if it were possible to be known what I sufferd when I was parted from you ; we did not speak (hardly) a single word all the way we came ; I fancy the two virgins had some secret inclination left behind, els they coud not so far have sympathizd with me for my known one ; and for my further mortification since I came here, I am advisd by my privy councellers not to think of going away on Sunday, and I beleive you woud be of the same opinion, if I had time to tell you all the reasons they give me ; but what I hope will be some comfort to you, Felly will dine with you on Sunday ; Lord Gage has promisd to carry him from Court, and nothing can hinder our meeting on Monday morning, for if you find your self not

---

*It is not clear whether this and the two next letters, all undated, are the last of the June batch or the first of the following August batch.—S.H.A.H.

disposed to take a hott dusty journey hither, you have but to send the coach for me, to be here between nine and ten a clock, and I will make your excuse of business, which you may easily pretend, for Mr. Grey (who was here with his lady to day) says we are certainly to have this estate, and he will come to Town on Tuesday to talk with you about it; Mr. Cliffen was also here to day, and says he shall be able to give you a particular account to morrow, and he will endeavour to find you. I am forced to finish this with my room full of company, therfore cant say so much as I woud do, but beg you woud let me know as soon as you can whether you send or come for me on Monday, that I may order my affairs accordingly, for I woud not be dressd before I come to Town, if I dont dine here first. I cant ask you to lye here on Sunday for many reasons, I will tell you when we meet. Adieu, my dear.

660.                                        London, Saturday evening.

My letter being seald before the receipt of yours, I sent you word by the bearer, (who tells me he told Matt so, not being able to speak to you himself,) that I was not sure whether your business or my own might not prevent my coming with the coach on Munday morning as I intend; but that in all events it shoud not faile of being there at the time you mentiond either with or without your most faithful Bristol.

Can there be no way of my seeing you to morrow at Kinsington? I'm quite forlorn when without you.

661.    Lady Bristol to Lord Bristol.

I find no answer to my letter of last night by Mr. Young, which makes me in pain you have not receivd it; I was called to the Princess before I coud finish it in the morning; I desird you woud let me know what you intend to do on Munday morning, whether you will

dine here or send for me ; if the last, I desire it may be early in the morning, for I woud not dress me till I come to Town. Jack is here, and woud
fain perswade me to dine at Mrs. Pultneys. I shall expect your directions
by the footman I will order to call at night ; or if that failes, you may write
by Mr. Cornwallis that meets us at Kinsington in the morning. Dont disappoint me in that, for I am enough so in not being able to say half what
I woud do now, for Mrs. Berkley and Mrs. Dives are come into my room,
and I expect every minute to be (I am) calld to the Princess.

Ickworth near Bury,

662.   To the Earl of Berkshire.                          June 30, 1722.

My Lord
I think my self obliged to take ye very first
opportunity of sending your Lordship my wifes and my own acknowledgments for ye favour of your Lordships letter, which has in every point
confirmd ye justice we had already done your Lordship in beleiving that,
as soon as you shoud be rightly informd of ye true state of our title, we
shoud need no other advocate with your Lordship than your own known
honour to quit ye possession as you have done to, my Lord, your Lordships
most obliged & most obedient servant, Bristol.

Ickworth near Bury,

663.   To the Honble Mr. Griffin.                          June 30, 1722.

In  pursuance of ye promise I made both to Mr.
Chauncey & Mr. Peach that I woud communicate every thing which shoud
come to my knowledge relating to ye estate lately descended in coparcenry
between your self & my wife, I herewith send you a coppy of Lord Berkshire's letter to me, (which I receivd but the last night,) that no more time
may be lost (now this great point of his Lordships quitting claim thereto is

so well over) in concerting all such farther measures as may be adviseable to be pursued in order to get & keep possession etc. Whatever Mr. Chauncey shall counsel us will meet with a ready concurrence from, Sir, your most humble servant, Bristol.

**664.**    To Mr. Henry Barrell.    Ickworth, July 3, 1722.

The terms you tell me the Dean and Chapter do at last insist on for my fine are so unprecedentedly unreasonable, that had I no other estate, I would rather chuse to lett my lease run out than endure any such farther impositions from a sett of landlords whose severities are endless. Should I have used my tenants as hardly from time to time as they have me without any stop or relaxation, notwithstanding the increase and continuation of taxes for above thirty years of all kinds, I ought to expect the inheritance would not prosper long in my family ; what my present masters thoughts are upon that head I am at a loss to imagine ; but this I can assure them and all such hard task-masters, that there is so universal a cry against the growing exactions and oppressions of all such arbitrary lords paramount, that some effectual course must and will be taken to confine their long abusd power within due bounds, as is the case of lay-lords already with their customary tenants. In order whereunto I am advised to print and publish the naked state of the case as it is and hath been between us ; first to lett the world see their estate was actually lett by lease during my aunts widow-hood for no more than £120 per annum, and even at that rent the tenant grew so poor that he was forced to leave it, and that at his going out I was obligd to expend near £200 in putting the premises into tenentable repair for his successor, notwithstanding the predecessors covenant to uphold, which I never receivd one penny indempnity from ; that from £120 fine only which my ancestors usd to pay I have been gradually raised to £159 .. 12, which I have twice submitted to rather than break entirely with them, as I must now do ; that after having treated with them in so very fair and candid a manner as to shew them the lease subsisting between me and my tenant, and done every other thing they desired, they should make so unsuitable a return as to catch at that covenant about the repairs, and thereout create an imaginary value of £20 per annum more, and to fine me for it accordingly ; whereas in truth and fact the repairs have not cost the tenant so many shillings yearly, all things being set by me in so substantial order before his entry. Besides turn that circumstance which way you will, it cannot alter the state of the clear yearly value as to me, (the rule which the Bishop of Norwich of his own accord agreed with me but this last winter upon,) for supposing I was to receive as much more in rent as the repairs come to, yet, if I were to do them instead of my tenant, the nett-profitt would come out just as it now does. Then the vast charge I have been at to improve their estate from £120 to £200 per annum is another material article they seem wholly to throw out of their consideration ; which how equitable in it self, or how political as to its consequences on all such precarious tenures, mankind must judge till such proceedings reach the last tribunal. Then to compleat the whole : they refuse to lett my lease go back in its commencement to Midsummer 1720, which I am willing to comply with, and would allow them full interest money for the old fine last paid from that time to this, altho' they ought to remember that their own irresolution and disagreement among themselves gave rise originally to the delays which since have happend, and insist on taking advantage of me for their own fault. Who would beleive all this? In short, since you, their Secretary, could bring them to no more reasonable measures after all ye arguments you urged on their behalf as well as mine, I despair of any agents of my own succeeding better, & therfore cannot think of sending one to treat farther with them ; but because I am resolvd to leave them without excuse in case I shoud be forced to break intirely with them, having a great opinion of your probity, & finding you have a through knowledg of ye meritts of ye cause in question, I dare make you umpire of all ye differences betwixt us, & so you may tell them with whatever else you think proper or prudent to be communicated to them out of this letter (and no more) from your assurd freind & obligd servant.

**665.** To Mr. Henry Barrell. July 16, 1722.

Having much company in my house, I have only time to tell you that as the first lapse was owing to ye dissension and irresolution of their own body about the manner of settleing their fines in the year 1720, I cannot but still hope for their own sakes as well as mine they will never persist in so unjustifyable a practice as to make me pay for a delay, which their conduct, not mine, renderd unavoidable; & to that first fault of their own creating ought indeed to be imputed the subsequent one; for had not the first thrown disputes and difficulties in the way, my fine might have been agreed & paid at its proper time or very soon after. Were Mr. Dean Pratt (to whom I desire my service) throughly apprisd of this and every other circumstance relating to my case, I cannot but yet flatter my self he would not only readily accept of, but induce the Chapter to do so too, what I am going finally for peace-sake to offer them ; which is that rather than to breake intirely with them, or to lett my lease run on till I shall find some other expedient, I will persuade my self to pay them two hundred pounds for the nine years elapsed, altho' that sum is near double the fine formerly laid upon any of the ancestors of your assured friend to serve you, Bristol.

**666.** To Lady Bristol. London, Aug. 8, 1722.

I grow so intolerably weary of the world the moment I am without you, that I can no longer bear it than till Friday morning; Lord Hervey says he will go with me. The affair hinted at in his last letter to me proves to be a matrimonial design upon your cousin Catherine Talmash, which he desires may be kept a great secret; what it will come to God knows; I have already prayd to him to succeed or prevent it, as may be best for my family. I send you the words sett to musick by Bononcini, which I not coming time enough from Lord Godolphins to hear, (who tells me my companions are the Earls of Burlington, Cardigan and Leicester,) Bononcini did me the personal honour to make the musicians and voices of the whole choir perform it over again, which being done in so particular a manner putt me out of countenance, being unusd to seek and consequently unacquainted with publick honours. There was a vast deal of company present; the young Dutchess of Marlborough, the Dutchesses of Grafton, Shrewsbury, Lady Darlington etc, together with all our Suffolke relations, whom I told you expected at Richmond, and that they shoud have the honour of kissing your mistresses fair hands, and of getting a buss from your honest master. Coud I gett one of you before I go, twere possible I might live upon't till we are to meet at sweet Ickworth, till when adieu I doubt must be said by yours for ever, Bristol.

**667.** Lady Bristol to Lord Bristol. Richmond, Aug., 1722.

By every wind that comes this way
Send me at least a sigh or two;
Such and so many I'le repay
As shall themselves make winds to come to you.

Woud that were so, tho' I blowd my self into a consumption, for I am upon the rack to know how to see you, for the Princess does not come to the funeral, so that I cannot come without it be in the morning before she wants me, or in the evening after she has done with me; pitty my forlorn

Vol. II.   DD

estate; I can no more, my room is full of company.—Pray let the inclosd
go to Mr. Grayhams, and the things sent when done.

**668.**    Lady Bristol to Lord Bristol.     Richmond, Aug. 11, 1722.

I am sure my dear dear angel will be glad to
hear I gott safe here on Thursday night, (which I did without any accident,)
if I shoud say well, I must forgett my usual sincerity, for I was so ill all the
way and all night that I calld up Catherine at six a clock to have sent to
stop your journey, for I really thought I shoud never see you more ; the
conflict I was in putt me into such a passion of crying that I was a sight
when I come to appear at Court, and I believe rather a jest than pittied
upon so uncommon an occassion ; thank God I am much better to day, but
so very low spirited that I was not able to write two letters in the morning,
(for I was obligd to write to Dr. Freind to patch me up for another week,)
so I am forcd to do this with company in my room this afternoon, and if I
shoud say more might loose the opportunity of saying any thing. My
dearest dear, adieu.

Felly is much better, I think quite well. Say what you think proper to
your company.

**669.**    Lady Bristol to Lord Bristol.     Richmond, Aug. 13, 1722.

I did not need the additional weight (to all my
other uneasiness) of not hearing how you gott to Ickworth ; where the fault
lies I know not, but either the Princesses footman forgott to call, or the
post (as he says) was not come in before he left London; however, I have
laid in by so many hands that come to morrow, that I hope I shall not fail;
but I dare not deferr writing till then, for fear some accident shoud hinder
me, for we have seldom two days together so little company as to day ;
indeed it happend well for me, for tho' I am a great deal better, yet I am still
so very low spirited, that the least thing in the world disorders me, even

the going to Kinsington yesterday, where there was a great Court ; perhaps you will think that shoud produce some news, but they were so imployd with looking at the new Embassadress from the Emperour's Court, that they coud think of nothing else, and indeed I dont wonder at it, for she is a most extraordinary figure, and talks so much and so loud that you may hear her two rooms off. The Dutch Embassador and his lady were here yesterday to take leave ; he enquird after you, and said if you had been in Town he woud have waited of you to receive your commands. My Lord Godolphin was here to day, and enquird after you also ; he has been putt under great difficultys by a most extraordinary humour of the Dutchess of Ma— towards the Duke of Argyle. He had a ticket sent him to come to the funeral, and accordingly came to Town, but the day before the cere-mony it was sent for back again, and told him the sending of it to him was a mistake ; I coud hardly think but the whole was so, till I had it from his own mouth.—I suppose you heard before you went out of Town that Lady Darlington had the ten thousand pound prize in the lottery ; this is all the news I know, except that the Queen of Prussia is brought to bed of a son (after having had five daughters), which is great joy at this Court. I dare not trust my self with telling you any part of what I feel, for fear it shoud make me unfitt to appear before my master, (who I attend every evening,) therfore will lett that alone till we meet, when the pleasure of seeing you will compensate for the torments I endure by your absence, which are greater, greater farr than ever. Pray thank Jack for the charming letter he writ to Pegg, which I shall keep for your diversion. I have such a horrid pen and ink that I am afraid you cant read this ; I am sure I cant, I have such a mist before my eyes that I can hardly see to bid my dear dear angel, adieu.—

I am not yet so happy as to have heard from London, and I dare not keep this to send by our company in the afternoon, for they are generally so merry that it may be forgott. I dont know but my last had that fate, for my Lord Sussex told me since, he was forcd to putt it himself into the Duke of Kents pocket.—If Cornfourth did not take out Fellys debenture, let him send word in writing where I am to have it by the next post, that I may (if it be possible) receive the money on Munday, when I go to London.—By the help of Dr. Freinds medicines I am much better, tho' the very smell of them is enough to strike one down.

**670.**                                        Ickworth, Aug. 13, 1722.

                    Your absence more than ever putts me in mind of what I have heard of the dismal effects occasiond by the bite of a tarantula, and tempts me to think there must be some relation in nature between them ; the patient is taken immediately with heavy anguish of heart, dejected sadness of mind, a plaintive voice, and sorrow seated in his face ; all which symtoms are succeeded by a continual melancholly hanging about the person, in spite of all the entertainments tryed to amuse him ; I know but one circumstance they stand differenced by, which is that my malady is rather renderd worse than curd by musick. This being my case before I receivd your letter last night, judg how the time will pass with me till I hear you are quite well again. I must do your son Jack the justice to tell you that as he finds I want comfort, so there is nothing omitted by him to divert me ; but tho' he coud succeed so well in it (as you saw) when you were by, yet now alass tis all in vain. Notwithstanding he has opend to me almost all the treasures of his compositions in verse and prose, (by which you may see he finds me very low in spirits,) and altho' they are both most ingenious, and woud with you have regaled me most sensibly, they cannot banish my fears about you, which will be uppermost and endless till we meet again.—I have had Aldermen with me here till late, so can only tell you, the Election coming on at Bury Thursday come sevenight, all my friends have petitiond and prevaild with me to go thither on Saturday night next, and to stay there till the day of Election, to secure some of the flying squadron to vote some sure friends into their body. If Lord Hervey be with you, lett him (with my blessing) know this, and that all his friends agree that he shoud be there at the same time with me; and therfore hope he will order his affairs accordingly; I woud have written to him, but that it is already too late to say any more than that I am more miserable than ever I found my self, for want of my sole satisfaction, thy only lovd company. Bristol.

671. Ickworth, Aug. 15, 1722.

How heavily the hours have passd with me till I can be assurd you have had no return of the illness your last letter mentiond, and that you are perfectly recoverd of all your complaints except that of our separation, which I can never wish you wholly indolent upon, your own heart may in some measure guess at, tho' none but mine can truely tell. One woud think that the more frequently absences recurr, the easyer humane nature shoud bear them; but alass! to affections so intire and so uncommon as mine, they only serve to make one more covetous of the company and conversation of its lovd object, and to dread the approach of any accident that may sever us from it, tho' but for a short season, especially when that of life (like mine) is so too. O! then tis the tarantula stings strongly; I find every bite makes daily deeper impressions, and diffuses its poyson so powerfully o'er all my thoughts, that they represent nothing chearfully to me, nor will nor can do so till I see you again; therfore pray make hast home, if you hope ever to see me revive enough to make you the companion I wish to be for the poor remainder of my daies.—Yours of the 13th instant is just now come, which I thank you most kindly for, but not those whose fault it is you did not receive mine of the 11th, which I took care to write before I eat or drank. I hope you know me too well to suspect it mine you had it not in time. Cornforth receivd Felle's quarter, but so dwindled by the Secretary's and other fees, that it came but to £25 odd shillings. Upon opening a letter from Tom, I have the additional uneasyness of knowing Lord Hervey has been dangerously ill; but how shoud it be otherwaies? It being now late, and you not being with me, together with Lord Hervey's disorder, has made my eyes misty as well as yours, so that musing, as I use, I know you woud have me leave off, which I will do as soon as I have told you, I am more unfit than ever to live without you, having no one pleasure in prospect but the seeing you this day sevenight, which will be accordingly longd for with the utmost impatience by your old friend and faithful lover, Bristol.

**672.**    Lady Bristol to Lord Bristol.    Richmond, Aug. 15, 1722.

Your dear letter, that brought me the welcome news of your being gott safe to Ickworth, came most seasonable to the releif of my poor spirits, for notwithstanding all the remedies I have taken, I was very much out of order last night and this morning, but am much better now. I can think of no cause for it but the having more company than ordinary, which alwaies (now) setts my spirits in a flutter; but I have never been wanting in my attendance either to my master or mistress. Lord Essex kissd the Prince and Princesses hand yesterday, for being Lord Lievtenant of Hertfordshire in the room of Lord Cooper; we are very impatient to see that ceremony over by a new lady; till that is, it will be very hard upon us old ones, for the Dutchess of Shrewsbury is taken very ill, and sent word she cant wait next week; so that there is none but Lady Grantham and me, till the Dutchess of Dorsett (who is to be sent for) comes to Town; if they think of keeping me it must be in my bed; but as I dont fear they will putt any such hardship upon me, I beg the coach & horses may be at London on Sunday night, in order to fetch me from hence on Munday; but if you had rather I shoud hire horses, you have but to lett me know by the stage coach on Saturday, which will be time enough for me to be accomodated.—The Dutchess of Grafton dind with me to day; I beleive you will not see her in Suffolke, for she says Sir Thomas Hanmer has left it to her choice, it being so short a time he shall stay himself. My Lady Sandwich has had a very unlucky accident; going over a foot bridge that was rotten, it broke, and she and the gentleman that led her both fell into the water, and she is very much bruisd; but poor Sir Gus : Humes's misfortune is far greater; for his eldest son fell off his horse, and (by a blow of his temple) died upon the spot. But why do I inlarge upon other peoples troubles, that have so many of my own, and the greater, because I have been partly the cause of some of them my self, by not accepting your kind offer to come and stay here with me; but I must not repent of that, since tis so much for your advantage to be where you are, which ought and ever shall be the first consideration of, my dear dearest, your faithful wife, E. Bristol.

Aug. 16. Thursday morning. Just as I am going to send my letter away, I receive yours, and will be sure to obey your commands to Lord Hervey by writing to him; for he has not been here since you went, being ill of a sore throat. I sent to him yesterday, and they brought me word he was better and hoped to see me this week.—What is to become of me, if you stay at Bury till Thursday? if you care I shoud come directly thither to you, pray lett me know, for I cant bear the thoughts of going to Ickworth and missing you. I am much afraid you will want the coach; if you do, pray dont send it, for it will be quite equal to me if I have but another servant to secure me from robbing. I have had but an indifferent night, but am pretty well now, but have neither room nor time to say any more. I have desird Lord Hervey to write you an answer by to nights post.

**673.**    Lady Bristol to Lord Bristol.        Richmond, Aug. 17, 1722.

I choose to begin my letter a day before the post, because I am never sure of my time, nor able to write long when I have it; tho' to day I am better, having had a better night, and my fitt not so bad or long as usual; you will wonder (I beleive) what I mean by a fitt, being unwilling to give you the trouble of knowing it till I was so near seeing you; they call it a fever upon the spirits, which I have before told you are extreamly low, with no stomach and a continual thirst; I wake about five or six a clock in the morning in a great sweat, and such an extream sinking within me that I can hardly stir or speak till I have taken drops or some other thing that Dr. Friend orders me. He came here last night, and has changd all my medicines; to day I have begun the bark with other bitters, but I hope on Wednesday for a more sovereign cordial, when I can once more see my dear dearest life again. The Doctor told me Lord Hervey had been worse than I had heard, but is now much better, which I suppose he told you last night, if he was able to write, as I desird he woud in my letter to him; but I will leave this melancholy discourse and tell you some news. The king begins his progress on Munday sevenight; he lyes that night at the Duke of Boltons, and goes the next day to Salisbury, when he sees the troups reviewd on Wednesday, and on Thursday he goes to Winchester, on Friday to Portsmouth, and lies that night at Lord Scarboroughs, and the next day he comes back again to Kinsington. Mrs Springs and Gage have been here to day; they kissd the Prince and Princesses hand; I did my best (as your relations) to entertain them the rest of the day; Felly showd them all the gardens and the wood, and the Princess did Mrs. Spring the honour to speak to her, so I hope they went away well pleasd; by good luck they mett some of their acquaintance, for the Dutchess of Grafton was here, and Lady Dalkeith, and Lady Isabella Scot.

Aug. 18. Saturday morning. I cant beleive it was from the bark or any other medicine but your dear kind letter, which gave me fresh spirits last night. I receivd it just as I was going to supper, and upon the strength of that cordial I eat a leg and wing of a chicken, a very great performance for me; I cant say I have missd my fitt this morning, but it came an hour later, so I had more rest, and consequently better able to bear it; however, pray be easy, for upon the whole I am very much better, and I hope no unforseen accident can happen to hinder me seeing you on Wednesday night. This being the last day, I have had such swarms of people all the morning, and so many are to dine with me that I am afraid I shall not have time to say much more to you, neither have I a word of news ; but I hope this ballad will supply the place of that, and give you some diversion. —Tis just as I feard ; the young Dutchess of Grafton, Lord Cadogan, Lord March and several others have dind with me, and are now in my room, that I have not time to say any more, or indeed to read what I have writ ; they have sett my spirits in a fresh flutter, as I beleive you will see by the shaking of my hand. Tom dined here, and says Lord Hervey is much better. I can no more; adieu.—My dear dear, dont be concernd, these disorders are frequent, and will go off soon again ; I have taken somthing, and am better already.

674.                                 Ickworth, Aug. 17, 1722.

I was hardly able to lett Tom Harvey come without me, notwithstanding the hourly wants this family must have felt without me, beside the absolute necessity my presence is now of at Bury ; much less coud I lett him go without telling you I can live no longer without you than untill Wednesday, when if any accident shoud prevent our meeting, (which I have prayd most earnestly Gods wonted goodness to us may avert,) I shoud (if possible) be much more miserable than since I

Vol. II.    EE

saw you.—Our son Jack was no sooner gott well but he wantonly tryed experiments to fall ill again, for on Wednesday he drove his lady about till late in the open chaize, with the coldest easterly wind blowing on them, which yet coud not make him putt on his great coate, in so much that we are not sure but he may have gott some slight return of his aguish indisposition ; he really seems to be careless of his constitution to an affectation, for the more his friends advise him to manage it with common discretion, the more he seems bent to expose it. All the rest, God be praisd, are very well. The only good news I have to send you from this place is that poor Fanny has puppd, and is well after it.—I have kept this open till Tom Harvey has been in bed two hours to see what your letter said about your self, which I have livd in most unexpressible anxiety about, and am releivd from most of it by hearing you are well enough to think of your journey hither at the time appointed. God Almighty send you safe to the longing arms of your most faithful Bristol.

I will gett leave to meet you at Ickworth Wednesday night.

**675.**                                    Ickworth, Aug. 18, 1722.

Altho' I wrote to you this morning by the coachman, yet fearing what I said about our son Jack might make you uneasy, unless you heard farther from me this evening, I can now give you the satisfaction of knowing he is better, and that Alderman Ray has just now assurd us that he will have no more fitts of his ague, the jesuits powder (which he has taken several papers of) agreeing so well with him. Shoud you want any excuse to gett away, I think this a sufficient one of its self, beside the additional one of sparing me the trouble of a disappointment I coud never brooke, but less than ever at this time, being more than ever yours the nearer my grave I grow. Bristol.

**676.** To Mr. Milles. Ickworth, Sept. 1, 1722.

I am still left so much in ye dark as to ye true state of my son's affairs, that I'm not at all able to give any manner of advice concerning them, not yet knowing so much of them as to understand what is meant by Wallers agents proposing to accept of £1500, any more than how farr he woud have me consent to a sale. I woud do much to extricate him out of his present difficultys; and if any consent of mine woud make him once more easy, when he or you will make me master enough of your scheme to know wherein I can do him effectual service, nothing on my part shall be wanting that can be reasonably requested of your friend & servant, Bristol.

**677.** Lady Bristol to Lord Bristol. Sept. 29, 1722.
The red Lyon at Hockerill. Saturday night.

I beleive my dear life will be glad to hear we are gott safe to this place (tho' a good deal fatigu'd) after the unlucky accident that happend. About an hour and half after I was seperated from my guardian angels tender care, the coach broke between Hiam-hedge and Kentford; the first thing I askd the coachman was, what we were to do, and all that his fatt head producd was to sett there till they went for the other coach; but with much to do we gott to Newmarket; what I did there, Lord Paggett and the two Mr. Mansells will give you an account of, for they intend to dine with you to morrow, so that it will be needless to tell you that Lord Or—y, as well as Lord N—, is taken up and brought to Town last night, and the messengers are out for several others; one of the cheif evidences against the Bishop, endeavoring to make his escape three story high by his sheets out of the window, fell into the Thames and was drownd; I beleive he woud have been of service, for tis certain he was not born to be hangd.—The Crown Inn is quite full with the Duke of Somerset

& several others, but thank God I have the prospect of a clean bed here, for I dont think I coud have gone a step farther in the coach, no more than my pen, so must bid my dear good night.

I hope both sick and well are the better for this summers day at Ickworth.

**678.**    Lady Bristol to Lord Bristol.

London.   Sunday night, Sept. 30, 1722.

I take the first opportunity to tell my dear angel I am gott well hither, tho' so very much tird that I was not able to go any where but to my aunt Effinghams, so can tell you no more news than what I writ last night from Hockerill, (which I hope you receivd ;) the two Lords are sent to the Tower, and they talk there will be several others. My Lord Hervey has been with me till tis now twelve a clock, but his company was so agreeable that I did not know how weary I was till now that he has left me. He has told me several things that are very pleasing, and what I hope will make the winter so ; the particulars of most of them you will have from him ; the overtures of the ministry to you I have from other hands as well as his, and that you seem to be at present the mistress they intend to pursue ; may they succeed, if their intentions be as just and right to you in particular, and the publick in general, as is wishd by your sincere and faithful E. Bristol.

General Whiteman died suddenly at Bath in two hours after he left the hazzard table.  I shoud be glad you woud seal up the key of your closet, and send me by this messenger.

**679.**                                    Ickworth, Oct. 1, 1722.

I must begin with telling how much I wanted the comfort of your letter from Hockeril brought me after having heard by Lord Pagett and the Messrs. Mansells (who dind here yesterday) of the accident of your coach breaking before you gatt to Newmarket; altho' they told me you made so good use of your time there as to feed heartily on mutton stakes, eggs and bacon, and had a suitable quantity of Widow Jackson's strong ale to digest them in. I'm sure they seemd so fond of both eating and drinking especially, that I was forced in doing the honours to take much more champaine and burgundy with them than you know I ever chuse to do but in such cases of necessity, for being of the Prince's family I was resolvd to give him the best welcome of all kinds this place coud possibly afford him, & I hope succeeded in it accordingly as yours and my sons fellow-servant too.  I will in the next place requite the good news of your being well at Hockeril by telling you our son Jacks recovery proceeds daily and visibly without a check.  God of his great goodness towards us continue it, and more especially since I find how inseperably and essentially your welfare is bound up with his from what I not only saw but felt yesterday was sevenight.  He dined below with us this day, and lookd much better than he did before his last relapse.  Dr. Pake visitts him but every each day, and can hardly spare so much as that of his time from Rushbrook, Sir Robert Davers lying desperately ill of a violent feaver attended with a dangerous diabetes, in so much as twas confidently reported this morning that he was actually dead.—What you send me word of with relation to Lord N— and G— did not much surprise me after the B— of R—; but if Lord O— has dippd in those monstrous measures against his countrys religion and liberty, where shall we find faith upon earth? It makes me sick of mankind, and were it not for you, I shoud have been so of womankind too long agoe ; but you have strongly bribd me to bear with them and the world too (wicked as they are) for the remainder of my life, which has no prospect of a pleasure in it but what is to result from your or your dear childrens happiness, the completion whereof engrosses both the thoughts and prayers of your most faithful friend and lover, Bristol.

**680.**    Lady Bristol to Lord Bristol.                Oct. 1, 1722.

If there were a courrier every hour, I shoud still find somthing to say, my head and heart are so full of love and you ; how much I want you is not to be expressd. This being a safe conveyance, I may venture to tell you reports as well as certainties. They say the messengers are out for Lord Str — d, Lord Ba — rs, Sir W. Win — , and that Lord Gower is absconded ; and I hear by one that knows, they are determind to meddle with no body they cant prove somthing against. The coach waits, I cant say more.

**681.**    Lady Bristol to Lord Bristol.        Richmond, Oct. 2, 1722.

I was unwilling to lett my dear angel know how much my journey had disorderd me, before I coud assure you I was so much better as to have slept very well to night without the assistance of my opium pills, which I was forced to make use of upon the road. I had besides the pain in my back (which has troubled me so much of late) a great pain in my side ; these complaints with that flushing heat made Dr. Friend think it necessary I shoud loose a little blood, which Mr. Grayham has been here this morning for, and I hope I shall have no complaint by night ; I want your dear company here, where you are so kindly enquird after by my master and mistress ; I dont know how the last woud have been servd, if I coud not have come ; for the Dutchess of Shrewsbury went away sick, and Lady Grantham is ill of a feaver, and Lady Essex coud not wait if she was declared, she is so near her time.—Mrs. Howard is just come in, and scolds me to death for writing, for fear my arm shoud bleed again ; but if I had any thing to tell you that coud be depended upon, I woud venture that ; but there are such numbers of reports one does not know what to give credit to ; but so far I beleive you may be assured that there has been the most villainous designs that can be imagined, and tis a frightful thing to hear such numbers as are concernd in it. Pray God they may be all discoverd, that you may injoy Ickworth in peace with the dear children & your faithful wife, E. Bristol.

We dont go to London till Saturday, when the King goes. Lord Peterborough supd with me last night, and has just now sent me a basket of fruit, but I shall not venture to eat any, so be in no pain that I shoud do any thing to hurt me. Mr. and Mrs. Clayton are with me, and give their service to you. I have nothing more to add but that the Council satt yesterday from eleven till four in the afternoon, and mett again at seven, and satt till eleven at night.

**682.**                                         Ickworth, Oct. 3, 1722.

The only pleasure I'm capable of feeling in your absence is the amendment of our son's health, which, God be praisd, proceeds to admiration. He dined with us to day in publick, and eats and looks very near as well as he did before his illness, neither did I ever see him in much better spiritts than he was all day yesterday and to day, which doubly delights me, as I know twill make you better too to hear of such uninterrupted alteration in him, which pray requite by telling me you are free from all complaints also. Sir Robert Davers dyed on Munday last at three in the afternoon, so that if our Lord Lieutenant ever hopes to putt this county upon a better bottom for the House of Hannover, this is the only critical season which has offerd its self since the happy Revolution to attempt it in successfully, for Torism must not be trusted.—I left the key of my closett with Bullen to be kept with yours when I came from London. As to the new Buzlums you mention, tho' you have often told me I am the greatest coquette that ever God made, yet unless they shall approve themselves true lovers of their country as well as of their new mistress, they shall never obtain the least kind regard from me, whatever allurements they may think to throw out to catch me with, which nothing can effect but such a behaviour as was yet never observed in any party in power by your faithful friend and constant lover (in spite of the coquette), B.

**683.**    Lady Bristol to Lord Bristol.          Richmond, Oct. 4, 1722.

I am so unlucky to be forced to enter upon a fifth letter before I have had the pleasure of receiving any; the missing one on Munday has given me a thousand fears that you might not be well, or Jack worse, else sure you woud have writ on Saturday night as well as I did, finding more and more every releif one can gett in absence absolutely necessary; I will give you that of knowing the bleeding has quite taken away the pain of my side, tho' my spiritts sufferd by it that night, notwithstanding I had the honour of the Princes company above an hour in my room.  I have taken my rheubarb to day, for my rheumatism pains has been very troublesome to me ever since my journey, tho' I dont think it was possible I coud gett cold, for it was as hott and dusty as at Midsummer, and so continues, which makes the Princess venture too much, for she is generally out an hour after tis dark, which I beleive woud kill me, if she were not so good as to dispence with my attendance.  I am sorry I have no news to tell you that I can depend upon, except we hear some when the Prince comes home; he is gone to meet the King in High Park, to see an exercize with hand Grenadiers.  The Duke of Rutland is come to Town to receive the blue ribbon.  I beleive there never was a thought of changing the Speaker, whatever you may have heard; but we have the good luck to have every one that is namd inclind to be a family friend, which I hope will prove well for my Lord Hervey; he was here yesterday, and looks better than I have seen him a great while; I am afraid you found it otherwise with poor Tom, which made me willing to indulge his inclination to go to Ickworth, which I hope will mend him.  I am just out of my witts;

Mrs. Howards man is come back, and tells me there is no letters, which makes it impossible I shoud write common sence, but I am desird by all here to tell you they much desire you shoud sett up my Lord Hervey for the county in the room of Sir Robert, who they here is dead; Lord Scarborough, Mr. Pelham and several others dind with me and desird me to write, but you are best judge your self what to do; they seem very pressing for your coming to Town, and in their desires to serve Lord Hervey upon this occasion; Lord Scarborough has writ to him himself, and so you will hear from him more particularly, for I am fitt for nothing; I have not eat, and I am sure I shall not sleep, without the messenger I have just now sent brings me some comfort. Adieu, my dear.

**684.** Lord Bristol to Lady Bristol. Ickworth, Oct. 5, 1722.

O that you shoud send me so many complaints, and I without means of cureing them, or coming with wings to assist you in them! which I hope Dr. Freind has so effectually performd that neither the pain in your back or side any more afflicts you; you may be rid of both, and I trust in God's goodness and my best prayers that you are so, ere this, but I must and shall feel on till I hear you are well again. Thank Mrs. Howard from me for chiding you that you ventured bleeding to lengthen your letter, which can never please me when it pains you. How often have I beggd of you never to sell me satisfaction at so dear a rate as to disease or inconvenience your self on such occasions. If our son's recovery coud restore you to ease as soon as his sickness disorderd you, you need undergo no farther fears about him, he being now, by his own confession, mended to a miracle. He enterd yesterday on asses-milk and Pyrmont waters, both which agree wonderfully well with him. He has been several times abroad in the coach, and was this day about the Parke on horse-back, to take the benefitt of the sweetest season sure that ere was known in this month and climate. I know your mistress is too wise not to take as great a share in it as any body; woud I coud give my self the same assurance as to one of her R.H.'s suivantes, whose health is dearer to me than any earthly blessing, and so essential to my own that unless yours goes well, every thing of course goes ill with your most faithful Bristol.

To morrow I am to dine at Sir Thomas Hanmers in order to take my leave of him, where I shall hear who the Tory-party intends to putt up in Sir R (obert) D (aver's) room. As to my Lord Hervey, many people have already been with me to desire he may appear; but I cannot think of engaging him in the management of a new county interest, who had not industry enough to preserve one in an old burrough, where never family had a more intire creditt than my own. He has not writ about it.—I hope by that time this getts to London, you will have found twas none of my fault you missd of my letters, I having punctually writt by every post. Tis now an hour beyond my usual bed-time, must therfore wish you a good-night.

**685.**    Lady Bristol to Lord Bristol.    Richmond, Oct. 5, 1722.

I was so miserable yesterday about your dear letter that I wonder I am now alive, for after my third messenger about it brought me word it had been sent the day before, I gave it for lost, till Matt's industry found out the mistery about ten a clock, that two water men had quarreld who shoud bring it, and so kept it 24 hours at Brantford, where I was forced to send at that time of night for it, and by great good fortune gott it just as I sat down to supper; the sight of your dear hand (before I read the pleasing contents within) gave me a joy I cannot express, from which I eat a very good supper, and slept very well till I was disturbd

by the packing up, the little Prince being gone this morning, and so is his
Majesty, which is a day sooner than he designd, but there is so much
business in the examinations that either the Cabinet or great Council setts
almost night and day. They say Mr. L—r squeeks finely; there are
several people more namd that they say are to be taken up, but that is too
tender a point to touch upon, unless it were done. Bononcini is dismissd
the theatre for operas, which I beleive you and some of your family will
regret; the reason they give for it is his most extravagant demands.—
Saturday morning. I have been awake ever since seven a clock in hopes
of your letter, which is to be brought me by some of the people that come
to carry us to Town, which I find now will be pretty late, for the Prince is
gone a shooting; however, we dine there, but as there is a talk of going to
the play, I dare not trust to finishing my letter till then, for fear I shoud
not have time to say so much as I woud, and as my Lord Hervey desires,
(who supd with me last night,) but I hope he will write himself, and better
explain to you what he woud have than he did to me; all that I can
gather is that he is quite determind against standing for the county himself, but very desirous that Jack shoud, which he says will be approvd of
as well, and that he will willingly go down to give him all the assistance
he can ; I find his present point is the being calld up to the House of
Lords, which I beleive he has some encouragement to hope for, and I
think he seems so impatient for that as to be inclind to drop the petition,
if the project for the county succeeds ; but I told him my opinion as to
that, (and I beleivd it woud be yours,) that it was giving up a great deal
too much to the Davers's interest; but to be as plain as I ought to be to
you, I found him so changd in every thing from what he was the last time
I saw him, that I was quite surprisd ; he has promisd to breakfast with me
this morning, where he will receive your letter to him, (for they have
brought it with mine just this minute,) which I hope will have as good an

effect upon his temper as what you tell me of your self and Jack has upon mine, tho' I own tis some allay to my pleasure not to hear a time sett for our meeting, since I am obligd to wait another (month?), being the only lady in a condition to do it at present, but I hope I shall not be disabled at the end of it to take a journey, if this fine weather tempts you to stay beyond a curiosity that all the world has at present, which has, they say, very much increasd the company in Town this week, tho' there was enough before to make a little assembly every night at some house or other.—

London. Saturday night.—My Lord Hervey was with me just before I left Richmond in a much better disposition of mind than he was last night, but I beleive his affairs giving him so much trouble had ruffled him, for now he seems inclind to go on with the petition, that Tom may come in at Bury, if Jack succeeds in the county; this is the present scheme. Lord Scarborough seeming to be a family friend, I showd him the paragraph in your letter that related to the affairs of Suffolk, which I hope you will not think wrong, since it was so well taken as to have him desire me to lett you know from my Lord Townshend that they never had a thought of setting up any body but one of your family, and which of them you fix upon shall have their assistance, but they hope you and the Duke of Grafton will have agreed about this affair before he comes out of the country, which will be on Munday. I hope my Lord Hervey has writ, (as he said he woud,) for to be sure he will be able to tell you more than is thought proper to be communicated to me; he promisd to come to me to night, but I dare not keep my letter open any longer for fear I miss sending it. Here is no news that is proper for a letter but that poor Lord Hinchenbrook is dead by a relapse he had of a fever six weeks ago, which I hope will make Jack more careful for the future. Pray God bless you all; I can see no longer, nor read what I have writ. I find I have spelt so ill you wont be able to find out some of the words.

**686.**  Lord Bristol to Lady Bristol.

I send you this copy of your cousin Griffins letter
that you may see by the different dates of my letter and his answer what an
hopeful man in business I am to act with.  The tenants having attornd,
and we being in quiet possession, I see no necessity for our going in person
to receive the rents due at Michaelmas last, thinking that part may as well
be performd by the stewards or agents appointed by either side.  The next
most material point is to gett an exact account of Mrs. Howard's joynture,
which you may find out by the Dutchess of Norfolke or some other of Mrs.
Howard's more intimate acquaintance, to whom her Grace can recommend
you.  The account you sent me in your seven-sided volume (which instead
of thanking I must chide you for) of Lord Hervey's irresolution is most
surprising, that part of the scheme especially which ever had a thought of
dropping the prosecution of his petition, which, if he does, after all the pains
and pelf I have laid out in retreiving (as I have done) so ill a lost game,
shall give me my quietus from ever meddling where such managers are
concernd.  I had not a line from him by the last post, but receivd a letter
from the Duke of Grafton this day, wherein he proposes setting him up for
this county, to which I have this night sent him the following answer to
London.—That part of the scheme which allotts this shire for our son Jack
seems to me to be as crudely considerd as all the rest; for in the first place
he is very little known out of our immediate neighbourhood ; then to think
of putting him upon going about and drinking with gentlemen at every
Quarter Sessions, and doing many other things necessary to succeed in
such an undertaking, as shifting his lodging often etc. after so dangerous
an illness as he has miraculously escapd from, is what I know not how to
encourage, had he the qualification of £600 per annum in land requird by
law, which I shall not in so short a time know how to accommodate him
with.  O ! what woud one give for a little judgment, one grain wherof is

worth a pound of any other faculty of the understanding in the conduct of humane affairs. Woe is me who am constraind to live and act with those who want it so; but more woeful still not to know when I am to see you again, the enjoyment of your sweet society being the cheif scheme for the short remainder of his life, who in his best daies never had a wish beyond being with, and in his last woud pray to dye with, the sole object of his love. Bristol.

**687.**    To the Duke of Grafton.    Ickworth, Oct. 8, 1722.

I am honourd with your Graces letter by Mr. Eldred, but knew not he was the bearer of it till he was gott too farr out of the messengers reach, I sent after him to ask the favour of his dining with me. The proposal your Grace is pleasd to make of setting up my son for this county is doing honour to us both; but he hath already one iron in the fire, and I cannot advise him to meddle with any more of that kind, least the first shoud burn for want of due tending, which is the only circumstance, I think, can make that unprecedented cause miscarry, unless his present friends shoud prove as loose and lukewarm to him on that occasion as others before him have experiencd upon many more; however, as nothing has been able to make me so where the safety of the King, his family, our religion, laws and liberties are concerned, so as soon as your Grace can fix on such a person as I believe will most uprightly assist in the preservation of all those most invaluable blessings, your Grace may promise your self all the interest that can be made for him by your Graces most obedient and most faithful, humble servant, Bristol.

**688.**    Lady Bristol to Lord Bristol.    London, Oct. 9, 1722.

Nothing but the pleasure I have to be any way conversing with you coud raise my spirits enough to be able to write to day after what I sufferd yesterday by being in two such heats and crowds as was at both Drawing rooms, ours in the morning and the Kings at night, which lasted till twelve a clock. I am unwilling to tell you how unable I was to bear it, for my rheumatick pains have been very bad these two days ever since the pain in my side left me, which returnd in my journey from Richmond, tho' I said nothing of it to you on Saturday night, hoping it woud go off, which it did the next day, so that I conclude by these pains coming in the room of it they are all from the same cause; my spirits will be but a small support to me, for they never were lower in this world, and your letter not mentioning any thing of your coming sunk them, if possible, yet lower ; sure to morrows post will tell me when I may expect you, or whether you woud have me come to you. Lord Cooper enquird much after you yesterday at our Court, (where the Arch-Bishop of York was also,) and when you came to Town, and said he hopd it woud not be long first, and desird me to give his service to you.—I think you are in the right not to think of setting up Lord Hervey for the County, for I beleive it woud lessen his interest here as to the petition, if not quite drop it ; but I cant see any reason against Jack, for sure there is no body (uningagd) in that county that has a better (or indeed so good) a pretension. I was sorry to find by Sir Thomas Hanmer, (who I went to see last night, and so did Lord Hervey,) that you had mentiond nothing of it to him, which made him very much surprisd when I did, and say it woud be the last misfortune that coud happen to him to be obligd to appear against any of your family. I find the person designd is either Sir William Barker or Sir Robert Davers. I was mightily pressd at Court last night to know what you intended to do; I told them I coud not tell, but I supposd they woud be better informd by the Duke of Grafton, if he had consulted you before you were ingagd ; if they had not, it was their own fault, for they knew what your opinion was, both by my Lord Hervey and me, in relation to this affair.—I have been walking in the Park with the Princess in a high wind and dust, and near a thousand mob to huzza the King to the House ; you will easily beleive this expedition has not mended my complaints. The Duke of Grafton has been just now with me to beg I woud second the letter he writ to you yesterday about setting up one of your sons for this election ; the reason why he namd my Lord Hervey was because he writ to him about it on Saturday night, which I own has peakd me a good deal that he shoud do that after what he said to me, and never tell me of it, tho' he was with me till I went to bed, and agreed to every thing I had writ, for I read it to him, nay, twas by his own desire what I did say ; but after what passd on Friday with him in relation to you, I can wonder at nothing ; but that I did not intend ever to have mentiond, if he had not compleated his in-gratitude by returning the sincerity of my friendship to him at this time in the manner he has. I have not seen him to day, so cant tell whether he will write to you this post any more than he has done any of the former ones. I was in his room at one a clock, and he was asleep, and when I came home to dinner he was gone out without leaving word where I might hear of him, tho' I said I wanted to speak with him, so that I cant tell you whether the petition is lodgd or not, for it was not drawn last night at eight a clock ; but I will say no more upon this subject for fear you shoud see so much what I feel as to make you uneasy ; so will only tell you the Duke of Graftons speech at parting, that is, I hope Lord Bristol will lett us have one of his sons, and by G— we'll dip and carry it in spight of their teeth.—Pray, my dear, tell Betty Dr. Friend is gone out of Town for some days, so I coud send her no answer ; I must beg you also to tell Harry that he had no letter with the cheeses.—The letter I have sent you to the Clergy is mightily commended. My dearest angel, for this time farewell.

I am in hopes you are coming, because you have sent me no note to receive the money as you said you woud. Pray lett Cornfourth lett me know how I am to receive my sallary, for I am at a loss. The length of this must excuse ye blunders.

**689.** Lady Bristol to Lord Bristol. Oct. 9, 1722.
Tuesday night, 9 a clock.

I am just come to my Lady Orkneys to play at ombre, and to hear what news I coud; I suppose it will be none to tell you Mr. Compton is chose Speaker; Sir John Packenton made a long speech, and said he had many reasons against Mr. Comptons being Speaker; one was he had £10000 a year as Paymaster, beside a very good imployment under the Prince, which showd his dexterity to be very great, (in his opinion too great for that chair,) to be able to carry his affairs so swimingly as to oblige the two Courts, when there was that difference between them; besides his having servd an apprentiship in that House, which might make him as good a cook as if he had livd at Pontacks to dress a dish to suit every ministers pallate as occasion offerd; there was several more things said to the same purpose, but really my memory wont serve me, and they make such a stunning noise that I am quite stupifyd, this being my first appearance in an assembly, tho' there has been one every night. Lord Stannup, they say, spoke like an angel; and now, my dear, I think I may bid you Adieu for this night. I have just been with my aunts, who are willing to use all their interest for Jack if he stands for the County, and they pretend to a great deal.

**690.** Lord Bristol to Lady Bristol. Ickworth, Oct. 10, 1722.

Unless you coud find as great a pleasure in beholding the characters only of my hand writing as I alwaies feel at the very sight of yours, (even before I've read one word,) the unreasonable length of my last letter must seem tedious and troublesome to a courtier as

Vol. II. GG

you are in strict waiting from such a mere country gentleman as I am, whom you fine folks may imagine has little else to do with his time; but if you knew what full imployment this family keeps mine in, you woud rather wonder how I find enough from it to correspond so punctually as I hope now you are throughly satisfyd I have done. To enter into a detail of particulars woud swell this to as large a volume as my former. Know only that Jacks footman is gone for refusing to make a fire even in his masters chamber; and Jack Offord run away from my service the last night to avoid fathering a bastard, which a Bury lady, as he heard, was coming as this day to have laid to his charge; but before his flight I wormd enough out of him to resolve to turn away his master and good example Emmet, altho his bastard shoud become by it a standing expence to this parish, the preventing of which was the sole reason of my bearing with him so long; then as to my only footman Will, I coud not help (contrary to all my resolution) chastizing him for sowing sedition in my family, by asking Syer, (when she was doing her duty and going to see if they behavd well at the 3d table,) in a very jocose tone, what that old woman had to do there, and rose and shutt the door against her, and have given him warning, but he begd I woud not discharge him till we return to London.—Tis now my bedtime, when both your letters are just now arrivd. Cornforth says Mr. Travers at the upper end of Bury street dispatchd Fellys first quarter for him; and I have written to Mr. Fowler that you may receive at any time all the money I have in his hands, either your self or by charging bills upon him for whatever you want.—As to the scheme of elections, I hope what I wrote to you and the Duke of Grafton have sufficiently satisfyd both that neither of my sons (at present) are fitt to undertake the County, which Sir William Barker was with me yesterday to declare his appearance for, and frankly told me he was sure to carry it, tho' several of his neighbours have refusd to engage for him till they heard from me. Sir R. Davers declines standing, and has promisd his interest to Sir William Barker.—I am glad to hear you were well enough to be at Lady Orkneys, and cannot go to bed; tho' much beyond my usual time, till I have told you our son Jack found himself so recoverd as to be on the coach-box this morning without any great coate on, till I made him putt one on, to drive his wife and child about the parke. They neither of them talk of removing, nor can I yet, if I woud, till the great affair at Bury be once again settled and secured beyond any future possibility of being broke into, tho' Collonel Norton and Lady Felton shoud joyn more strength then they have already done to supplant instead of supporting (as they ought) the family interest of your faithful friend and lover, Bristol.

Say nothing of this to your aunts till I see you, be sure.

691.    Lady Bristol to Lord Bristol.    London, Oct. 11, 1722.

If your letters were not alwaies so just & fitt to every subject, I shoud say a great deal of this in particular to the Duke of Grafton, which I think so right that even you your self cant mend it, and (which I am over joyd at) intirely takes off the scandal laid upon you, (and they say affirmd by Sir Thomas Hanmer,) that you were at a meeting at his house to sett up Sir William Barker; you have intirely convincd me the scheme of setting up my son ill-judgd in every particular you have mentiond; but I own I was weak enough to be pleasd with it at first, knowing the desire he had to be in Parliament, tho' you can be my witness it was never with design to prejudice my Lord Herveys interest, but to bring in both, for you know my first letter mentiond none but himself, nor never shoud but at his own desire. I wish he had dealt as sincerely by me, or at least had known his own mind better than to have made me write one thing for him to you, whilst he was acting another way for himself; but I said enough (I am afraid too much) upon this disagreeable subject in my last letter ; but I have not seen him since, so cant tell whether he has writ to you or not; but I can tell you the petition is lodgd, for I askd the Speaker yesterday morning, having some doubt about it, for it was not drawn up on Munday night at eight a clock, and they say if it had not been lodgd the next day at twelve it coud not have been at all, neither do I beleive it will be of any signification now, if you're not hear to solicit your self.   I dont find but that every body is of your mind, that that and the County coud never both have done, and that it must have weakend your interest very much at Bury to let the petition drop.   They say you will have a great deal of business very soon in the House of Lords ; both Houses are fuller than ever was known at the beginning of a sessions ; but dont think I say this to save a journey, for I will certainly see you at Ickworth, if I cant do it here next week, tho' they shoud say I did it to save a birth-day manteau.   My other expences here will not be great, for I am invited abroad to dinner every day ; to day I dine with Lady Orkney, to morrow with Mrs. Clayton, Felly and I are both invited, besides a general invitation to Lady Cobham and the Bed-chamber womans table. I was last night at the Play with the Princess, where there was the vastest audience that ever was seen, and some of the new blue ribbons to show themselves ; there was three given yesterday to the Dukes of Roxborough, Bolten and Rutland ; they talk much of Mr. Howard being made a peer and Lord Godolphin a duke.   Lord Townshend has been twice, if not thrice, to introduce Lord Suffolke to kiss the King's hand, but before he coud gett into the Closet and out again he was gone, so very mad he is. The bride, Lady Parker, was at our Court to day, as was also Sir Thomas Hanmer, who was up in the corner from the company with the Prince for above half an hour ; tis plain how he has been wrongd as to not returning my Lord Herveys visits, for he was here yesterday morning to see him, tho' his calling upon him on Monday night was purely accidental, and by a mistake of a message. The whole world is in great expectation of the Kings speech to day ; I hope to be able to give you some account of it before night.—Mr. Lear (Layer) has equivocated so in his last examination before the Council that he is again putt into irons, and his tryal (by an Essex jury) to come on next week, which they say is to be the opening of what is to be laid before your House; I am very glad to hear from good hands that they have very strong and sufficient evidence to justify all they do. There is certain advice that the Pretender is gone out of Italy, and tis so confidently reported that he is imbarqued from Spain that all the stocks are fallen, and they apprehend a run upon the bank, which gives me great trouble that you have not sent me orders to receive the money at your goldsmiths ; however, we seem to have the hearts of the mob, for I believe there was two or three thousand to day in the Park, huzzaing the whole royal family, and were ready to pull the Princess to peices as she was walking.—I am desird by her Royal Highness that when the family comes up, she may have some cream brought, as she had last year, boyld and putt up in a bottle, and I fancy some that is clouted might come up in a pot.—I am afraid if you were dissatisfyd with me for writing so much by Saturdays post, neither the length nor contents of what I writ on Tuesday woud please you ; but I hope you receivd them all ; there was three parcels from me besides the news, and I beleive you will have almost as much to night before I have done, for I am resolvd to send you word what is done at the House of Lords, tho' it is not up yet, and tis now seven a clock. I am going back to Lady Orkneys on purpose to hear. Dr. Freind has just been with me, and writ the inclosd prescription for Betty ; as to my self, he tells me I must not expect to be quite well till I have been at the Bath, but must continue the Spaw waters and drops he has orderd, a melancholy winter prospect for your poor, forlorn E. Bristol.

The Duke of Grafton sent me word he woud see me this morning, if it were possible, and that he had receivd your letter, but I conclude they were too full of business, for the Council satt before the King went to the House, but I am not sorry to have no more to do with those affairs that have given me so much trouble already. I say nothing of Mr. Griffin, for I am sure you are best judge what to do. The Duke and Dutchess of Norfolke are not come from Bath.

Oct. 11. Thursday night 8 a clock. The House is just now up, but tis so late the Speech wont be out to night, but they say tis the finest that ever was writ, tho' very long, and setts forth the convincing proofs the King has of this plot, not only from his informations at home but from all his ministers abroad, that several of his allys have been solicited to joyn in this plot, but have been so firm to his Majesty and his government as to refuse it, and that he will very soon lay before them the most execrable designs against his person and government that ever was known, upon which their Lordships have suspended the Hapas Corpus Act till the 24th of Oct : 1723; there was 67 for it and 24 against it, in which number was Lord Letchmore, Lord Cooper, Lord Trever, and Lord Batters they say spoke remarkably well ; the Duke of Grafton movd it, and they say spoke very long and well ; Lord Harcourt and the Duke of Argyle admirably; this is all the information I can give you ; sure it woud be no new one if I shoud fill another sheet of paper with telling you how much and dearly I love you, and with what impatience I long to see you, more if possible than ever was felt by your tenderly affectionate E. Bristol.

They make such a noise I am afraid you cant make out what I have writ. I forgot to tell you that Lord Presedent and Lord Anglesey spoke mighty well for their different sides. Lady Orkney says if she were in your place, she woud forbid me touching a pen.

**692.**  Lord Bristol to Lady Bristol.       Ickworth, Oct. 12, 1722.
What you have written and I have heard and seen of Lord H— (Carr) woud long ago have cured me of concerning my self in any thing that relates to him but his reformation, were it not that his dear mothers meritts towards me were so very farr surpassing every other wifes, (but what I have found favour with God to see renewd in you,) that I must still for her sake feel almost the same tenderness, whenever I woud go about to rend him from my heart, as if he never had faild towards me or himself. The faults I can least pardon must be those committed against her, who has so worthily succeeded and so well supplyd her place in my heart. Sure there must be some mistake on his or your part. It is impossible he coud do what you imagine, unless advisd and putt upon it by some after he had seen you. God's omniscience and my own heart alone shall ever know how many cruciating torments it has silently groand under, to see the most hopeful gentleman that ever appeared in this or any other nation throw himself (and all the admirable talents he is so abundantly endowd with) away in such an irretrievable manner as he has done, notwithstanding all my frequent freindly admonitions to the contrary; but as he is the son of such a mother and in distress (tho from his own follies), I must beg you woud be present when Mr. Milles comes to search ye writings as I have describd and directed him to in my closett, and to make him leave a receipt with you specifying every deed or other paper he may find necessary to carry away in order to satisfy the purchaser of Aswarby estate. Were I not still engagd here about his affairs more than my own, it shoud not be long before I woud make my self happy again; but things are not yet brought to bear, nor cannot. I hope by this time you are not quite so sorry as you were that I had not spoke to Sir Thomas Hanmer any farther than I did about our County election; if I can judg at all, tis better as it is in all respects, especially since you have already allowd I was in the right

as to L: H:; and sure you must do the same now you have read all my reasons against Jacks appearing also under so many hazards to his health, uncertainties as to his freinds activity and interests, and difficulties as to his qualification in so short a time, besides many more considerations I must reserve till we meet, not proper for this place.

Saturday morning. Both your kind letters came safe to me last night; by the first of which I find my self farther obligd to the world for the new peice of injustice they have done me, and fathering of it upon one of my best freinds, which was designd as a two edgd sword; but as his love to truth will do me right as to what passd at Milden-hall, so I trust my letter to the Duke of Grafton .will blunt the most malicious story on both sides. You can witness for me how sick I have been of this depravd wicked world for many years; but this last groundless outrage will so finish my aversion to it, that I must and will resolve to have no more to do in it but to make you and our children as happy as I can, and my self so in you all. There is no comparison can justly sett forth the joy I shoud feel in having your lovd company here again, coud it be contrivd without hazard to your health; but to think of such a journey at this late season of the year with so crazy a constitution as you complain of, and to expose it to getting cold and other inconveniences by short days and dark nights, woud prove such allays to that pleasure that I know not (upon the whole) how to perswade, whatever I desire. Birth-days have commonly cost you, as well as our daughter, so dear one way or an other, that I coud wish you were out of the way of hurting your self by this which is approaching, were I not so strongly bribd as I am by the hopes of seeing you sooner so than can be otherwise contrivd by your faithful Bristol.

Poor Lady Davers dyed of a feaver last Thursday; our son Jack is, I thank God, so well recoverd of his, that he has been every day abroad in the open chaize (tho' against my will) without being the worse for it again, which is a sure sign of a thorough cure. His wife goes on well with her breeding.

**693.** Lady Bristol to Lord Bristol. London, Oct. 13, 1722.

If I had not had such a long experience of your wondrous love and constancy, I shoud suspect you were changd, or at least thought me so, when you coud say, (for I cant beleive you thought it,) you feard the length of your letter must be tedious and troublesome to me. O that you coud but see with what pleasure I devour every line, and what regret I feel when I am come to the end; then you woud be convincd how much tis in your power to please in every thing you do, tho' I must own tis some allay to that happiness when you tell me how many troubles you daily meet with in your family; how very unlucky am I then to be forcd to give so large an increase to it; but where woud you find a friend besides my self sincere enough to tell you such a misfortune; but tis too certain that Lord H. [Hervey] is utterly ruind both in reputation and fortune, if your wisdom dont find means to retreive him; tho' the life he leads must soon putt an end to his trouble (if continud), but as that will be but an increase to yours, I hope you will find some way to recover so lost a sheep; dont give your self the uneasiness to think there is any difference between us that makes me say so much; I do assure you (for your sake), had it come in my way, I woud never have reproachd him for what he did to me; but tis so far from having been so that I have not seen him since Sunday, nor heard from him till last night after one a clock he sent to me from the tavern to know if I had any commands to Ickworth, for he shoud send early this morning; I was but just asleep, for I did not come home till twelve a clock from the most painful drawing room I ever underwent in my life, for I was upon the rack in my limbs all the time; I turnd so pale as I satt at play that the Princess thought I was going to sound; I beleive this sudden

Vol. II. HH

change of weather makes me so bad from an extremity of heat to be so very cold to look like snow, which I hope will make you less unwilling to leave the country, which I find all your freinds here very impatient for; I was told by more than one, why will my Lord Bristol that has always expressd himself so zealous, and means everything that is right to the Protestant succession, be absent at a time when tis expected every body that is of that mind shoud with a more than ordinary warmth exert themselves; besides the giving a handle to malicious people to say you are unwilling to see how great villains your late new freinds will be provd; and that I verily beleive you may depend upon, even to the destroying of the whole Royal family, either by poyson or assassination; I beleive you will think they have been too far provokd to suspend the Habas Corpus Act for such a length of time, but there may be reasons unknown to me; therefore will leave their justifications to themselves; but tis certainly thought so necessary at present that if the time had been shorter, (for that occasiond the whole debate,) they woud have found very little opposition, except my Lord Batters, who was so warm as to say he woud rather live in Turkey with the bow string about his neck than give his vote upon that occasion for so detestable an Act; he was so heated that in the middle of another speech he was forcd to set down, and said his concern was so great that he coud go no farther; the Bill was read three times, and passd the same day.—The Duke of Grafton was to see me yesterday morning, but not finding me he followd me to Court, and said he thought upon what you had writ to him and me it was best (tho' very unwilling) to meddle no farther in the County, since twas impossible to attend it as it ought to be, there being so much business here; he among the rest seems mighty pressing for your coming to Town for many reasons as he says, but the petition in particular, which is impossible to be carried in such hands without your assistance; this is what he bids me say, tho' he intends to write to you himself, if it be possible. I am going now to meet him for the christening of my Lady Inshequeens child, with the Princess Ann who is godmother. I am mightily concernd that any body shoud go to Ickworth without somthing from me, but you see by what I told you how impossible it was without breaking a rest so absolutely necessary for me to take; however, I hope this will come to your hands before you have sent your answer, as it may be of use to you, tho' I am wholly ignorant what the message is about, but guess tis concerning the sail of his estate, which he seemd mightily dissatisfyd you shoud lay any restraint upon him in.—I dind yesterday at Mrs. Claytons with Lady Burlington; she had provided an ombre set for us till the Drawing-room. Felly eat like a porter, and I never saw him look so well in my life, and I think to do him justice he now behaves as well; I wish I coud say the same of his tutor. To day I dine upon my chicken at home, as I generally do of post-days, for I find my time much too short (tho' as you justly say I write volumes) to say what I woud; ages woud be so to express how much and tenderly I love you, and how unalterably I am yours, E. Bristol.

I am surprisd to hear you say your company has not spoke of moving, for by the account they have writ to Mr. Pope they are expected to night; I have not had the honour to hear from either since I left them. Lady Burlington has again miscarried of twins, and Lady Essex is now in labour.

**694.**                    Ickworth. Oct. 15, 1722, our sons birthday,

who I hope has written to you by Tom Pritchard (as he promisd me) to excuse me to you for not doing so my self, having been engagd in more messages and visitts to and from such as we are working with to retreive the interest at Bury than ever I experiencd in settling it so well as I had once done. J. Davers has sollicited more in ten days (tho' both father and mother lay by the walls most part of the time) than ever

Lord Hervey did in so many years, otherwise all the pains and expence I am now at might have been spared. Tis now past midnight, and I am but this minute gott out of my coach from Bury, and so fatigued that I am very sure you woud rather have me go to bed and rest my self than say any more to you now, unless it be to tell you that nothing coud have enabled me to undergo what I have mett with and been forcd to upon this occasion, but to bring matters to bear to morrow (a hall being then calld), wherein more difficultys have arisen than is possible for any one not privy to them all to imagine ; insomuch that coud they have been foreseen, I shoud hardly have imbarked so farr as I have done in them, but I hope by next post to send you word they are all surmounted ; in the mean time, methinks the keeping of this important burrough out of suspected hands may be a sufficient answer to all those malicious comments you say are made on my absence at this critical juncture. I shall have a double pleasure in this victory (if it proves one), as it will shorten my stay here, intending to make my self happy in thee again the first moment tis in the power of thy most faithful Bristol.

**695.**    Lord Bristol to Lord Hervey (Carr).

Ickworth, Oct. 15, 1722.

Dear Son

You need not have thought it necessary on the account you mention to putt your self to the charge and inconvenience of sending your servant on purpose with your letter, since none of the many particulars it contains required either the dispatch or secrecy of an express; however, the good will of it is receivd as well as you can wish it. I sent Mr. Milles by the last post all the instructions and directions I coud recollect about the remaining evidence of your estate, which I hope you have found the fruit of by this time. Were it not for the important affairs you know I am engagd in at Bury, which (after many unforeseen clashing interests intervening) I hope to bring to bear in a very few days, I would lose no time in coming to assist you all I am able, both in the sale of your estate, (which I am much afraid you will be otherwaies be as ill used in as you have been in those occasions which have made such sale necessary,) and in the prosecution and management of your petition, (which I a little wonder you woud not let me see a draught of before twas presented,) on the success whereof every thing I am and have been doing here so much depends, that I am amazd there ever was the shadow of a thought to drop it. Tis very much that after all which has passd relating to that part of your scheme which concerns a candidate for this county, the Duke of Grafton shoud never have had conference enough with you about it to tell you he never had any with me further than by a letter, which upon the answer I sent him to it after many days elapsd, he has (by my wife only) let me know at last he thinks it best to meddle no farther in it, a conclusion I am always readyer to joyn in than to proceed, where I know judgment, steadyness & industry will be wanting. The objections raisd by Lord T. to the other part of your scheme, I am apt to believe are owing to personal respects, but not such as you imagine. I never found but difficultys were started upon all occasions, whenever the promotion of any part of my family was proposd, as if on sett-purpose we were to be kept low that others might rise, whatever the disparity of merit might appear in every competition between us; my own personal pretensions have been so very few, that surely something more might modestly have been expected in favour of such sons as all the world well wonders have been neglected, at the same time that a sett of empty, ignorant, worthless fools have been employd, (only I suppose because they woud be such,) and advanced to all the posts of power, profitt and trust in the Kingdom, to bring all things into that desperate, disaffected condition we find them. How many of that vile character and viler conduct have, like Gideon's fleece, ingrossd all the

precious dew for assisting in all such wrong unpopular acts as have
alienated the hearts of so many of his Majesty's good subjects :

> Whilst those who have his interests trulyest servd,
> May thank their own estates they are not starvd.

You see since you have sent a messenger on purpose, I am resolvd to make
some use of it by what I've said ; I kept him thus long, not knowing what
the last nights letters might bring.—J. D. and his friends are more
industrious, and bid more for votes against the intended filling up than ever ;
but 1 hope your friends will help you to throw water into his wine, when
your petition comes to be heard.  Collonel Norton has at last thrown off the
mask, which I know not how he can well answer (at this time especially) to
his Whig friends ; and J. Davers has so far opend himself to one of my
friends as to ask his vote for Colonel Norton in case Serjeant Reynolds
should dye or resign, who has given no sort of help to your most
affectionate father, Bristol.

**696.**    Lady Bristol to Lord Bristol.        London, Oct. 16, 1722.

I find the tender regard I have had to your quiet
made me so  nice in what I said  in relation  to my  Lord Herveys  conduct,
has made you  think there may  have been some  mistake one  way or other
to occasion what has happend to me.   I wish to God for his sake as well as
yours there were room for such a suspicion, or that the rest (nay almost all)
of his friends that he has treated in the same manner were as ready to
excuse him as I am ;  but  to be very plain, the only thing can  be said for
him is he never gives himself time to be cool enough to know what he does ;
judg then how fitt such a body is to dispose of an estate without your assistance,  and  not only that, but to be sure the  money he receives  for it be
made a right use of ;  for tis certain he has many more debts than you know
of ;  one I have lately heard of, which I am  much  concernd  for ;  tis to a

fine lady,* who is so highly disobligd by it as to tell me, tho' she thought by his manner of living she had not much reason to expect to be paid, yet sure she might be civily treated; you may easily believe what effect this has upon her fond husband, who always professd himself (and I believe really was) one of his best freinds; I never care to name any body in a letter, but I believe you may easily know who I mean; but I must beg of you (tho' I believe I need not) that you will never give any hint of what I have said in any of my letters relating to these unhappy affairs till we meet; then I shall be able to tell you a great deal more than is proper to write, and give you (too) convincing proofs of what I have told you already, which I woud never have given you the disquiet of knowing, if I had not thought it absolutely necessary for your familys sake, and how impossible it was for such a behaviour to be long conceald; then how false must I have appeard to you, (God forbid that shoud ever happen,) that have seen and know so much of it, had I not let you know it. I met him last night at Court, where I let him know I had receivd your orders to deliver some writings to Mr. Mills for his use that were in your closett, and that I woud be sure to be at home, whenever he woud lett me know he woud be here, but I fancied he had better wait the return of his messenger (who is not yet come back), to know if you might not have somthing to add to the instructions you had already given us.—I believe you will wonder I was at Court the day I was out of waiting, and in such continual pain all the while I was so; but being obligd to attend the Princess at Lady Inshequeens, I was forcd to follow her on to the Drawing room as all the rest did, tho I took my rheubarb, which I think I am somthing better for to day, and intend to go to the Banyeau at night; Dr. Freind woud have me take stronger, but I choose rather to take my rheubarb the oftner, for fear the other shoud sink my

---

* Lord B's pencil note in margin says, Pultney.—S.H.A.H.

spiritts beyond what I am able to bear, which is pretty near compassd already, especially when I had read your letter yesterday, and found no time fixd for your coming, and my self so unfilt for a journey, tho' that woud have but little weight, if I had not upon sounding their minds a little at Court found it woud be very ill taken, if I shoud not appear at the Birth-day, which you know is now so near, besides another publick day a Saturday for the Corronation ; but I flatter my self, when you have receivd my last letter, that I shall have an answer to morrow that I shall soon see you upon much easier terms than a journey to Ickworth woud be this very cold weather. However, if that cant be, I beg you woud write me somthing, that may give me too just a pretence for coming to you to be refusd it. I dare not trust your tenderness towards me with knowing with what impatience I long to see you, nor how miserable the want of it makes me, for fear you shoud leave some necessary thing undone, that I may reproach my self for afterwards ; yet sure, since you say it is my Lord Hervey's affairs more than your own that keeps you, I have enough convincd you how necessary your presence here is to that.—I dind yesterday with the Dutchess of Grafton and Sir Thomas ; I find by him there will be a great struggle to day in the House of Commons to shorten the time for the suspencion of the Ha : Corp : Act, and they think they shall carry it ; there never was known so full a House ; there is not above 30 members wanting besides those that are dead or chose for two places ; it will I fear be impossible to give you any account of their proceedings, for they say they will very likely set till twelve a clock at night. I am to dine with Mrs. Howard to day at the Duke of Argyles, where if there is any thing to be learnd, you shall hear from me again. As to private news, there is none but that Lady Essex and Lady Rich are brought to bed of daughters ; Durestanty is arrived, and the rest expected in a day or two, so that opperas are intended to be begun next week. Lady Hillsboro is expected to morrow ;

I find his worthless Grace of Wa—n (Wharton) has left her lord in the lurch, and joind with Mr. Earl, who tis thought will carry his petition against him; there never was known such a number as is now before the House, so what will become of ours, (if not taken more care of than it is at present,) I know not; but to show you what lies in my power has not been wanting, I hope I have gaind Sir Thomas; at least he has promisd to attend it; Mr. Mills (who has just now been here) tells me he had so short warning for the writing of it, that he was forcd to sett up all night to gett it done in time; by that & several other things that he has seen he thinks it quite improper to go on with any thing till you are upon the place, which he says he has already told you, and intends to repeat by a letter to night, so that he has taken but one deed, (which he has given me a receipt for as you orderd,) and says that will be sufficient till you must necessarily be here, which has given me new life; (tis an ill wind that blows nobody good;) pray God this journey may prove as successfull and as much to your satisfaction in all things as it will be to the pleasure and delight of the most tender, loving heart of your E. Bristol.

I write so much I am afraid I somtimes repeat the same thing over twice, therfore cant tell if I told you the A. B. of York and Lord Cooper both attended the address to the King.—I have writ and spelt this so abominably, I am afraid you can hardly read it, my hands are so very cold, tho' I writ a great part in bed; what is it then for Jack in an open chaize?

**697.** Lord Bristol to Lady Bristol. Ickworth, Oct. 16, 1722.

I cannot suffer a second messenger to go from hence without saying something to you by him, tho' very weary, and late as it was, I wrote every thing I coud think then of, unless it were that Harry finding himself forgotten by Lord Cadogan, and hearing there are new regiments to be raisd, desires to try his fortune among his friends, which was what I knew not well how to deny him. I hope if matters go well to day at Bury, it will not be long before I shall follow him; therfore think not of a journey hither, but depend upon my making my self happy once more in thy much belovd company at London the very first moment I can gett from hence, which without thee is farr from being so much as tolerable to thy constant lover and most faithful of freinds, Bristol.

**698.**   Lord Bristol to Lady Bristol.      Ickworth, Oct. 17, 1722.

Altho' this place discovers fresh beautys every day, and not a week passes but art is employd to perfeĉt what nature begins, yet since the moment I wrote to you not to think of coming any more to it this year, and those pleasing hopes I livd upon hitherto are turnd into dispair, every thing seems so alterd about me that I can hardly perswade my self I am at Ickworth ; in short, so very burthensome and disagreeable is it become that I can bear it no longer without you, and do therfore intend with Jack and his wife to sett out to morrow towards you ; they being two invalids will retard my happiness till Saturday, but so long as I am getting nearer you, a day will seem shorter than a second now. O ! let us never part more, to comfort me for what I've lost already. Yesterday, pray tell Lord Hervey, we gaind a compleat victory at Bury, having chosen in no less than four new friends, viz. Mr. Barnardiston, Jackson, Grigby and Malfongratt, by the help of several old enemys ; insomuch that tho' there were 14 to 8 against us in the 24 when I came hither, now we have a majority of 13 to 10 there, and of 8 to 5 in the Aldermen ; this has so incensd the other side, that there is no resentment we must not expect when the petition comes to be tryed ; wherein I conjure Lord Hervey to behave with all temper, especially till I come, tho' the Torries shoud speak never so freely of this proceeding. I cant write to him now.—I have taken a place for your maid Betty in Fridays coach, and hired a waggon to bring your maids and goods to be here on Munday. Betty and Tom choose to stay till the weather alters, and you send for Nan and Bab etc.—I have sett up till so late for the coming in of your dear letter, that as it requires no answer but what the first part of this I hope will satisfy you in, I will bid you Adieu till we meet. A good night to my dearest.

**699.** Lady Bristol to Lord Bristol. London, Oct. 18, 1722.

I long with the utmost impatience for to morrows post, not only for the pleasure I hope from it of hearing of your intire victory over those pack of villains that have kept us so long asunder, (for which I hate them if possible more than ever,) but for the agreeable consequence that attends that conquest, by inabling you to fix the time when I may be once more happy in your dear lovd company; for tho' my friends here are infinitely kind to me, I still feel a want which makes me incapable of tasting any other pleasure; however, that I may return their favours as far as I am able, I must desire you, when you have any venison fitt to kill, you woud order some here. I am sorry to find you have been brought under the necessity of parting with your Park-keeper and so many other servants, for fear that shoud occasion another delay, before you can settle (almost) a new family. The best account I can give you of the little remnant that is here, will (I am sure) be to tell you that my pains has been so much better these two days that I did not venture to go to the Banyeau, the weather being so very cold; but I may now own to you they have been intolerable, tho' I have kept my self as much as possible from giving way to it, & for the sake of my spirits (which are so very low) gone abroad when I have been much fitter to be in my bed; nothing less than this shoud have prevented me seeing you at Ickworth, which I am certain woud only have provd a trouble to you in the condition I then was; the greatest proof I can give you of it is that I had once resolvd (upon what Dr. Freind told me) to desire you woud give me leave to take a winter journey to the Bath ; and now to convince you what a change I feel, I must lett you know that with all the bussle Harry made in the family (to gett his bed made & somthing for him to eat or drink) between two and three a clock, I never wakd till nine ; when I did, the poor creature had little rest, such numbers of questions I wanted to ask; but, thank God, he is very well after it ; nay, was in such spirits at that time of night as to send for my Lord Hervey home, to give him your letter, which he gott from Tom upon the road.  I dind yesterday at Lord Cobhams, so had an opportunity to inquire into his affairs, and find there is no design of raising any new regiments, but only to have an addition of men to every old company, and by that to save the expence of more officers ; from which I conclude you will have him stick to his first scheme of the Guards ; but as your coming (thank God) is now so near, there shall be nothing fixd till then, as I hope your interest at present will be able to assist him.  I am sorry mine can do no more for Mr. Buttses friend, for I am told by Ch : Churchil Mr. Warpole does not meddle with the excise, and I dont know who to apply to in that office ; I woud however have spoke to him, but that both he and she are in such affliction for their daughter, who is at last dead of that long illness, so very like poor Betty's case that I cant help being in pain, tho' I hope without reason, and that I shall see her soon in health, and that she will remember to take care of the Princesses cream.—The House of Commons satt too late on Tuesday night for me to give you any account of the Bill being passd by a majority of 53 ; Sir Thomas Hanmer (I hear) did not speak at all, Lord Morpeth dreadful bad ; other particulars woud not be proper for a letter, if I had a head good enough to relate them.  I hear no other publick news but the great expectations there is from Mr. Lears tryal.—Mrs. Clayton (who is in waiting) has sent to me to meet Lady Burlington there at dinner; if I can pick up any thing more, you shall hear farther from your faithful E. B.

I hope Syer will not forget I bid her send all the thick cheeses that were made last year, and all the hams that are left and dryd toungs. The butler I told shoud putt up ten dozen out of each hogshead of the pale ale. I am sorry to find you have not your wine sent till this week, for it did not go to the carrier till Friday, which was the day after they sett out; where the fault lay I know not; but if you had given me your orders, you shoud not have been disappointed.

700.    Lord Bristol to Lady Bristol.    Ickworth Parke, Aprill 15, 1723.

I hope you found your self so well after I left you that it made you resolve to sett out on your journey to Bath this day as you proposd, & that that was the reason why you had not time to write on Saturday night, knowing how much preparation is necessary for an expedition of that kind. I am under a double concern till I hear how you are, both as it will be so much longer before we can meet again if you are not gone, & that your bruises must mend but slowly to prevent it; therfore pray put me out of pain as soon as you can, since pain must be my portion still when ever I am from you. As for my self & all ye children, we are well, God be thanked, & gott safe hither; but my journey seems to affect my bones much more to day then yesterday; age is coming upon me, & tis welcome.

701.    Lady Bristol to Lord Bristol.    London, Aprill 16, 1723.

I cant tell how to beleive Nan forgott how ernestly I disired her to lett me know how you (in perteculer) & the rest in general passd your first days journey; the missing of that account gives me a thousand fears which I am at present in a very il condission to bear, for I was so full of pain and my legg so swelld and red that Mr. Brown woud not undertake for its not breaking after all I had sufferd; so that I have been forcd to return to polteses again, which with phisick being repeated & keeping quite still ever since the unhappy moment of our seperation has brought me now almost to the same condission you left me in, & he now gives me hopes the worst is past, however, begs I woud give my selt another days rest, & take ruebarb again to morow.   I have been ye more willing to comply, not only for the fear I had of being laid up upon the road, but that I coud not gitt a place for Squire to go the same stages with me till Thursday, & it was quite impossible for me to bear four in ye coach; even as it is I have such a dread of ye journey that I beleive if my things had not been gon, I shoud have given over the thoughts of it.   I have another griveance upon me besides, which is that you may want the coach before it can gitt to you; in short every thing helps to break ye brussed read, but I hope you cannot want a conveyance, since so many people will be coming from Newmarkett; however, I shall be oblidgd to travell so very softly that I beleive one days rest at Bath will be enough for the horses; theirfore I propose their setting out on Monday cross the country, if no unforseen accedent hapens to prevent it.—Now I think it is time to begin to inliven this maloncholy episell by wishing you joy of your new (and as tis said) most beautyfull grandaughter; at least I hope she will seem so to you, since she has what you so much disird, black eyes & a dimple; but you will have a fuller account from Jack, who ses he will write to you to night; she has hitherto given her mother very little trouble, for she was but 2 hours il.—What I coud pick up for your entertainment I have inclosd; they are both much commended.—I have sent Harry twice to Mr. Fowler, who tells him the ballance of your account is paid, & that he has receivd no mony since; so that I shoud have been at a loss if Lord Hervey had not been so kind to lay down the mony for me, & take my note upon

Fowler for the £ 100.—I write this in my bed, where I have laid most part of the day to rest my legg ; but, however, I have been in a good deal of pain ; to sattisfy myself as well as my frinds I have had Dr. Alburthnett to see my leggs ; but neither he nor Brown woud have me venter to stir this week, tho' they both agree the Bath will be of infinett servis to me, so I have ditermind for my self & will sett out on Thursday, since I can go now in the coach & never be oblidgd to putt my leggs down, & they both think the swelling will dispers without breaking if I keep to the methoud proscribed ; but all their remedys will make a slow progress till I am again blesd with the sure remedy for all my pains ; till that long time farewell to my dearest life.

Hear is another papar that they say sells very fast, but Sally for my mony.

**702.** Lord Bristol to Lady Bristol.

Ickworth Park. Wednesday April 17, 1723.

Tis now near ten at night, and I yet have not receivd one word concerning you since we parted. I shall sitt up till the post comes in, let it be never so late, not being able to compose my self to rest without first knowing how you are, and whether you were well enough to sett out on Monday as you intended. Doubts and fears are the bane of all my quiet, in spite of all the philosophy, moral or divine, which I, when with you, think I'm so through a proficient in ; but sure I ought to be ashamd to owning I am troubled with either after so long an experience of God's most gracious providence towards me & mine.—Your letter is at last arrivd and welcomo, tho' tis near midnight, and two hours beyond my (now) ordinary time of being in bed. I find by it that this will not reach you till you are at Bath ; pray be in no manner of pain about the coach, for I shall have no use for it, I hope, till you have done with it ; keep it as long as you please ; or if I should, you judg right that I cannot want a conveyance to London when so much company will be going thither from Newmarket, where I only stayd to get my travelling nursery a dinner, without seeing one soul of them all but Mr. Walker, who made me a visitt at the Greyhound, and told me all I care to know of that place.—God grant every thing relating to our grandaughter may answer as well the prayers as it has the prophecy of your old Jacob.

**703.**　　Lady Bristol to Lord Bristol.

　　　　　　　　　　　　　　Wensday night, Aprill 17, 1723.

　　　　　　　It was some comfort in all my troubles that I did not miss of your dear letter to day, for I was very much afraid you would have sent it to Bath. Could I have immagened you had any expectation of hearing from me on Saturday, I had not faild to have writ, though I am sure it woud have been more trouble to you to have known ye condission I was then in; for I kept my bed allmost the whole day, and the rest of it was not able to see any body, my pain was so great, besides that I had cryd my eyes out with fright; but thank God I am so much better with what they did last night that I shall sett out to morow morning early, that I may bait the longer. I find Mr. Mansell intends to go with us to diner, but he will have but indifferant company of me between the pains of my body & those of the mind aded to them by going so much farther from my dearest life; how then can you be so cruell to me as to talk of old age; endeed I had enough before to overwhelm me; theirfore will say no more upon that subject, but begg what you feel from that may make you resolve that we may part no more, so draw that good from the present evell; good night to my dearest.——I have paid the mony to Mr. Gardner for Harry this day. I made a hard shift to gitt a sight of my grandaughter to day, who is realy the prittest thing I ever saw. Lady Bell was marred yesterday; I think Nan shoud write to her.

**704.** Lord Bristol to Lady B.　　Ickworth Park, April 20, 1723.

I have just got my dinner after having been to visitt & take order about the repairs of my estates at Read and Chedburgh, and am returnd so very weary and unusually fatigued that I have hardly strength or spirits left to vindicate what I said in relation to old age, tho' what I now feel is the best proof of what I told you of it; but since I find tis news more unwelcome to you than me, you shall hear no more of it after having justifyed what I said of it by the following examples. Agamides & Trophonius having built the chancel or oracle in the temple at Delphos with five whole stones, and desiring of Apollo to have what he judgd best for their reward, were three daies after found dead in their beds. Also Biton and Cleobis (sons of Argia the priestess), who when she was going to Juno's temple to sacrifice, the horses of her charriot being tired, her two sons drew it up themselves, for which pious labour she prayd the Goddess would procure the best thing ye Goddess could give to man for her two children; at night, after supper, they went to bed and were found dead next morning. Likewise Pindar, the Theban poet, making an implicit prayer that God would do by him as he knew best for him, dropt down dead immediatly.—Were not a dozen Bury Aldermen broke in upon me, I could accumulate authorities without end to make good what I said on the approach of old age; but as I have askd their leave only for one minute to finish my letter to you, I will only add by way of corroboration;

> If righteous souls in their blest mansions know
> Or what we do or suffer here below,
> And any leisure from their joys can find
> To visitt those whom they left lost behind,
> To view our endless greifs and boundless fears,
> Our hopeless sorrows and our fruitless tears,

Vol. II.　KK

With pity, sure, they see the kind mistake,
Which weeping friends at their departure make ;
They wonder why at their release we greive,
And mourn their deaths who then begin to live.

**705.**   Lady Bristol to Lord B.        Bath, April 20, 1723.

I am, thank God, got safe to this place, though
with a good deal of pain and tird to death ; yet considering the very bad
condition I set out in and the hazards they all told me I run in coming, I
am better then I could expect.   The fright I have been in to day has set
my spirits in a flutter ; for besides the most violent tempest that ever I saw
or heard in my life, the house at Sandy-lane had like to have been fird
about our ears, so that we coud scarce get a bit to eat, and after staying in
this condition between 3 & 4 hours we were at last forcd to set out before
the thunder and lightening was over ;  & very well we did, for the ways
from thence (by this extremity of weather) is as bad as they were at Christmas, and tis now past 9, so that I have not time to say what I woud
before the post goes, but I hope Harry writes to you to night as I orderd
him, because that will be with you a post sooner then this, and he will tell
you we got well to Reading, for he and Mr. Mansel went so farr with us.
Betty gives her duty ; she is very uneasy with swelld legs as well as my
self; however, she has been in very good spirits all the way, which I dont
expect to have till we meet ; till that long time farwell.

**706.**   Lord Bristol to Lady B.       Ickworth Park, April 22, 1723.

There can be no end of my uneasynesses till we
meet again, for till I hear you passd your journey to Bath without any ill
accident, Major Davel on the rack will not feel much more torment than I
shall suffer, especially after the description you made me of your legs

before you undertook it, since if any overthrow should have happend, or but one of your company thrown upon them in those rugged, joggy roads, worse consequences might attend on bruise upon bruise than the Bath would make good again; it had need work wonders to compensate half the injuries it has done me, but if at last it will procure you a healthful, painless end of your life, I will freely forgive all its offences towards me. Did you know how much thoughts and care dear Nann has bestowd upon me, both in my journey hither and providing for me all the good things she can get or hear of since my being here, you would not chide her for any neglect; she has too tender and too sensible a soul any more to bear than to deserve any thing of that kind, and therefore I've suppressd what you said about her not writing on the road, and desire it may never be revivd, for if it was an omission, the fault was not hers but Cornforths. She is hitherto an excellent creature, and it were great pity the world or the modes of it should ever alter her from that right byas she would for ever run in. Yet let not what I've said of her make me forget my blessing to Betty, tho' I've not had a line yet from her.

707. Lady Bristol to Lord B. Bath, between 8 & 9 a clock,
April 22, 1723.

I have kept the coach till the post came in, (which it is now by 8 a clock,) not knowing but you might give some other orders about it, or not think one days rest enough for the horses; if I were to judge them by my self I should be of that opinion, for besides the wearyness in my bones after lying still so long, the pains in my legs are very bad even now, though in my bed, where I beleive I shall be forcd to remain most part of the day, as I did yesterday, and when up lay upon the couch till I went to bed again; yet they were swelld to a vast bigness; I wish I may be able to give you a better account of my self by the post in

the  evening, which I reckon will be with you before this, so will keep them
no longer but to bid adieu to my dear.

**708.**    Lady Bristol to Lord B.              Bath, Aprill 22, 1723.

Tis but very few hours since I wrote by ye coach,
and I beleive their will be yet less distance of time in the receiving of thees
two letters; so that you will not (I hope) expect a better account then you
had of me in the morning ; all I have to hope is not to fall into any more
surgens hands; at present I wholey depend upon Mr. Skrine, who has
orderd me a fomentation when I go to bed ; he sais he hopes a little more
time and patience will releive me ; if it weir only to stay at home I coud
very easily submitt to that ; for by what I hear and what I have seen (which
I beleive has been the best) their is little temptation abroad, especially
when one can have Grantam by the day at home.   Their is so little company
hear that I coud easily give you a list of them ; the Duke of Queensborough,
Lord Carlton, Lord Dunbarton, & General Evans, are all the men I know
but Lord Abington, who is come with his lady ; poor Bishop Nevell can
scarce be reckond among the living, being (in my oppinion) wors then dead ;
they say he sitts at Lindseys with one to hold his cards & another to give
him snuff; palsey & gout have brought him to this missirable condition.   I
had like to have forgot Mr. Duncomb, tho' he lodges in the house; he & Mrs.
Smyth inquird after you.   The news of this day is full of Lord Scarboroughs having lost £13000 to Lord H. Manners, Charters & others; this
you have, I sopose, from better hands then mine; as alsoe of our poor
grandaughter being in danger ; I own my weakness in being so fond of her
to have it give me a good deal of pain ; and though I have taken ruebarb
& writ so much already, yett I cant help giveing Jack some advise about
her, but wether that any more then any other from me will be taken I

cannot tell; but as long as my dear angell loves me all other troubles can be submitted to by your faithfull E.B.

**709.**   To ye Dutchess of Marlborough.          April 24, 1723.

I am honourd with ye favour of your Graces letter, & should (I fear) in strict good manners say, I am sorry your Grace thought it necessary to give your self that trouble to distinguish me from the rest; but the least mark of esteem or friendship, where I've alwaies been so justly ambitious of deserving either, ought to make me too proud to part with any portion of it, even but in compliment. I must therefore own it was extreamly welcome to me on that score, and shall accordingly take care to comply with ye contents of it as soon as I gett back to London, which I propose to do by ye beginning of next month, when I shall hope to have a personall opportunity of assuring your Grace with how sincere and constant an attachment I have ever been etc.

**710.**   Lord Bristol to Lady B.      Ickworth Park, April 24, 1723.

Having spent this evening in answering a billet doux sent me by that great and agreeable lady who lately sat so long by our bed-side, the conclusion whereof was in the strong terms following, viz. " I take this opportunity my self of assuring your Lordship that I am with all imaginable respect yours etc.", I hope a wife of near 28 years wearing will not expect much from me to night at least; and therefore must put you off with the short allowance only of knowing your family here is, God be praisd, very well in health; but I cannot say much of the good order I find things in, either within or without doors, neither indeed can it be expected where the master's and mistress's eyes are so often missing. Tis now past eleven, and I have not got my letters yet from Bury, so that I am still under the most uneasy uncertainty how you passd your journey to Bath, which (to be a little serious) I had rather know, and that the waters and bathing

are doing you all the good you want and I wish you as to the lengthening
your life, than to be happy in all the bonne-fortunes the rest of your sex
have to bestow, were there no sin in the enjoyment of them.   But this being
a secret slipt in haste from my pen, I hope you will not expose your Joseph
to the laughter or incredulity of a vicious world ;  but if you should, I would
as freely own it to them as to you, and therefore do by me in this, as in all
other things, just as you see fitt, being unalterably what God's goodness has
been pleasd to make me, yours alone.

711.    Lady Bristol to Lord B.            Bath, April 24, 1723.
              If my dear angel were to hear it from any hand
but my own how very ill I have been, your accustomd tenderness towards
me woud make you immagin I were worse then I really am at this time,
which is as well as I can hope after so severe a shock ;  I was taken this
morning at 4 a clock with a violent fit of the cholick, which provd to be
hysterick, for it immediately threw me into fits ;  about 8 a clock my opium
got the better and laid me to sleep for 2 hours, since which I have been
pretty easy ;  I coud almost wish I had been so indiscreet to have given
occasion for this disorder rather then it shoud be natural to have such
frequent returns ;  it shows me what abundant need I have of this odious
place, and grieves me the more not to be able to make a right use of it by
drinking the waters at the Pump, which till my legs is better is impossible ;
but they are so much mended this 2 days that I hope soon to be carried in
a chair, and Mr. Skrine assures me I need not fear a return of this illness ;
what he has given me will secure me, so that I hope next post to be able to
give a better account of my self ;  till when, my dearest, adieu.—— To
morrow morning will give me great relief, if it brings any wellcome news
from you ;  I am now up, and (thank God) much better.  Wednesday 9 a
clock.

712. Lord Bristol to Lady B.    Ickworth Park, April 27, 1723.
    Let vulgar friendships flatter and dissemble; mine with you has been of a more severe and sacred sort than to practise or approve of either. I must therefore own to you, I cannot think Mr. M. (Mansel) offering or being permitted to accompany B. (Betty) so farr in your journey was well judgd on either side; publick particularities should never be sufferd to pass between young people unless all other preliminaries were first settled, which I suppose is not the present case; because there is no circumstance more rebuting to the rest of us conjugal pretenders than to hear or imagine one man is receivd on any foot different from themselves; had I ever heard of your and your aunts being so attended to Boxted, you might still have been Betty Felton for all the silly Suffolk swaine; and suppose my friend (who I have prayed to God may be destind to make one of my daughters happy) should have the same just delicacies, (as I believe he has,) what an irrepairable loss might we all suffer, tho from so innocent an accident! Neither has this been all the prejudice resulting from such unwary steps; since those who find they are like to wear the willow have often raisd malicious reflections to indempnify their vanity on being rejected; and the blue-mourn on female reputation is of so very nice a nature, that the least touch takes off that lovely gloss which art nor time can n'er restore again.—The account you send me of your self is as farr from making me easy as that I last treated of; however, I have one constant cordial, which I hope springs not from too much presumption, since I live with all the innocence human nature is capable of, that all things will end well for such at last; in that firm belief you are dayly recommended in the prayers of your best friend, Bristol.

713. Lady Bristol to Lord B.    Bath, Fryday night, Aprill 26, 1723.
    I think when I gave that maloncholy account of my self on Wensday night, I said at ye end of my letter I hoped for some

releif from yours the next morning; but alass, the subject (with ye in-
ferances from it) had a quite contrary effect upon my poor drouping spiretts,
for I fell into such a passion of crying that it threw me into another fitt,
which I find comes so frequently upon me on ye least occassion, that I nead
not dispair of what your authors cote as the greatest blessing the Gods can
bestow, at least as soon as old age will bring it upon you; & if it arives to
us both together I shall account it happyness endeed; but as I hope yours
is a great way off, I must thank God for the present blessing of being out
of pain all this afternoon, though so il in ye morning; a continual purging
I have had for three days has brought me very low & dispiretted; but
burnt ruebarb has had a very good effect, & I shall repeat it again at night
with somthing quietting, which Mr. Skrine tells me will prevent a return,
& that I may begin ye watters again to morow morning. I beleive the
thoughts of having lost a whole week in this place has contributted a great
deal to my ilness, for sure their never was any thing like it; all the entertainment I have had (when I have been able to take any) was one evening
at half crown omber with Lord Carlton & Mr. Syms, who lost 16 g:, which
made him sweat & sigh so bitterly that Betty had more deversion in sitting
by & hearing him then we had that won his mony. Another day I had
Mrs. Pagett & Mr. Boucher; I beleive you will be as much surprisd at his
being hear as I was when he came to see me; it was a visett to his mother
that brought him to this place; he is gon now to London, & talks of coming
back in a fortnight; I am thus perteculer, becaus you said you had some
affairs with him. The Duke of St. Albains came last night, but that will
not add much to the diversions of ye place, which I hear is as dismale
abroad as to me that keep home. Betty has been out twice; she is gon to
the ball to night with Lady Grantam.—— Saturday ye 27th. I began
this letter (as you will see) yesterday for fear I shoud not be able to do it
all at once, & say so much as I had a mind to, for tho' the spirett is willing

the flesh is week, yett I beleive a greater amendment was never known in 24 hours, for I not only begun the watters again this morning, but I went in a chare & drank them at ye pump, where I alwais find they agree infinetly better with me, but I cant alow the raising of my spiretts to be wholey oweing to that, for I am sure your dear kind letter has the largest share, though at the same time it gives me a good deal of pain to think what so much tenderness must suffer from Bettys letter and mine on Wensday till this gitts to your hands, which I hope will put you perfectly at eas, for I can assure you with great truth I find my self much better then I have been this month; however, I shall not venter out any more to day for fear of my leggs, for they are apt to swell more towards evening, tho' nothing to the degree they have done. Mr. Duncomb has been with me this morning; he would give one great faith in thees watters, for he sais he is perfectly recoverd both of his cholick & ruemattisem, which he was extreemly bad off when he came; & for my further incouragement (that have been so very il) he tells me he was much wors the first fortnight; I find many people of the oppinion that when the watters do most good they give great disorders at first; pray God it may prove so with me; in order to merett that blessing (as farr as I am able) is to be truely thankfull for the dangers I have past; so that I intend the going to church shall be the first use I make of my leggs.—I do not wonder at my being disapointed of hearing of you upon the road, when it was left to Cornfourth, but I hope Harry was not so for-gittfull on Saturday night to give you an account of us as farr as Reading, for mine that was writ the same post coud not reach you till Wensday. I dont remember wether I told you in any of my letters that Lord Cadoggen sent to me before I left London to invite me to his house in my way heither; their is a great deal of company their as you must have heard; the cheif of what this place affords has been with me to day to play at wish. Lord Carlton is as good at that as at omber, & chid his poor nephew Quensbor-

ough often.   I have continued  very well  all day,  and hope  to trouble you
with no more complaints then what your absence causes, which till we meet
you must bear with from your faithfull E.B.

**714.**     Lord Bristol to Lady B.     Ickworth Park, April 29, 1723.

The  unwelcome  account  I receivd of  you by the
last nights letters would have kept me  from sleeping (tho' I go to bed tired
every  night at ten) had it  not been for  your postscript,  which I hope was
not added to flatter or deceive  me, those  being practises  you know by my
last banishd by our faithfuller friendship.   I would  not  have  you at all
allarmd at the frequent returns of your hysterick disorders because you have
not lately  been indiscreet enough to  occasion them, they  being alass !  the
natural remains of that fatal course of life, which to my knowledge and
sorrow  you  have ledd for  near  28 years ;   your  winterly irregularities at
London having generally disabled you from making use of those necessary
helps the summer  season and  country  exercises  might  otherwise  have
administerd.   But as I know  the  many  truths  I have to  urge upon this
topick will  not at  present serve to  lessen your distemper, I shall  wave
saying any more now than that, as you know the whole peace and happiness
of my life depends entirely upon the continuance of yours, I will hope that
consideration  alone (tho' there  are many more)  must at  last prevail with
you to  think of nothing for  the future but  how to re-establish  a health so
essential to my own.—I hope your son has  made you  easy, as he has me,
about the black-eyed girl.—Pray fail not to show Lord and Lady Abingdon
all the civilities in your  way for their kindnesses to our son Harry, tho' he
wrote not to me as you  desired him and he promisd.   Mrs. Kinsman too
being at Bath, I hope you will not forgett, as she  loves  and has used our
boy Charles well.   Neither forgett  to Mrs. Smith,  Mr. Duncombe etc. the
compliments of your Bristol.

715. Lady Bristol to Lord B. Bath, April 29, 1723.

Tis hard to be denyd the only pleasure one has, but such is my unhappy fate at present, for they tell me writing such long letters do me a great deal of harm while my spirits are so low; but the truth is I never know when to have done when I am any way conversing with you, nor do I feel any uneasyness when I am so; yet they will lay my being out of order on Saturday night to that; my Lord Carleton was p‑esent when I foulded up my letter, and said he woud not write so much in a month if any body woud give him £500; he is really very diverting with his method of living, which is by an exact rule from morning to night, and by what I hear of the place, (for as yet I have not seen anything,) he will be under no temptation of breaking any of them. I have been at the Pump again to day, but yesterday I was not able, I was so vastly dis‑piritted, besides a good deal of uneasyness in my legs, which I beleive proceeds from this change of weather, it being now wet and cold, and all last week the very finest that ever I saw, which made me grudge the being here more than ever, instead of partaking the pleasures of Ickworth with you and the dear babes; but I am surprizd not to hear you talk of leaving it, since the Duke of St. Albans (who was to see me last night) told me there was a vast deal to do in the House of Lords concerning the Bishop of Rochester next Thursday; I never saw so dismall a spectacle as his Grace; if you were to see him you woud think your self so very young a man that you woud not wonder at your receiving a billet-doux; but I cant help being peakd enough to mortifye your vanity a little by telling you Mr. Nash has receivd one (since I came hither) from the same person; but I think I ought not to mention this, for it woud have gratifyd my pride the more to have had it particular, since you are so to me in the preference . between us by so many kind and tender expressions, which woud revive me almost from the dead, and has done wonders with me too day, for I am better this evening, but cant expect much benefit from the waters while this flux (tho' I have taken rubarb) continues upon me, and till I have some success in drinking they will not allow me to bathe for fear of my hysterick disorder, tho' it woud certainly do me great service for my legs ; I am to take a bollus night and morning, which Mr. Skrine says will both strengthen me and raise my spirits, and assures me this disorder is what frequently happens at the first taking the waters, and that they will succeed never the worse afterwards. Betty is gone to the play with Lady Grantam.— 9 a clock. Though I am a perfect St. Martin when I am writing to you, yet I left this blank to give you the last account I coud of my self, which I do with pleasure, since I am sure it will be so to you to know I am much better of all my complaints.

**716.**　Lord Bristol to Lady B.　Ickworth Park, May-day, 1723.

Altho' I prepard you before our parting not to expect a letter from me by every post, yet as I know you had much rather receive one from my hand than two from any body else, I cannot omit giving my self as well as you that satisfaction whenever I am not necessarily prevented from doing so ; were I at all inclind to let an other do this agreeable office for me, my present weariness would justly excuse me, having been above twenty miles to look after a celebrated padd for the Dutchess of Marlborough, who unlike most other things even answerd beyond expectation, insomuch that I gave the gentleman his price (which was no less than fifty pounds) for him at first word, lest, as I was told he had done formerly, he should change his mind, and not sell him on any terms. He has every good quality that you like, and you having had so many to my mind, I cannot for that reason but give you the refusall of him, being confident that constant rideing would do you more service in retrieving your constitution than the Bath-mineral or all the other medicines in nature. Therefore send me word if you will make use of him, for, if you will, her Grace must stay till I can find another for her. Tis now near an hour beyond my ordinary time of going to bed, and no letter from you, which till I see and know how you are, I cannot sleep, tho' I should, tho' what you told me of Mr. Skrine's assurance that you should hear no more of your disorder, has made me not quite so uneasy as I must have been but for that and your postscript.—Your letter is just come, and I have only time to tell you I have read it with joy ; shall give my ever good God thanks for your being so much better before I go to rest, and then shall hope to take more than has been felt these 3 weeks by your Bristol.

717. Lady Bristol to Lord B. Bath, May 1, 1723.

I think it is as much pleasure to me that I am able to tell you I am better as to feel my self so, after so many letters of complaints and such a long confinement ; I got abroad yesterday in the evening and went to the ball, but such a parcel of creatures as there was got together is impossible to imagin without seeing them, and when you do, as impossible to imagin from what parts of the world they are gathered together, for except my Lord Grantam's family there is not a creature that can walk, and the two male kind of them are boys to fill up the set ; in the other extream is my clumsey Lord Dunbarton and the thin awkard Duke of Qu—gh, besides 50 little hoppers that outdo any harleqine in their motions ; but I did not stay to see them shew their shapes in country dances, for I thought I should be as ridiculous as themselves to venture my poor swelld legs, who still give me a good deal of uneasyness being very sore, but I hope for great relief from bathing when I may venture with safety, which Mr. Skrine thinks may be on Monday ; in the meantime I fret and tease my self to think how unlucky I have been to loose ten days in this hatefull place, and cant find in my heart to wish you here to comfort me, which is a sign I love you much better than my self.—Lord Abingdon enquird after you, and run on for an hour in praise of Harry, who I find is a great favourite with him; I wish he may deserve it better than he has hitherto done.   Mr. Lee and his two daughters are here, but he is so exceeding ill that they seldom stirr; that being my case too, nothing but messages has yet passed between us.   Mrs. Long and Mrs. Gibson are come last week, the first of which has been to see me; the latter is very ill.   The diversions of this evening is the Poppet show, which I am unable to partake of, it being in Mr. Harrison's upper room ; Betty is gone with Lady Torrington ; the wiskers have promised me some diversion after tis over, if it be done in time ; if not, this day must pass like the former with your forlorne E.B.

   If it shoud happen you dont go to London, I hope you will remember the servants that wait for your directions, and poor Fanny that did not forget you.

   **718.**    Lord Bristol to Lady B.       Ickworth Park, May 3, 1723.

                 The relief your last letter brought me I first thankd God's goodness for, and now you for sending me the alteration of your health in such strong, and I hope sincere, terms.   I truely wanted the necessary effects it has been attended with, having slept more soundly in an hour since than in a night before.   May your recovery proceed to that perfection my prayers for you daily implore; and that nothing may retard it, I beg you would not write so much, knowing nothing spends the spirits more, and yours are not robust enough to bear the least fatigue ; I shall hereafter take care to manage them with so due caution as never to write or speak (whenever I am to be so happy again) to you any more on a melancholly subject, since I find nothing of that kind can be touchd upon without tears ; if the kindness my letters carry with them have a greater share in raising your spirits than taking the waters at the Pump, sure you need never want a cordial of that sort, if you have carryed that voluminous bundle of them with you as usual; look into them and tell me if ever love was like unto my love ; if ever faithfullness (on the male side) exceeded, nay, so much as equalld, mine; or if ever true tenderness was to be found in any humane heart to that incredible degree mine has constantly been possessd with for thee and thine. If my kindness will co-operate with the waters towards a speedy and certain cure of your complaints, pray let your own imagination supply the defects of language, and make that ingredient in your doctors bills stronger than any words of mine can possibly reach.

**719.** Lady Bristol to Lord B. Bath, May 4, 1723.

I have been now a fortnight at this hatefull place without the least sign of any amendment, and am now interupted again from drinking the waters or bathing so soon as I hopd for, having great dependance upon the later for my poor legs, which are still in a sad condition, though I am now able to walk without a stick; but they swell so extreamly (especially my left) when I have been up but a few hours, that before night I am scarce able to bear the uneasyness they give me. I was last night forcd to leave the ball and go to bed at 9 a clock, where I now am, and shall continue till I go to dinner, taking this opportunity, when I cant go to the Pump, to rest my legs as much as I can, so that I may not loose a moment in relieving some or other of my complaints, which I much fear are too many and great to be conquerd in the time I have here, which can be but 5 weeks drinking the waters, though I shoud meet with no more interruptions, my waiting coming about again the 17th of June, so that I must necessarily (to comply with that) leave this place the 13th; I am thus particular that you may order your own affairs and mine as is most agreeable to your self, which will make it entirely so to me, for I have very little to hope, since they say it must be a length of time here to cure my distempers, which (from a long and provd experience) I am sure without you woud rather be increasd, so that you may be assurd I dont mention this with any design of staying, since tis impossible I can wish you any thing so disagreeable as to desire you to come to this place, which is more so than is possible for me to discribe ; yet my Lord and Lady Grantham find time so necessary here, that they have lengthend out theirs (I believe) beyond mine, though they were here so long before me ; but I dont think I shoud have the same favour shewd me, though I had never so much occasion, nor indeed woud I at this time desire it, for if we are to have any summer, one may expect it by the middle of June, though tis now as cold as Christmas, which I am very much concernd for, since I find you are still at Ickworth, though I believe it is better for us that are here than heat woud be, which I found very uneasy at my first coming.  I shall be sure to obey all your complimental commands as far as I am able ; I have already done one part by having Mr. Duncomb to dinner, but have not seen him since ; where he bestows his person is impossible to guess, for he says he is never at home, nor no body ever sees him abroad.  I had Mr. Nash to dine here with him, who has been particularly civil and more than ordinarily obliging in everything ever since I came ; while I kept the house he never missd a day coming to enquire how I did; as to my Lady Abingdon, she was here before me, and has neither sent nor been to see me, so that I can only make her a courtsey when I know her, which at present I dont, for I have been but twice at the publick diversions, which was the balls, so that I coud only see her at the distance of the room, chuseing to sit at the lower end to be at liberty to go away with more ease ; my Lord and I have a vast deal of conversation every day ; he tells all his misfortunes at billiards, and how much money he looses ; I am in the same case with Mrs. Kinsman as the former lady, so that if she does not make her self known to me, tis impossible I can pay her the civility you desire, and I am inclined to do.  I am sorry

I cant give as good an account of my first setting out as I have done in these affairs, since you thought it wrong; I can only say I did all in my power (that was civil) to prevent his coming, though I did not think there was much in it, since she had a brother to accompany him, and was to have had two, if he had not been more than ordinarily lazy in the morning; there is a report here to day that the eldest brother of that gentleman is dead. I will keep my letter open as long as I can; if I meet with anything that is come by this post, you shall know it, not being out too day. My Lord Carleton (who is President of the Wiskers as well as the Counsell,) has sent me a message to know how I do, and where I will be attended, which must be at home, for though my present complaint is natural, yet coming upon so many others and lowness of spirits, it puts me a good deal out of order, which I believe you will hardly credit when you see this long letter; but if it had not been to you, my pen had long agoe dropd out of my hand, and now will hold no longer then to bid my dearest life adieu.—Pray put your letters in a cover, for by their coming thro' two posts they are often crackd in the foldings, & they are to precious to me not to be preservd.

**720.** Lord Bristol to Lady Bristol. Ickworth Park, May 6, 1723.

Your last letter brought me a most convinceing proof of the infallibility of my good genius towards you, for you will find I had already prevented your friends right advices against writing such long epistles to me, even tho' you say tis a pleasure to indite, and I best know that of receiving them : however, I once more beg you would never send me above a side or two at most, so much above my own satisfaction do I value your health and ease. I can readily give credit to the person, who said he would not write so much in a month for £500 as one of your dispatches to me containd, in case he thought twould make his blood beat one pulse the faster towards his death's-march. How can you be surprisd at not hearing

Vol. II. MM

of my leaving this place yet? since tis the only one where you are not can keep my mind in tolerable tranquility, with all the due submission I have taught it to God's wise providence.  Were you at London, it could not have kept me near so long from you; but as you are not to be found there when I come, tis so discouraging an exchange as I can never think of making but on necessity.  The Publick cannot want the attendance of such a cypher as I am to secure it, when at the same time it dispenses with the absence of so considerable a figure in its affairs as my Lord P.; besides, I am told the M. are broke almost into as many minds as there are men in it, which I take to be good news, for now Britain has many chances that one at last may think of her true interests.   Contrary to my own injunction I must begin a third side to tell you Harry has at last written to me, but twas not till he was driven to it by fresh wants, ( a liste whereof is inclosd,) which I must go to London and provide for him, being very confident they may be purchasd at much under-rates than thus given in by the agent, who in all regiments are mere hucksters, and he being so careless a novice in all management must at first see what may be saved by prudence, or he will never prove wiser in expences than he has been, which must end in want and a jayle.—That you think it as much pleasure to be able to tell me you are better as to feel your self so, must be doubly welcome to him who has (comparatively) no hopes nor fears left but what relate to your love & length of life, the continuance of both being become essentially necessary to his, who lives not but in you & for you.   Bristol.

**721.**    Lady Bristol to Lord Bristol.        Bath, May 6, 1723.

As I have not seen a mortal since I seald up my last letter, I have nothing but my (at present) unhappy self to furnish out another, which when I shall be able to do without complaints, God only knows, for my legs continue extreamly bad still, though I have not been out since Friday, and have been in or upon the bed almost all the time, for I was resolvd to take this opportunity, when I did not drink the waters, to try what rest woud do, for I fancyd getting up so much sooner to go to the Pump might make them worse; but since I find little or no difference, I shall return to that again, as it agrees so much better with my other complaints, which I find great encouragement here to hope that though I may not be quite cured, yet I may find so much relief as may make me spend the rest of my days more agreeable to my self and with more satisfaction to you than they have been of late. Though there is several people for the same complaints of the nerves that have found benefit here, yet none can give so great an instance of the good effect of these waters as Mr. Lewis, who they thought could not live when he came here last season, but by the help of that and this (for he is now here with his lady) Mrs. Lewis tells me he is almost quite recoverd, and indeed he appears to be so, for he is very gay and chearfull, and used only to amuse himself with playing upon the organ in the Church ; I believe you know both him and her, at least I am sure you will when I tell you tis she that always was very justly calld, pretty Mrs. Lewis; she is not only that but very agreeable, (which in my mind is better,) her name was Dashwood; so much for that.—Now I must give my dear angel a million of thanks for the kind preference in such a jewell of a horse, which I am entirely of your opinion woud infinitely contribute to my cure, if I coud conquer my fears; but as they are unsurmountable, tis impossible I coud find any benefit from riding, that puts me in such eternal terrours, and the least thing that does that, or makes me any way uneasy, I immediately feel very severe effects from, my nerves being so extreamly weak that I feel a most intolerable wearyness all over me when I wake in the morning, and such a weakness in my joynts that I can hardly hold any thing in my hands; but thank God I have had nothing of my hysterick disorder (beyond lowness of spirits) since I gave you the last account, which

I know you woud always have me very particular in, else I woud not have filld my paper up with all this stuff. I dont hear this post produces any thing but another change in the Duke of Wh—n, (which cant be calld news ;) it seems he is become a protesting lord again ; Lord Pomfret being so is more surprizing. The deversions of this day being a Popet-show, I cannot be a sharer in it, for I dare not aim at anything that is not upon even ground, so that I must content my self with reading and answering your dear letter, which is sufficient pleasure for your faithfull E. B.

722.    Lord Bristol to Lady Bristol.    Ickworth Park, May 8, 1723.

I must in the first place desire that neither you nor Mr. Skrine would do anything to put a final stop to that flux you say has been upon you ; tis a beneficial method nature has found out to discharge her self of all those morbifick humours, which a London life of laziness and luxury contracts in all our constitutions, and which I have had the advantage of since my being here ; check it you may in case it be too violent, but pray take great care not to lock up any feculent remains that may produce future diseases, if the Bath-waters should not at last prevent any such dismal consequences ; I have sufferd by them long and often in vain, but as my sole trust is in God allmighty, I'm confident, if those should not secure you, he can and will find out that which shall for my peace. Will Oliver is returnd from your estate in Staffordshire, which he likes much better than that in High-Suffolk ; I am, as I ought, equally thankfull to bounteous Providence for both, but above all for that happy conduite thro' which they have passd into the Hervey family. He receivd for your moytie of the half years rents due at Michaelmas last £138..16s..8¾d.,which was very welcome.— I have sent you inclosd the best account Cornforth can give without book of what you desird.—Since melancholly matters are improper for you, I send you these verses to enliven you ; I told the author his sentiments were strong, but diction weak; he said they were all of his own inditing, and that he had nothing but his poetry left to live on; which being the case, I'm afraid he'l dye not much richer than most of his fraternity. The letters are not come, and tis past my bed-time, therefore health and peace be with you. Amen.

**723.** Lady Bristol to Lord Bristol. Bath, May 8, 1723.

This being the disagreeable post that one writes two letters for one, I should be under a difficulty (if that coud ever happen ‧ from me to you) of knowing what to say, but that I have the good news to tell you of my being in the bath too day with less disorder than I coud possibly expect to my spirits, and with as much ease as I coud hope to my legs, for they dont feel so stiff, though they are so very much swelld, but Mr. Skrine gives me hopes even for that by telling me, if I will give him but time and patience, he is pretty sure (having had such success with my Lady Renelaugh) he coud not only cure me from what is occasiond by my fall, but alsoe what has so long troubled me; if he is able to perform the great things he promises, I believe it will reconsile you as well as my self to this hated place, which they say will not be long so dismall as it has been, but as they always talk so, I dont give much credit to it, though Mr. Skrine's great house has been taken for some time; the Dutchess of Rutland has one great appartment, and General Wills the other; the first is kept away by being so ill, the later by the Parliament; there is great expectation from too morrows letters to hear how the B. of R. behavd in your House; I have heard since I writ last my Lord Essex was a deserter as well as the other lords I mentiond in relation to Kelly; but I dont know why I pretend to write you news that are so much nearer it than we; and Jack is a very good correspondent if he pleases, though I cant say I am the better for it; I had a letter from his lady the last post to know who I woud appoint to represent me for their Christening, without telling me who was to stand with me either for godfather or godmother, or mentioning the name of the child, so that I conclude it is to be Lepell,as they had before thought, and upon which I told them my opinion, that in that case Mrs. Lepell woud be properer than me ; you may remember I told you what had past the night before we parted ; however, I writ Mrs. Hervey word, if they had alterd their minds, I still remaind at their service, which was as much as I coud say upon this occasion, and I hope you will be of the same opinion ; and that we may never differ in this or any thing else shall be the constant prayers, as well as endeavours, of your faithfull E. B.

**724.**     Lord Bristol to Lady B.      Ickworth Parke, May 10, 1723.

If length of time be ye only circomstance which can make the Bath waters operate so effectually as to cure all your complaints, I am sure by my consent you shall never leave them till that much desird point is gaind, whatever may be ye consequence of your staying elsewhere ; is there any thing to be putt in ballance with your health & ease, especially weir ye case as you suppose, that you shoud not have ye same favour shewn to you with others. Would one venter much to serve where one can suspect so little a peice of justice or humanity coud be denyed ? Try but ye request in time, & it cannot be refusd ; & if my company is ye other necessary ingredient to compleat your cure, (would nothing else do) I woud even live at Bath ye rest of my life to effect it,—You will see by ye inclosd that our son Will is arrivd at Portsmouth ; he has been there some time, and to excuse his not writing to me sooner has made a lame excuse of having hurt one of his fingers in their passage home ; he says their ship is orderd for ye Buoy at ye Nore, & to proceed thence for Woolwich, there to refitt, & to be one of those who are to convoy his Majesty to Holland ; he hopes I or you have a promis of something better for him than a Lievtenancy, having servd longer so than any man's son of my quality has been usually known to do; my answer must be (I know not what yours will be) that ye duties on preferments have been so very high ever since I servd in either House of Parliament, that neither my honour nor conscience would ever give me leave to trade in them for my self, and that it woud be unreasonable at my time of day to press me to begin that traffick for others, tho' ne'er so near or dear to me as one of your sons must ever be to B.

One of my best blessings alwaies attends our daughter Betty.

**725.** Lady Bristol to Lord Bristol. Bath, May 11, 1723.

I am sorry I cant end the week so well as I begun it, for the swelling of my legs are extream bad, and consequently very uneasy; but I woud fain flatter my selfe that it proceeds from an accident that I have occasiond, for finding my self better I attempted to return my visits yesterday and Thursday, and walkd once to the Pump and twice to Church; whether this has put me so much back again I know not; but tis certain my legs last night were as bad as ever except the soreness; this happening when I thought my self in so good a way of recovery has (as you may imagin) put a good deal of damp upon my spirits, though I am easier too day, having been in the bath again; I am to take my rubarb too night, and a Monday begin with what Mr. Skrine has such faith in, and that it may have a fair tryal I shall keep my self as still as l can; in order to it I am going to spend the evening with Mrs. Paget, who keeps the house; Mrs. Smith and she live together, and were both very kind to me when I was laid up, and as I reign Queen of the whisk party, I have (at her request) appointed them to meet me there. Granthams dont succeed so well in their Sovereign power over the balls, for though Mr. Nash appointed they shoud not begin last night till 8 a clock, (now the weather is warm,) yet they woud insist upon 7, (since they always retire at 9,) and accordingly there was not any

French dances above half an hour, and some time between before they coud gather 5 couple together (of creatures) to dance country dances, so that Mr. Nash was forcd to say aloud, This dance it will no farther go; for which reason they should have balls but once a week. He and the Grantham family are gone with 2 coach-fulls too day to Mr. Blathwait's; I put in broad hints for poor Betty that had a mind to see it, but they were not so kind as to ask her to go with them. The Dutchess of Rutland and Lady Betty Maners are arrivd, and so is my Lady Barrymore; I dont think any of them will contribute to the diversions of the place beyond three-penny ombre.—I find insensibly I have broke into your orders about writing, yet I must add the good news I have heard too day of Will's safe arrival at Portsmouth. Here is one Mr. Cleveland, who belongs to the Admiralty; he has had letters of it; his wife is a very agreeable woman, and very civil to me, (though we dont visit,) but I must do justice to every body else that is here, for they are all particularly so, which woud be a great addition to the place, if any thing coud be agreeable, where you are not, to your E. B.

**726.**    Lord Bristol to Lady B.        Ickworth Park, May 13, 1723.

The baths agreeing so well with you, and the punctual performance of Mr. Skrine's promises, would make me ask pardon of the place for all my past aversion to it, and force me to think of it hereafter with as much pleasure as it has given me pain; for should the restoration of your health faile, in vain would all the beauties of this sweet place court my senses; I find a great abatement in their usual effects upon me from your temporary absence only; what horrour then in every thought which will sometimes intrude when you are away, and suggest a possibility of my suffering a longer one. The only balm I have to pour into so deep a wound as that reflection never failes of making in my mind, is my through belief in and dependence on the infinite goodness and mercy of God, that such an irrepairable loss is not reservd in his providence for so true a penitent as I am.—Our dear daughter Ann having got cold by being later abroad in these sharp evenings we have had here than she should have been, has been a little feaverish with it these two or three daies; but Mr. Ray having given her what Mademoiselle told me never failed with her, she is apparently better, which has not a little relievd my poor heart, which I own cannot help being allarmd whenever she is attackd by any distemper one knows not how it may end, since I would fain have her live to shew the world an example of a perfect good woman, for such I am sure she'l make, if ever there is to be an other; her soul so gentle, and the elements (as Anthony said of Brutus) so justly mixd in her, that nature may boast to all the world and say, This is a worthy woman.—Having staid till this time here, I think not now of removing till this day sevenight, when I intend to take Felle with me to London, altho' I am not sure when there that they may think his face yet well enough for a drawing-room; however, I shall have your representative with me, which is alwaies a true pleasure to your Bristol.

727.    Lady Bristol to Lord B.        Bath, May 13, 1723.

I am (if possible) more dispiritted to day after my bathing than I was last time, and that I believe you might see by my letter was enough, for I hardly knew what I writ, but think I told you I was to spend the evening with Mrs. Smith and Mrs. Paget, where they found me so bad that they held a consultation for me, and found it absolutely necessary I should be as much in the air as the weather woud permit me to sit abroad; (being not able to walk,) Mrs. Lewis was so kind as to desire I woud try a coach, which I readily accepted of; so she carryd Mrs. Smith, Betty and my self to vissit Mr. Skrine and his wife. They have a very pretty place at Clarkendown, but I not being able to see all the garden, lost (as they say) several beauties; but it had need be as fine as Chatsworth, for the way to it

(I think) is almost as bad ; I am sure my poor legs found it so ; that and being 4 in the coach made them in a sad condition, for which I cryd about an hour after I came home, and as much this morning, though Mr. Skrine tells me my Lady Rochester's legs were as bad as mine, when she came here last year, and that he quite cured her before she left the place with the same medicine he begins with me too night in a glass of the Bath water, and the same in the morning at the Pump. . . . But I think I have said enough of my self, unless I coud tell you something better ; besides that I have chosen a very ill time to transgress the rules you laid down to me about writing, which I should never have been able to do, if your dear, kind prose had not been much more enlivening than your heroick verse.

**728.**    Lord Bristol to Lady B.    Ickworth Park, May 15, 1723.

After what I told you in my last of our dear daughter Ann's indisposition, I must begin this with the good news of letting you know she is much better, even so well as I hope to be able by the next post to tell you she is quite recoverd. The evenings have been so terribly cold here, that twas almost impossible to preserve ones self from feeling some inconvenience or other by them ; but since cool weather is so necessary to you where you are, it hath been welcome to me here, tho' by it and the drought we have little or no grass growing, besides many trees who have not yet put on their summer liveries. You will wonder to hear this place should want moisture, but it really thirsts after rain as much, if possible, as my soul does to see thee again. I have seldom differd in opinion from you but with great reluctance, and when that happend, (which sure has been as seldom as was ever known between man and wife in 28 years time,) I alwaies thought at least that reason was strongly on my side, which you have afterwards been ingenuous enough to own ; and as to the matter depending between you and your son and daughter about christening the pretty dimpled black-eyd girl, I think them very much to blame never to have acquainted you who they intend should stand with you ; tis but a common civility due to every one in your scituation as a gossip ; but as you are a parent, they ought to have consulted with you who would be most agreeable to you, as well as told you who they were to be. But now I must say that since you was askd, you should have done it without any conditions, and so left them without excuse for having omitted their duty towards you, which pray forgive this time for the sake of your Bristol.

**729.** Lady Bristol to Lord Bristol. Bath, May 15, 1723.

It being but a day & half since I wrote last, I hope you will not expect a much better account of me, for I can only say I am not worse ; when I shall be well, God only knows ; for till we meet again I dispair of it ; tis then (if ever) I must feel the good effect from thees watters; I have begun the pills, which are to do wonders; they made me very sick at first, but Mr. Skrine tells me that must not discourage me, for he will answeir for their succes, tho' at present they cant have a fair tryell, I am in such affliction for my Lord Pres—t, who has left us this day. You cant easily believe how much he will be missd, especially by me, not only as a whisk player but for his company at ye Pump, where he used to be very entertaining with all his lorms, for he has done every thing to a muinett by his watch ever since he came, .... Mr. Low is come, but he is good for nothing, for he refuses a half crown raffell when askd. Mr. Hamilton (Harry's Captain) is hear in his way to quarters. I thought it woud be right to return ye civelety he has & may shew his cornett, to invite him to diner, (for he had made himself known to me before;) I tooke that oppertunetty to shew him ye list of ye things which you sent me; upon that he writ me down this inclosd with such prises as he paid himself; but if his understanding be no better in that than in conversation, tis not worth much.

Hear is nothing talkd of hear but the Bishop of Roch : fine speach, which I sopose you have a better account of then I can give you, or you woud care I shoud, since I have already broke into your orders ; but as that proceeds from a kind caus, it will, I do not doubt, meet with as kind an excuse for your E. B.

**730.** Lord Bristol to Lady Bristol. Ickworth Park, May 17, 1723.

How could you be guilty of so double an indiscretion, when you found your self better, to venture a relapse, only to satisfy the senseless mode of returning Bath visits, whether well or ill, in such a time after ones arrival; and when you had done so and found your self the worse for it, to tell me of it ; for I must needs acquaint you that my spirits begin to be disorderd as much upon hearing any ill news concerning your health as yours can be on reading what I write on the most melancholly subject ; therefore pray take more than ordinary care of your self, and not compliment away my quiet with your own safety. I live not one day without you but to teach me how very miserable God could make me, and to deprecate with the most intense devotion so supreme an evil. My London letters are come in, but none inclosd as usual from you ; judge what a disappointment that must be to me, and how well I am like to sleep after so good an opiate; were it not that I have Robins sottish stupidity to accuse for the mischance, I should not be at ease one moment till I knew the true reason of it. I told you the Post-Officers would prove the safest conveyers, as I hope you have constantly experienced by never missing any of mine. I shall get the better of my extream leaning towards continuing in this sweet place, were it only to be so much nearer to you as I shall be at London, and that then I shall be no more liable to such tryals of my philosophy. You did our son Jack but justice when you said he could be a very good correspondent if he pleasd ; for (after several others) I receivd a letter from him by this last post, which gave me as full as clear yet succinct an account of the B——'s tryal, together with the passages in the other House relating to the Papists Bill, as, had I been present, I could not have understood them better ; therefore, as I verily believes he loves you in his heart, (otherwise I should be farr from being his advocate,) but has been forced to stifle some appearances of it, since he thought you wrong in some points towards his tender part, I once more desire you to live so with her, and to forgive him, as that he may shew you truly what an affectionate dutyfull son he can make, were matters once sett upon a reasonable foot between her and you. You know my maxim that quarrels would seldom last long, were there not some small faults on both sides ; endeavour to correct yours towards her, and then she'l be left excuseless. Our dear daughter Ann grows daily better, God be praisd, in all sorts of senses ; whoever is to be blessd with her, will never shoote themselves, as Jack tells me poor Lord Tenham has done. Farewel. Bristol.

**731.**  Lady Bristol to Lord Bristol.  Bath, May 18, 1723.

I give my dearest life a thousand thanks for the kind indulgence you give to my (present) ill state of health, by making me so vast an expression towards my cure as the coming to this hatefull place, especially at this time of the year, and in the dullest season that ever was known, so very bad that Mr. Nash talks every day of leaving us; but I shall have a greater loss to morrow, which is Mrs. Smith and Mrs. Paget going away ; they have been here almost 3 months, and have found a greate deal of benefit; I hope I shall do it in less, for I have determind to set out from hence the 13th of next month, if that sutes with your convenience of sending the coach, which I believe it will, because you say you shall go to London upon Harry's account, who I find by Mr. Hamilton is very much wanted at quarters; however, he is not to mind that but his Collonel's

orders.   I conclude Felly does not fail to put you in mind that he is to go
into  waiting  the  first  of  June;  but  I  believe  he  can  give  you no account
about the mourning, which is to last till the 16th June, then we go out ;
therefore I hope you will remember he will then want some summer cloaths,
for  sure  by  that  time  we  may  have  some  sign  of  it,  though  at  present  we
have  none,  but  are  forcd  to  have  fires  almost  all  day,  and  an  easterly  wind
that  has  been  ever  since  we  came,  which  makes  everybody's  complaints
worse,  and  they  tell  me  occasions  my  giddiness  in  my  head,  which  has
been  very  troublesome  to  me,  and  hinderd  my  bathing  for fear of increasing
it, but I have taken my rubarb again and am something better.  Mr. Skrine's
medicine  has  done  very  well  with  me  in  making  me  eat  and  sleep,  and
consequently  gives  me  spirits,  which  indeed  I  want  very  much  if  post-days
did  not  revive  me,  though  this  of  too  day  has  put  a  damp  by  finding  poor
dear  Nan  has  such  frequent  returns  of  her  feaverish  disorder;  any  ailment
to  such  a  treasure  must  alarm ;  I  wish  my  prayers  and  blessing  may  have
the  same  success  towards  her  as  yours  has  had  for  Betty,  who  is  so improvd
in  health,  looks  and  spirits  since  her  coming  hither,  as  is  hardly  to  be
imagind.   I  hope  to  be  able  to  give  you  as  good  an  account  of  my  self  in  a
little  time,  having  been  in  the  bath  this  morning  for  a  little  while  without
any  disorder  in  my  head,  though  I  was  a  good  deal  shockd  at  my  first  going
in  at  the  surpriziug  death  of  my  Lord  Tenham ;  there  was  a  poor  lady  (who
it  seems  was  a  relation)  sounded  away,  and  was  forcd  to  be  carryd  out.
I  have  so  much  exceeded  my  orders,  that  if  my  head  be  ill,  I  shall  think  it
a judgement upon me, therefore will bid my dear good night.

    **732.**   Lord Bristol to Lord ——      Ickworth, May 19, 1723.

        I am sorry your Lordship has given your self so
much  trouble  in  a  matter  I  cannot  serve  you  in  as  you  would  have  me,
since  I  have  yet  never  given  my  proxy  to  promote  or  prevent  any  bills

passing into a law, of whose fitness or inconvenience I had not first some
competent knowledge.  I intend to sett out hence for London to morrow,
& hope to arrive time enough to give my assent or negative to ye bill in
question, as shall appear most reasonable to, my Lord, your etc.

733.    Lady Bristol to Lord Bristol.        Bath, May 20, 1723.

        I avoided saying any thing in answeir to ye
begining of your last letter, because I must have undeceivd you in the kind
pleasure you took in believing ye Bath agreed so well with me ; for tho' I
have softend every complaint for your ease (as much as I coud with truth),
yett tis very sure I have not had one tolerable day since I came to this
place till thees last three ; & now I can sincerly assure you I am vissibly
mended, & hope I shall continue to do so since the thing I most apprehended
(which was my legg swelling so immoderately) begins now to abate, as
Mr. Skrine assurd me they woud, & tells me he never knew this medicen
fail in that complaint, & thinks it woud be very hard to begin with me, who
am the most reguler pattient he ever had, which I hope will prove some
sattisfaction to you.—I have done all that lay in my power to find out Mrs.
Kins—n, but in vain ; I applyd to Mrs. Long to help me, but she knew
nothing of her ; but upon inquirey we found out yesterday that she was gon.
I dont know upon what terms you & Mr. Gibson are now, but I think laitly
it has been but indifferant ; if any civellety that I can show his wife will be
of servis to you, I hope you will lett me know, (we do visett ;) Mrs. Pagett
remains still hear, for instead of having the coach come for her on Saterday,
her husband writ her word he woud come and fetch her ; we live very sociably
together as people of a family (in my oppinion) shoud, tho' Grantam dus
not seem to be of that mind, for he has taken no nottis of us, either for
breakfast, diner or super, which is pritty remarkable in this place, where
tis so common a thing, & he has his whole familey hear, even to his house-

keeper, & has a constant table, but few that eats of it besides Mr. Evans that lives with him ; I have the sattisfaction to find he pleases no body, yett we are very great to outward appearance; but how sincer that is you may judg from what I have told you.—I wish I may ever prevent your desirs by instink, as I have done about ye christening the black eyd girl ; for they have chose (I having left it to them) Lady Hillsborough to be my repre- sentitive, & Mrs. Brook for the other godmother; but who is ye godfather, or what the name, I am still to learn ; however that appears to me, shall, since you disire it, never be mentiond by your faithfull E. B.

**734.**   Lord Bristol to Lady Bristol.       London, May 21, 1723.

I was no sooner gott to my house hear but I found every room in it so intolerable without you that I could not bear being in it an hour before I went to seek some solace in Bond street, where I found your fair representative * the very thing my fancy had describd ; she has not a feature in her face but is yours in miniature, & as such receivd [from] every one in their turn so many kisses as made her ready to cry; & when I found by your letter which I mett hear how long it must yett be before I coud see ye original, to tell you the truth, I could hardly refrain from doing so too ; but lett this be a secret to all but your self; at my return home I felt my self so very much fatigued with my journey hither & thither, that I did not think I could have had strength or time to have filld the other side ; but begining any kind of convers with you has unwearyed both body & mind so much, that since ye first bell is but now ringing, I shall be early enough to tell you I receivd your last letter together with another before I left sweet Ickworth, which was some compensation, especially that which tells me you are better ; if you can eat & sleep well, those amendments

* Lord Bristol's pencil note in the margin says Miss Hervey ; meaning I suppose his eldest grand- daughter, Lepel, afterwards married to Constantine Phipps, 1st Lord Mulgrave. S.II.A.H.

alone will help to cure your imagination of those dispairing thoughts about your health, which would otherwise retard ye intire establishment of it, so devoutly prayd for by your only true friend, Bristol.

**735.** Lady Bristol to Lord Bristol. Bath, May 22, 1723.

By the account I gave of my self last post, I am affraid you will expect a better by this than I am able to give; for I cannot yet get the better of bathing without being disorderd ; for I was so ill after my last letter that I had much to do to write the superscription, and was forcd to have Betty do it up; my head and spirits are so affected with it, and gives me such tremblings, that were it not for my legs I should leave it off, though upon the whole I am certainly better, and Mr. Skrine gives me fresh assurance every day that with time and patience and the use of his medicine I shall be as well as ever I was in my life ; he will pawn his credit upon it, of which he has a large share with me, being so very care-full of me ; he never fails to see me once a day, and oftener when there is occasion. I am going to a play of the Dutchess of Queensborough's bespeaking, but dare not deferr writing till after it, for fear I should not be able, for I have been but at 2, and the last I was forcd to leave before it was done, but I hope I shall be better too day, for I go with the Dutchess of Rutland and Lady B. Maners. Betty continues very well, though she has been a little disorderd with a pain and a swelld face, but it has provd nothing but the cutting of a tooth; I believe she will be perfectly recoverd, for she has equipd her self for riding, (all the ladys do it here,) and dame Lindsey has lent her a very pretty pad and saddle; her dress becomes her very much, but it can be of no use to her, for here is no body worth making a conquest of, till last night Mr. Mansel arrivd, and I think that is not worth much, for according to the old proverb, while the grass grows the steeds may starve. I long more than ordinarily for too morrow's post to hear of dear Nan's recovery; and then I shall want to know how much poor Lew's beauty is affected by the small pox.—I kept my letter open till I am come from the Play, to tell you (what I am sure will please you) that I am come well from thence, and have passd the day so, but dare not venture to say more, for fear it shoud prove otherwise, therefore will only bid my dearest life good night.

**736.**    Lord Bristol to Lady Bristol.        London, May 23, 1723.

I think after your having ownd that the loss of my Lord P—'s company has provd such an affliction to you, I need no longer make a secret of my being fallen in love with much the most beautiful young woman now in the world ;....the strength of my affection for this new lady arises from the resemblance she bears to you ; to keep you no longer in so painful a suspence, tis my grandaughter.    Her godfather was Mr. Pulteney, who (by what you have told me) could not have been originally intended by her parents for the he-gossip ; for in that case they would never have kept you any more in ignorance about him than the godmother ; but as they themselves might be divided, or not determind in their choice, so could not sooner tell you certainly who it was ; should not this have been the case, you know already my thoughts upon their omission towards you ; however, I am better pleasd your instinct prevented my advice than that you should have done right, only because I desird it.—Felle is here with me, but whether his face be yet fit to attend the Princess with, I know not who is to resolve us ; your breach with Mrs. H——(Hervey), and the coldness between you and Grantham, will make us at a loss many a time for hints upon these occasions ; but as long as you grow better, the rest·are trifles to your Bristol.

**737.**    Lady Bristol to Lord Bristol.        Bath, May 25, 1723.

The last post gave me infinite pleasure in the bringing two of your kind letters to my hands ; that of Saturday from

Ickworth, which brought me the good news of dear Nan's mending so fast, was very welcome to me; but that of Tuesday, which gave me an account of your much dearer self being safely arrivd at London, was much more so; tis some comfort to be so much nearer; when we shall be yet more so remains with you to determine; for tho' I namd the longest time for my stay here, tis in your power to make it as much shorter as you please, and consequently more agreeable to me, who long most passionately to see you; in the mean time I am glad any part of me has contributed so much to your entertainment; that I do assure you will cover a multitude of falts towards me, were they of a much higher nature and without your desires added to it, which are most sacred to me, though it touches very nearly to receive so little where one has paid so much.—I wish this post might pass without mentioning any thing of my self, since I have nothing good to tell you; but I should be guilty of a breach of trust if I did not let you know that I am at last forcd to give over all thoughts of bathing; I believe I told you in my last that it always disorderd me; but last Thursday I was worse than ever with it, though I was not in half an hour; for I fell into the most violent hysterick fit I ever had in my life, which has put me into great disorder ever since, and quite taken away both appetite and rest, so much has it affected my spirits, though I have done all that lay in my power to help it, by being as much in the air as I was able; we have had two fine days, but this is a very bad one again. Betty looses no opportunity of riding, for when the Dutchess of Rutland baths and does not venture to do it, she goes with Mrs. Cleveland ; her husband was an old sea officer, and is now a commissioner of the Navy; she is so obliging that when Betty rides with her Grace, she is always ready to carry me in her coach ; indeed it is impossible for me to express how very kind my new acquaintances are to me; they are like so many nurses when ever I ail any thing, (which alass is but too frequent;) tis a melancholly reflection, after so long and tedious an absence, to be able to give you no better account of my self; but what I do to mend one complaint increases the other ; but that I may leave nothing untryd, I must beg you woud get Mr. Graham to go to Doctor Friend to know if I may venture to pump my legs, since tis impossible I can hold on bathing ;....My Lord Grantham told me too day our Court goes to Richmond Wednesday sevenight ; therefore I hope you will borrow my Lord Hervey's house there (at least a room in it) for the time I am to stay, for it will be impossible to bear an additional fortnight to what I have already sufferd by your absence. I spoke about Felly to his Lordship, and he agreed with me that Sir An: Fountain shoud see and give an account of him to the Princess. I receivd a letter from Mrs. Hervey too day dated for last post, to tell me the child was christend, but what the name is I know not. I desire you woud make my excuse that I dont answer it, for I am not able to say more (even to you) than bid you farewell.

**738.** . Lord Bristol to Lady Bristol.       London, May 25, 1723.

Since you shew so much faith in Mr. Skrine, which they say is half a cure, you must persist in what he prescribes, altho' at first it may not answer expectation ; his confidence being so strong as to stake his reputation upon the success of that method and those medicines you are now in the course of, has given me very great and comfortable hopes too that those, together with my devoutest prayers, will not begin to faile in your case after his having had so good experience of his humane means, and I of my divine. My universal recipe for all my wishes of importance is, Put thy trust in God, my soul, and he will bring it to pass. He best knows of what vast consequence your life is to my happiness, and his goodness will mercifully ordain accordingly. I receivd a letter by the last post from Mr. Ray, that our dear daughter Ann mends daily, and he hopes to let me know in a short time she will have her perfect health again ; that

Betty is in that condition I am glad to hear. I wish I could say as much of the news you sent me of a certain person's being with you ; you see how right your friend judges of those matters, and how one particularity draws others after it, which ought all to be chargd to the account of the first, that I must again say should neither have been offerd nor accepted. Louisa's spots were very fresh when I came away, but that they dye away no faster is oweing to the unseasonable cold winds we have had, which have made Felle's face (as I told your mistress last night in the King's drawing-room) hardly fit to waite on her R.H. next month. Mr. Cornwallis, I find, is willing to waite on, if she should find him so. The world is, as I feard, an odious scene of dull satiety without you, and must continue so till you return to your Bristol.

**739.** Lady Bristol to Lord Bristol. Bath, May 27, 1723.

My letters come to you like a fit of an ague, a good day and a bad, for I am really as much better now as I coud hope, considering how very ill I have been since my last bathing ; till yesterday I have scarce eat a bit, and indeed one had need have as good a stomack as Betty to be able to eat at this house, for such a cook never was in a kitchen, and woud almost have tempted me to change my lodging, for we are (if possible) worse servd than ever ; however, I stick by them this time, as I do by Mr. Skrine's perscription, and am very glad to find your opinion is that I shoud do so, though all my friends here tease me to death to have more advice, but I dont think I can have better than one that has had so long experience and practice as he has had of the effects of these waters, which has never yet faild to do me good, nor do I think they woud have lost their good effect now, if I had not been under the necessity of bathing for my legs, which has checkd the progress of the waters towards the cure of my nerves and cholick, (which is all from the same cause ;) and I see daily before my eyes such vast success in those cases that I cant despair but that your kind and pious prayers will at last meet with their desird end, nay, I hope have begun already, for I have held out these two days much better, and have great hopes I may continue so ; too morrow will be a tryal of it, for they promise mighty things for his Majesty's birth-day, and any crowd or bussle puts my spirits in a flutter, which makes this empty dull season much more sutable to me than a fuller woud have been ; but that you may see we have not been quite without diversion, I have sent you our fine Opera performance ; it is at least as good poetry as your bell-man's. I dont know if you have met with this piece of wit upon Lair's head, so have sent it you ; I dont pretend to send you any other news, now you are at the fountain head.—I cant but be very uneasy for fear dear Nan has been worse than you represented to me, since you say still nothing more than that she is of the mending hand, which I know (by my self) comes but slowly on this bitter weather, and makes me unable to say more than bid my dearest life adieu.

**740.**    Lord Bristol to Lady Bristol.        London, May 28, 1723.

After so many repeated ill consequences as you had experiencd from bathing, I wonder why Mr. Skrine should advise your using it so long.    I sent for Mr. Graham immediately on the receipt of your last ; but knowing he could not be admitted to Dr. Friend (in ye Tower) without leave from Lord Lincoln, I sent him to tell his Lordship (with my service) that you had desird his advice in a point which concernd your health very much, and begd he would order he might see him for that purpose ; his Lordship was not to be found yesterday, but this morning he told Mr. Graham he could not do what I desird without the King's consent, but that he would ask his Majesty's permission, and did not doubt of obtaining it ; so that I fear twill not be practicable to send you the Doctor's opinion upon your quære by this post, but neither Graham nor his Lordship shall have any rest untill I can get it for you against the next. Finding your spirits want every help to raise and relieve them, I send you the inclosd from our dear daughter Ann, as a cordial to support them from any uneasyness might lye upon them on her account ; my prayers you'l see have been graciously answerd for her, and I doubt not but the same infinite goodness (in which I alone confide) will prove as propitious towards those put up for you. I intend to send the coach for you from hence on Saturday come sevenight the 8th of June to be at Bath the 10th, and to take two daies rest there in order to set out with you the 13th of June ; could I possibly leave the businesses which brought me hither undone, I would have gone sooner in it myself, having much more impatience to see you again than ever I felt in my life, having now been longer from you than ever, and could not bear it but from a hope God's goodness will order the future so as the like may never be the lott of your almost despairing friend, Bristol.

> **741.** Lady Bristol to Lord Bristol. Bath, May 29th, 1723.

I should not do justice to our fine entertainment last night if I did not begin my letter with it ; to do it in form and like a news writer, I must say the morning was usherd in with ringing of bells, which provd no small trouble to me, for I was disturbd by 5 a clock with them ; about six in the evening all the company made the best appearance they coud at Harrison's room ; at seven the ball began, where the most extraordinary thing of all was Betty, to make the greatest compliment she coud to the day, dancd 4 minuets ; the first time she trembld and was so out of countenance I thought she woud not have been able to go thro' with it ; out the second time she performd very well ; the supper was at 9, (for we dont break into hours upon any account,) and a very handsome one it was ; there was 2 large tables besides little ones ; the best of the company sat at one, and the rest were dispersd ; Grantham, as well as the rest of the gentlemen, condescended to wait upon the ladies ; I held out pretty well all day, but towards the end of supper the heat and noise, with such a load of meat, quite overcame me, and I was ready to sound when I got down stairs, for my nerves and spirits are still very weak, though they have mended ever since I left off bathing ; but that and these cold easterly winds does not do so well with my legg; but I trouble you too often upon that melan-cholly subject, so will return to the diversions again, which concluded with illuminations and a large bonfire before Westgate house, where my Lord Grantham lodges ; but they were so insolent that when the fire was almost out they broke all the windows in the house ; but as the servants knew 2 of the people, Mr. Nash said they shoud produce the rest, and be put in jail too day ; what they done in it I cant tell, for I am so much tired I have not been out yet, though Mr. Nash invited me to breakfast, and they say this is a much more celebrated day (here) than yesterday.    Betty is so well after her performance that she is gone a horseback with the Dutchess of Rutland and Lady B. Maners, who has her lover here to attend her; tis one Mr. Munckton ; they say he has a good estate, but I cant say much for his person ; the match is all concluded, and she is to be married as soon as she goes from hence.    I am sorry you give your self any uneasyness about another gentleman being thought of that sort to Betty, for there is nothing remarkable in his coming hither, for he did the same thing in the winter, not only to see his sister, (who lives hard by this place, and is extreamly ill now at Bristol, where he is gone too day,) but for his health, which is really but bad, for he has the cholick extreamly.    Mr. Lee continues very ill, but I have obligd his daughters for ever by providing them with tickets, and carrying them to the ball and supper ; I was mighty glad to find how much they were pleasd ; I was doubly so by their being your relations, for you cannot have any part of you that will not be alwaies infinitely dear to your faithfull E. B.

742. Lord Bristol to Lady Bristol. London, May 30, 1723.

The getting leave for Mr. Graham to be admitted to speak with Doctor Friend would have been a matter of much more difficulty than you seemd to imagine, had it not been for the industry of your own friend ; which being at last obtaind, you will receive the result of by the Bath-coach on Saturday. There is sent by it a box of pills, a bottle, a copy of the Doctor's bill, with directions how they are to be taken, as also the two pounds of chocolate you desird. Since I cannot yet be so happy as to be where you are, the only thing can make this odious place tolerable must be to find I can be of any use or benefit to you where I am, and must remain for some time, your son Harry's wants (and my own to supply them) being like the hydra's head, multiplying on being cut off; I was yesterday to see some horses for him, (none of those hundred I have at Ickworth being proper for his service,) but such awkward beasts I never beheld as he had found out to buy. You cannot imagine how very well pleasd I have been with my self (which is a weakness I'm sure I have been as little guilty of as any man) for sending you so authentick a relief for the uneasy jealousy you were under for our dear daughter Ann as her own letter, which I hope has fully quietted your mind on her account; I wish it were in my power to do so on every other, for then I'm sure all the prescriptions for your body would take place the sooner and more effectually ; and without a hopefull prospect of that, (which thanks to my gracious God your last letter gives me a comfortable view of,) I find neither my poor body nor mind can live together with any sort of satisfaction ; no body can tell the anxiety but those who have felt it of having their last stake of happiness depending on a single chance, but more exquisitely so, if dureing the suspence they know they have the worst on't; but this aggravating circumstance cannot come into my case, being firmly persuaded, whoever depends so intirely upon God as I do shall have the better in that great chance of your

Vol. II. PP

life against all other accidents whatsoever.—The child's name is Le-Pell, which as much disposd as you know I have alwaies been to pour oyl into those wounds which mutual warmths have made, I cannot but say you should not so long have been kept a stranger to.—Since you think me at the fountain's head of news, I suppose you expect some from me; and tho' I care to hear little (unless twere better) and to communicate less, yet having a most extraordinary piece at present to tell you, I cannot refrain from letting you know that all the dreadful allarms of plots and conspiracys have at last ended in letting the rest of the supposd criminals go free; and as a future discouragement to all machinations of the like kind, Lord Bolingbroke is come over with his Majesty's pardon in his pocket.—Lord Waldegrave this day in my sight kissd your mistress her hand on being a lord of the King's Bed-chamber in the Duke of Richmond's room.—I beg you would write me no more long letters, however my present practice be contrary to the precept of your faithful monitor, Bristol.

**743.**   Lady Bristol to Lord Bristol.        Bath, June 1, 1723.

I am very much concernd to find I have given my dear angel so much trouble, but I never thought that there coud have been any difficulty in speaking to Doctor Friend out of a window, since tis what has all along been allowd him ; and not being so now I am afraid is a bad sign for him, which I am extreamly sorry for; but one of his patients here assures me he will be very soon at liberty.   I am glad to hear so good authority to try pumping, which I shoud do to night but that I have taken rubarb, for I am very impatient to find some relief for my leg, which has been worse since I left off bathing ; so unlucky am I that what is to do me good in one complaint hurts me in the other; but how can I hope for success in any thing, when my guardian angel is at this distance from me ; however, it gives me the next greatest pleasure that you say you would have been with me if you coud. I joyn with you most sincerely in praying that the like absence may never happen again, and with the utmost impatience long for our meeting more, if possible, than ever; especially since you order me to shorten this way of conversing, and I am afraid I am under too great a necessity of obeying you, now I drink the waters again, which I did not when I writ those 2 long letters. This shall be supplyd with some Bath wit and gallantry upon Molly How; the author is yet unknown, (at least to me;) I can hardly think it is her fat-headed admirer my Lord Dunbarton; if he comes in your way, he will give you a full account of my nerves as well as his own, for we have had very frequent and learned discourses about them, among which what I am now doing was agreed to be very bad; therefore for this time necessity must get the better of inclination, and force me to bid my dearest life adieu.

I cant help adding this postscript, (hopeing it will be as great satisfaction to you as to me) that Mr. Skrine says tis a certain sign this extream swelling in my leg is only from my fall and bruses, since one is so vastly worse than the other, and still persists in the faith of his medicine, whether it be from that or any other cause.

744. Lord Bristol to Lady Bristol. London, June 1, 1723.

I am just going to ye great lady in whose favours you say Mr. Nash has equal share; be it so; I have at present ye advantage of him by his absence, this being ye third time I shall have been with her since I came, & might have seen her oftener, coud I have accepted of several other invitations she has made me for want of better company; but my business hear increases daily, & what between Harrys affairs & ye several claims made on your Staffordshire estate, Hetleys & Sir William Barker's suites, I have little or no time to spare. I made a final end with that worthy gentleman, Mr. Minshul, yesterday, the discharge of whose judgment upon our £500 wager (after paying ye purchase of Harrys commission) has left me more bare of mony than ever I was in my life, neither do I know what shift I can make till Michaelmas term, when I am resolvd to sell & make myself easy. I hope you receivd the things safe I sent you by ye coach, & that ye success of Doctor Frind's prescription will pay for all ye trouble I was at in procuring it; if you have any more advice to ask of him, twill now be easy to come at it, even he being (in this honey moon) to be baild out, after all that was said with so much confidence of his guilt & legal proofe of it upon his commitment. You cannot do me a greater pleasure than to send me more commissions for your service till we are to meet, which I trust in God will not be longer than till this day fortnight; but that's an age computed by ye same tedious time I have spent here without you; I really never found fourteen days before of near so long seeming duration. Tell dame Lindsey I cannot find my self in fancy enough to answer her letter till you come to put it into me; but then she shall not faile of my thanks for her good news.... Your Bristol.

**745.**    Lady Bristol to Lord Bristol.        Bath, June 3, 1723.

As I have already told you the least trifle puts me out of order, you will not wonder that I am so much so too day from what so vastly concerns me, which was the being like to miss of your dear letter, for after their being twice lookd over, I was told it was certain there was not any, but still persisted and sent again to the Postmaster, who then said he believd there was one, but in the hurry of giving them out he coud not tell what was become of it; but before I had quite done my waters at the Pump, (for the uneasyness I was under made me very late there,) I receivd the welcome tidings of your being well, and for the first time in my life felt a pleasure in what you say gives you so much uneasyness, for twere impossible to feel that tenderness which I alwaies hope to receive and pay without suffering a great deal in the absence of what one loves; to shorten that, though but for a day, woud have given me some pleasure, and I once intended it, but I cannot set out till Thursday (the day first mentiond), because of the convenience of Squire going in the stage coach, for I am almost as little able to go 4 as I was when I came hither; what alteration pumping will make, I cannot tell, for I coud not make tryal of it till too night, but I find the extream heat we have had for this 3 days has agreed very ill with all my complaints, for it put me out of order to go but 2 miles to dine with Mr. Skrine yesterday; Mr. & Mrs. Lewis carried Betty and I; we shall have a great loss of them, this week they go away; I cannot say so much for the Granthams, who set out this morning at 3 a clock, and General Evans with them; they dine with him at Windsor in their way to London; I shewd my Lady Grantham my leg, and my Lord part of it, to convince them both how impossible it woud be for me to wait, if I were not better, or met with more than ordinary favour, which that I may not fail of, if you give some hints to that purpose, it may prove of use to your E.B.

Dont let Betty forget my hoop that belongs to my riding cloaths, when the coach comes.

**746.** Lord Bristol to Lady Bristol. London, June 4, 1723.

The very warm weather we have here adds daily to the great impatience I am under to have you out of that frying-pann I know you are in. O how I shall regret the sufferings I have felt for your absence in case that odious place should not at last return you safe and sound to me again; I cannot but flatter my self with the same comfortable hope Mr. Skrine does, that the leg you so complain of is solely the effect of your fall, and for the same sound reason too, because otherwise its partner woud have shard more than it has done, were it oweing to any natural disorder in your blood or constitution; but be it one or t'other, I am glad to find his faith continues strong as to the efficacy of his medicine, which I beseech God of his wonted goodness to us to vouchsafe his effectual blessing to. Fervent prayers is a more salutiferous ingredient than can be mixd with any humane help, and if that will co-operate more successfully to your cure than all other drugs put together, you will for my own sake, as well as yours, find you'll gain ground hourly.—I send you another of dear Nann's letters to satisfy you of her entire recovery, having (as you'll see) rode abroad again. My grandson already shews he partakes of me in something, since he is so fond of being in Ickworth air; but even that begins to be infected from the general contagion of roguery abounding in the world, for W. Oliver writes me word that your cheese chamber has been broke open, and upon search made fifteen of them found in Larner's house, who conscious of his guilt has made his escape out of our poor old Constable's Goodchild's hands, and left his wife and children to be maintaind by your most affectionate longing husband, Bristol.

**747.**     Lady Bristol to Lord Bristol.     Bath, June 5, 1723.

Sure never poor creature that took so much pains to be well ever succeeded so il; I tryd ye pump in as gentle a maner as was possible. . . ; so that I was forcd to take an oppium pill, from which I gott a pritty good nights rest, & am better to day, tho' not without some remains of pain & sickness, which by the heat of ye wether makes me very faint, & unable to inlarge so much as I shoud do upon an affair that happend this morning. Mr. Mansell came to breakfast with me, & at ye same time to offer some proposals in regard to Betty, which was done in a very oblidging maner, at least I thought so, since he flatterd my vanetty so much as to say he did not doubt but makeing his sute to you threw me woud be more agreable than by himself; besides that he did not think it so proper an undertaking at this time till he had first spoke to his father, to see what he woud do for him, for tho' he was determind to marry no other woman, yett he lovd her too well to make any proposale to you that had not a prospect of makeing her happy as well as himself, & I find he dus not dispair of finding so much favour from Lord Mansell to bring this matter about in a maner that (he hopes) will not be disagreable to you, and then you are to hear from him in form; he depends much upon being ye favourett child, & showd me a very kind letter from him; he is so much in ernest as to lett me into all ye affairs of his familley, but as that is nothing to ye present bussiness, I will deffer it till we meet, which, as it please God, shall be dead or alive on Saturday senett.—I have been out since I wrote this, & find I am much better, & hope to give a good account of my self by next post. Wensday, 9 a clock.

**748.** Lord Bristol to Lady Bristol. London, June 6, 1723.

       Having disabled my thumb yesterday in cutting a piece of Mrs. Bullen's very hard cheese, you must not expect a long letter from me. Tis a sign indeed that every trifle can put your spirits into a disorder, if only the mislaying or missing one of mine can occasion it; were you mistress of my Christian philosophy, (which I must beg you would endeavour to practice,) such an accident would not (as you confess) so vastly concern you; for tho' I feel as great and as true a pleasure in receiving your letters as you can possibly do at the sight of mine, yet when I was disappointed lately by the post as you by the postmaster, I trusted in God you were well, kept my mind resignd, and made a virtue of necessity. If any hints I can give will be of use to you, you may be sure I shall make as large ones as your leg will afford; but should you find your self after your journey hither unable or but the least unfit to wait the week after, I should think laying the bare matter of fact before those concernd would be alone sufficient to get your self excusd for that turn; besides, as

you have often servd out of course to supply the absence of such who out of
laziness or vanity have not thought fit to do their own duty, sure twould be
but justice and no favour (as you call it) for them to repay you in this time
of need.  I have given Betty order (in your own words) about your hoope,
which shall come by the coach on Saturday next from hence ; how I shall
long for that day sevenight your own heart (I hope) can tell you something,
tho' never in near so strong terms as is suggested by the impatient soul of
your, till then, disconsolate partner, Bristol.

> **749.**    Lord Bristol to Lady Bristol.        London, June 7, 1723.

It still being uneasy for me to write with my cutt
thumb, I shall only trouble it to tell you how tediously time passes with me
every where in your absence; even at Ickworth every hour seems a day,
but hear each moment more than a month; how long a week this will be
till Tom who brings you this conveys you to me again can only be felt but
never well discribd, so shall not be attempted by your most impatient
freind, Bristol.

> **750.**    Lady Bristol to Lord Bristol.        Bath, June 8, 1723.

I was so very ill after my last pumping that I
durst not venture again till last night, when I did it with so much better
success that I intend doing it again too night : I took a different method,
for I suppd first and went directly to bed after I came from the Pump, and
took a cordial bollus to fortify my stomack, which had so good effect that I
think I am better too day than I have been since I came to this place,
except yesterday that I was quite as well.  I wish I may continue so, for I
have but a heavy day upon my hands, being to dine with people I have no
acquaintance with beyond a formal visit; tis Mr. Mansell's sister Mrs.
Talbot and her husband, who are come too day from Bristol to make him a

visit in the way to their own house at Lacock, where they have invited us to dinner in our way to London ; but that my infirmities (especially upon a journey) has given me too just an excuse for, which has made this too day unavoidable, (as I hope you will think,) for as I woud not seem too forward as matters now stand, I think it woud be as wrong to do any thing that might shock. I have had fruit and carp twice from their house, extream good in their kind ; I find she is very well married, having a fine place and (which is better) an extraordinary good husband.—I hope I explaind myself enough in my last letter for you to understand that it was by his desire I writ, that I may have some answer by the next post to give him, which I believe he will expect, though I did you justice in letting him know the good opinion you had alwaies expressd to have of him, which I hope you will think was right for me to do; he sets out for Wales (to his father) the later end of next week. We have now but 3 families remaining here, the Dutchess of Rutland, Lady Torrington, and Lord and Lady Barrimore ; Tuesday and Thursday carry them off as well as your impatient longing E. B.

I believe I shall set out a Thursday before the post will be come in here ; therefore that I may be sure to miss none of your dear letters, pray let that of Tuesday night be directed to me at Marlborough, which will unweary me when I come there.

**751.** Lord Bristol to Lady Bristol. London, June 8, 1723.

Altho' I sent a letter this morning by Tom Harvey, yett computing that ye post will be with you before him, & finding how vast a consequence (as your partiality termd it) your weakend spiritts drew from ye disappointment of one of them, I had much rather putt my thumb to ye pain of writing a second than expose your freindly expectation to ye uneasyness of missing such a trifle again. What you write to me of Mr. M (ansel) shews how great a rarity judgment is in humane nature, for sure no overture shoud have been made (even to you) till he had first broke his purpose to his father; then indeed he would have judgd right that no suite can come so well recommended as thro' your hands to ye heart of your indulgent Bristol.

**752.**    Lady Bristol to Lord Bristol.        Bath, June 10, 1723.

I am sorry to find you still complain of your thumb, and more so that you shoud put your self to pain for my pleasure, tho' it came very seasonably to me this morning, to relieve me in the disorder I wakd with, for I cannot yet be free from some returns of my old complaints upon my nerves, though I am as much mended in every respect within this 4 days as is possible to imagine, so much that I almost wish the weather and my impatience to see you would admitt of my staying a little longer, though I really believe this sudden alteration for the better proceeds more from the time drawing near of my being to be happy again in your lovd society than from the waters or any other medicine,

> Since life's not worth the pain which I endure
> By being sent from you to seek my cure,
> Yet when I recollect how farr above
> The rest of moitals I am blest in love,
> By being possessd of all that heaven can give,
> I think it worth my while to strive to live;
> And by my care, if I prolong my days,
> Each added hour an age of pain repays.

I believe you will wonder at this piece of poetry; but what will not love inspire; yet such as I feel for you cannot be discribd either in verse or prose, but only in the heart of your faithfull E. B.

The coach and all the horses are safely arrived, and were doubly welcome to me by the dear kind letter they brought, for which I thank you most heartily.

**753.**    Lord Bristol to Lady Bristol.        London, June 11, 1723.

This is to thank you for giving me an other opportunity of writing to you (the only pleasure I can take till we meet) than I coud otherwise have contrivd but by your direction ; I will in return tell you I am just now come from taking my leave of the Prince & Princess, who are gone to Richmond, & our son with them ; they both inquird after you, & I faild not to drop such hints as you desird; but wether they will turn to such account as we woud have them, I know not. I am ingagd in law business as soon as I have gott my dinner; therfore can only tell you, if my prayers prevail, you will have a safe and easy passage to your longing lover, Bristol.

Lord Tho: Maners is dead of ye smal pox.

**754.**    Lady Bristol to Lord Bristol.        Bath, June 12, 1723.

I believe I may judge of your heart by my own, that a letter will be agreeable to you, though I am to follow it so soon : the very thought of that gives me new life and spirits, and contributes greatly to the amendment I now daily find ; but I cant help being uneasy (after the account you have given me of your affairs) that I am under the necessity of drawing 2 notes upon Mr. Fowler for fifty guineas each to discharge my expences here, and to be able to carry some money with me to Richmond. You may remember I receivd no money before I left London, and that this was the method you orderd me to take; however I deferrd doing it till the last day, thinking to make it more easy to you ; they are drawn ten days after sight, and cannot be in Town before Friday, though they shoud take the first post to send them. The goods will be in Town on Friday, and I have sent 6 cheeses, which I believe will sute your taste and not hurt your thumb to cut ; it will be proper they shoud be unpackd as soon as they come. I must give you a little more trouble, which is to

beg you woud put Betty Morris in mind to have my mantoe and pettycoat
brought home a Saturday, for I conclude I am expected at Richmond on
Monday, where I hope you have orderd your affairs so as to go too, for
another seperation will be death to your faithfull E. B.

I must beg you woud order Cornforth to get me a footman against I
come to Town, for if I can bear with Will : till that night, it is as much as
I can possibly do.

**755.**   Lady Bristol to Lord Bristol.   Richmond, June 19, 1723.

It has been no small disappointment to me the
not seeing you to day after this rain ; I so much depended upon it that I
dressd me by 12 a clock to have the more time with you ; but I hope you
pass your time as agreeably as (my Lord Sunderland tells me) you did on
Monday ; if you do that and are well, I ought to be satisfyd, though I am
afraid I cant be truly so till we meet again ; till that long time farewell, my
dear.—Wednesday, 5 a clock.

**756.**   Lord Bristol to Lady Bristol.   London, June 20, 1723.

You must wrong your own judgment as much as
you do my heart to suppose I can spend my time agreeably without you,
after having passd so many years with pleasure in your company only ; if
Lord Sunderland speaks truth, tis more than his father before him ever did.
I am staid for to attend her Grace again this morning to hear some more of
her exceptions to ye Master's report argued, her first being unjustly over
ruld by ye Court in ye opinion of your lawyer & lover, Bristol.

**757.**   Lady Bristol to Lord Bristol.   Richmond, June 26, 1723.

I find so many diffecultys in gitting to you that I
have now quite laid it aside, tho' to day I might have had a very good

oppertunety, for Lady Rumney & Mrs. Dunch would have caryd me this evening, but I have so many reasons (besides a friends advice) that I am sure you will think me in the right to deffer my pleasure & happyness till Sunday, when I hope you will come to fetch me, for I can hold out no longer from seeing my dear dearest life, tho' tis unreasonable to aske you to come again in ye dust to your impatient E. B.

**758.** Lord Bristol to Lady Bristol. London, June 29, 1723.

As I shall see you so much sooner & be with you so much longer in ye short space of life which remains, I will come not only thro' dust but dangers rather than not do what I hope we both desire. I shall bring our daughty Betty with me, if you dont contradict it by this messenger to your faithfull freind & lover, Bristol.

**759.** Lady Bristol to Lord Bristol. Richmond, June 29, 1723.

I cant let any messenger go without saying something, though I hope Mr. Methwin did not give you the pain of knowing how very ill I was yesterday, having had a very severe fit of the cholick from 7 a clock till near my bed time; then it came into my limbs with that violence that I have had very little rest all night. I cant give any reason for this except it be drinking new claret ever since I came here, but to prevent that while I stay, Lord Scarborough has given me some very good Spanish wine. I am better too day, and intend to secure my night by an opium pill; too morrow I hope for a Sovereign remedy for all my pains, till when adieu, my dear dear. I hope you will come early.

**760.** Lord Bristol to Lady Bristol. London, Aug. 27, 1723.

They tell me tis my birthday; but I must alwaies keep it with double pomp of sadness when seperated from you. I went to bed at eight last night hopeing to recover so long loss of sleep as you know

I had sufferd, but found my pain returnd with so much force, (whether from
the phang he had left in my gum or the other tooth next that he drew, I
know not,) that I was obligd to send for Emmet, (who lay at Marybone,)
so they brought me his son, who stopt my tooth with the most nauseous oyl
I ever smelt or tasted, which at first caused more pain, but about one it
ceasd, and let me sleep very sound till noon.    I am  in all conditions ever
most intirely yours, Bristol.

**761.**    Lady Bristol to Lord Bristol.    Richmond, Aug. 27, 1723.
                                This day must ever be held sacred where ever I
am, and tis what I have much more reason to be wishd joy of than you, as
being not only the birth but foundation of all my happiness ; it will prove
the continuance to it, if I hear by the messenger (which I every moment
expect) that you are out of pain and every way better than when I left you ;
I wish I coud say I were so, but really I am so very low spiritted that
nothing but the thoughts of what this day brought forth coud support me
with life ; nothing I meet with hear can help to bear me up ; till I see you
I hope for no relief, for I find they are brutal enough to think of pawning
me here, because I did not jump over the stick the Dutchess of Shrewsbury
and Lady Grantham held out for me ; but why should I trouble you with
my grievances that have but too many of your own to oppress your poor
heart with ;  but I will not give way to my sorrow of this blessed day ;
besides that I have a flattering hope that tells me I shall see you too day,
since tis now past one and the groom not come, and I conclude you woud
not keep me in suspence of what so nearly concerns me, if you did intend
to be the welcome messenger your self.

Half an hour past 4.  I have been kept upon the rack till now to hear of
you, and find very little satisfaction in the account you give of your self ;
therefore beg I may hear again from you in the morning, or by Lord W.

Manners in the evening, who I will desire to send to you before he comes away. I have now my room full of company, and can say no more but bid my dearest life adieu.

762.    Lord Bristol to Lady Bristol.     London, Aug. 28, 1723.

    The very moment I was out of bed I set me down to write to you the letter which you receivd, and therefore you were not on the rack a minute longer than was possible for me to prevent. But why, after all I have said to you upon the subject of resting on Providence, will you still give your self more trouble than by your own experience from past events you found you need or ought to have done. There is no living long, easy or happy without learning that necessary lesson which I once again conjure you to become a better proficient in for your own sake as well as mine. I passd the last night in as sound a sleep as I ever can hope for; if it had any interruption, twas not from the pain of my teeth. Doctor Arbuthnot is just gone from me, who came to tell me he has advisd our son Jack to take the Bath waters, in order to secure him from feeling any more returns of those dangerous fits of the cholick in his stomach; and I believe, by his way of speaking, that they would be glad you could contrive to have him and his wife, if not in the same house with you, at least so near us as to save them the expence of keeping any table of their own. I told him I intended to see you to morrow at Richmond to take my leave of you, (an alwaies heartbreaking occasion to me,) and would impart their purpose to you, and doubted not but you would do every thing in your power to accommodate them, whereof you or I would give them notice.—The account you send me of your self, and of the state of your matters with relation to your waiting longer than is consistent with your Bath journey, gives me more uneasyness than I care to express. I cannot conclude without sending you a piece of good news to comfort your spirits, as I must own it did mine.

Mr. Barricave begd an audience of me, and twas to tell me that our son Felle was fallen into so deep a course of melancholly from finding he had forfeited the Prince and Princesses good opinion of him, and that we had withdrawn all sort of countenance, or so much as common affection for him, that he was grown weary of his life, and not only hoped but prayd that God would take him out of the world, but desird first that he would make the innocence of his intentions known, that he only meant to make a joke of it at first, but finding it made a serious matter of, gott rid of it where he told me, that it might not be known who had it. Mr. Barricave added that being of so violent and determind a spirit, if I did not abate of my late usual severity towards him, he could not answer that he would not do himself some mischief, which you may be sure was done accordingly by your etc, Bristol.

**763.**    Lady Bristol to Lord Bristol.    Richmond, Aug. 30, 1723.

I give my dear angell a thousand thanks for his good news, & I can receive no addission to that pleasure but ye seeing you on Sunday, that being an idle day, I hope it will put you under no diffeculty, but if it shoud, I would not purchace my pleasure by giving you trouble; may you never know ye least of any kind, but all your days be as prosperus as my fond wishes can pray for; adeu, my dear dearest, I am calld away to my mistress.

**764.**    Lord Bristol to Lady Bristol.    London, Aug. 30, 1723.

Knowing how much you want comfort of all kinds, tis no small one to me that I can with all manner of sincerity assure you our son Will is in ye very best way, & has ye very best sort of small-pox that his nurse says she ever saw on any body she has attended; they are risen so much, & those few on his face (not above 25) so well filld already that she is sure ye eruption must have been many days sooner than was perceivd by those about him, for she reckons they will be at their height by Monday or Tuesday; he is so very well & easy that he can hardly beleive tis ye small pox ; if a turn of any kind should happen for ye worse, you may depend upon hearing from me, otherwise you will not expect nor nead I give you or my self any farther trouble. Altho' God knows my heart has no sensible pleasure left but in seeing & being with you, yett that satisfaction meets with so many allays & interuptions where you now are, (besides ye (to me) uneasy indecorum of appearing there when ye small-pox is in my family,) that unless it will very much lighten that load I left you with on your poor mind (wholly untraind to trouble), I hope you will not insist on seeing Sunday next your ever faithfull Bristol.

**765.**  Lord Bristol to Lady Bristol.  London, Sept. 2, 1723.

How much my fond foolish heart has paid since my parting from you last night, & must still feel till we meet again, you shall never know, because unfitt entertainment for a mind like yours already over laden with concern, tho' of a different nature. The inclosd are just come to hand, which I desire you woud return me when read. I think not of going hence till Thursday morning, as well because Will's distemper will not till Wednesday be past its crises as becaus you see by that time Jack will be here to settle his journey either to Ickworth or ye Bath, as I shall be best advisd by my good genius for him, which, as he is so essential a part of you, can never dictate amiss, since my prayers have ever been to guide me right in all things that concern you. I have not only been to see but swung in ye chariott Cornfourth told you of, & find it much more roomy & of an easyer motion than I ever mett with any of those kinds of hired voitures. I have also taken care you shall have his safest, soberest coachman, and good horses with holsters & buckets for carabines

Vol. II,   RR

& pistols, as you desird.  If there is any thing els can be done by me to make you easy, lett me know it, having no comfort left in life but ye thoughts of my having done every thing I ought towards you.  Adue for an age to your disconsolate freind, Bristol.

**766.**   Lord Bristol to Lady Bristol.     London, Sept. 3, 1723.

I can lett no oppertunity pass of giving you any ease or comfort, knowing by my self how much you must want them.  This is therfore to lett you know Will is as well, if not better, than can be imagind in ye height of such a distemper; & as both Mr. Grimes & his nurse assure me there can be no danger, (nor endeed never was,) I intend to go on Thursday towards Ickworth in order to meet you ye sooner at Bath, till when I must subscribe my self, as I must be, your most disconsolate freind & lover, Bristol.

**767.**   Lady Bristol to Lord Bristol.     Richmond, Sept. 7, 1723.

I should have been tempted to have followd my dear angel with a letter by Thursdays post; but before Cooper got hither to tell me you were gone, I was taken so very ill with my old complaint that I was not able to write, but I have been very easy since yesterday morning, and slept very well too night, so that I hope all is over for this time, and to contribute towards it I am made very easy in all affairs here; but as you left it wholly to my management, I thought it much better the child* shoud not wait any more, since I coud not be upon the place with him at the time; for it woud have been very unreasonable to expect Mr. Cornwallis shoud have waited on till I came back, though the Princess was so obliging as to say she desird his stay might be as long or as short as woud be most for his advantage; for she shoud alwaies think her self

* Her youngest son Felton, who was a page to the Princess of Wales.—S.H.A.H.

obliged to do him any good, or shew him any favour, whenever it lay in her power, as if he had continued in her service; yet she coud not but think we had done a right thing in taking him away, though she was sorry to part with him; and at the same time with a great deal of warmth fell upon those that had done so much towards the spoyling him, and said they deservd more to be hangd than any body that went to Tyburn that coud endeavour to ruin so fine a youth. She is satisfyd now that I have done my part towards waiting, for I offerd to stay another week rather than she shoud run any risk of being disappointed by the Dutchess of Shrewsbury's illness, but she has undertaken it and I am acquitted, and after that the Princess told me, if they shoud grumble after I was gone, she shoud think them very unreasonable, since I had done my part so obligingly; therefore she desired I woud not loose a moment in my journey to Bath, for she was convincd I had too much need of it. If I can gain a day by leaving this place too morrow in the evening I will, in order to have the benefit of this rain, which I hope came time enough for you to have the good of it; may that and every other blessing in life attend you. Jack and Mrs. Hervey are come; I hear they were to see Will yesterday.

**768.** Lord Bristol to Lady Bristol. Ickworth, Sept. 7, 1723.

Knowing you will be glad to hear of our safe arrival here, I take ye first opportunity of telling you so. My body bore ye journey better than most men at my time of day shoud reasonably expect; but my mind was never less at ease than now, and must always find it self so (even here) where you are not. I found our female family all in perfect health, (except Betty who has had a little rash upon her for 2 days,) among whom your representative already makes a flaming figure; I never saw so fine nor so good humourd a child; we were (I hope by natural sympathy) extreamly well pleased with one another at first sight. Betty desires if you see Doctor Friend before you go to Bath, that you woud ask him if she is to go on with his prescription after she getts there, or what other method she is to pursue. You cannot imagine what additional inquietudes my poor heart has sufferd from reflecting on ye uneasy condition I left you in, & ye fears I have been under, least being already so any new degouts shoud extort from you any words or actions that might put you in ye wrong, ye very point your ill willers woud joy to drive you to; but hoping I said enough to you on that subject to keep you from splitting on so dangerous a rock, I hope no more need now be added to it by your only true & faithfull friend and lover, Bristol.

**769.**    Lord Bristol to Lady Bristol.    Ickworth, Sept. 9, 1723.

Twas very necessary for ye support of my present stock of spirsit to send me word of your recovery at ye same time that you acquainted me with ye return of your old complaint. I begin to be as unfitt to be trusted with any ill news as your self; therefore pray spare me all you can to what concerns others, tho' I woud never be kept in ignorance (cost what it will) of any circumstance relating to your self. I daresay your being made easy in your mind as to your waiting contributed as much to your cure as ye many disagreeable alarms you had about it servd to throw your body into that disorder; since then you see how influential your soul is upon it, I beseech you to preserve that in as much tranquility as possible. We have without doubt made other people (in return) as easy by withdrawing our son, who, twas manifest to me from ye beginning, had it in their view to oblige some other family with his vacancy. I always wishd he had never filld it, seeing from his first appearance in that destructive school he woud be ruind. Having got cold in his journey by going out at night into ye yard at Newport without his hatt, or by ye fore-glass being broke by Mr. Barricave, (who poor man was in such confusion I said not one word about it,) as we stood still in ye inn at Harlow after baiting, he has had a sore throat ever since; but Mr. Raye has been with him, & he is doing well again, as I hope & pray every thing else may, where you or yours are concernd, so strong is ye faith of your friend and lover, Bristol.

**770.** Lady Bristol to Lord Bristol. London, Sept. 10, 1723.

I beleive my dearest life woud be surprisd at a letter from this place, were not Jack & his wife to be with you before you can receive this; he will give you an account how much I have been out of order before & since I left Richmond. I beleive the coming to this desolate house where I have been so happy contributed greatly to all my complaints, for I have not been able to stir out or see any body since I came, though I was in Town pretty early a Sunday evening, which I spent with my 2 sons. Mrs. Hervey I have not had ye honour to see since I came; tis pretended there was a mistake in ye message I sent to both of them the moment I came to Town, & where one is so indifferent any excuse will serve, tho' I beleive it as sincere as all ye compliments I sent you word of in my last letter had passd between a great Lady & I; however, I am very glad my warmth of temper (which did not want provocation) took ye turn you seem so much to desire it shoud; may I forever by a secret impulse do what you think best, as I beleive this will prove, for I daresay my enemys are diss-appointed by it; however, you will find Mr. John's opinion is that I shoud have pursued my first hasty resolution; but there is time enough for that when we have an opportunity to talk over & well consider all circumstances, which is both too much for a letter or my spirits at present; but I am so very much better that I hope nothing will hinder my setting out to morrow, nay, I beleive I coud have done it to day, but that Doctor Friend thought this most secure, and that it could be no hindrance as to my drinking ye waters, since if I had not taken my rhubarb to day, I must have done it before I begun them, which I can now do (by his direction) the day after I get there. I have been forced to change ye chariot for a coach, which is full as easy, for I have been in it to try; had I not done this, half my things must have been left behind; besides I have another satisfaction in it, which is carrying Kat : with me to stay till you come, when I am sure J shall need no other assistance, tho' I really do at present, if it were only for my journey, for it woud be a very melancholly thing to be left aloue with a stranger if I shoud be ill; I had Mr. Benny's consent; he said he woud with all his heart for as long as I pleased, provided I woud prevail with her to marry him before she went, for he found he was like to stay as long without her if she stayd as if she went; so this morning the knot is tyed, and I hope will prove a happy one, for honest & faithfull servants are treasures in this bad world.— That you may be sure to meet with no disappointment in ye want of a letter, I hope you remember Saturday is ye first post I shall have from Bath, but I hope I shall meet with that of Thursday at some of ye inns; if I do you shall not fail to hear from me; but that being an uncertain way, if you miss of a letter, conclude it ye post & not ye fault of her, who I hope will never have oue towards you. I conclude Jack will tell you of ye Dutchess of Marlborough's fall & hurt, and what was said upon it by a great man.

**771.**     Lady Bristol to Lord Bristol.     Reading, Sept. 11, 1723.

According to my promise this comes to let my dear angel know I am safe got to this place, & better in health than I coud hope for after so very indifferent a night as ye last, which made me apprehensive of being out of order in a strange place, else I coud not have resisted the pressing invitation I had from Mr. Grey to lye at Billingbear ; I met him at Maidenhead, where he dined with several other Justices ; I chose to dine there, because I might have ye less way to come after dinner ; he told me Mr. Elwes & Master Megot were both with him, and well. They say there is an infinite of company gone to Bath, but here is no sign of its increasing, for there is not one coach at any of ye inns in this town to night, so that I hope to rest in quiet, which tempts me to go to bed, tho' it is but 9 o clock, and I hope it will contribute to make my legg continue as well ye rest of ye journey as it is to night, which is much better than I have known it after going so long in a coach ; this is news that I am sure will please you, as I hope every thing of or from me will always do by my constant prayers & endeavours for it.—

Thursday morning, Sept. 12, I cant say I have slept well, for I was so bitt with buggs yesterday at Maidenhead when I laid upon ye bedd, that has so swelld my neck & all one arm that I have been very uneasy all night ; but as to my most material complaint I am very much better, & have not needed to take one slop since I set out, which is saying a great deal, if you knew how frequent they had been since I saw you ; I hope this account will be to your satisfaction, & that I shall be able to give you yet a better next post from Bath ; tis 8 a clock, & I am just going to drink your dear health in chocolate, and then set out. Adieu, my dear.

**772.** Lord Bristol to Lady Bristol. Ickworth, Sept. 11, 1723.

Having told you in my last that our son Felle was out of order, you will expect a further account of him in this. Mr. Ray thought at first it might prove ye scarlet feaver, that distemper being at present very rife in these parts ; but that heat, which was upon him during ye continuance of his sore throat, is gone quite off him since that grew well, & you need be in no farther pain about him. I hope this will find you safe & well at Bath, & in a lodging to your mind, for that is a circumstance of great importance, bodily cures proceeding slowly where ye mind is not intirely at ease ; whatever makes yours otherwise must at ye same time destroy ye quiet of mine, it knowing no peace but when you are pleasd & prosperous. Sir. T. Hanmer dind with me yesterday, for whom our daughter Betty provided so very good a dinner, that I was doubly concernd you had not your usual share both in ye eating & ordering of it. I am making so much hast to get into Lincolnshire, (Monday next being ye day I set out,) that I desired he woud excuse my not waiting on him at Mildenhall to thank him for ye favour he had done me, which he with his accustomed goodness very readily and reasonably assured me he shoud not expect, since I had so little time to turn me in here, the greatest part whereof hath already & must yet be bestowd on Corporation business, Saturday being wholly dedicated to that service, being to receive all my friends at my old house in Bury ; but that nor nothing else shall retard my moving nearer towards you on Monday, having neither life nor soul without you. Adieu.

**773.**    Lady Bristol to Lord Bristol.        Bath, Sept. 14, 1723.

I am glad I can return ye pleasure my dear angel gave me this morning in hearing you were safe & well at Ickworth by telling you I am so at this place. I had not only a very easy coach, but by your kind care a very sober & carefull coachman. I wish I coud give you as good an account of my lodgings, but they are really extream inconvenient, but I must submit to necessity till I can better my self, for at present there is not a room to be got if I woud give £5 for it, so that it was lucky Jack did not come with me, for he must either have lain in an inn or a garret, & ye room kept for Betty, which is within mine, is impossible to make shift with, but ye town is so full as was never known, yet by what I can guess no company; however, by ye messages I have had this morning I expect a swarm of such as there is this afternoon, therefore write now for fear of being disappointed in all the pleasure I propose till we meet, which I hope will be as soon as it can sute with your convenience ; but I am afraid this accident of your glass being broke may keep you ye longer till you get it supplyd, for it will be impossible to travel without; nay, I am afraid, though you do not give me ye pain of knowing it, that your tender jaws may have sufferd already by ye want of it. My coucheé last night, & levy this morning, has been as much crowded with visits & compliments as if I were ye Princess of ye place; Cutzona has been one, Mr Nash was also here to know what commands I had to Bristol, where he was going at a visit to ye Dutchess of Marlborough; he showd me a letter with compliments to us, which I returnd in the best manner I coud. I have just been at Church to thank God for my own good journey, & to pray for yours with all the fervency so affectionate a heart is capable of to ye dear lovd object of all its wishes.

774. Lord Bristol to Lady Bristol. Ickworth, Sept. 14, 1723.

The frequent returns you have felt of your hysterick and chollical disorders since you were at Bath give me no great faith in those waters ; and unless this second season does you much more service than the first seems to have performd towards cureing your complaints, which have cost me so much concern and anxiety of mind, I shall be tempted to fall out as much with them as the place it self, which nothing can reconcile to me but prolonging a life so necessary to the bearing of my own. I saw by Jack's manner, when he was giving me the reasons why you stayd so much longer in London than you intended, that he softend the representation all he could, finding me dejected enough before. How likely Lincolnshire is to mend any of my melancholly moods, I would not have you think enough of to guess at ; or if you should, to remember I carry one comfortable hope with me, which is that the nearer I get to you, the farther off will all my disagreeable ideas vanish, one of which is that as I shall set out thither on Monday, I shall not be able to hear from or write to you in many daies, which I mention by way of the same caution you gave me in your last, that you might not be disappointed should you miss two or more posts of receiving letters from me. I have sent Bullen word as you desird that Nann goes to the Bath as well as Betty, but what Jack and his wife will do here without us is another uneasy thought to your faithfull Bristol.— I beseech you to write no more long letters.

**775.** Lady Bristol to Lord Bristol. Bath, Sept. 16, 1723.

I am sorry to find your journey into Lincolnshire put off to this day, for what ever stops you meet with in the progress of your business, must necessarily deferr my happiness here; but as I am sure you will let that be the first moment you çan, I will not say so much upon it as my inclination woud otherwise lead me too. I always apprehended Mr. and Mrs. Herveys going to Ickworth woud keep you longer than you designd; he had some thoughts of going with you to Sleaford, but as you say nothing of it I conclude tis laid aside; I pressd his coming hither, but found him very averse to it. You tell me nothing of dear Nan, whether she comes with you or not, for all the kind commendation you give her sister cannot make her loose one inch of ground in my affection, and consequently wish to see her, though as they are to come with you, they will have but little proofs of it, for your dear lovd presence will so fill my heart with joy that it will leave no room for any other pleasure, notwithstanding all the blow coals I meet with here, which says you only take this in your way to Bristol, whither you and Lord Harborough (for they joyn the 2 rivals together) are going in all hast; and by the accounts I have she* has abundant need of some resource, for she is reducd to go down to the wells every day to pick up a little hazard, and cuts when ever she has pickd up

---

* I presume the Duchess of Marlborough ; see letter 773. S.II.A.II.

a pair of pieces; the discription of that, and of a party she made at ombre, must be deferrd till we meet, for tis too long for a letter, and I am afraid you will think I have writ too much already, if I dont tell you for my excuse 1 have not yet been in a condition to begin the waters or make tryal of any of Doctor Friends prescriptions; but I hope to be able too morrow or next day at farthest. I was yesterday in Bedlam, which is Harrison's room; tis much beyond whatever you saw or can imagine; they pretend to calculate that there is near 7,000 strangers here, and out of every 100, 99 that never were seen before; but I got out of this hurly burly very soon, and was very agreeably entertaind, for Cuszony, who I found there, was in high good humour, and went with Lady Gage, Mrs. Berkeley and my self and Mrs. Upton to Lindseys, (who never has any company of a Sunday;) there she sent for Whyburn with his lute, and sung for 2 hours like a nightingale; she has learnt two English ballads, which she makes the agreeablest thing you ever heard; these wanted nothing but your dear self to make the entertainment compleat, without which all other pleasures are tastless to your forlorn E.B.

The Master of the Rolls did me the favour to make me a visit this morning.

**776. Lord Bristol to Lady Bristol. Wisbich, Sept. 16, 1723.**

Knowing by my own experience how welcome your letter from Reading was to me, which gave me the satisfaction of knowing you were got well thither, I flatter my self it will not be much less agreeable to you to hear my daughters and I are come well hither, and that we left all our family so at sweet Ickworth. The news of your legs bearing so much of your journey without being the worse for it will enable me to go the better through with mine, especially since at the same time you tell me your most material complaint is mended without the help of taking one slopp, and that too after having been frequently attackd by them lately.

Keep but your mind easy by the practice of my pious principle, and assure
your self all things will do well at last for those who can bring themselves,
as I have done, by God's grace to depend on and resign my self intirely to
his most wise and merciful providence, which I trust will soon bring us
together again, never to be parted more till death shall make the seperation;
and as to my own life, were it not for your dear sake, he best knows how
indifferent that term would stand in the future wishes of your ever faithful
Bristol.

**777.**    Lady Bristol to Lord Bristol.        Bath, Sept. 18, 1723.

        I hope to  morrows post will  bring me some
welcome tydings, by which I may guess when I may hope to see you, for
I own tis a dread upon my spirits to think that after so long an absence
from that country, you shoud find more business there then you expected;
but as I find you judge so right of me that, if I am not easy in my mind, my
bodily cure will go on but slowly, I am very well satisfyd from ye kind
indulgence you have always showd that you will not loose a moment you
can save towards the making me happy in your much lovd society, without which ye being so much better, as I really am, will not continue long.
I have drank ye waters at ye Pump these 2 days, which I shoud hardly
continue to do if there was not such a vast difference to me in it, for tis
most intolerably troublesome, for in all ye times that I have been at ye
Bath, I never saw any thing like ye crowd there is now in every place;
there has been a play and musick since I came, but I was at neither ; the
ball I have been at, though you know tis not one of my entertainments, and
they are now more disagreable then ever, tho' there is 2 such fine dancers
as L— F— Hamilton & Miss St. Johns ; they are both very impatient to see
Betty, but I beleive there is one here that is more so ; all ye gamesters are
here as usual, yet they complain that play goes on very dully ; however,

bad as it is, poor Nash is almost undone, for tis allowd by all that he has lost £1400, which I beleive made him very indifferent company at Bristol, where he was 2 days to wait upon her Grace of Marlborough, whose patience is quite worn out, so that she resolves to stay no longer then ye latter end of next week, but has been so obliging to desire an appointment with me first; Mr.ǂNash has undertaken it at a half way house, and to borrow a coach for me; but I fancy, if I continue to mend, I may venture to go quite there, if I can have any convenience for it; the compliment will be ye greater, & I shall have ye pleasure of seeing a place I have so long desired to go to; but I cannot yet determine anything, for even ye writing of this has put my spiritts in a hurry, though at ye same time it gives me infinite pleasure to express ye tenderness of my heart to its dear lovd object. Since I writ this, I receivd another summons from her Grace for ye half way house. Lady Orkney, Mr. Nash & my self are ye party, but she sends me word she woud not depend upon me, neither shoud I have any thing to do with it, if you was here: your not being so she regretts extreamly; but who suffers most from that is easy to guess.

**778.** Lord Bristol to Lady Bristol. Sleaford, Sept. 18, 1723.

I wrote to you from Wisbech, which I hope you receivd. This is to let you know we all got well hither, excepting that Betty, after drinking some ale & eating a bit of cheese (neither of which she shoud have done) at Swineshead where we baited yesterday, complaind of being sick in her stomach, till her rash appeard, & then she found herself better; we kept her warm ye remainder of our journey, & put her to bed as soon as we arrived. I staid in her room till I heard she was in a very sound sleep, & has so continud till nine this morning, when she awakd & is ashamed to say she ails anything after such a nights rest. I shall be so throngd (as this country phrase is) with business during my abode here, that you must not expect above six lines at a time from me ; neither woud I have you send me more in return as long as you are drinking ye waters, which I desire you'd do with ye same care & caution of Lord Carlton, if you hope to reap that effectual lasting remedy from them which I pray for & expect, that so we may never more be under ye fatal necessity of parting again, or of my leaving our family, friends & sweet Ickworth for that odious place ye Bath ; yet whenever ye conflict returns, my choice must for ye future be to follow you, since I find there is none of ye common comforts of life to be found, where you are not, by your faithfull Bristol.

**779.**    Lord Bristol to Lady Bristol.    Sleaford, Sept. 20, 1723.

Having been this day at Aswarby to remove all the evidence relating to my estate in this country, my spirits are this evening in as bad and low a condition as ever you felt your own. I stood in need of all my Christian philosophy to bear the sight of a place where, let my eyes turn which way they would, reminded me of some pleasing passage or other of my life, spent for five and thirty years in the sweet society of two the worthiest women that ever it pleasd God to bless one man with. There was not a corner we ever were together in that was not visitted by me with uncommon veneration paid to Providence for the happiness 1 had enjoyd with innocence in thy lovd company ; and to think those daies were never to return was a reflection not to be borne but by a mind, like mine, so intirely resignd to God's wise dispensations. My affairs here prove like the hydra's head, for I no sooner dispatch one but two more rises in its room ; and so I expected it would happen after a six years absence, which has made it necessary to spend at least as many months as I have allowd daies for setting things into the good order I then left them, which being the case I must e'en resolve to adjourn the consideratic n of the least material ones till next year, and apply myself to rectify the more important wrongs, that I may be able to be with you by the latter end of next week, the only hope that will enable me to go through with so much fatigue as will in the interim fall to the share of him, who is in all humours and scituations of life most unalterably and only yours, Bristol.

Betty is very well again.

**780.** Lady Bristol to Lord Bristol. Bath, Sept. 21, 1723.

I am just come from waiting of her Grace at the halfway house; but as my spirits is not very well able to bear any fatigue, I am now tird to death ; what has made me the more so is that, not being willing to loose a day from drinking the waters, I got up by seven a clock to compass them before I went, for she named a 11 a clock to be at the place appointed, and we were all so exact that we met at the door. You were very much wanted, and your health begun by her Grace; she says she woud add a few days to her time there if she coud hope to see you, and that she might be sure of you woud feign have tempted me to come and expect you there ; but as I cannot admit of so powerfull a sharer in my happiness, I shall wait with impatience for that pleasure alone, and if my calculation dont deceive me this letter will not find you in Lincolnshire. Wherever you are may all the blessing my fond wishes can think of ever attend you and yours.—Dont think I am ill because my letter is shorter than usual, for I really am not, but much more tird than with my journey hither, but I guess by my own heart what yours may apprehend from the slightest accident. I give you a million of thanks for the kind relief you gave me from Wisbich.

**781.** Lord Bristol to Lady Bristol. Sleaford, Sept. 23, 1723.

It gives me much concern to hear how little pleasd you are with your lodging; I was alwaies afraid your new friend, Mr. Skrine, had too much business of his own to take due care of you in that necessary accomodation ; but pray tell your blow-coals that were it worse than such imaginations as even theirs can represent, I had much rather be lockd up for life with you in it than enjoy all the finest Princesses and pallaces in the world without you; ney, they shall see and know I am leaving my affairs here imperfectly settled to hasten to that Bedlam you describe rather than bear your absence any longer.  This for your blow-coals.  Having John my footman ill of a feaver by getting drunk since he came, and lying asleep three hours on a tomb-stone in a cold night, I know not what to do with him, were my business here dispatchd ; but in the condition both are I cannot yet fix the day I hope to see you ; in the meantime you have done my heart right in concluding twill be the first possible, and after the prayers you have put up to Heaven for my sake and good journey to Bath, I shall not fear any more adverse accidents to retard it ; and considering how graciously all our petitions have been answerd, and how happy Heaven has made us (I hope I may say) both, I think we ought to spend the remainder of our daies mostly on our knees in thanks and praise to that infinite goodness, which has set no bounds to his blessings towards your happier partner, Bristol.

Since I find you lay so much stress on being certain what day you are to expect me by the letter I have just now receivd, I have opend my letter again to tell you (tho' this is market-day and I am throngd with more business than you can imagine,) that whatever business I leave undone, you may depend (God willing) on my making my self happy by being with you on Sunday next ; sooner will not be in the power of your impatient lover, Bristol.

**782.**   Lady Bristol to Lord Bristol.   Bath, Sept. 23, 1723.

Being so very unused to dissemble, I am afraid my letter the last post discoverd more of my infirmities than I designd it

shoud, for I really was so disorded with that little expedition that I have
not yet quite recoverd it; but as my chief complaint is a most extream
lowness of spirits, I have this day receivd a cordial for that, not only what
your dear kind letter brought me of your safe arrival at Sleaford, but a large
pacquet from Mr. Jodrell directed to you here, by which my pleasing hopes
is confirmd of seeing you in a few days ; but for fear any unforeseen accident
shoud keep you to another post, I chose rather to loose my labour in writing
than you shoud ever meet a disappointment where I am concernd ; but this
being the last I think of writing, I hope you will excuse my exceeding the
6 lines which you prescribe, and I shoud yet go farther in news had I any
thoughts of this coming to your hands. Our company increases daily, so
that people of fashion is forcd to be content with garrets, and I shall remain
where I am, for the people of the house are so unwilling to part with me
that I believe they woud do any thing rather than I shoud leave them ; tis
very airy, quiet and free from stinks, but there are some inconveniencies,
which tho' they are very well for me alone, cannot be made sheift with when
you are here; but as a remedy for that those that are in the upper part of
the house are so very obligingly civil to offer to change with me at an hour's
warning. O that that happy hour were arrivd, when we shoud meet to part
no more. Till that long time farewell to my dearest life.

**783.** To Alderman Ray. Bath, Oct. 10, 1723.

The full and friendly account you have been so
good to send me of all affairs at Bury recalls to my remembrance the long
and usefull correspondence carryed on with me by your worthy partner Mr.
Batteley, whose loss (though very great) I see may be supplyed to me, and
I hope will prove so, by the kind continuance of yours in its room. The
choice of your brother and Mr. Discipline into your body was very welcome
news to me, which with my hearty services to them both I desire you would

Vol. II. TT

let them know, as also that I shall depend on their favour towards me and my family as long as we pursue the publick interest of Bury and Great Britain, and no longer. Alderman Hovell being calld to give an account of his past conduct, I shall leave him to that great tribunal with this short remark, that I have been young and now am old, yet did I never see any man prosper after deserting truth or his professed principles for any worldly interest whatsoever, an observation honest Mr. Hall would do well to consider of in time. When you have penetrated into the seeming mystery of the enemies appearing at your late hall to concur in the election of our own candidates, I shall depend on your imparting of it to your etc.

I desire you woud make my kindest compliments to all true friends.

**784.**     To Sir Thomas Hanmer.          London, Nov. 30, 1723.

Altho' I have been some time preparing my self for what has happend,* yet it could never come without giving me great concern. My sons natural and improvd abilities were once in a way of being great enough to have made him what I alwaies wishd, and therefore proposd to him for his pattern, a man of as much weight and usefulness in his generation, if possible, as your self; and I daily flatterd my self with the pleasing hope his good understanding woud some time or other gett the better of those destructive habitts courts & the common course of this world leads young men into; but death preventing that long expected turn has had its full effects on a nature you are farr from being a stranger to. I know no greater consolation I am capable of at present than what arises from those fresh assurances this sad accident hath brought me of your invaluable friendship and affection towards me and the rest of my family, which must ever be rememberd by me and them as the chiefest comfort and treasure remaining to us in life, but in a more particular manner by, Sir, your etc.

---

* Carr, Lord Hervey, died at Bath, Nov. 14, 1723. S.H.A.H.

**785.** To Serjeant Reynolds. London, Dec. 26, 1723.

The occasion of my giving you this trouble is to make you a proposal, the success whereof I hope may prove a mutual satisfaction to us both. There is at present a Judge's place vacant, for which, as I am informd, Mr. Walpole's recommendatory interest is not yet promised. If you have any mind for this thing, and that I can be of any assistance to you in procuring it, you may depend on any service I can doe you. Your advantage alone would be sufficient to engage my utmost endeavours; but I shall have a double satisfaction in bringing this matter to bear, as your promotion to an attendance in the Upper House will make room for my son to supply your place in the lower. I find him very sanguine in this affair, but before I would suffer him to sett any step in it, I was resolved to know how you stood affected, and if it suited with the plan of life you may have laid down to your self. I can only add that if there is any thing which your absence makes necessary to pass through a third persons hand, you can not be servd with more pleasure or faithfulness than by your etc.

**786.** To Sir Thomas Hanmer. May 23, 1724.

My satisfaction in Betty's match is now compleat, since it has occasiond so many fresh & freindly professions of kindness from you to me & my family, which are alwaies welcome because I'm sure they are sincere. If ever marriage promisd happiness, theirs has as many hopeful ingredients to make it throughly so as I've observd in any since ye blessd daies of my most chast & pious parents. I must with gratitude to heaven own Mr. Mansel was ye second man of our whole species that I would have chosen for her, & in justice to her will tell my friend that I am confident she will well deserve him.—Your inquiry after my journey into Wales is made in such obliging terms that, had I not intended it before, it

would alone have made me resolve upon one thither, whenever I find it
possible to undertake it; but as my daughter Herveys being brought to bed
of a boy ye last Tuesday in her husbands absence will necessarily require
my attendance here till ye christening is over & he returnd from Bath,
(where he has recoverd much health & strength,) I begin to fear ye remainder
of this summer will be too short to settle my affairs in Suffolke & Lincolnshire
in, so as to make it practicable for me to begin it before you'l be thinking
of coming back again. Whatever dispatch ye strongest desires to see & be
with you can make in my domestick concerns, you may depend on from
ye utmost industry of, Sir, your etc.

My wife returns you her best respects; I beg mine to my good Lady
Bunbury & all that belong to her.

**787.**   To Lady Betty Mansel.                    June 2, 1724.

So pious, so pretty & polite a letter, from so fair,
so fine & flourishing a young married lady, to a superannuated antiquated
father, should have been sooner answerd; but to tell you truth I even yet
know not how. You seem to have displayd ye whole artillery of your brain
as strongly on me to make me admire that part of you as much as Mr.
Mansel felt from ye irresistable lightening of your eyes when they deignd
to flash their luster on him; you see I am sett upon making you think there
is something in what I say, since flattery becomes a never failing pasport
with your sex to make even nonsense acceptable, so it does but appear in
that charming dress; but how if it should appear that I have made use of
this roundabout way to introduce a real commendation instead of a compliment, by confessing I never saw that poyson employd on any body,
where it ever mett with so many sure antidotes to render it successless, as
in your self. Contemplating of you in this view, Mr. Mansel must give me
leave to value & admire you as much as I hope he does; to love you as

much as you may make him do I will not pretend to, for reasons you can best by this time give your self. The delicacy you express by way of jealousy in ye share he possesses of my heart is very welcome news to me ; & as it is ye only uneasyness of that sort (I verily beleive) he will ever give you any just occasion to feel for him, I conclude you will gladly compound ye present difference by dividing it as equally between yee as it is already disposd of by your most affectionate father.

If you can speak as well as you write, pray say all you know I would say to Mr. Mansel.

**788.**   To Lord Hervey.                     July 12. 1724.

Dear Son

Altho' the subject matter of your two last letters seem more proper to be discussd by word of mouth, yet since you desird an answer to them in this way I readily (you see) comply with it, as I woud most willingly with every other thing that can make you easy & happy; but in doing that at present I must not so far deceive you by concealing the true circumstances of my estate from you as to lett you imagine the additional anuity you mention can possibly be allowd you out of my revenue (which hath already for some years past fallen short above £ 1000 per annum to make good my own necessary expences occasiond by new & unforeseen disbursments on account of the many children I have had to educate, wherein your share hath made a most considerable article,) without makeing you much more uneasy hereafter than you now seem to me to be aware of; for if more of my lands must be annually sold off (after those now on sale for payment of debts already contracted, and to raise your sisters portions, & to discharge the accidental load laid on my estate by the arrear decreed to be due on the demand of Hetley's rent-charge,) to supply the yearly exceedings of my own and their expences, what coud remain (should it please

God to lengthen my now useless life a few years longer than you know I have reason to desire) to support the Earldom in any decent degree of independency, which after my example I most seriously recommend to your continuing in, as the best preservative of your honour & conscience in the faithful discharge of that sacred trust which the constitution of your country hath placed in every peer, and which, if not well and wisely executed, can end in nothing but the destruction of the publick, & in the curse & punishment of those & their posterity who abuse it. I see then no way left to leave you & my family in that free & innocent condition it can alone at last prosper by but in your mutually resolving to retrench every unnecessary expence, & in order to that to live constantly in the country, which for your sake I would willingly submitt to, were Ickworth as disagreeable to me as London or the Bath ; but then your wife and you must do so too, or else the scheme will prove abortive, and never be rightly rellishd by those who must & shall comply with it as well as we. If it shall be found that this expedient shoud not enable you to live within your income, (your own & all your servants diet costing nothing & your children being wholly maintaind in every thing by me,) rather than you shoud e'er be driven to what you so much apprehend of breaking into any part of your wives fortune, you may at any time have recourse to whatever remains of mine, to which you shall always be most welcome, being your most affectionate father, Bristol.

If this should not satisfy for ye present, say what will.

**789.**    To ye Dutchess of Marlborough.        July 14, 1724.

    Madam

            As things but trifles in themselves become considerable when freindship happens to be concernd in them, your Grace has this trouble to sett your late misunderstanding of me right. That I never could think you capable of doing that for kingdoms, which your sudden warmth supposd me to say of you for counters, I appeal to all who have ever heard me speak of you. That I only askd whether after a card is once playd any discard could be taken back again, I must & do referr my self to ye lord who lead it; but so ready were you to putt me in ye wrong on that occasion, that you were pleasd to pronounce me guilty of beginning ye dispute ye night before; wherin I must also appeal to ye same noble lord, if he did not first move ye question as to spades being ye trump, & whether after that I did not lay down my cards for some time, & at last respectfully askd which of ye two suites mentiond I was to discard for. If this was acting wrong, I am sure it was not so towards your Grace, whose freindship I have always sett so just a value upon, that I would preserve so precious a possession on any terms but ye exposing my self to such misconstructions as (were they well founded) must make me thought unworthy of it, the only price I could not pay for ye continuance of it to, Madam, your etc.

**790.**   To ye Honble. Mr. Mansel.   London, July 25, 1724.
   Dear Son
                              The dispute between you and your wife (I hope she will give me leave to call her so) who should write first to me was so very kind, that (throwing all other circumstances out of the case) I ought naturally to wish, as I not only sincerely do, but verily hope, that as it is the first it may prove the last strife between yee, unless it be who shall love and esteem the other most. She has writt me so welcome an account of her reception in Wales, that I cannot doubt of her doing everything in her power by way of return to deserve it, which I shall take the liberty to tell her when I next write to her, altho' I'm sure she wants no such monitor to remind her of, because your judgment in chusing her for your wife, as well as her own character, is concernd in doing every thing that may answer

that good opinion you have given the last proof any man can show of her supposd meritt.  Your kind present of the Welch salmon hath not yet been opend, but you have so prepossessd me in favour of whatever that country produces, that I may safely thank you for it beforehand as the best of its kind.  Speaking of such things must put one in mind of Mrs. Duncombe without forgetting Lady Betty Mansel, to whom & to your cousin Stradling & self I am even much more than that nice Master of the cerimonies could possibly prescribe to your most affectionate father & faithful servant, Bristol.

I expect a nice geographical, historical & political account of your country from my son Tom, to whom I give my blessing.

791.    To the Hon. Brigadier Waring.      London, July 30, 1724.

The kind assistance I receivd from you in preparing my defence intitles you to be made acquainted with the event of it; which, as you are more concernd in than my self, gives me double disappointment.  By this you'l see the fate of law is quite as uncertain as that of warr, and that wise men shoud have as little to do with either as can be contrivd.  Whenever necessity forces you to one or t'other, my good wishes for your success in both shall alwaies attend you for the civilities you have shewn on this occasion to, Sir, your most obligd humble servant, Bristol.

P.S.  I have orderd my attorney to take great care of your papers.

792.    Lady Bristol to Lord Bristol.           Aug. 2, 1724.

I was unwilling my dear angel should hear by any hand but my own how very ill I have been since I came home yesterday in my usual manner, only the cholick excepted, tho' I have a little of that too this morning.  I have had some sleep since 5 a clock, which I hope will do me good, but it woud do me more to see you here, which I hope you will not deny me, for I shall have the day to my self.  I was afraid you might hear by some body from Kensington that I was not able to attend the Princess thither, made me willing to send this as soon as I coud for fear you shoud think me worse, when I am really better, and I know what your dear tender nature woud feel for me, having seen me so lately in this condition.—Sunday past 8.

**793.**   Lord Bristol to Lady Bristol.        London, Aug. 2, 1724.

Altho' I give my self the ease (which God only knows how much I want of all kinds) of thinking your yesterdays disorder will be attended with no farther ill consequences, yet I would have come in the place of this, had not I lent my coach this day to carry Lord Hervey and his lady to Lord Berkeleys, where they are to stay till near the time of their going to Bath, without going to Ickworth at all ; to which place (having settled most of my material affairs here) I should have been glad to have set out for to morrow, had not your ilness made it necessary for my quiet to come and see to morrow how you are after it, tho' of all things Courts and company are grown more than ever disagreeable to the plain, honest, sincere soul of your old friend, Bristol.

> Still bashfull virtue would from Courts retreat,
> And only to be usefull would be great.

**794.**   Lady Bristol to Lord Bristol.        Richmond, Aug. 4, 1724.

There is seldom any pleasure that does not find some alay; that which I had yesterday in your company met a great one; for when I came from the Play and saw how dark it was, I had ten thousand fears which multiplyd every danger that might attend my dearest life in his journey home; and when I reflect that what ever accident might happen proceeded from your dear kind indulgence to me in staying so late, I am quite out of my wits till I hear you are got safe home, which I hope this messenger will bring me the welcome news of.   I will not ask you to come again in the heat and

Vol. II.      vv

dust, but if it rains I beg (and am not usd to be denyd) you woud, for I am sure the journey will do you as much good as the seeing you will do me, for I love you more than words can express.—I hear Clack intends me the honour of a vissit, which I hope you will prevent, for she is too free of speech for a Court. Since I writ this, the heavens have favourd my wishes with rain, and I hope you will second them by coming.

**795.**   Lord Bristol to Lady Bristol.          London, Aug. 4, 1724.

Mum with his 3 horse-men left dear Nan and me with only two on your side of the water, after which we heard no more from them, tho' you know we staid purely to strengthen their escorte. However, as we both (I hope) relyed upon a stronger guard than anything human, we passd our journey (tho' late and dark) as safely as if we had come in the midst of our army of 18000 men.—I shall take care to keep Clack from coming to your Court; as to my own doing so any more, did you know what new troubles I'm engagd in to pay off all Bullen's tradsmen as well as my own creditors, you would no more dream of it than I can of ever being happy again, unless in the persuasion that I am at last got into the way of being eternally so.

**796.**   Lady Bristol to Lord Bristol.          Richmond, Aug. 4, 1724.

Nothing but the extream desire I have to hear of my dearest life coud tempt me to set pen to paper with such an intolerable head-ache as I never had in my life. I believe tis occasiond by a cold I got here yesterday with coming to a wet room, which joynd to the uneasyness of my mind I have had no rest too night, and am very unfit to entertain my company too day, tho' it is but small, for our whole family is gone to Windsor. Lord Falmouth was here yesterday, and is so much of our opinion as to Mrs. Dunch, that I think him worthy seeing some of Harry's letters; if you think it proper, pray send me those you think best against he comes again, which he says shall be very soon.—I find you were expected to come here yesterday, therefore I hope you will yet do it, if you stay long enough in Town, not only for their sakes but of one that is for ever and ever yours.

797.   Lady Bristol to Lord Bristol.   Richmond, Aug 5, 1724.

I was much disappointed yesterday by the Princess's footman forgetting either to let me know when he went, or to call upon you ; they come now to me in a great hurry to say they are going, so that I have only time to tell you the Dutchess of Marlborough was here yesterday in high good humour; she told me, woud you think it, your Lord has never been near me since you went ; I take that to be a sign you have no interest in him, or that you have played me false, and used it against me ; — pray go and convince her tis neither.   I hope this rain will bring you either too day or too morrow; I am sure it will do you good as well as me.   They stay, so must bid my dear Adieu.

798.   Lady Bristol to Lord Bristol.   Richmond, Aug. 6, 1724.

I cannot miss any opportunity to know something of my dear angel, tho' my last inteligence was not in the least to my satisfaction, first that you had no thoughts of coming here again, and the conclusion of your letter, you may easily believe, was mortification enough, and what at this time I was very ill able to bear either in body or mind, for I have had an unlucky blow of my breast, which has given me some pain ; the history of it is too long for a letter, but I must again beg to see you here after the sweet rain ; I am sure it must do you good, as well as give me a great deal of pleasure; but then I desire it may be too morrow, for Saturday I am to go to a great christening of Baron Sparr's to be godmother with his Majesty and the King of Sweden.   If you coud tell me any

thing extraordinary of Mum, it woud be their leaving you in the manner
they did after what had passd ; but you had (as you rightly judgd) a better
security ; may the same guardian angel protect and bless you wherever you
go and whatever you do. Adieu, my dearest life ; thank God there is but
three days more.—If Lord Sussex returns too night, he will send to you for
a letter, else I must content my self with the waterman. I wish Betty woud
find time to mend my things before she sends them. Sure you will come if
it is not very inconvenient ; I dont go to London for the christening, tis at
Twickenham.

**799.**    Lord Bristol to Lady Bristol.        London, Aug. 6, 1724.

I have still sympathy enough left (I find) to feel
more pain from the unlucky blow (you mention) on your breast than you
can do ; and tho' I shall be most uneasy till I can hear it is not like to have
any ill consequences, yet I cannot possibly come to morrow to satisfy myself about it, having appointed to meet Mr. Pemberton, who is come out of
Cambridgeshire on purpose to make a final end by paying him the principal
and interest money decreed him. Saturday you say you are engagd, and
Sunday no proper day at your Court, and on Monday I expect you here,
where every hour seems a year to me even with dear Nann, without whom
I had been most finishtly forlorn ; but as melancholly storys are not good
for hurt breasts, you shall know no farther concerning me.—How came
your accident ?

**800.**    Lady Bristol to Lord Bristol.        Richmond, Aug. 7, 1724.

My dearest life, I receivd your letter just as I was
going to bed, which made me sleep the better. I am very sorry since I
coud not see you yesterday that I mentiond anything of my engagement
too day, for I might have had your company for some hours before I went,

since I dont dine there, tho' I was invited with the rest of the company to a vast entertainment, but I did not think it proper to leave my own table, which I found the Princess thought very right. She complimented me last night upon the commendations she said she had heard of me for these two days past, how perfectly well I had done the honours to all the foreigners who have been entertained here at dinner with me; she told me they were so charmd with me that I had made several conquests. The French Abbot said so many obliging things to me of you that I believe it inspird me with spirits the better to entertain them. I find the Princess is very desirous you shoud show them your medals; she wanted to speak to you about it; it sutes with your own rules to go to Court at going out of Town; why therefore shoud you not meet us too morrow at Kensington, and come back with us to dinner; then, perhaps, I might get leave to go home with you at night, which I cant otherwise do; but if you dont like of this proposal, which I think very reasonable for you as well as pleasing to me,.I must desire you to send the coach here on Monday morning for me to set out about ten a clock, that the lodgings may be got clean for Lady Hertford. I hope the present I sent you yesterday came safe to your hands, for I am sure it must be good; I sent it just as I receivd it from Mrs. Vernon without opening.— My breast, thank God, is pretty well again, and I hope no farther consequence will attend it, for I venturd to put my stays on yesterday, and I am very easy too day; neither my time nor paper will admit of my giving you an account how this accident happend, but when you know it, I believe it will increase your present aversion to Courts.

**801.**    To Mrs. Duncombe at the Honble. Mr. Mansel's lodgings in Bath.

Ickworth, Sept 24, 1724.

Madam

No mind less moral & ingenious than your own could ever have hitt upon so happy a method of paying debts as yours has done; for you abundantly inrichd me without att all impoverishing your self. The welcome account you send me of my daughter's prudence and perfections will add to my days, altho' I read them with just allowances to your partiality & painting, which even the pencil you wishd for could never have drawn in more amiable colours ; may you prove as true a prophetess as to the duration of her wisdom & happiness, (they being like Hippocrates's twins, that must live or dye together,) as she was when she told me how much she relyed on your friendship & kindness towards her. Your letter woud have been faultless as the persons it describes, had it not supposd the lines of it too many, or that twas possible to be tired with them, since I can safely swear the sole allay I found in it was Mr. Finis's* appearing much too soon. The permission you gave me to show it to my second self naturally ledd me (as a friend is deemd an other self) to impart it to Sir T. Hanmer, who tho' he gave me all sorts of good entertainment, yet I reckond I regald him full as well as he had done me. The verses you sent me are very pretty, & much more `poetical than country muses commonly produce ; but the prose they were accompanyd with had so far prepossessd me in favour of its inimitable beauties, that I could not be touchd to that degree with them so as to alter my first affection for that, according to the constant nature of your most obligd kinsman & most obedient servant, Bristol.

I would beg the liberty of sending my blessing by you to all my children but that they'l want none as long as you are with them.

**802.**                                    Ickworth, Sept. 26, 1724.
          Dear Harry
                    I take this first opportunity to tell you I hope the sight of your mistress and the kind reception you mett with have quite dispelld those melancholy apprehensions under whose power your last letter to me was indited ; but shoud she at last prove false and ungrateful, sure

---

* Lord Bristol's marginal note says, She signd hers Finis. S.II.A.H.

such a woman would be no great loss, were her fortune yet much more considerable than it is to be. I am very confident I could never grieve the missing of such a wife (no more I trust in common sence will you) as she woud prove, supposing her capable of breaking through all those solemn and sacred tyes, by which she has so firmly and repeatedly bound herself before God & man to be yours. What is to be hopd for from a heart so lightly ballasted as to be tossd to and fro by every blast of known, designd detraction too? Such a soul I'm sure could never have made you totaly or lastingly happy, had she the command of the philosopher's stone to bring in dower with her; and if her love had never taken deeper root than not to stand steady proof against all the storms of maternal malice in your disfavour, how coud it have withstood the tryals and temptations that time never fails to throw in woemens way, to make them forgett their former vows, and feed their vanity, and satisfy their new desires at the expeace of their own honour and the peace and reputation of their old discarded inclination. These being the sentiments you must draw your consolation from, should she forsake you, they are recommended, ney, injoynd you, by your most affectionate father, Bristol.

P.S.—If she insists on the return of her letters as the sine qua non, I withdraw my advice as to that point to make yee both easy.

**803.** Lady Bristol to Lord Bristol. London, Sept. 28, 1724.

I was unwilling to trust your dear and tender nature with seeing the pain I felt at parting from you, more, much more (if possible), than ever, and I was willing to hide as much as I was able from Mr. Macroe, tho' some woud break forth. I believe the constraining my disease increasd it, for I was so extreamly ill at Hockerell, that when I had sence enough to think at all, it was that I shoud never see you more; but thank God I am now safe arrivd at this place free from any bodily pain, but that of my mind will know no ease till I am again in the center of all my happiness, your dear lovd arms, which I hope will be in a fortnight and two days, therfore I shall count every minuit till then. As much as my spirits coud be revivd after so great a shock, has been by seeing Harry so happy in finding his mistress every thing he coud wish her after all the doubts and fears he has labourd under; the particulars I will leave him the pleasure to tell you. I chuse to send my letter this way both as tis the safest, and that I have not alwaies an opportunity to send my letters to London of post days. I was not able to go anywhere last night but to my aunt's, who I think in a very bad way, and by her own description going apace; she wants mightily a companion, and desired me to think of somebody to be with her; she askd me if there were no such body in Suffolk; I recommended Ickworth to her, tho' she is not in a condition to be movd so far; she told me my Lady Playters had sent to offer her service, but I hope she will not be driven to accept of it; therefore wish you coud think of any body; Mrs. Griggs has left her in a very ungratefull manner.—I find spirit of Hervey has done me more good than spirit of lavender, for I am much better too day. I thank God I can have pleasure in others happiness, tho' I want it so much for my self at this time. The post too day I hope will give me some relief; in the mean time God Almighty bless and prosper you and all the dear babes, whatever becomes of your poor E. B.

**804.**    Lady Bristol to Lord Bristol.    Richmond, Sept. 29, 1724.

Tho' tis not many hours since I wrote you a long letter, yet I cannot let a post go without something from me, if it were only to keep up an old kind custom, the remembrance of which is and must be ever dear to me; those thoughts and the pleasing hopes of renewing those days again is all I have now to keep up my drooping spirits with, tho' my reception here was very gracious, both from my master and mistress.

I got some of my sausages made ready, and carryed them in myself when they were at dinner, which they were extreamly pleasd with, and said a great many obliging things upon it; both Prince and Princess are so extreamly fond of them (and considering the condition of the later,) I believe it woud be very acceptable if you woud order some to be sent by the stage coach, and give Matt notice to fetch them from thence; I can easily have them brought hither, if I know when they will be in Town. I cant name Matt without telling you I find he has behavd in a most scandalous manner; some particulars I sent you word by Harry, (if his thoughts are not too much taken up to remember,) which made me not trouble you with it in my letter yesterday; besides that he has promisd to reform; I shall be able to give you a better account when I go back again, which depends upon his Majesty, who leaves Windsor and goes to Kensington Thursday or Friday next, and tis thought he will go to London the later end of next week; if he does, our Court will move alsoe; that may possibly fill the Town, but in the whole way that I came through I dont think I saw 6 coaches but hacks. Thursday next is to be a great wedding at Twickenham, Miss Verney and Mr. Bowes; there has been another at Bath, Mrs. Rolt and Lord Somerfield; the greatest part of our Court and neighbourhood are now at that place, which was never known so full in any season with people of quality; Lady Fitzwilliams has disposd of her daughter there; the match is concluded between her and Mr. Edwin (Lady Kath—n's son); she is to have £10000, a great fortune, I think, where there is another daughter and two younger sons; God I hope will bless ours with a less. Pray remember me kindly to all with you; but dear Nan must always have Benjamin's mess from her fond mother and your affectionate wife, E.B.

I am under the last impatience till I hear how you do of your pain in your stomach I left you with, and how you got off that misserable wet day at the funeral.

Vol. II. WW

**805.**   Lord Bristol to Lady Bristol.     Ickworth, Sept. 28, 1724.

Knowing how very heavy late disappointments sit on my own mind, I am pleasd to find my fund of good nature not so farr exhausted by them as not to take all due care to prevent other people's meeting with any from me; so since you desird me to write, you see I do, tho' I have nothing to say but that I hope you passd your journey safely and gat well to Richmond. The little peace I hoped for here has been disturbd by a very melancholly letter from Harry, which I have sent him the most consolatory answer to that my own experience of the world and womankind could suggest to me, and which I hope will in the worst event can happen have all the due success designd by your etc.   Bristol.

**806.**    Lord Bristol to Lady Bristol.     Ickworth, Sept. 30, 1724.

Had you seen the very despairing letter Harry had left with Bullen before his journey into Kent, and by her officiously conveyd (contrary to order) to allarm and disturb me, as I told you in my last, you would have been as much surprisd as I was to see him this day, while we were at dinner, in the coach-box, flogging Coe and Carter to arrive in pudding-time, with Mr. Macro in the chariot, when God knows my own melancholy foreboding fears had rather figurd him, when next moving hitherward, in a herse than such an equipage, with an air of joy and gladness spread over all his countenance. But this is a fresh instance of the truth of my maxim ;

> Those souls shall all their misery transcend,
> Who God adore, and on his will depend.

Nothing less than the same supreme power can restore pleasure, or even peace, where tis more wanted.

**807.** Lady Bristol to Lord Bristol.  Richmond, Oct. 1, 1724.

Hope softens every care and eases every pain; therefore for my own sake I will indulge that only pleasure I have at this time in thinking you had more and stronger motives for writing than my desires: but be it from that or any other cause, still it must be kind; that thought alone was sufficient to give me more spirits than I have had since I left you; and it was so remarkable that they said at supper, nothing but your letter coud have given them, (for I receivd it just as I was sitting down;) Stanhope said, *Yes, yes, you may depend upon it, my lady goes on in her old way of at least four sides of paper every post; I found her at it the other day*; and that was true, for I was writing when he came to fetch me to play with the Prince, which is the only diversion we have now, there being very little company, and few of them care to stay dinner, the days are so short, so that we live like a good sociable country family within our selves. The King comes to Kensington too day, and the weather being so extreamly fine, tis thought he will stay till the later end of the month; but I think the Princess will run a great hazard if she does so, being (as she told me yesterday) to be brought to bed the first week in November, which will make my stay in the country very short, when I am so happy as to get to my dearest life again; but I hope I shall not come up alone, being so near the meeting of the Parliament, which they say will certainly sit at the time appointed. The Speaker dined with me a Tuesday, and he begun a health to all our friends at Ickworth as what he thought woud be the most agreeable toast to me. I was very sorry to find there was a letter gone to you from Harry, for by his own account of himself at that time I guessd it must be in that melancholy strain you describd; but as you were soon relievd from that trouble, so may you be from all others which may interrupt that happiness, as will ever be most devoutly and constantly prayd for by, my dearest life, your most affectionate wife, E. Bristol.

God bless the dear children. The Duke and Dutchess of Grafton set out next Saturday to Euston for 3 weeks; you may make what use you please of this intimation, for I told him he went so often backwards and forwards that it was impossible for you to know when he was there without he sent to you, which he said he shoud certainly do.

**808.**    Lord Bristol to Lady Bristol.    Ickworth, Oct. 3, 1724,
(dear Bell's birthday).

I am sorry you can send me no better news of Lady Effingham; would she please to accept either of the Pladd-room here or my house at Bury, (both which I offerd her in my last letter,) I am confident the air of this place or that would soon cure her of all complaints for want of health; and for a companion, if she likd my conversation but half so well as I have alwaies done hers, she need not enquire any farther about one. But alass! if ever it was tolerable, it must at present seem tedious. As dismal as the day of Mr. Lee's funeral provd in all respects, yet according to Squire's maxim I receivd no sort of harm, (being in the execution of my duty towards God and a dead friend,) neither from the wetness of the weather nor the dangers of the night, being under the conduct of old Frost my day-labourer, who even by day-light is none of the safest pilots. Had he survivd, would he have run such risques to follow me to my grave? Since you think my bodily pains worth enquiring after, I can tell you that in my stomach has been less violent than it used to be; at least it seemd so; but whether from the weakness of the humour, or the mind's inattention to lesser evils, I wont determine. The sausages could not be made fresh time enough to go by yesterdays coach; but I have taken care that two dozen shall be made on purpose to send by Tuesday's coach, which Matt must call for on Wednesday at night. They are so apt to make people sick who love & consequently dare eat many of them, that

I wish their consequences may not make me repent the pains I have taken about them. I gave dear Nann the pleasure of reading what you wrote about her, who deserves as much as her dear sister who was born on this day did, which is as full an encomium as can be bestowd by me on any one. O that the name of Hervey could be adornd by the Bettys as it hath been by the Isabellas!

**809.** Lady Bristol to Lord Bristol. Richmond, Oct. 3, 1724.

I hope those devout and pious maxims you are blessd with will deliver you as happyly out of all your troubles as you are from those that relate to Harry. I thank God your wise and good instructions has given me faith enough to believe it, else I should not care if I were to go down to Ickworth in the same conveyance you expected poor Harry in. That you may know (as well as he) how sincere a part Mrs. D— has acted in this affair, I must tell you that while she was doing so many vile things to make this young couple miserable, she at the same time told the Duke and Dutchess of Newcastle that she thought the match was too farr advancd for her to pretend to prevent it, and that all she had to do was to make the best of it she coud; this l had from one they told it too; but now I am upon the subject of incensere and double dealing, I must give you some account of the Bath. Duke Desney dined here yesterday, who is just come from thence; he says Lord and Lady Hervey are in perfect health and spirits suted to the gaiety of the place, and that he is grown fat, and looks so well that tis surprizing ; he says they keep a very good house, which he as well as the rest of their acquaintance have had the benefit of; I dont call them friends, for those lye in a much narrower compass than I find their entertainments have been; for out of 1500 strangers which is at this time computed to be upon the place, they may alwaies find enough that will be glad of a good dinner; I shoud think such a number of breaths, and few of them I believe very sweet, should rather increase diseases than lessen them

in that little close place; but one woud not believe many people went there
for health by the daily reports we have of such infinite numbers of diversions;
the constant balls does not satisfy, but the old fashion is renewd of giving
the boucket, which some that are not quite so lively as the rest are not very
well pleasd with, the Duke of Rutland in particular, who absolutely refusd
it, and Lord Scarborough took it up; since that. Lord Essex has given a
great entertainment to Peggy Pelham; but all these things (according to
custom) displease (at least) as many as they please; if you have not a fuller
and better account than any I can give you from your son, tis not through
his contempt of these pleasures, (as he seemd to insinuate in his letter to
you,) but tis rather from the large share he has in them that will not give
him time for so unfashionable a thing as duty and affection to parents ; but
I hear he is much taken up in pursuit of the same lady he began with in the
spring, who they say is there in great beauty; but as there is many new
ones, I dont know how long her reign will last; however, I am told they
leave all these joys, and intend to be in Town next week; if that is so I
suppose you will hear of them, because Ickworth may be made shift with
now the Town is empty, and I believe by their way of living their pockets
must be so too.—Thank God, among all these disagreeable things I have
the pleasure to hear my daughter Betty is in good health as well as looks,
and the report continues of her being breeding, which I wish may be true,
not only as I am fully persuaded it will recover her entirely, but alsoe be an
increase of Mr. Mansel's happiness, who deserves so much from her that I
hope she will ever be endeavouring to pay it with the same heighth of
affection as is at this moment felt towards you in the heart of your most
tender and faithful wife, E. Bristol.

I hope I may conclude the dear children well, since you say nothing of
them ; but I expected an account of the family from my young house-
keeper. Tom and Will are both at Bath.

**810.** Lord Bristol to Lady Elizabeth Mansel.

Ickworth, Oct. 3, 1724. Your elder sister's birth-day.

Dear Daughter

I once justly thought no day of the year could ever produce a more perfect humane creature than this did in the person of your faultless sister Isabella, a name must always be dear to me for hers, your most excellent grandmothers, and my most virtuous first wifes sakes; but Mrs. Duncombe has drawn so beautiful a picture of her sister Betty, that were she not in a place exempt from grief or envy, might feel both to see her self surpassd. I know every feature has solid grounds of likeness, but sure such lines as she describes must be larger than the life; are they not? speak and make me once more know true joy again before I dye. Could that demy-miracle ever come to pass, it must proceed from seeing such uncommon meritt as you are mistress of multiplyd by the production of a broad-eyd boy to make Mr. Mansel as happy every way as you can contrive. I have given my self the pleasure of hoping your not daring to drink the waters has been more owing to that cause than to the cold you took in crossing the Severn ; if it be so, permitt your husband to confirm it, as twill administer one of the most cheering cordials to the drooping spirits of your most affectionate father, Bristol.

**811.** Lord Bristol to Lady Bristol.      Ickworth, Oct. 5, 1724.

I have made so great a tour too day at my estates of Barrow, Heigham groves, the Brooms and Tuddenham, to quiet several disputes and to settle new tenants in the latter, that I am much more tired than I used to be in going thrice as farr, even tho' my dear daughter Ann accompanyed me throughout the whole expedition, who trusting to Mrs. Syer's prudence for our provisions at night, after having fasted the whole day, gave her, Harry, Charles and my self (besides three servants that

attended us) litterally but a leg of mutton, a pudding and a grape-tart for
our dinner and supper blended together, altho' we killd a bullock but the
day before, and had 3 roasting pieces in the house.   Sparing at the spigget
and letting out at the bunghole was the motto I at first assigned her, and
she deserves it.   If I were not very weary, I could contradict your panegyrick
upon hope with no less authority than Cowley's and my own experience.
Does he not justly term it

> Brother of fear, more gaily clad,
> The merryer fool o' th' two, yet quite as mad ;
> Sire of repentance etc.

Are there not more odds against those who trust in it than to the ad-
venturers for the top-prize in a state-lottery ?   How few, very few, have not
been deceived by it !   It may be your son may be drawn in by it in pur-
suing the pleasure of a conquest, which when gaind can at best but purchase
pains and uneasinesses here and punishments hereafter, the inseperable
penalties annexd to such sins ;  but if I have any hope surviving in me, tis
that he will not, cannot so much degenerate from his (in all those respects)
most faultless father, Bristol.

**812.**    Lady Bristol to Lord Bristol.    Richmond, Oct. 6, 1724.

If my memory deceive me not, (and sure I ought
never to forget so great a blessing,) this is the happy day wherein you had
so wonderful a deliverance at Newmarket,* which prevented my being made
the most miserable of women ; may the same good God for ever protect and
preserve you.   I hope to hear by your dear letter he continues to do so to
you and yours :  but I was not so lucky as to meet with any body that coud
bring it me last night, so I sent Robin after dinner and expect him this

---

* See his diary, Oct. 6, 1698.—S.H.A.H.

morning with the tide. I dont know whether I shoud tell you of an accident that happend to me of Saturday after I had writ you that long letter, which alwaies gives me as much relief as my mind is capable to receive in your absence, and consequently I thought my self better than I had been since I left you, and eat my dinner with a better appetite; but just before I riss from table Mrs. Howard perceivd I changd colour, and that my mouth was drawn a little of one side; she askd me how I did, but I had such a faltering in my tongue that I coud not speak to be understood, tho' I felt neither pain nor sickness at that time; but after it was over my jaws were as if they was breaking to pieces. The Princess woud feign have persuaded me to be let blood, but I was afraid it might sink my spirits more, which are still very low, tho' I have not neglected any part of my duty by it, for I was at Kensington with the Princess on Sunday, where we found his Majesty in perfect good health and humour, and as great a Court as the emptiness of the Town coud afford, but not a word of news stirring; the most welcome I coud have is just arrivd with the glad tidings of your health after the hazard you put it too that dreadfull day, which I think you had very ill luck to meet with, for in my whole life I think I never knew such weather at this time a year; I wish it dont tempt the Princess to stay hére too long, and that she shoud be catchd here, which woud be dismal for us; I never saw her or anybody else near so big in my life, but as she is under no apprehension of having two, (but rather wishes it,) she is in no trouble about it. They have spoke often of the goodness of the sausages; I told the Princess I had sent for more, depending upon your never failing fund of kindness, which has alwaies rememberd every thing desired by, my dearest life, your most affectionate wife, E. Bristol.

I wish you had spared the conclusion of your letter, my heart was too full before; I beg if you feel never so little pain in your stomach that you woud take the rhubarb pills; they stand upon the corner cupard in our room.

Vol. II,     xx

**813.**   Lord Bristol to Lady Bristol.        Ickworth, Oct. 7, 1724.

I congratulate you with truer joy on the faith you mention to have acquird by my maxims and instructions than if I could have made you Empress of the world without it; may it increase like the grain of mustard seed, and even then it cannot surpass that superlative degree of belief with which God's grace has touchd my heart. There passes not a day but some one or other of my observations on his providence are verifyed either by the rewarding of virtue or punishing of vice ; and if there were no other means of teaching me those divine truths but by the severe discipline I have been tryed with, tis welcome, and I can most sincerely say and think, Tis good for me that I have been so sorely afflicted and troubled. I find your faith hath brought forth hope ; but alass ! every comfortable thought must prove abortive unless to both those you can joyn charity, without which, and a through stock of it too, all the other virtues are but dead and useless acquisitions.   Had I not been a wholesale dealer in it, some must have sufferd as much as I have done ; but as Christianity enjoyns forgiveness, and as our former friendship obliges me to advise every duty that ought to be practisd by a parent, take example from me, and endeavour to forget and forgive every thing you think your son has been wrong towards you in ; and if he is conscious of much misbehaviour, that being pardond will of course make him love you much for the future.   You (now) know, next to securing the salvation of my own soul, the peace and prosperity of my family is what I have most at heart ; and do but reflect what a melancholy prospect presents itself to my imagination, when to all the undeservd disappointments I have met with from my most obligd friends, the necessary pains and infirmities incident to old age, etc., must be added the cruciating contemplation of leaving you and my heir on ill unnatural terms with one another, after all the pains that have been taken to raise and strengthen it by your common friend, Bristol.

The sausages were sent by the Coach yesterday morning.

**814.** Lady Bristol to Lord Bristol. Richmond, Oct. 8, 1724.

The pleasing hour draws so near that I must put you in mind (tho' I hope I dont need it) to send the horses for me to be in Town on Sunday night, that I may leave this place early on Monday morning, to settle all my affairs that I may be able to stay the longer at Ickworth, where I long more to be than words can express, and have a much more pleasing prospect in every particular of this journey than I had in my last. Pray let me know by Saturday's post whether Lord Godolphin expects us to meet at dinner at his house at Newmarket on Wednesday, that I may order my journey and time accordingly; because, if that appointment is off, I will contrive (by lying at Newport) to reach Ickworth in as exact pudding-time as Harry did, and I hope as welcome a guest, for he was not in more danger of coming in a herse than I have been; but thank God I have been better than I coud expect after such a shock. Poor Lady Grantham has left this place with very little hopes ever to return to it again; Mr. Hill remains here without a prospect of ever removing again; Lord Paget they say is given over with a feaver and vomiting blood, so that death is aiming at the young as well as the old; and we have nothing left to enliven our dismal abode but (George's friend) Paine, and he goes on with the same gaiety of temper as usual, to supply for what Newmarket and the Bath has at present robd us of. I hear Will has left the last of these places to go above 200 miles with Mr. Vane to Lord Bernard's seat in the North, instead of going into Suffolk as he ought to have done; so farr does the contagion of folly run through our family; Lord Scarborough (who is just returnd) is my author for this, as well as that Lord and Lady Hervey will be in Town too morrow or next day, and intend to honour Ickworth with their presence, but I conclude not for long, because they say the Operas and the Parliament will open together, and there is two new singers, a man and a woman, the finest that ever was heard, but that will not make up for my loss in the death of poor Pinkerman.—I thought you woud like to know what money you had in Mr. Fowler's hands, therefore have sent you the inclosd account, but I suppose there may be more receipts before I get to London, therefore if you woud have any more money disposd of than what you gave me your note for, if you will let me know by the next post, your commands shall punctually be obeyd in that and every thing else in the power of your most affectionate wife, E. Bristol.

Since I writ this I have considerd the coachman will come to Town so many hours before the post that I hope to receive your orders by him.

**815.**    Lord Bristol to Lady Bristol.        Ickworth, Oct. 9, 1724.

The sixth of this month in the year 1698 was but one of those dangerous accidents from which I escapd death; the 25th of this same month in the year 1717 I was yet in more imminent danger from being some time under water in my new-made canal here, with the boate (out of which I fell topsy turvy) driven by the wind over my head ; but God's infinite goodness thought fit to deliver me from both, for what ends he best knows; one I hope by his grace to secure, which is heartily to repent of all my former follies and transgressions, and to prepare myself by innocence and vertue to appear a likelyer candidate for heaven than hell, when he pleases I should leave this world I am weary of for a better ; if so worthless a creature can be reservd to any farther good purposes, his power alone can produce them.   The sad state of mind you have so long known and alwaies leave me in needed not the additional weight of woe which the last account of your self has plungd me into ; for were the relations of lover and friend quite exstinguishd, yet to my foolish fond nature that of a thirty years companion only would make a seperation intolerable, being left without resource whenever that shall happen ; to prevent which pray come and use air and exercise, which will alone ridd you of all complaints, and preserve your life at least till there is an end of mine, and of your daughters educations, to whom I cannot doubt but your future course of living will be as edifying as the common examples set them by the rest of the world have been destructive, to be a witness whereof would furnish a fresh reason why God has so often spared his now sole servant, Bristol.

I shall see how much you profitted by the sermon I sent you in case you bring Lord Hervey and his wife with you ; if they should not fill your coach, you may bring the maps upon the fore seate; they lye tyed up in poor last Lord Hervey's closet, the key of which is in the drawer of the table which Lord Lonsdale gave him, which stands in my closet; but if they should be troublesome in any manner, you may leave them.

816.    Lady Bristol to Lord Bristol.    Richmond, Oct. 10, 1724.

I was so disorderd both in mind and body when I wrote the second sheet of paper last post, that I really cant tell what I said in it; but I fear there was enough to make you doubt whether I have profitted so much by your wise instructions as I ought to have done, at least not enough to prevent some sallys of human frailty to break forth upon a fresh occasion, especially one that touchd me so nearly as a disappointment where I had laid the first foundation of all that pleasure hope had given me; for if you, my tutor, friend and benefactor in all that's good or valuable in life, can quote authors as well as prove it by your own experience to be a vain shadow only for fools and mad-men, where shall my poor heart that's torn to pieces with a thousand racking thoughts find a sanctuary ; I dare not think without returning to hope again, that as you esteem charity to be the most Christian virtue, and the Scripture tells us it will cover a multitude of faults, I in that may find a resource in the full persuasion that it will be returnd to me with as much truth and sincerity as I have ever made it my endeavour to practice it towards others ; and if it can extend it self so farr as to forgive such injuries as I have receivd from ———— (O, that ever I shoud have occasion to mention that name in this place;) but I will leave it a blank, and carry my precepts so farr as to wish (for his sake) it may remain so in the book of fate, where the secrets of all hearts are laid open. May I not then hope (my dear confessour) to be forgiven all my follies and transgressions which fills my soul with continual shame and remorse; but I cannot reckon the duty of a parent (especially towards him) as one of my faults; therefore I hope you will (for your own sake as well as mine) as strongly inforce what is due from children; for those to whom much is forgiven, of them shall much be required; and I hope to practice that as farr as I am able, as well as preach it; but as I expect nor desire nothing for my self but through an acknowledgment as well as true repentance for all my faults, so I hope no more can be requird of your most sincere and truly affectionate wife, E. Bristol.

Lord Abergavenny is given over of the small pox. I suppose you know Mrs. Duncomb goes with Lord and Lady Carteret to Ireland; they dined with me, and left several compliments for you when they came here to take leave. You must excuse all my ill spelling and every other defect, for I have not only been often interrupted, but have such a cold in my head that I can scarce hold it up. Pray thank dear Nan for her letter, as I do you for the sausages. I have much to say, but have time for no more, which you may be glad of.

817.    Lord Bristol to Lady Bristol.        Ickworth, Oct 10, 1724.
Seven at night.

Altho' I wrote this morning by Tom Harvey, yet finding by your letter to day that you desird to know by this night's post what you were to depend on with relation to dineing at Lord Godolphins on Wednesday, I was obligd to dress my self and send away Thomson to

Newmarket, who brings me word that Lord Godolphin went this morning to London with Lord Devonshire, and that he is not to return till Thursday, so that you are at liberty to divide your journey as will be most convenient to you. The Dutchess dowager of Marlborough is in the right never to hamper her self (as she calls it) with any appointments in travelling, and this last instance confirms it, as it was not a little incommodious to part with one servant out of two for nothing. You have done very well in getting an account how much money is in my goldsmith's hands to answer any future emergencies ; at present I have no occasion for any of it; but if you can make any use of the whole or part, tis all at your command, as hath been every thing else that I have been owner of ever since I promisd or professd my self to be yours and only yours, Bristol.

**818.** Lady Bristol to Lord Bristol. London, Oct. 29, 1724.

I found the ways so extreamly bad that I think I never was more disorderd with any journey in my life, tho' I met with more amusements in it than I coud expect; for at my baiting Mr. Walpole and Mr. Dodington seeing my coach stopd and came in to me as I was at dinner ; and at night we met again at Hockerell, where they took me out of the coach and carryd me in to supper, which they had got ready just as I came. I was not sorry to have that opportunity to get Harry so considerable an acquaintance, for when the Duke of Grafton arrivd (which was soon after) and put him forward, they seemd very well pleasd with his company ; but alass! the case is now quite alterd with him, for after Mr. D——t, himself and I had spent the evening in penning an epistle to the worst of women, and took care to have it deliverd into her own hand, it was at last sent back unopend ; he has sent to her again too day pressing to see her ; I have not heard yet of any answer, but he will write you every particular, so that I have nothing more to say in this affair but to desire your advice and commands how we are to act under such extraordinary circumstances, particularly what you woud have him to do, which is the only thing keeps me here till Monday's post, for I intended otherwise to have surprizd you with my company on Sunday, tho' I fancy you coud not but think I intended it, since I pressd no farther as to your coming here, which has been mightily enquird after too day by the Prince and Princess; the latter is so very well that I believe I may venture another fortnight, tho' that, she says, is the very longest, and the Prince told me I was so skilfull that I was a very necessary person upon that occasion; but having got off my waiting I hope nothing else will prevent my setting out a Tuesday, and that you will not be dissatisfyd with my keeping the horses for that purpose. My aunt is thought to be better, tho' she seems to me to be going a pace; she was extreamly pleasd with my kind care for her; that and the obliging reception I had too day at Court woud, if any thing coud, recompence the pain of body and mind which has been felt in this journey by, my dearest life, your most affectionate E. Bristol.

Will came to Town last night.

**819.  Lord Bristol to Lady Bristol.  Ickworth, Oct. 31, 1724.**

You best know how little able my mind has been of late to judge soundly of any matter; but at present I am renderd altogether incapable of advising in Harry's unlucky affair or any other thing by his brother's condition, who lay a dying with the cholick from 2 a clock yesterday morning till near noon, when the violence of his pain began to cease, after having taken one hundred and ten drops of laudanum and a turpentine glyster. In this scituation I was forced, nevertheless, to receive and entertain the Bury Corporation, to whom your young deputy gave one of the finest dinners I ever saw at Ickworth or any where else. I opend the treat with a brimmer to your Master's health, tho' I had not recoverd my taste for claret since I was obligd to do the honours here to the Duke of Bolton. Your son did not rest well last night, but was pretty easy. As to Harry's business, had I my best spirits and understanding about me, (which whatever I possessd formerly of either are now near quite decayd,) I know not how to guess at such a creature as with all the fruitfulness of her sex in riddles farr exceeds any I have ever yet mett with or read ot before the age of twenty. I think tis now pretty plain, writing will avail but little, and therefore the only way left for him is to press an interview, and that upon the foot of a legal right he may and shall set up to her as his own by solemn publick contract, which shall not be deemd his but my act ; and this you may acquaint the mother with as the last ressort, in case she and her daughter persist in their base, contemptuous usage of him and his family ; but this must not be mentiond till the daughter has confirmd to him by word of mouth the contents of all her last most barbarous letters, which will read very well in a Court of justice, (if that method must be taken at last,) and make a strong contrast between them and the foregoing ones whilst the warmth of the contract subsisted. This, I once again repeat, must pass as a course taken by us against his will, since it will necessitate the publication of her letters, which he should not consent to, and as you know he once wrote to me to return unseald in case he dyed, which request I should religiously have complyd with, before I knew how unworthyly she would use us. Perhaps all these appearances may have been advisd and consented to by her as probations to try the strength and sincerity of his · passion, and then all hasty or violent resentments and desperate measures on his side will be donner dans le panneau, which ought to be judiciously guarded against and avoided. Yet at the same time he must take care to use none of those expressions before any witness his letters are too full of ; as *I can resign you, tho' with a great struggle. You need not fear the exposing your letters. I beg to see you to take my final leave of you, and if she will grant*

Vol. II.    YY

*an interview, promise not to mention so ungrateful a story as the repetition of his love, etc.*—these being all inconsistent with the only scheme capable (I see) of bringing such mercenary minds to reason, which is to allarm them with the just retaliation of making the whole proceeding publick in a legal prosecution to recover his mistress or damages, one of which the law will give him. But this, I say again, must be reservd as the last resource after a flatt refusal upon an interview. Amidst all these difficulties and distresses Lord Cornwallis and Mr. Lehoupe, who were to have dined here yesterday with the Corporation but for a mistake his servant made in my answer to his message in the morning, has wrote me word that he will do so to day, which I am most unfitt for in all respects, but necessity has no law. Mr. Barricave alsoe begs of me that you would give a sister of his (who will attend you with a letter from him impowering her to receive it for him) an order on my goldsmith Fowler to pay her fourty two pounds, which you must take her receipt for on the back of his letter to her, and keep it as my voucher.

**820.**    Lady Bristol to Lord Bristol.    London, Oct. 31, 1724.

My dearest life

I am very glad you will see by my last letter that my inclinations and design of returning back again was before I knew your desire for it, which might have made my choice look like necessity; if my journey was not necessary I have paid very dear for it, for I can safely say I have not known one easy hour since I left you either in body or mind; the later is so affected to see poor Harry in such a condition as is past belief for the last of womankind; the loss of her is in my opinion a considerable gain, and the greatest mercy God Almighty coud bestow upon him; he sets out a Tuesday for quarters when I do for Ickworth, without either of us receive any other commands from you; if you coud find horses to bring you in Lord Hervey's calash to Newmarket I should be glad to meet you a Wednesday to dine with Lord Godolphin, (who is still there ;) Williams may go home in your conveyance, and you with me in the chariot. As my walks have lain in a very narrow compass I can tell you no news, for my aunts, Mrs. Cockburn's and home is all the places I have been in except the necessary duties at Court, which was yesterday by much the very finest appearance I have ever seen. The Dutchess of Montague was the most magnificent of any, tho' all was very splendid, and Miss Heriot not the least so, in order to a new conquest as I suppose. You know my ear too well for me to pretend to give you any account of the Opera farther than that the new man takes extreamly, but the woman is so great a joke that there was more laughing at her than at a farce, but her opinion of her self gets the better of that. The Royal family were all there, and a greater crowd than ever I saw, which has tired me to death, so that I am come home to go to bed as soon as I have finishd this, which I cant do till I have told you Will has lain out every night since he came, but does not know that I know it, so you may make what use you please of it. I askd him if he did not design to go to Ickworth ; he said he did not know if he should not go to his ship; he and Harry dined with me too day ; I woud tell you more particulars about Harry but that he said he woud write himself. Mrs. Pulteney has had a fall from her horse, and they say is much hurt. The last bell is gone by, so I have time for no more than to bid my dearest dear good night.

**821.**    Lady Bristol to Lord Bristol.      London, Nov, 21, 1724.

Near 10.

             At my arrival I found the inclosd letter with a long bill out of the Exchequer Court, (too big for the post ;) you will see by the date how long trusty Matt has had it in his hands without giving you any account of it himself or telling Bullen a word of it; all he had to say for himself was that he told Mr. Harry of it, and thought he had writ you word. I hope you have receivd his letter (since I came away) wherein he gives you an account of all his own affairs. Bullen says she saw him write it, and another to me the beginning of last week; I find by Bullen he was very uneasy at his going, and said he believd if he had staid he might have had some hopes; what grounds he had for it I know not. Mrs. D—h was here to see him, but he not being at home she sent to desire he woud come to her. I find the chief business was to get her daughter's letters; but she said her daughter woud not see him, tho' she had left her entirely at her liberty; therefore she hoped he woud think no more of her; he told her, till he had it from her own mouth he shoud go on, and as to the letters you had them in your possession, and that his first reason for ever shewing them to you was to make the better and kinder impressions upon you in favour of Miss Heriot; she told him she was very sorry he had done so, and it was the only wrong thing that she or her daughter had to accuse him of, for she feard you woud make some use of them that he woud not have done, for she did not know how farr a parent's resentment woud carry them, so that I find she is very much frighted. This is all I can learn of this matter either of Mr. Mansel, Betty or Tom; they have been with me ever since I came to Town, and we are going to eat a barrel of oysters together; they all present their duties to you; Betty I think looks better and is in better spirits than ever I saw her; the sight of it has almost unwearyd my body from a most tedious journey, but God and you can only ease my mind; but I will not tell you what I have sufferd since we parted, for I am sure it woud give you as much pain as it woud others pleasure, if you were to tell it. If you are at the expence of bringing other people's children only for their humour, tho' tis to hurt them, I hope you will indulge me so farr as to let mine partake of that convenience, since they are of years to have some good from it, besides the being a pleasure. I hope you will make enough out of these blunders to give me farther direction about it ; there is come a letter from Mrs. Dunch, which is gone after him.

**822.** Lord Bristol to Lady Bristol.    Ickworth, Nov. 21, 1724.

If my prayers were heard, (which I endeavour by all the innocency of life humanity is capable of may be favourably receivd,) this will find you safe and well where you wishd to be. I have sent as you desird to enquire more particularly of the house-keeper at Mrs. Godfrey's, who in the main gives a good character of her; but as one of the chief reasons assignd by her self for leaving Sir W. Gage's service was that she must have coffee every morning, and could not but at her own expence, I shall not think it reasonable to add that article, where necessary ones already (as you know) exceed my income. What will the next generation come to ? You must send down the same set of horses (if they performd well with you) with the coach you went in, to be here at Ickworth on Monday come sevennight at night, being the 30th instant, I designing to set out for London with Lord Hervey and his children the next day, being Tuesday the first of December, and hope to be with you on Wednesday the 2d at London. In the meantime farewell. Bristol.

**823.**    Lord Bristol to Lady Bristol.    Ickworth, Nov. 23, 1724.

For fear mine by last post might miscarry, I must here repeat what that containd, viz. that I in the first place hoped you gatt well to London, that in the next you would order the same set of horses and drivers (if they performd well with you) to bring the coach you went up in to be here on this day sevennight to bring Lord and Lady Hervey, Nan and my self the next day towards London. You must also direct that the same livery saddles and bridles which went through with you should be sent down in the said coach, for otherwise we shall want enough for our journey.—I hope the omission Matt's idleness producd will not have any very ill consequences ; but if it had been otherwise, the same accident I dare say would have happend.  I neither heard from Harry concerning that, nor his own affair ; and must believe all the uneasyness he shewd at parting was only to exchange London for Gloucester or Hereford.—The account you send me of my most valuable daughter Mansel has had power enough to revive some ray of comfort, which has of late been an utter stranger to my breast.  If ever woman was born to be wise and happy, she (by God's grace) seems to be cut out for that rare lott ;  may Mr. Mansel never be disappointed, whatever falls out to those less worthy.—Young Granny has so violent an oppression fallen upon her chest and lungs, (whether from teeth or great cold caught I know not,) that were I to govern she should not see London this winter for her portion.  Your son went to Bury this afternoon to treat the Corporation again, not being able to attend them on the Prince's birth-day. Adieu.  Bristol.

**824.**     Lady Bristol to Lord Bristol.     London, Nov. 26, 1724.

I receivd your letter at my daughter's, and imparted your kind expressions and wishes to them both, tho' there was something that touchd me more sensibly than I was at this time well able to bear ; for tho' I endeavourd to conceal my grief before those I knew it woud give pleasure to, yet I have (to my cost) vented it since I was alone. Mr. Mansel still keeps the house, but is much better ; he having an ombre party Betty and I went to my aunts ; I thought she spoke more hearty than I have heard her, but to be sure she is in a very bad way, and Lady Playters sticks close.  You will see by my letter last post that I have taken the best care I coud to obey your orders, and shall do the same by your next command about the saddles ; but since you are to come in the coach your self, I will not venture your own, because the best that can be expected from it will be to keep you 2 hours the longer each day upon the road, or perhaps leave you upon it, which will prove no small disappointment to me. Pray let me know if you come to Hockerell the first day, and whether you bait or not the second day; if you stop at Epping, pray let it be at the Crown, for the woman at the Cock was very impertinent as I came up. I was alwaies of opinion it was rediculous to bring up those little children, but now sure it will be monstrous to bring the girl; I hope for dear little Granny's sake you will prevail, and that once in their lives they will act with common sense and reason; the duty and respect they owe to your opinion they have shewd already in bringing either; I leave it to you whether tis not more reasonable for me to hope you will bring mine, since you are to be at all the expence, which I hope you will set down among the unnecessary ones. Here are three assemblys going forward, but they dont afford any thing worth repeating; only Mrs. Kemp (Sir Mar: Wyvile's sister) who has a house with but two little rooms of a floor, and all the people of quality in Town goes there, and the deepest play that ever was seen. Lord Cadogan lost £1500 yesterday was seven-night; it was pretty deep last night, but not quite so extravagant; I went with the Dutchess of Dorset and Lady Betty Germain; I lost the small sum I venturd; too day I have a summons for crimp, but I expect no better luck at that; for till I am happier in the chief concern of life I must be in every thing unfortunate, and remain your most forlorn and wretched E. B.

I hope you will remember to have some ale put up for our selves, and a hamper besides for Mr. Mansel and your daughter; but I desire the hogshead that was first bottled may be kept entirely for our own drinking, for I am sure it will prove very good, and I woud have Will Oliver see to the bottleing of the 3d hogshead before you come away. I have taken care too day that you shoud have the same coach I had, or as good a one; if you

woud not have them come to Ickworth till Tuesday morning, you had best
to prevent them, for I forgot to ask you time enough to have an answer, I
was so very ill all day on Tuesday.  From Soho, where your health was
drank, and their duty desird; I have the comfort of a very valuable son
restord to me for the loss of an unworthy one.

**825.**    Lord Bristol to Lady Bristol.      Ickworth, Nov. 28, 1724.

I have been every day since you left me litterally
up to the knees in examining tradsmen's bills and Will Oliver's accounts;
they all shew how necessary it is to let neither run on above one year.  I
have not yet so conquerd them as to have written to you at all by this post,
had not yours which I receivd this morning made it necessary to tell you I
design to get no farther than Newport the first day, and that we must bait
at Epping the next, which shall be at the Crown.  As to the coach coming
here on Monday at night or Tuesday morning, since we intend to go no
farther than Newport, it will be indifferent let it happen how it will, tho' in
both my letters about it I said to be here on Monday the 30th instant, not
then knowing whether we should gett to Hockeril or not the first days
journey.  I have taken the same care of the ale etc as hath alwaies been of
every other thing you ever yet desird of your etc.  Bristol.

**826.**    Lady Bristol to Lord Bristol.      London, Nov. 28, 1724.

I receivd your letter at the usual place where
pleasure and happiness abounds, and nothing is wanting to compleat it but
your dear and much lovd company; I think I long more to see you at that
little board than ever I did for anything, for I am sure it will give you a
new set of spirits; they are not only every thing they should be to one
another, but are also so to me in a very agreeable manner, which makes me
hope my daughters and their husbands (for I am sure my dear Nan will

come in for her share of every thing that is good and kind) will make up
the deficiencies of my son and his lady; but if I go on with the commendation
of one part of my family and the ingratitude of the other, I shall leave no
room for news, the chief of which at present (and indeed all the talk) is of
Mr. Yonge's divorce; the bill was brought in yesterday to the House of
Lords, and they say will pass without any opposition ; the families (they
say) are agreed he should not return the portion, only pay her the interest
of it for life. Now I am upon this parting couple I must tell you of as
extraordinary a joyning, which is the Duke and Dutchess of Wharton; he
is quite reclaimd, and as Mr. Sharden (who is an intimate of theirs) told us
at Mr. Mansel's, he believes there is not a happier couple in the world,
which she confirmd to me in a visit yesterday morning, and told me at the
same time the luck her lord had in his copper mine that he found in the
North ; he is to receive a hundred thousand pounds from it the third of next
month. Lady Gertrude Huthem is come 6 weeks before her time of a dead
son ; I expect every moment to be calld to imployment of that sort, (tho' I
hope with better success,) for the Princess has been very uneasy this 2 or 3
days, so that I am forcd to leave word where I am to be found, which is not
very difficult, for my walks lye in a very narrow compass. I am going to
day again to my Lady Orkney's to crimp, tho' I had very bad success last
time, as I told you I expected, and I am not in a humour to hope for better
luck, since you can have any thoughts of leaving my two poor girls behind,
which I will never beleive till I see. Betty was so mortifyd at the mentioning of it that Mr. Mansell offerd to send his coach for them ; but I told
him that was unnecessary, for if you had a mind to bring them, the coming
of a stage coach day was conveniency enough. I own to you, as well as I
love little Granny, if I see those children preferrd to the place of my own
by your choice, it will shock me so that I shall hate the sight of them ; the
reason you give for their not coming into the world is contrary to the maxims

of the Spartans, and I hope you will find as much wisdom and virtue in them, nay, I may answer for it, if they take example by their 2 elder sisters. I have had Robinson with me this morning that I might be sure you had the same coach and horses I had; the saddles and pistols I have also taken care to send; the guns I thought woud be troublesome to carry, and that you woud not want them with so large an equipage; the coachman desires you would let him have a night's lodging at Ickworth, for he says it is 6 miles extraordinary to go to Bury, which will be very hard for his horses with 4 days journey and the roads so bad, and days so short that if you dont set out by 5 a clock in the morning you will be in the dark, which I beg you would not; if you had come in your chariot without luggage, you woud not have had all these difficulties; pray God send you well out of them and safe to your affectionate wife, E.B.

Lord Rumney died to day at one a clock.

**827.**    To ye Honble. Mr. Griffin.    London, Feb. 11, 1724/5.

I have hitherto avoided giving any trouble of this kind that I did not think absolutely necessary, and woud not now interrupt the pleasures I know you take in the country but as I think it for your service and interest, as well as my wifes and my own, that you woud come up to Town your self, or authorize some able agent here to act in concert with us touching the defence or allowance of the many claims and demands made by Mr. Howard's creditors on the Staffordshire estate. I wrote you word what had been agreed on when I mett Mr. Webb at Mr. Chauncey's chamber; but now the time draws near your presence will be necessary to hear the cases which are drawing up argued by the councel to which they are intended to be referrd, and to admitt or disagree to the several claims made by Mr. Howard's creditors; and if we shoud be advisd to controvert many of them in law or in equity, it will require our whole time to take care of so many suites as may happen.—There is also another matter of consequence which I formerly mentiond to you, with relation to the Mastership of Magdalen Colledg in Cambridge; tis worth our stirring in and retrieving, as we have an evident right to it ; but how farr that right may be weakend by time is left to your farther consideration by, Sir, your most humble servant, Bristol.

My wife is your servant.

**823.**    Mr. Alderman                    London, March 6, 1724/5.

You having a double title to be troubled on the present occasion, both as Cheif Magistrate of Bury and as one of my firstrate friends in the Corporation, makes me address this to you, to let you know there is a very near prospect of Mr. Sergeant Reynolds's being declared a judge, and that you would be so kind as to convene all our fast friends together at your own house or any other place you or they shall think more proper to drink a glass of wine together, and then & there to acquaint them that I intend to sett up my son, the Lord Hervey, to supply the Serjeant's vacancy as your representative in Parliament; and that as soon as the warrant is signd for his being a judge you and they may depend on seeing both my son & me at Bury to sollicite his election, which is as firmly depended on by us & all other friends to the present Government as you may reckon upon being reimbursd whatever charges you may be at in doing what is desird of you & them by your most obligd friend to serve you & them, Bristol.

My son sends his most humble service to all our friends.

**829.**    Mr. Butts                      London, March 9, 1724/5.

Mr. Sergeant Reynolds's patent for being a judge not being yet compleated, my son and I are both detaind here to sollicite the dispatch thereof, which shall no sooner have passd the broad seal but he and I intend to be at Bury to offer him for his successour, whereof you may give all our fast friends notice, (as I have already done by letter to the Alderman,) and in the mean time try what impressions you can make upon your friend Hubbards or any other of the adverse party ; & tho' I know you want no spurr to quicken you in what concerns the interests of my family and the Government, (which I take to be both at stake in the present case, should any opposition happen,) yet I am commissiond by the Duke of Grafton to assure you from him that in case you will be serviceable on the present occasion to promote the present Lord Hervey's pretensions to be the next burgess for Bury, you shall certainly be one of his Majesty's chaplains, which hath been formerly & formally requested of him by one who you shall always find punctual to his promises, even in this which I now make you, and which I have heretofore made to all our friends, that should they reject this as they did my last Lord Hervey, they should never have the opportunity of refusing a third son from their and your affectionate friend, Bristol.

I need not caution you to make a discreet use of this.

**830.**    Lady Bristol to Lord Bristol.    London, March 13, 1724/5.

I hope I shall hear by Monday's post that this will find you safe arrived at Ickworth without any of ye accidents that you were threatend with from ye crassey coach ; I am so much so both in body and mind that I cannot pretend to give you any entertainment, for I came home from ye Princess last night so much out of order that I did not attempt looking in at my Lord Strafford's, tho' even at that time of the night there was the greatest crowd I ever saw.    Lord Carlton is extreamly ill ; he was taken on Thursday morning with a swimming in his head, for which he was let blood, & went the same evening to play at the Dutchess of Marlborough's; but the heat of her room overcame him, and he was thought to be quite gone; there was every thing done that is proper on those occasions, yet he had another attack yesterday; but this morning I sent and he was better, but is since that fallen into an extream dosing, & is to be bled again. Pray God preserve you from any such accident for the sake of your family, as well as your poor disconsolate but ever affectionate wife, E.B.

831. Lord Bristol to Lady Bristol. Ickworth, March 15, 1724/5.

The coming hither in a day & half at sixty, & the state of mind I have lived (I cant so properly say as labourd) under for some years, had both together brought me to this place so very tired & dispiritted that, had things been as in times past, I know not if I could have found strength enough to have told you that the crazy coach we came in provd to have more than I; for that performd its journey beyond expectation, but I'm afraid I gave my company reason to think otherwise of me: but no more of that.—I find my friends all so faithful here that I am like to meet with little if any opposition.—Least you may have forgott what you were to tell ye Dutchess of M. when you deliver the particular I left with you, tis briefly thus: that as I must sell some of my lands in Lincolnshire to pay for those I have purchasd near this place, I have resolvd to part with such members of my Lincolnshire estate as are mentiond in that particular; and as the two Hales which make the greatest part of the rental consist of lands yearly improvable, & that they are much more easily taxed than other estates are in all that neighbourhood or county, (whereof her steward or whoever she intends to intrust with ye survey of them may be satisfyed from ye town's duplicates to the landtax,) I will not take under thirty years purchase for them; and in case she should not think them worth the sending one to see and survey them, (tho' they lie so near Evedon that no estates can be more convenient for her,) lett me know by the next post, for when by this I have

performd  my  promise  that  she  should  have  the  first  refusal of any lands I
should  dispose  of  in Lincolnshire, there are others who have long desird to
have  the  nay  of  them  after  her  Grace.   A  clear  title,  long and peaceable
possession, with the circumstance of such low rates to the land-tax, (it being
now  no  otherwise  chargd  than  when  the  estate  lay  open  and  unimprovd,)
are  such  conditions  as  few  other  estates  can  boast of ;  but  as  all  these  rare
circumstances  concurr,  beside  that  desirable  one  of  its  vicinity to what she
hath  already  purchasd,  no  less  terms  must  be  expected  from  her  and  your
friends,  and  one  that  must  always  be  the  best  he  honestly  can  to  his  poor
numerous family.   Bristol.

**832.**     Lady Bristol to Lord Bristol.     London, March 20, 1724/5.

May  I  for  the  rest  of  my  life  ever prevent what
you  wish  or  desire  I  shoud  do,  as  I have done in this ; for you will find by
my  letter  last  post  that  I  had  executed  the  whole  of  my  commission,  and  I
think  the  answer  was  too  peremptory  to  trouble  her  Grace  again upon that
subject  without  I  receive  your  farther  orders ;  but  I  believe  I  shall  see  Lord
Godolphin,  and  will  let  him  know  what  you  have  proposd ;  &  that  you  may
know  what  he  says  by  this  post,  I  will  keep  my  letter  open  till  the  time  of
our  meeting ;  till  then  I  wish  I  coud  find  any  thing  in  this  dull  town  &  my
duller  selfe  to  entertain  you.    The  present  discourse  is  upon  a  plot,  there
being  a  quantity  of  gunpowder  discoverd  in  a  cellar  under  the  Parliament
house.    The  Dukes  of  Devonshire  and  Kent  are  named  for  President,  but  I
dont  find  many  people  of  opinion  it  will  be  either  of  them.    The  last  lord
dyd  very  rich,  but  I  have  not  heard  all  the  particulars,  only  that  he  has
left  Lord  Burlington  £30000  in  money  besides  a  great  estate  in  land,  which
fell  to  him  of  course ;  he has also left the Duke & Dutchess of Queensborough
£5000  a piece, but to his other nephews & neices only £500.    Tho' I conclude
you  have  the  account  of  the  burning  the  town of Buckingham, yet there

is something so remarkable in it to Lord Cobham that I cannot forbear mentioning of it. I was at dinner there when the news came of above 150 houses being destroyd ; there only remaind the Church, the Town-house & School, with 4 houses belonging to himselfe, which were all he had in the town. As none deserves so distinguishing a mark of the favour of Providence better than your selfe, that it may happen to you in every accident of life shall be the constant prayers of your affectionate wife, E. Bristol.

I am now at Lady Goars, & have spoke (there) to Lord Godolphin ; he says what ever answer I had from the Dutchess of Marlborough must be his, both as to the land & the money, therefore you are at liberty to make the best of the first, and to give six months notice in form for paying in the money.

**833.** Lord Bristol to Lady Bristol. Ickworth, March 20, 1724/5.

Our daughter Mansel having caught a violent cold by going out in the open chaize her brother got his feaver by, has been very much out of order, even to ye degree of having brought back her former fainting sick fits, accompanyd with shortness of breath etc, insomuch that last night Dr. Pake was sent for, who being gone to Yarmouth the messenger was sent again to Bury for Dr. Clopton, who not arriving till it was near one a clock in ye morning, I hearing she was easier & not very well my selfe was advisd to go to bed, where I was no sooner laid but I heard the Doctor's coach rattling on the stones before our door ; he was prevaild on to stay with her all night, and having blistered her hath been better all this day. Tis now past seven at night, and her feaver not returnd. Her poor husband was last night almost frantick with the fear of loosing her, which if ever woman did or can deserve, she seems to have grace and wisdom enough to merit from him. Such being my opinion of

her, judg how much concern falls to my share on this occasion, which
nothing but my great Catholicon for all evills that have or can befall me in
life can any ways alleviate, and that, thanks to his goodness, rather
increases than abates in Bristol.

**831.**   L)rd Bristol to Lady Bristol.     Ickworth, Wednesday.

11 at night, March 24, 1724/5.

Dr. Clopton is just now come out of our daughter
Mansel's chamber, & tells me upon the whole he thinks her better than he
found her yesterday, her short breath and sick fainting fits being both considerably abated; & in order to make shorter and surer work of her
recovery, he hath prevaild with her to put on blisters to her wrists, which I
must do Dr. Clopton the justice to witness for him he early declard for,
long before Dr. Friend advisd ye application of them.  We are very much
easier to night than hitherto; her poor husband hath been almost distracted,
but I have prescribd him my great Catholicon—trust in and submission to
God's wise will etc, which will do him more good than the blisters can do
her.. He sends his duty to you; I have set up for your letter, which is
fuller of resentment than needs by farr.  Would you have been allarmd and
put into your fits because Mr. Mansel feard more than we did?  Was it not
sufficient to hear & receive three times in a week from me how she did with
all sincerity?  If all this was not satisfactory, why did not you come to her
to be better informd?  Would you have had the messengers, who went
express and were not to lose a moment's time, delay their return for your
dispatches, or only to tell you what you knew from me?  I could put more
questions, but am already two hours past my usual time, and have very
little rest or spirits to spare at any time, but more especially now.  Therefore a good night is wishd you by, tho' seldom now known to Bristol.

**835.**   Lady Bristol to Lord Bristol.                    March 27, 1725.

Your letter yesterday gave me a most seasonable reliefe (when I needed it very much), both in Betty's amendment & the kind reason you give why I did not know the worst of her condition; the messenger being hindred by it could be none, for he went much more out of the way with dispatches, & I believe waited longer than he would have done for me upon such an occasion. That I did not go my selfe, you know too good (or I may more justly say too bad) a cause for; but as that will, I conclude, be removd now ye election is over, which I hear was to be Thursday last, if you are not coming back, (as I hope you will let me know by Monday's post,) nothing shall hinder me from being with you as soon as I can get an easy conveyance. I have this day taken physick by Dr. Friend's direction and begun Bath water, & am to have the same emulsion made with it which Sir David orderd me in this case. Nurse Tuer usd to make it, and has the receipt, which I desire may be sent, if you come your selfe; otherwise it may be kept there for me. Tis not the fear of death that makes me do all this; God knows I am not happy enough for that; but I woud avoid by all means I coud to prevent dying in so much pain & anguish as such a disease woud bring upon me, & I have already enough in my mind for one poor mortal to endure; but I will say no more upon this melancholly subject, for I know your tender nature is such that it will add more weight to your present uneasiness, which if I could lighten or relieve by anything in my power, it woud be counted such a blessing as I coud not purchase at a price too dear. The Dutchess of Marlborough is extreamly kind to me; I dind with her yesterday, & she has desird I woud come every day, yet sent again a particular invitation for to day, with a very obliging message, saying I knew no body was more welcome than my selfe; but I was not well enough, so Tom dind with me at home; he came yesterday to Town & looks miserable, but says he is as well as ever he was in his life; he presents his duty to you ; may none of them ever want it towards you, whatever they do to me. The Dutchess of Marlborough had a large share of ye mutton and sausages that came last, and likd them so well that she hopes you will bring some more of both ; when you come for me your selfe will be enough, for beleive me, my dear, I long to see you with the utmost tenderness of affection.

**836.**    Lord Bristol to Lady Bristol.    Ickworth, March 27, 1725.

That I may never faile in any point of duty towards one I once solemnly vowd to cherish in sickness or in health till death us do part etc, I send this to give you ye releife of knowing our daughter Mansel's feaver is visibly abated ; but she is very low in flesh and spirit, and will not so soon recruit either as most other people woud do, by not taking nourishment near so often as she ought.    Rest being what Dr. Friend found most beneficial to her in her last illness, we have so much indulgd it in this that she hath slept or slumberd away most of the time since she was first attackd.—The precept not coming to Bury till yesterday, the Election cannot be till Thursday ; how many days after I may be obligd to stay on Betty's account cannot yet be foreseen, any more than when the grief and concern & disappointments will end of Bristol.

**837.**    Lord Bristol to Lady Bristol.    Ickworth, March 29, 1725.

If my prayers can prevail, your pains will abate ; for they had already prevented your relation of the return of them by a devout application to the throne of grace, that you may pass the remainder of your days without tasting deep of that bitter cup of discipline which Providence sees fitt to inflict on others as their most proper preparation for eternity.—The receipt you mention of the emulsion Nurse Tuer has mislaid, if she ever had one, which she is not sure of, but hath sent you a copy of the .paper you gave her for mixing the ingredients. Mr. Ray says they are the cold seeds, & certainly Mr. Graham must have Sir D. Hamilton's prescription on his file, should you have lost the coppy of it which you suppose you gave to Nurse Tuer. Could I tell you what more to do in this matter, you should know it. Mr. Mansel sent a servant this day to London, who will be with you by to morrow morning, with an account how his wife did till this morning. I can now tell you she hath passd the rest of this day without any fainting or sick fitts, & that ye feaver is dying away apace instead of her doing so, as her distracted husband thought woud be the case, tho' my presaying mind never once suggested so since all her sickness. I have had such and so many experiences of its truth and God Almighty's never failing mercies to me and mine, that it woud be an irremissible sin to distrust either in Bristol.

**838.**    Lady Bristol to Lord Bristol.    March 30, 1725.'

I find tis impossible for me to receive any pleasure or comfort without an allay, for tho' I feel as much of both as is possible for poor Betty's amendment, yet I cannot but be very uneasy at your saying you dont know how many days you may be forcd to stay upon her account after the Election is over; [i] sure any is too much, and nothing can add to the extravagance of such a journey (whence nothing coud be expected better then what has happend) but the suffering you to stay an hour after your business is over; it was their choice to go once alone, and now they have the addition of two sisters, and may also have that of a brother, who is not in the least wanted here, for things go on extreamly well without him; but I am at last grown wise enough to hear & see and say nothing, tho' I have the satisfaction of hearing every thing I have already said justifyed, and every other party concernd condemnd, even to the saying Bradshaw ought to be sett of her head, as ye Berkley family had threatend to do so many

years ago; but she is an insignificant part of my resentment, and I thank God
last week has given me so much time for reflection, that I find it not so hard
a matter to forgive injuries but I can very sincerely & heartily say the
Lord's prayer, Forgive us our trespasses as we forgive them that trespass
against us; but that can neither be expected or requird, either by God or
man, without a sincere repentance, which that those may feel who have
offended, for their own & their posterity's sakes is most devoutly prayd for
by your affectionate wife, E.B.

I am something better of the complaint I most dreaded, but this rainy
weather makes me extreamly lame, which I believe is a good deal owing to
the Dutchess of Marlborough's keeping me up so much beyond my time,
for at one a clock she proposd a second round of beasts ; I complyd with
half because I won.

**839.**    Lord Bristol to Lady Bristol.    Ickworth, March 31, 1725.

Doctor Clopton observing that for four nights last
past there were some remains of Betty's feaverish fitts constantly coming on
about ten a clock, I saw he was very desirous she would suffer him to lay
on one blister more to make as he termd it safe work ; but as she had already
endurd the pain of two applications of the same kind on her shoulders &
wrists, & would (I knew) doubly dread a third, as it would allarm her to be
thought yet in danger, beside the vexation of dressing them, I proposd not
to disturb her last night's rest by the proposal, but in case he found them
necessary this morning then we would all press the use of more, & put it
purely upon her shortness of breath to releive that, without frightening of
her as to the continuance of her feaver ; my advice was so successful (with
God's assistance) that she has passd this day with more strength & better
spiritts than any since she was seizd, and I have kept my letter open till near
eleven to tell you what the Doctor (who is just now come from her) says ;

which is that there is some small attack again, but less than last night, &
believes part of it may be imputable to sitting up longer to day than she
should have done, & hopes the point may be weatherd without more blis-
tering, which she is so averse to that she seems resolvd to stand any hazard
rather than to comply with it.   She spoke to ye Doctor with more good
humour than usual, which I construe to be playing cunning with him to
gett ye blister excusd.   I have made your apology both to him and Mr.
Mansel, & am glad to hear you have made yours where tis much more
necessary and of greater moment.   Good night.—The Election is put off
till Friday.   I am glad your pains are abated, tho' mine continue.

**840.**   Lady Bristol to Lord Bristol.                    April 1, 1725.

Your kind prayers (as those of such pious souls
must ever find) have had in a great measure their wishd success, as you
will see in my last letter, before I knew ye cause of so sudden a change for
the better; tho' I had a little return of my pain last night, tis nothing to
what it was, and I shall now try Mr. Skrine's pills for the swelling of my
leg and the lowness of my spiritts, both which are extream, but I hope for
a better cordial for the last by to morrows post, that I conclude must tell me
when I may hope to see you ; for tis surely impossible that Mr. Mansel can
suffer you to stay from all your business both publick and private only to
attend Betty's recovery of her strength, which by Dr. Friend's as well as
your account is all that is now wanting.   Our doctor has gaind immortal
honour in saving the Dutchess of Rutland when Sir Hans Sloane had given
her over ; she is now out of all danger ; Mr. Spencer never was in any, tho'
very full of a very indifferent kind ; Sir William Windham is in great
danger, which perhaps may bring the Duke of Somersett to Town; then I
shall not forgett poor Squire.   I heard there was to be a call of the House
to day, therefore took care with Lord Cobham & Lord Strafford that if any

excuse were necessary for you, that they woud make it upon ye account of your daughter's illness, for I thought an election was not so proper to mention. I hope I have done right; tis my wish so to do, and shall ever be my endeavour in every thing relating to you, while there is life in your most affectionate E.B.

Lord Strafford sends me word the call of the House is put off till this day sevenight, but their lordshipps were very sowre, & had a great mind to send for you up by messengers, there being a great day on Tuesday next upon the City Bill, they are appointed to meet at ten a clock.

**841.**　　Lord Bristol to Lady Bristol.　　Ickworth, April 3, 1725.

Sincerity & faithfulness being the only good qualities I ever had to value my selfe upon, nothing must make me forfeit either of them; and therefore I will tell you that poor Betty was more uneasy last night, & hath been worse to day, than I have known her for four days last post, occasiond, as the Doctor apprehends, by some return of her feaver. He staid some hours to watch such an abatement of it as to give her the bark about half an hour after four this afternoon, which she took another dose of at 7 this evening, and is to repeat it every two hours and an half; it agrees, God be thankd, very well with her hitherto, and she is now asleep. My son was yesterday chosen Burgess for Bury in the most honourable manner, as his father and good grandfather had always been before him, having had the votes of every member of that substantial Corporation, to which choice the Town gave their universal approbation by lining every street and window between my house (from whence he was attended by all the gentlemen and clergy of Bury and its neighbourhood) and the Guild-hall, crying as we passd along with musick, drums and morrice dancers before us, A Hervey, a Hervey, long live & flourish that noble and honest family, etc. Mr. Mansel having felt a slight fitt of an ague was not with us, which with his wife's illness continuing as it does makes it uncertain when I can be with you.

**842.** Lady Bristol to Lord Bristol. April 6, 1725.

I am so very faint and low spiritted that I am very unfitt to give you so melancholly an account of my selfe. I was taken on Sunday night in my usual manner with extream pain of ye cholick, which lasted about 3 hours, & then threw me into violent convulsions. Dr. Friend was calld up and stayd with me a great while, & at last with a large quantity of laudanum laid me to rest. At my waking from it I receivd your letter, which provd no small disappointment to me that you coud not yet tell me the day of your being here, tho' I hope & conclude you will find by my last letter that it is necessary for you to be here on Thursday morning, for I find the lords are determind to spare none that are absent, and Dr. Friend (who I told Betty's case to) says he reckons her illness quite over, since there is intermission enough for the bark, & that it agrees with her. I congratulate your success at Bury, and hope you will always find the same upon every occasion. My head is so extreamly heavy that I am able to say no more but to clear my selfe of not having done any one thing to bring this disorder upon me, so that it seems purely owing to my heart and spiritts being more oppressd than they coud bear, nature took this violent course to discharge it selfe; but I have had no return of my fitts since yesterday morning at 10 a clock, & by the help of my quieting medicine rested very well till 6 this morning, then my spirits was a little disorderd, but taking what I was orderd went to sleep again, so that I hope my present danger is over if I am to make you happy; if not, the sooner death comes the welcomer to your poor E.B.

The Dutchess of Richmond fell in a fitt as she waited upon the Princess at chappell on Sunday, and I was calld out of the next closett; that surprize helpd a good deal towards my disorder, tho' I dind after with Mrs. Warpole, yet I was ill all day.

**843.**    Lord Bristol to Lady Bristol.    Ickworth, April 7, 1725.

J have been at Bury all this afternoon to make vissitts and return thanks to the gentlemen etc. who shewd such signal respect to me and my son on occasion of his election. Tis both late & I am so weary & dispiritted that I can only confirm to you the good news of my last that Betty is out of all danger by the help of the bark, and mends visibly every day, so as to dine on butterd chicken to day. She knows nothing of her husband's having had three fitts of an ague, but as he missd entirely of it yesterday, and hath been very punctual in taking on the cortex, tis very probable he will hear no more of it.—Tis now past eleven, and the servant I left at Bury not come with the letters, so that I must bid you good night.

**844.**    To Mr. Ambrose Ray.    London, June 5, 1725.

So true a friendship as you have constantly maintaind towards me and mine, even to have stood proof against the powerful influences of an elder brother at the most critical junctures, justly deservd the best returns I could at any time make you or yours. If what I have done in favour of your nephew gives you so sensible a pleasure as you express, it much enhances my own satisfaction in having bestowd the living in my gift on one so every way worthy as I find him of it. The right remark you make that steadyness seldom fails of its reward, reminds me of a Scottish proverb which says, Honesty may be dear bought, but can never prove an ill pennyworth ; a truth I have livd to see so often confirmd by my own experience, that I would not but have made that purchase (as little present maintenance as it has afforded me) for all the other riches and honours this world could have supplyd the absence of it by.  That my posterity may fare the better for it is sufficient comfort to your faithful friend and obligd servant, Bristol.

**845.**  Lord Bristol to Lady Bristol.  June 19, 1725.

I have just now, and not till now, receivd so confusd an account thro' Betty Morris from Williams of your having been out of order by something of the mobb, that I can make neither head nor tail of, that not being able to come my selfe till to morrow, having appointed Lady Wrottesley to meet her this afternoon upon the subject of the enclosd, I send this messenger on purpose to know how you do till I can see you to morrow.

**846.**  Lord Bristol to Lady Bristol.  Friday July 2, 1725.

The Dutchess of Marlborough being gone to an auction yesterday, and not returning soon enough to resolve your question before Robin's departure, I send this messenger on purpose to let you know that she will dine with you at Richmond to morrow, and that she will be troubled with my tedious company in her own coach, tho' at the same time she desird I would have my own also ready, least she should have more to bring with her than her own would hold.  Being last night at her house, Harborough told me he was to be this day at Richmond, and that he should take it amiss if you did not invite him to dinner, tho' he could not do it if you did.  Forewarnd forearmd.

**847.**  To Lord Hervey.  Ickworth, Sept. 6, 1725.
Dear Son

The incredible character you have met with of my ducal friend* smells so rank of the resentments of those disappointed

---

* Lord Bristol's marginal note says, Bedford.  S.H.A.H.

politicians who tryd to lead him in a string, that I could hardly read it without the indignation due to all such immoralities, tho' this is not the first instance by many within my own experience how far party interests will carry men to asperse & villify those who have too much sense & honesty to be governd by them. How many have I known who will no longer acknowledge the least good quality in any man than he will drudge on with them in every measure, tho' never so dirty; one step in opposition to such schemes (tho' consonant to their common principles) is sufficient to become at once with them a ridiculous ignorant vaus rien, without faith, honour or constancy; but such a man's consolation may be that those people's prejudices are now so very well understood that their satyrs are panegyricks, since being their known fools at all turns is the only way left to exempt one from all other faults or defects. These are the men whom a most ingenious modern poet must collaterally have pointed at when he thus sung of some other of our cotemporaries.

> * Affix some specious scandal on their name,
> And baffled by their virtue triumph o'er their fame.

The thorough approbation you have heard me often express of that author's works whereout this distich was taken, must be the only reason your modesty can assign why you ought to suspect I should be ever weary of his prose ; but to undeceive you once for all, know I like both, and can never have too much of either, when you can afford them to your most affectionate father.

**848.**    To ye Right Honble ye Lady Diana Spencer. Nov. 6, 1725.

If any thing could compensate for the disappointment of a letter from the Dutchess of Marlborough, it must have

---

* Lord Bristol's marginal note says, His own lines; i.e., Lord Herveys. S.H.A.H.

been the agreeable surprise of one from Lady Diana Spencer; for which unexpected honour this comes to offer you my best acknowlelgments, and to promise, if you'l have goodness enough to pardon the present preferrence I've allowd, it shall (as tis the first) prove the last competition wherein you can ever be made second to any other mortal in the esteem and admiration of, Madam, your Ladyship's most obedient and most obliged servant, Bristol.

**849.** To the Dutchess of Marlborough. Ickworth, Nov. 8, 1725.

If any thing could tempt me to suspect you were not mistress of that through good understanding all the world allows and which I have long admird in you, it must arise from the great wrong it does it self in supposing it can want, much less receive, any assistance from mine, which, if it ever had a being, has since subsisted purely on the gleanings from your own ; as therefore you have a right not only to employ it in all the under-uses you find it fit for, but to all the other services its unprofitable master can ever do you, I shall not fail of being at London to receive your Grace's farther commands within the time prescribd to, Madam, your Grace's most obligd & most obedient servant, Bristol.

**850.** To Baptist Lee Esq. , London, Dec. 2, 1725.

I have studiously consulted my dearest daughter* on the several particulars you recommended to my care, and am glad to find she has so just a sense of those good qualities we both think you possess to so uncommon a degree as alone can make one of her tender nature happy, and which also serve to make the distinction you have shewn her much

---

* Lady Hervey writing to Mrs. Howard from Bath in October, 1725, says; " Arm yourself with "faith to believe me when I tell you that Bab, our own lean, pale-faced Bab, has been queen of a ball, & " has been the object of sighs, languishments & all things proper on such occasions ; & to surprize you "yet more I must inform you that her flirt is master of ten thousand pounds a year." Suffolk letters, 1, 195. Two more letters to Mr. Lee will be found, viz. Nos. 852, 854. S.H.A.H.

more valuable than it could otherwise have been to either of us. As to her constantly living in the country, she is so early wise as to have made that her choice already apart from any other consideration, that the merit of her complyance in that point on your account will be lessend, if not quite destroyd by it.—We are all very much concernd for the melancholy occasion which has kept you in the country, to which we wish as speedy and prosperous an event as to every other thing wherein your ease and happiness is concernd, being with all sincerity and true esteem, Sir, your most faithful friend and humble Servant.

**851.**   To Mrs. Carus.*                      London, Dec. 4, 1725.

The unwelcome news you sent me of your good husband's ill state of health equally surprisd and concernd me. I took him to be blessd with as sound a body as mind, and if there had been a man I could allowably have envyed, I always thought twas he, especially since I knew of his uncommon good fortune in finding so excellent a wife as I am throughly satisfyd you are to him in all essentials requisite to his happiness. Had I known of his distemper in the beginning, the violence of its progress might more easily have been checkd by the early advice of our very best physicians here (which he shall never want as long as I can purchase it) before any ineffectual medicines or mistaken methods prescribd by others less skilful; but even as his case now stands, I would not have him or you despair of relief; in order whereunto I sent for Mr. Graham immediately on the receipt of your letter to show him the relation therein given of your husband's disease, and find it exactly the same in all its circumstances with that his brother Malthus labourd under. I desird him to have recourse to his file of bills, and to send me a copy of those receipts and of that regimen

---

* Lord Bristol had a domestic servant named William Carus in 1705—1710. S.H.A.H.

whereby he found most ease and benefit, which I have here inclosd; but if on tryal he should find they are of little or no service to him, let me know it together with an exact state of his case from the physicians who have had him in hand, and an account of what he hath taken from them without effect, and then I shall take care to lay the wholê either before Dr. Mead or Dr. Friend, the two topp physicians of this town, (which of them he has most faith in,) and doubt not but somthing may be hit upon conducive to his cure, which (unless it be to your self) would prove the most sensible satisfaction that could be felt by his & your friend & servant, Bristol.

My wife sends you her service & thanks for your present, which is received; and in return will send you 6 pounds of the best chocolate which Mr. Malthus found ease by, and, if it agrees with him, will furnish him with what more he wants.

**852.**   To Baptist Lee Esq.         London, Dec. 11, 1725.

That no misunderstanding might arise between us in the course of that treaty you seemd so desirous to enter into, I took care to be very clear in our first conference concerning the portion, which you may remember I then told you could be but four thousand pounds without distressing the head of my own family, which 1 can never consent to do on any consideration. The reason of my exceeding that resolution in ye case of my daughter Mansel I acquainted you with, but I then resolvd never to give above £4000 with the rest of my daughters, (having so many younger sons to provide for besides,) a rule if ever I would make a breach in, should be on the present occasion, but even here it cannot, must not be transgressd by, Sir, your faithful friend and humble servant Bristol.

All our services here attend you and your family.

END OF VOL. II.

+

www.ingramcontent.com/pod-product-compliance
Lightning Source LLC
Chambersburg PA
CBHW031350290326
41932CB00044B/862